PIGOT & CO.
of
England & Wales.
WITH PART OF
Scotland
INCLUDING THE NEW LINES OF CANALS, RAIL ROADS &c.
EXPLANATION.
Mail Roads
Turnpike Roads
Cross Roads
Rail Roads
Rivers
Navigable Canals
Cities in Capitals, as CHESTER
Market Towns in Roman Print, as Manchester
the figures attached denote their distance from London, as 186
Borough Towns are described by stars, which denote the number of Members returned by each Borough, as Wigan
NORTH SEA OR GERMAN OCEAN
NORTH RIDING
DURHAM
LINCOLN
NOTTINGHAM
DERBY
YORK
Berwick
Newcastle
Sunderland
Hartlepool
Whitby
Scarborough
Bridlington
Flamboro' Hd.
Spurn Hd.
Humber Mouth
Hull
Lincoln
Nottingham
Sheffield
Leeds
Bradford
Halifax
Huddersfield
Wakefield
Doncaster
Pontefract
Selby
Howden
Beverley
Driffield
Malton
Thirsk
Ripon
Richmond
Stockton
Darlington
Bishop Auckland
Durham
Alnwick
Morpeth
Tynemouth
Gainsboro'
Grimsby
Louth
Horncastle
Spilsby
Wainfleet
Boston
56°
55°
54°
53°
2°
1°

COMPRISING THE

COUNTIES OF ENGLAND,

(UPON WHICH ARE LAID DOWN ALL RAILWAYS COMPLETED AND IN PROGRESS),

WITH

Large Sheet Map

OF

ENGLAND AND WALES,

AND

A CIRCULAR ONE OF THE COUNTRY ROUND LONDON:

THE WHOLE ENGRAVED ON STEEL PLATES.

ACCOMPANIED BY TOPOGRAPHICAL AND STATISTICAL ACCOUNTS OF EACH COUNTY;

RAILWAY INFORMATION;

TABLES OF DISTANCES OF THE PRINCIPAL TOWNS IN GREAT BRITAIN;

AND

AN ITINERARY OF THE MOST USEFUL AND GENERALLY TRAVELLED ROUTES

Throughout the United Kingdom.

PUBLISHED BY J. PIGOT & CO. 59, FLEET-STREET, LONDON, AND FOUNTAIN-STREET, MANCHESTER:

And sold by them and the following Booksellers:—

SIMPKIN AND MARSHALL, STATIONER'S-COURT; LONGMAN AND CO. AND SHERWOOD AND CO. PATERNOSTER-ROW; ARTHUR VARNHAM, 61, STRAND; AND HATCHARD AND SON, PICCADILLY.

PIGOT AND CO. PRINTERS.

ADDRESS.

THE Proprietors, in placing their BRITISH ATLAS *before the Public, beg most respectfully to state their pretensions to its patronage--to secure which neither expense, labour nor anxiety have been spared in every department of the Work. The Maps have been engraved from the very latest surveys of England, Ireland, and Scotland; whilst every improvement and correction that it has been possible to acquire a knowledge of, subsequently, have been laid down with scrupulous fidelity. It has also been an object of consequence with the Proprietors to introduce interesting originalities, not hitherto embodied in other Atlases. The convenience of the traveller and tourist has been consulted with solicitude, and assistance in various ways has been effectually afforded them, in one novel mode especially—that of exhibiting, on the Maps, the main roads diverging from one county to the principal towns in others adjoining. Nor have they been unmindful of the important change effected in travelling, by the operation of* RAILWAYS: *every line already opened, and others which they could confidently rely upon as progressing, being faithfully and distinctly delineated, according to the best official authorities. The several Distance Tables, Routes, and Topography of the counties, will likewise, they trust, be welcomed, not only as powerful auxiliaries to attain the object desired, but as possessing interest of no common character, as well as proving valuable and appropriate appendages to the Work. In the general detail of the Maps, it is presumed that correctness and perspicuity will be recognized throughout the entire series, and that they will be found invested with all the information furnished by larger and far more expensive publications.*

Messrs. Pigot & Co. having thus briefly described the principal features of the British Atlas, may be excused in presuming to anticipate that it will be received as a valuable acquisition to the private library; useful in point of reference to the man of business,--and a Work conveying interesting information to the general traveller.

☞ **Attention is invited to the Explanatory Remarks, Example, &c. on the Distance Table Sheet.**

This edition published in 1997 by Bramley Books
Origination by Scantrans Pte Ltd, Singapore
Printed and bound in Italy by Rotolito Lombarda
ISBN 1-85833-659-7

CONTENTS AND THEIR ARRANGEMENT.

THE FIRST PAGE OF THE DISTANCE TABLE SHEET CONTAINS ROUTES FROM LONDON, & PROVINCIAL ROUTES.

UPON THE FULL FRONT OF THE DISTANCE TABLE SHEET APPEARS THE LARGE RECIPROCAL DISTANCE TABLE OF THE PRINCIPAL TOWNS IN ENGLAND, SCOTLAND AND WALES.—A TABLE EXHIBITING THE DISTANCE OF THE CHIEF SEA-PORTS IN THE UNITED KINGDOM, FROM OTHERS IN FRANCE AND GERMANY. —A TABLE SHEWING THE DISTANCE FROM LONDON (BY CHART) TO THE CAPITALS OF THE PRINCIPAL COUNTRIES IN THE WORLD.

THE LAST PAGE OF THE SHEET CONTAINS ROUTES IN IRELAND, FROM DUBLIN.—ROUTES IN SCOTLAND, FROM EDINBURGH.—ROUTE FROM THE LAND'S END IN CORNWALL, TO JOHN O'GROATS HOUSE, IN SCOTLAND.—TOUR FROM EDINBURGH TO INVERNESS, BY THE FORTS AND THE CELEBRATED FALL OF FOYERS.

Maps of England and Wales

WITH

A CIRCULAR MAP OF THE COUNTRY ROUND LONDON.

AFTER WHICH APPEAR, IN ALPHABETICAL SUCCESSION,

THE COUNTY MAPS,

TO EACH OF WHICH IS PREFIXED A TOPOGRAPHICAL ACCOUNT.

ROUTES FROM LONDON.

The first column of figures gives the distance from place to place, the second column the entire distance.

London to Edinburgh.

Place	Miles	Total
Waltham	11	
Ware	10	21
Royston	17	38
Caxton	11	49
Huntingdon	10	59
Norman's Cross	13	72
Stamford	14	86
Witham Common	11	97
Grantham	10	107
Newark	14	121
Tuxford	13	134
Retford	7	141
Bawtry	9	150
Doncaster	9	159
Ferrybridge	15	174
Sherburn	6	180
Tadcaster	6	186
York	10	196
Easingwold	13	209
Thirsk	10	219
Northallerton	9	228
Darlington	16	244
Ferryhill	11	255
Durham	7	262
Newcastle	14	276
Morpeth	15	291
Felton	10	301
Alnwick	9	310
Warrenford	11	321
Fenwick	9	330
Berwick	10	340
Eyeton	8	348
Dunbar	20	368
Haddington	12	380
Musselburgh	11	391
Edinburgh	6	397

London to Glasgow,

By Leeds Mail Route.

Place	Miles	Total
Barnet	11	
St. Albans	10	21
Luton	11	32
Bedford	19	51
Higham Ferrers	15	66
Kettering	9	75
Uppingham	15	90
Oakham	6	96
Melton Mowbray	10	106
Nottingham	19	125
Mansfield	14	139
Chesterfield	12	151
Sheffield	12	163
Barnsley	14	177
Wakefield	10	187
Leeds	9	196
Harewood	8	204
Harrogate	8	212
Ripon	11	223
Royal Oak Inn	10	233
Catterick Bridge	11	244
Smallways	11	255
Bowes	8	263
Brough	13	276
Appleby	8	284
Penrith	14	298
High Hesket	10	308
Carlisle	8	316
Longtown	9	325
Ecclefechan	14	339
Dinwoodie Green	11	350
Moffat	11	361
Crawford	15	376
Douglas Mill Inn	13	386
Hamilton	18	407
Glasgow	11	418

London to Manchester.

Place	Miles	Total
St. Albans	21	
Dunstable	12	33
Woburn	9	42
Newport Pagnell	9	51
Northampton	15	66
Market Harbro'	17	83
Leicester	15	98
Loughborough	11	109
Derby	17	126
Ashbourn	13	139
Leek	15	154
Macclesfield	13	167
Stockport	12	179
Manchester	7	186

London to Carlisle & Glasgow.

By Manchester.

Place	Miles	Total
See preceding route, London to Manchester	186	
Bolton	11	197
Chorley	11	208
Preston	9	217
Garstang	11	228
Lancaster	11	239
Kendal	22	261
Penrith	26	287
Carlisle	18	305
Longtown	9	314
Ecclefechan	14	328
Moffat	22	350
Hamilton	45	395
Glasgow	11	406

London to Birmingham and Holyhead.

Place	Miles	Total
St. Albans	21	
Dunstable	12	33
Brickhill	10	44
Stoney Stratford	9	52
Towcester	8	60
Daventry	12	72
Dunchurch	8	80
Coventry	11	91
Meriden	7	98
Birmingham	12	110
Wolverhampton	14	124
Shifnal	12	136
Watling Street	7	143
Shrewsbury	10	153
Oswestry	18	171
Llangollen	13	184
Corwen	10	194
Cernioge Maur	13	207
Capel Cerig	14	221
Bangor	15	236
Canca Mon Inn	13	249
Holyhead	12	261

London to Liverpool.

Place	Miles	Total
St. Albans	21	
Dunstable	12	33
Brickhill	10	43
Stoney Stratford	9	52
Towcester	8	60
Weedon	8	68
Daventry	4	72
Dunchurch	8	80
Coventry	11	91
Wishaw	17	108
Lichfield	11	119
Wolseley Bridge	10	129
Stone	12	141
Newcastle-under-Lyne	9	150
Congleton	12	162
Knutsford	14	176
Warrington	11	187
Prescot	10	197
Liverpool	8	205

London to Falmouth.

Place	Miles	Total
Brentford	7	
Staines	9	16
Bagshot	10	26
Hartford Bridge	9	35
Basingtoke	10	45
Whitchurch	12	57
Andover	7	64
Salisbury	17	81
Woodyates Inn	10	91
Blandford	12	103
Milbourne	8	111
Dorchester	9	120
Bridport	15	135
Axminster	12	147
Honiton	9	156
Exeter	16	172
Crockernwell	12	184
Oakhampton	11	195
Launceston	18	213
Bodmin	21	234
Truro	23	257
Falmouth	12	269

London to Norwich.

Place	Miles	Total
Epping	17	
Harlow	7	24
Hockerill	6	30
Newport	9	39
Bourn Bridge	10	49
Newmarket	12	61
Barton Mills	8	69
Thetford	11	80
Attleburgh	14	94
Norwich	14	108

London to Brighton.

Place	Miles	Total
Croydon	9	
Ryegate	11	20
Crawley	9	29
Hickstead	9	38
Patcham	10	48
Brighton	4	52

London to Hull.

Place	Miles	Total
Waltham Cross	11	
Ware	10	21
Buntingford	10	31
Royston	7	38
Caxton	11	49
Huntingdon	10	59
Norman's Cross	13	72
Peterborough	6	78
Market Deeping	8	86
Bourn	8	94
Falkingham	9	103
Sleaford	9	112
Lincoln	18	130
Spittal Inn	12	142
Brigg, or Glandford Bridge	12	154
Barton	10	164
Hull	7	171

London to Portsmouth.

Place	Miles	Total
Kingston	12	
Ripley	11	23
Guildford	6	29
Godalming	5	34
Liphook	12	46
Petersfield	8	54
Horndean	8	62
Portsmouth	10	72

London to Bath & Bristol.

Place	Miles	Total
Brentford	7	
Colnbrook	10	17
Maidenhead	9	26
Reading	13	39
Woolhampton	10	49
Newbury	7	56
Hungerford	8	64
Marlborough	10	74
Calne	13	87
Chippenham	6	93
Bath	13	106
Bristol	13	119

London to Milford Haven,

By Bath, Bristol, New Passage, and Cardiff.

Place	Miles	Total
See Route London to Bristol	119	
New Passage Inn	11	130
Black Rock Inn	3	133
Newport	15	148
Cardiff	11	159
Cowbridge	13	172
Pyle Inn	12	184
Neath	12	196
Swansea	9	205
Llanon	13	218
Carmarthen	13	231
To Milford as the succeeding route	40	271

London to Oxford, Gloucester and Milford Haven.

Place	Miles	Total
Uxbridge	15	
Beaconsfield	8	23
High Wycomb	6	29
Tetsworth	13	42
Oxford	13	55
Witney	11	66
Northleach	16	82
Cheltenham	13	95
Gloucester	8	103
Ross	16	119
Monmouth	11	130
Abergavenny	17	147
Crickhowell	6	153
Brecon	14	167
Trecastle	11	178
Llandovery	9	187
Llandilo Vawr	14	201
Carmarthen	15	216
St. Clears	9	225
Narberth	13	238
Haverfordwest	10	248
Milford Haven	8	256

London to Harwich.

Place	Miles	Total
Romford	12	
Brentford	6	18
Ingatestone	5	23
Chelmsford	6	29
Witham	9	38
Copford	8	46
Colchester	5	51
Bradfield	12	63
Ramsey	5	68
Harwich	4	72

London to Dover, Calais & Paris.

Place	Miles	Total
Dartford	15	
Gravesend	7	22
Rochester	8	30
Sittingbourn	11	41
Feversham	9	50
Canterbury	6	56
Dover	16	72
Calais	26	98
Marquise	13	111
Boulogne	10	121
Cormont	16	137
Nampont	17	154
Abbeville	19	173
Flixecourt	15	188
Amiens	14	202
Fleurs	11	213
Breteuil	8	221
Saint Just	14	235
Clermont	11	246
Chantilly	15	261
Saint Denis	18	279
Paris	5	284

To Paris, by Brighton and Dieppe, 227 miles.

PROVINCIAL ROUTES.

The first column of figures gives the distance from place to place, the second column the entire distance.

Birmingham to Cambridge.

Place	Miles	Total
Stonebridge	10	
Coventry	8	18
Lutterworth	14	32
Market Harboro'	13	45
Kettering	11	56
Thrapstone	9	65
Spaldwick	9	74
Huntingdon	8	82
Fen Stanton	5	87
Cambridge	10	97

Bristol to Margate.

By the Coast.

Place	Miles	Total
Bath	13	
Warminster	17	30
Deptford Inn	11	41
Salisbury	11	52
Romsey	16	68
Botley	12	80
Wickham	4	84
Havant	12	96
Emsworth	2	98
Chichester	7	105
Arundel	10	115
Shoreham Bridge	12	127
Brighton	8	135
Newhaven	9	144
Seaford	4	148
South Bourne	8	156
Bexhill	13	169
Hastings	6	175
Winchelsea	7	182
Rye	3	185
New Romney	11	196
Hythe	8	204
Folkestone	4	208
Dover	8	216
Deal	8	224
Sandwich	6	230
Ramsgate	5	235
Margate	5	240

Hull to Bristol.

By Lincoln.

Place	Miles	Total
Barton	7	
Glandford-Bridge	11	18
Spittal Inn	12	30
Lincoln	12	42
Newark	16	58
Nottingham	20	78
Ashby de la Zouch	20	98
Tamworth	14	112
Birmingham	15	127
Bromsgrove	13	140
Droitwich	6	146
Worcester	7	153
Tewkesbury	16	169
Gloucester	11	180
Newport	16	196
Bristol	18	214

Hull to Holyhead.

Mail Route.

Place	Miles	Total
Beverley	9	
Market Weighton	10	19
York	19	38
Tadcaster	10	48
Leeds	15	63
Bradford	10	73
Halifax	8	81
Rochdale	16	97
Manchester	11	108
Warrington	18	126
Chester	21	147
Holywell	18	165
St. Asaph	10	175
Aberconway	19	194
Bangor	15	209
Holyhead	25	234

Hull to Newcastle-on-Tyne.

Place	Miles	Total
Beverley	9	
Market Weighton	10	19
York	19	38
Easingwold	13	51
Thirsk	10	61
Northallerton	9	70
Darlington	16	86
Fennyhill	12	98
Durham	7	105
Newcastle	14	119

Liverpool to Newcastle-upon-Tyne.—*By Carlisle.*

Place	Miles	Total
Ormskirk	13	
Preston	18	31
Garstang	11	42
Lancaster	11	53
Kendal	22	75
Penrith	26	101
Carlisle	18	119
Brampton	9	128
Haltwhistle	12	140
Hexham	15	155
Corbridge	3	158
Newcastle-on-Tyne	17	175

Liverpool to Harwich.

By Manchester.

Place	Miles	Total
Prescot	8	
Warrington	10	18
Manchester	18	36
Stockport	7	43
Macclesfield	12	55
Leek	13	68
Ashbourne	15	83
Derby	13	96
Loughborough	16	112
Leicester	11	123
Market Harboro'	15	138
Rothwell	8	146
Kettering	5	151
Thrapston	9	160
Huntingdon	17	177
Cambridge	15	192
Linton	11	203
Haverhill	9	212
Halstead	15	227
Colchester	14	241
Manningtree	9	250
Harwich	11	261

Liverpool to Norwich.

By Manchester.

Place	Miles	Total
Prescot	8	
Warrington	10	18
Manchester	18	36
Stockport	7	43
Chapel-le-Frith	13	56
Chesterfield	24	80
Mansfield	13	93
Newark	20	113
Sleaford	19	132
Falkingham	9	141
Bourn	9	150
Spalding	11	161
Holbeach	8	169
Lynn, over Cross Keys wash	20	189
Swaffham	15	204
East Dereham	12	216
Norwich	16	232

Hull to Norwich.

Place	Miles	Total
Barton	7	
Glandford bridge	10	17
Spittal Inn	12	29
Lincoln	12	41
Green Man Inn	9	50
Sleaford	9	59
To Norwich, as by previous route		100

Leeds to Norwich.

Place	Miles	Total
Pontefract	13	
Doncaster	15	28
Bawtry	9	37
East Retford	9	46
Tuxford	7	53
Newark	13	66
Sleaford	19	85
Then to Norwich as by previous routes		100

Leeds to Southampton.

Place	Miles	Total
Wakefield	9	
Barnsley	10	19
Sheffield	14	33
Chesterfield	12	45
Mansfield	13	58
Nottingham	14	72
Loughborough	15	87
Leicester	12	99
Lutterworth	12	111
Daventry	16	127
Banbury	17	144
Chipping Norton	13	157
Woodstock	11	168
Oxford	8	176
Abingdon	6	182
East Ilsley	10	192
Newbury	10	202
Whitchurch	13	215
Winchester	13	228
Southampton	12	240

Leeds to Newcastle-upon-Tyne.

Place	Miles	Total
Harewood	8	
Harrogate	8	16
Ripon	11	27
Leeming Lane	15	42
Catterick Bridge	6	48
Darlington	13	61
Durham	18	79
Newcastle	14	93

Manchester to Birmingham, Bristol, Exeter & Falmouth.

Place	Miles	Total
Wilmslow	12	
Congleton	12	24
Newcastle-under-Lyne	12	36
Stone	9	45
Stafford	7	52
Penkridge	6	58
Wolverhampton	10	68
Birmingham	14	82
Bromsgrove	13	96
Droitwich	6	102
Worcester	7	109
Tewkesbury	16	125
Gloucester	11	136
Cambridge Inn	11	147
Newport	5	152
Alveston	8	160
Bristol	10	170
Red Hill	8	178
Cross	9	187
High Bridge Inn	9	196
Bridgwater	8	204
Taunton	11	215
Wellington	7	222
Cullompton	12	234
Exeter	12	246
Moreton Hampstead	12	258
Tavistock	21	279
Callington	9	288
Liskeard	8	296
Lostwithiel	12	308
Grampound	14	322
Truro	9	331
Falmouth	12	343

Manchester to Leeds, Selby, and Hull.

Place	Miles	Total
Oldham	7	
Delph	6	13
Huddersfield	12	25
Leeds	16	41
Peckfield	10	51
Selby	10	61
Thence by Steam Packet to Hull, communicating with the following places:		
Long Drax	12	73
Booth Ferry	4	77
Goole	4	81
Whitgift	4	85
Blacktoft	2	87
Whitton (*Linc.*)	4	91
Hull	20	111

York to Carlisle.

Place	Miles	Total
Boroughbridge	15	
Leeming	15	30
Catterick Bridge	8	38
Smallways	11	49
Bowes	8	57
Brough	13	70
Appleby	8	78
Penrith	14	92
High Hesket	10	102
Carlisle	8	110

York to Lancaster.

Place	Miles	Total
Tadcaster	10	
Harewood	11	21
Otley	8	29
Addingham	9	38
Skipton	6	44
Gargrave	5	49
Settle	11	60
Thornton	12	72
Hornby	8	80
Lancaster	9	89

York to Liverpool.

Place	Miles	Total
Tadcaster	10	
Leeds	15	25
Bradford	10	35
Halifax	8	43
Rochdale	16	59
Bury	7	66
Bolton	6	72
Wigan	11	83
Prescot	14	97
Liverpool	8	105

Or by Huddersfield and Manchester.

Place	Miles	Total
Leeds	25	
Huddersfield	16	41
Delph	12	53
Oldham	6	59
Manchester	7	66
Warrington	18	84
Prescot	10	94
Liverpool	8	102

ROUTES IN SCOTLAND.

FROM EDINBURGH.

⁂ FOR ROUTES FROM LONDON TO EDINBURGH, SEE LONDON ROUTES.

The first column of figures gives the distance from place to place, the second column the entire distance.

TO ABERDEEN,
By Perth and Queensferry:

Place	Miles.	Total.
Cramond Bridge	6	
South Queen's Ferry	3	9
Inverkeithing	4	13
Kinross	14	27
Damhead Bridge	6	33
Bridge of Erne	7	40
Perth	3	43
Inchture	14	57
Dundee	8	65
Arbroath	17	82
Montrose	12	94
North Esk Bridge	3	97
Inverbervie	10	107
Stonehaven	9	116
Dee Bridge	13	129
Aberdeen	2	131

And from Aberdeen to Inverness,
By Banff.

Place	Miles.	Total.
Bridge of Don	7	
Old Meldrum	11	18
Turreff	17	35
Banff	11	46
Cullen	13	59
Fochabers	12	71
Elgin	9	80
Forres	12	92
Nairn	11	103
Inverness	16	119

Or by Huntley and Keith.

Place	Miles.	Total.
Greenburn	5	
Glasgowego	5	10
Inverary	6	16
Pitmachie Inn	9	25
Huntley	12	37
Keith	10	47
Fochaleers	8	55
Inverness	48	103

From Edinburgh to Inverness,
By Dunkeld, and by the Forts—see route to John O'Groat's, &c.

TO INVERARY,
By Stirling & Callander.

Place	Miles.	Total.
Stirling	35	
Doune	9	44
Callander	8	52
Locherne Head	13	65
Liangarston Inn	8	73
Crianlarach Inn	10	83
Tyndrum	5	88
Dalmally	11	99
Clady	7	106
Inverary	9	115

TO INVERARY,
By Glasgow & Luss.

Place	Miles.	Total.
Glasgow	43	
Kilpatrick	9	52
Dunbarton	5	57
Luss Inn	12	69
Tarbet	8	77
Arroquhar Inn	2	79
Glencoe *(passage of)*	4	83
Rest and be Thankful	3	86
Cairndow Inn	7	93
Inverary	10	103

TO PERTH AND BANFF.
By Fifeshire.

Place	Miles.	Total.
Leith	2	
Petty-cur *(ferry to)*	7	9
Kirkcaldy	4	13
Plasterer's Inn	6	19
Falkland	5	24
Bridge of Erne	12	36
Perth	4	40
Cupar Angus	13	53
Forfar	18	71
Brechin	12	83
North Esk Bridge	6	89
Bridge of Dye	13	102
Banchory Ternan	9	111
Kinarny	10	121
Monymusk	5	126
Pitmachie Inn	11	137
Marnoch Bridge	18	155
Banff	11	166

TO STIRLING AND BANFF,
By Falkirk.

Place	Miles.	Total.
Linlithgow	17	
Falkirk	7	24
Bannockburn	9	33
Stirling	2	35
Dumblane	6	41
Green Loaning	5	46
Crieff	10	56
Amulrie Inn	11	67
Aberfeldie	10	77
Cushie Ville	5	82
Tummel Bridge	8	90
Dalnacardoch	10	100
Dalwhinnie Inn	13	113
Bridge of Spey	10	123
Pitmain Inn	3	126
Aviemore Inn	13	139
Grantown	14	153
Cromdale	4	157
Bridge of Aven	9	166
Aberlour	8	174
Keith	13	187
Banff	20	207

TO ST. ANDREW'S,
By the Coast.

Place	Miles.	Total.
Leith	2	
Pettycur *(ferry to)*	7	9
Kinghorn	1	10
Kirkcaldy	3	13
Dysart	2	15
East Wemyss	4	19
Largs	7	26
Pittenweem	8	34
Anstruther	1	35
Crait	4	39
Kingsbarns	3	42
St. Andrew's	7	49

TO GLASGOW,
By Mid Calder.

Place	Miles.	Total.
Hermeston	6	
Mid Calder	7	13
Blackburn	5	18
Kirk of Shotts	9	27
Holy Town	6	33
Glasgow	11	44

TO GLASGOW,
By Linlithgow.

Place	Miles.	Total.
Corstorphine	4	
Kirkliston	5	9
Linlithgow	8	17
Falkirk	7	24
Loanhead	6	30
Cumbernauld	3	33
Bedley	7	40
Glasgow	7	47
Or from Loanhead as above.		
Kilsyth		30
Kirkintullah	5	41
Glasgow	7	48

TO GLASGOW,
By Bathgate.

Place	Miles.	Total.
Corstorphine	4	
Uphall Inn	8	12
Bathgate	6	18
West Craigs Inn	5	23
Airdree	9	32
Glasgow	11	43

TO GREENOCK AND AYR.
By the Coast.

Place	Miles.	Total.
Glasgow	43	
Paisley	8	51
Port Glasgow	14	65
Greenock	3	68
Innerkip	6	74
Largs	9	83
West Kilbride	7	90
Saltcoats	6	96
Kilwinning	4	100
Irvine	3	103
Monktown	8	111
Ayr	4	115

TO AYR AND PORTPATRICK, also LANARK.

Place	Miles.	Total.
Currie	6	
Little Vantage	5	11
Causeway End	2	13
Carnwath	12	25
Carstairs	3	28
From hence to Lanark is 3 miles, making		31
Douglas Mill	10	38
Douglas	3	41
Muirkirk	10	51
Cumnock	11	62
Ayr	15	77
Maybole	9	86
Girvan	12	98
Ballantrae	12	110
Lochryan	9	119
Stranraer	8	127
Portpatrick	6	133

TO DUMFRIES & KIRKCUDBRIGHT.

Place	Miles.	Total.
Pennycuick	9	
Noblehouse Inn	7	16
Blyth Bridge	5	21
Crook Inn	13	34
Tweedshaws	9	43
Moffat	7	50
St. Ann's Bridge	8	58
Kirkmichael	5	63
Dumfries	8	71
Crocketford	9	80
Castle Douglas	9	89
Bridge of Dee	3	92
Tonguetand Bridge	5	97
Kirkcudbright	2	99

ROUTES IN IRELAND.

FROM DUBLIN.

☞ *Eleven Irish Miles are equal to Fourteen English.—The first column of figures gives the distance from place to place, the second column the entire distance.*

TO SLIGO—*By Mullingar and Longford.*

Place	Miles.	Total.
Lucan	7	
Maynooth	4	11
Nineteen Mile House	9	20
Kinnegad	9	29
Mullingar	9	38
Longford	20	58
Rusky Bridge	8	66
Carrick on Shannon	11	77
Boyle	7	84
Ballinafad	3	87
Colooney	12	99
Sligo	5	104

TO DROGHEDA—*By Naul.*

Place	Miles.	Total.
Glassnevin	2	
Brackenstown	4	6
Ballyboghill	4	10
Naul	4	14
Dardistown Bridge	5	19
Drogheda	3	22

TO LIMERICK AND KILLARNEY.

Place	Miles.	Total.
Rathcoot	8	
Nass	8	16
Kildare	9	25
Ballybrittas, *Queen's Co.*	8	33
Maryborough	7	40
Castletown	8	48
Roscrea *(Tipperary)*	11	59
Moneygall	7	66
Silvermines	11	77
Newport	9	86
Limerick	8	94
Patrick's Well	5	99
Rathkeale	9	108
Abbyfeale	16	124
Castle Island	10	134
Killarney	10	144

TO GALWAY—*By Athlone.*

Place	Miles.	Total.
Kinnegad	29	
Beggar's Bridge	8	37
Kilbeggan	7	44
Athlone	16	60
Ballinasloe	12	72
New Inn *(by Kilconnel)*	10	82
Athenry	10	92
Galway	11	103

TO GLENHARM, &c.

Place	Miles.	Total.
Belfast	80	
Carrickfergus	8	88
Larne	10	98
Glenharm	8	106

TO WATERFORD.

Place	Miles.	Total.
Leighlin Bridge as in Route to Cork	45	
Gowran	7	52
Thomastown	7	59
Mullinavat	9	68
Waterford	7	75

TO BELFAST & DONAGHADEE.

Place	Miles.	Total.
Swords	7	
Balruddery	7	14
Drogheda	10	24
Dunleer	7	31
Castle Bellingham	4	35
Dundalk	6	41
Newry	10	51
Loughbrickland	7	58
Dromore	8	66
Lisburn	7	73
Belfast	7	80
Newtounardes	7	87
Donaghadee	7	94
Or by Bangor.		
Belfast		80
Hollywood	4	84
Bangor	6	90
Donaghadee	5	95

TO COLERAINE AND GIANT'S CAUSEWAY,
By Antrim.

Place	Miles.	Total.
Banbridge	60	
Lurgan *(Armagh)*	7	67
Glanevy *(Antrim)*	10	77
Antrim	7	84
Randalstown	4	88
Ballymoney	19	107
Coleraine	7	114
Giant's Causeway	8	122

TO LONDONDERRY—*Through Armagh.*

Place	Miles.	Total.
Dundalk	41	
Johnston's Fews	10	51
Newtown Hamilton	2	53
Armagh	9	62
Dungannon	11	73
Cookstown	8	81
Stramore Inn	10	91
Dungiven	8	99
Clady	9	108
Londonderry	7	115

TO CORK—*By Kilkenny and Clonmel.*

Place	Miles.	Total.
Racoole	8	
Naas	8	16
Timolin	14	30
Carlow	9	39
Leighlin Bridge	6	45
Kilkenny	13	58
Nine Mile House	13	71
Clonmel	11	82
Clogheen	11	93
Kilworth	12	105
Rathcormuck	6	111
Cork	13	124

TO WEXFORD—*By Bray, Wicklow, Gorey and Wells.*

Place	Miles.	Total.
Donnybrook	2	
Bray	8	10
Kilcoot	6	16
Wicklow	8	24
Arklow	12	36
Gorey or Newborough	10	46
Wells	9	55
Wexford	12	67

Route from the LAND'S END, in Cornwall, to JOHN O'GROATS' HOUSE, in the North of Scotland.

Place	Miles.	Total.
Land's End to Penzance		10
Marazion	3	13
Helstone	11	24
Truro	16	40
Bodmin	23	63
Launceston	21	84
Oakhampton	18	102
Crockernwell	11	113
Exeter	11	124
Cullompton	12	136
Wellington	13	149
Taunton	7	156
Bridgwater	11	167
Axbridge	17	184
Bristol	18	202
Newport	18	220
Glouoester	16	236
Tewkesbury	11	247
Worcester	16	263
Droitwich	7	270
Bromsgrove	6	276
Birmingham	13	289
Lichfield	16	305
Burton-on-Trent	12	317
Derby	12	329
Chesterfield	24	353
Sheffield	12	365
Barnsley	14	379
Wakefield	10	389
Leeds	9	398
Harewood	8	406
Harrogate	8	414
Knaresborough	2	416
Boroughbridge	7	423
Topcliffe	7	430
Northallerton	12	442
Great Smeeton	7	449
Darlington	9	458
Rusheyford	9	467
Durham	10	477
Newcastle-on-Tyne	14	491
Morpeth	15	506
Alnwick	19	525
Belford	15	540
Berwick	15	555
Houndwood	14	569
Renton	2	571
Dunbar	14	585
Haddington	11	596
Edinburgh	17	613
South Queen's-ferry	9	622
North Queen's-ferry	2	624
Inverkeithing	2	626
Gairney-Bridge	12	638
Damhead-Bridge	8	646
Perth	11	657
Auchtergaven	8	665
Dunkeld	6	671
Monlinearn Inn	7	678
Blair Athol Inn	11	689
Dalnacaroch Inn	11	700
Dalwhinnie Inn	13	713
Bridge of Spey	10	723
Aviemore Inn	16	739
Bridge of Carr	7	746
Freebairn Inn	9	755
Inverness	14	769
Beauley	10	779
Dingwall	9	788
Invergordon	14	802
Tain	12	814
Bonar Bridge	16	830
Dornoch	12	842
Golspie Inn	10	852
Port Gower Inn	14	866
Berridale Inn	10	876
Dunbeath Inn	8	884
Wick	16	900
Freswick	10	910
John o'Groat's House	9	919

Tour from EDINBURGH to INVERNESS, by the Forts, and the celebrated Fall of Foyers.

Place	Miles.	Total.
Linlithgow	17	
Falkirk	7	24
Bannockburn	9	33
Stirling	2	35
Callander	17	52
Tyndrum	36	88
Bridge of Urchy	6	94
Inverouvan Inn	3	97
King's House	10	107
Glencoe.. *(passage of)*	9	111
Ballychelish ferry	5	121
Fort William	14	135
Letter Findlay	15	150
Fort Augustus	14	164
Inver Morrison	6	170
Drumdrochit	12	182
Inverness	14	196
Or from Fort Augustus as above		164
To the General's Hut	18	182
Inverness	14	196

About one mile and a half from the General's Hut is the celebrated Fall of Foyers, well worth the attention of the curious.

J. Pigot & Son, Printers.

Names of Towns	Counties	Market Days	London	Aberystwith	Ashton-under-Line	Barnsley	Bath	Bedford	Berwick-on-Tweed	Birmingham	Blackburn	Bolton	Boston	Bradford	Brighton	Bristol	Burslem	Burton-on-Trent	Bury St. Edmunds	Cambridge	Canterbury	Carlisle	Chelmsford	Cheltenham	Chester	Chesterfield	Chichester	Colchester	Congleton	Coventry	Derby	Doncaster	Dorchester	Dover	Dumfries	Durham	Edinburgh	Exeter	Falmouth	Gainsborough	Glasgow	Gloucester	Halifax	Harwich	Hereford	Hertford	Holyhead	Huddersfield	Hull	Ipswich	Kendal	Kidderminster
Aberystwith	Cardigan	M. and S.	208																																																		
Ashton-under-Line	Lanc.	S.	187	144																																																	
Barnsley	York	W. and S.	177	175	30																																																
BATH	Somerset	W. and S.	106	123	170	181																																															
Bedford	Bedford	M. and S.	51	185	135	127	118																																														
Berwick-on-Tweed	North.	S.	337	325	195	176	364	292																																													
Birmingham	Warwick	M. Th. & S.	110	110	83	90	90	69	266																																												
Blackburn	Lancaster	W. and S.	209	160	30	58	192	157	187	105																																											
Bolton	Lancaster	M.	197	148	18	46	180	145	196	93	12																																										
Boston	Lincoln	W. and S.	116	214	117	88	179	75	248	105	139	127																																									
Bradford	York	Th.	192	172	30	24	205	153	161	114	41	37	109																																								
Brighton	Sussex	Daily.	52	236	240	231	122	103	390	169	263	251	168	246																																							
BRISTOL	Gloucester	Daily.	119	110	163	177	13	115	353	87	183	171	180	197	135																																						
Burslem	Stafford	M. and S.	152	113	36	59	132	109	237	46	58	46	100	69	207	127																																					
Burton-on-Trent	Stafford	Th.	125	128	58	62	120	71	239	28	88	76	78	90	178	114	30																																				
Bury St. Edmunds	Suffolk	W. and S.	72	238	174	156	171	56	315	127	197	186	93	172	123	171	152	116																																			
Cambridge	Cambridge	W. and S.	51	210	153	134	144	29	289	97	175	163	72	148	105	143	141	92	27																																		
CANTERBURY	Kent	W. and S.	56	264	242	233	164	107	388	165	264	252	170	247	71	171	208	179	126	106																																	
CARLISLE	Cumberland	W. and S.	301	236	122	134	293	262	89	196	99	108	217	110	362	285	150	192	276	272	357																																
Chelmsford	Essex	F.	29	231	189	170	136	61	329	137	210	198	113	188	81	148	164	132	42	40	85	301																															
Cheltenham	Gloucester	Th.	95	113	126	135	41	85	311	45	148	136	140	159	131	43	85	73	142	113	150	242	126																														
CHESTER	Chester	W. & S.	182	99	46	78	155	137	226	75	51	39	139	75	240	150	32	75	187	170	236	137	212	113																													
Chesterfield	Derby	S.	150	160	46	26	162	100	203	64	69	57	70	50	205	156	39	36	134	106	206	159	154	109	77																												
Chichester	Sussex	W. and S.	61	214	248	238	90	112	395	142	270	258	178	253	30	103	213	162	134	113	100	341	92	113	222	193																											
Colchester	Essex	W. and S.	51	258	203	180	162	76	337	145	226	214	120	196	105	169	192	143	32	48	79	304	22	147	221	154	112																										
Congleton	Chester	S.	162	122	27	47	141	121	228	58	47	35	115	68	216	136	10	40	155	150	217	143	173	100	33	42	200	196																									
COVENTRY	Warwick	W. and F.	91	137	97	87	92	50	263	18	119	107	88	114	150	95	60	29	106	79	147	209	112	51	91	64	132	124	69																								
Derby	Derby	F.	126	140	57	50	131	74	226	40	79	67	66	78	181	127	34	12	116	96	182	174	135	85	72	24	169	147	39	40																							
Doncaster	York	S.	159	182	46	16	97	119	177	93	69	62	73	34	212	191	72	66	140	114	213	136	160	139	88	30	228	162	61	96	54																						
Dorchester	Dorset	W. and S.	120	178	220	253	55	150	406	143	242	230	210	236	113	64	187	174	194	172	176	342	149	99	221	207	82	171	193	146	183	237																					
Dover	Kent	W. and S.	71	279	258	248	177	122	405	181	280	268	187	263	80	190	224	195	143	113	16	372	100	166	252	222	110	95	233	163	198	229	192																				
Dumfries	Dumfries	W. and S.	338	273	166	170	330	299	109	233	136	145	274	146	398	322	187	229	319	309	399	37	340	279	176	196	378	341	178	243	212	179	381	415																			
DURHAM	Durham	S.	259	258	113	98	286	215	78	188	104	116	172	83	310	275	161	161	238	213	311	67	258	233	159	125	318	261	144	187	148	98	332	327	104																		
EDINBURGH	Edinb.	Daily.	393	328	249	235	385	343	59	289	192	201	309	203	448	377	243	285	375	350	449	93	394	336	232	261	435	398	236	302	267	235	436	465	71	137																	
EXETER	Devon	T. and F.	172	185	238	253	82	198	429	163	260	248	254	273	182	76	203	190	248	225	227	364	202	116	224	227	144	223	212	175	203	270	54	243	401	351	457																
Falmouth	Cornwall	T. Th. and S.	269	278	333	348	177	294	524	258	355	344	348	368	276	170	298	284	342	318	323	457	296	211	317	322	238	316	306	270	298	366	150	339	496	446	553	96															
Gainsborough	Lincoln	T.	150	187	66	35	189	107	196	87	103	91	51	54	201	163	71	65	124	104	202	162	145	116	71	22	210	152	71	88	47	20	232	218	199	118	255	262	358														
GLASGOW	Lanark	Daily.	402	337	227	235	394	367	103	297	200	209	318	211	459	386	251	293	383	357	460	101	402	343	240	260	445	405	243	310	275	243	444	476	72	164	44	465	560	263													
GLOUCESTER	Glo'ster	W. & S.	103	165	128	142	36	93	318	52	150	138	148	163	132	34	93	80	148	121	158	252	131	9	116	116	118	154	102	58	92	154	92	174	289	240	345	111	207	139	353												
Halifax	York	S.	194	165	22	26	208	146	169	110	31	29	109	8	248	189	62	59	124	152	249	112	196	155	66	46	240	198	52	110	70	36	248	265	149	97	211	305	401	56	213	155											
Harwich	Essex	T. and F.	72	279	224	201	183	97	358	166	247	235	130	210	126	191	178	158	38	69	100	318	42	167	236	170	134	21	212	147	167	183	192	116	362	271	412	244	340	170	419	175	214										
HEREFORD	Hereford	W. and S.	135	73	128	145	61	105	317	49	148	136	152	160	136	48	91	79	161	136	190	234	165	40	95	119	150	186	100	70	95	152	116	206	271	243	327	124	220	142	335	32	152	206									
Hertford	Herts.		21	210	168	156	120	28	314	104	191	189	96	174	74	126	144	106	56	32	77	286	32	100	174	128	83	49	154	85	110	140	142	98	327	236	375	194	291	128	384	107	158	70	139								
Holyhead	Anglesey		261	107	138	170	227	219	316	161	144	131	230	166	328	209	122	163	276	258	319	228	292	190	87	165	300	312	122	152	181	170	278	335	265	249	321	285	380	198	329	188	158	314	163	256							
Huddersfield	York		189	162	21	17	206	138	173	102	38	32	108	16	243	187	59	74	173	144	244	120	188	147	74	38	231	195	49	102	62	33	245	260	157	95	213	263	359	53	221	153	8	214	148	166	153						
Hull	York		171	218	87	64	235	131	183	122	105	98	78	64	225	214	107	102	147	128	226	157	168	175	133	78	235	177	108	123	82	49	257	242	194	105	242	297	393	35	258	180	72	185	174	152	227	70					
Ipswich	Suffolk		69	264	189	182	177	83	343	154	221	209	114	200	122	190	174	146	26	54	126	303	40	165	224	158	130	18	184	135	140	166	189	140	340	263	400	241	337	158	409	172	202	21	190	67	304	199	173				
Kendal	Westmoreland		261	193	82	90	238	209	132	152	55	64	173	66	315	234	104	148	239	232	316	44	260	196	95	114	298	278	99	161	136	99	294	332	81	67	137	309	405	119	145	199	68	276	190	242	184	76	125	264			
Kidderminster	Worcester		126	101	88	105	80	82	279	17	109	97	122	121	178	76	51	45	140	113	182	201	149	39	75	80	149	161	60	36	57	110	132	197	238	204	295	152	248	101	302	40	113	182	35	117	132	111	139	170	160	
Lancaster	Lancaster		239	170	60	72	216	187	154	130	33	42	176	64	293	212	76	84	126	210	294	66	249	174	71	99	276	256	76	139	114	97	272	310	103	87	159	287	383	117	167	177	68	266	168	220	162	76	125	252	22	138
Leeds	York		186	187	37	19	207	146	157	109	51	47	102	10	240	196	78	81	168	142	241	115	184	154	80	45	238	190	65	109	69	28	252	257	152	79	208	272	368	48	216	161	18	204	164	168	169	16	54	194	71	125
Leek	Stafford		154	122	32	57	147	101	226	51	55	43	96	62	209	135	10	35	144	127	210	151	167	96	38	30	195	180	10	64	28	60	190	226	188	148	244	211	307	70	252	98	54	201	96	139	137	53	111	170	107	60
Leicester	Leicester		98	154	85	76	118	48	248	44	108	96	61	104	152	120	65	27	86	82	153	204	108	77	99	53	161	119	74	26	28	72	171	169	241	178	297	196	292	64	305	82	100	134	98	83	187	92	98	124	160	61
LICHFIELD	Stafford		119	121	72	74	107	76	250	16	94	82	88	98	173	103	35	12	135	107	174	183	140	61	63	48	158	158	42	27	24	78	161	190	220	172	276	179	275	71	284	69	94	173	67	112	151	86	114	162	139	28
LINCOLN	Lincoln		130	191	88	52	182	89	214	81	110	98	36	73	183	176	81	65	106	87	184	181	127	133	122	41	193	135	83	81	51	38	215	200	218	136	273	252	348	18	282	142	75	144	133	110	210	72	41	132	137	98
Liverpool	Lancaster		205	117	43	73	191	156	208	97	41	33	147	71	259	177	50	90	206	180	260	119	218	141	18	77	241	230	42	106	87	90	241	276	156	141	212	253	349	104	220	149	63	251	134	191	105	61	131	228	75	99
Lynn	Norfolk		98	225	151	128	184	75	289	114	173	161	40	146	150	188	131	102	44	46	154	248	88	140	163	107	160	76	142	96	97	112	218	169	285	211	348	266	362	98	349	149	148	76	160	78	252	145	116	64	211	131
Macclesfield	Chester		167	130	11	29	149	115	219	66	42	30	104	54	222	145	18	56	157	138	223	138	180	109	43	34	208	191	8	78	41	53	202	239	175	139	231	221	317	67	239	111	47	208	109	152	131	42	101	183	94	68
Maidstone	Kent		35	244	222	212	141	85	367	145	244	232	150	227	52	151	187	160	107	86	27	336	64	130	217	185	72	86	197	126	161	193	154	43	373	294	428	205	301	185	439	138	234	107	170	57	296	224	206	104	296	161
Manchester	Lancaster		186	137	7	37	166	134	198	82	23	11	116	35	240	160	35	65	177	152	241	119	191	125	38	46	224	203	24	96	56	51	220	257	156	120	212	237	333	72	220	128	27	215	125	167	128	25	94	198	75	85
Margate	Kent		72	280	259	249	178	123	404	182	281	269	188	264	87	191	224	197	143	123	16	373	102	170	254	222	115	123	234	164	199	230	192	21	410	331	465	240	336	222	476	173	266	144	207	93	333	261	243	142	333	198
Milford Haven	Pembroke		256	72	216	240	158	230	396	144	221	209	277	227	280	145	180	196	264	231	311	309	284	161	170	240	249	307	194	176	216	270	212	327	346	329	402	221	317	269	410	153	236	328	125	260	166	234	304	325	265	165
Monmouth	Monmouth		127	92	140	155	43	118	331	66	162	150	174	176	165	30	105	93	174	147	184	271	157	35	113	129	144	178	115	84	106	159	99	199	295	253	355	106	202	153	359	26	168	200	19	133	183	164	187	199	212	55
Newcastle	Stafford		150	110	38	62	120	107	240	46	61	49	103	72	204	124	3	36	153	138	204	153	168	88	35	42	189	189	12	57	37	75	182	221	190	156	246	200	296	71	254	90	64	202	88	142	125	62	110	178	109	48
Newcastle-on-Tyne	North.		273	272	127	112	300	229	64	202	118	130	186	97	324	289	175	175	252	227	329	57	273	247	173	139	334	275	158	201	162	112	345	341	94	14	123	365	460	132	158	254	105	289	257	250	265	109	119	278	81	220
Northampton	Northampton		66	158	117	108	98	19	279	50	139	127	77	137	120	97	91	61	78	53	121	235	80	63	120	83	130	97	100	31	60	104	143	137	272	207	328	173	268	92	336	71	129	117	86	50	208	121	127	107	191	63
NORWICH	Norfolk		108	270	201	179	207	90	340	159	224	212	82	197	170	205	200	145	42	64	164	306	82	175	224	154	177	62	187	140	145	163	234	157	350	261	398	288	384	159	406	183	199	56	198	98	312	196	159	42	262	176
Nottingham	Nottingham		124	150	59	38	147	74	220	48	91	79	49	77	179	144	43	28	108	82	162	187	122	111	99	26	189	130	54	54	16	43	198	196	224	145	280	220	315	39	288	107	73	145	101	102	187	65	74	134	143	65
Oldham	Lancaster		191	144	4	34	173	139	191	88	30	18	123	26	246	167	42	72	184	158	246	126	195	132	45	50	231	210	32	101	60	50	227	263	163	113	219	244	340	70	227	135	19	222	132	174	135	17	87	205	82	92
OXFORD	Oxford		55	150	145	138	64	56	314	62	167	155	118	162	113	67	111	83	107	86	111	260	85	39	141	112	81	106	120	50	88	147	98	126	297	237	353	147	242	139	361	47	158	127	76	56	220	150	163	124	216	68
PETERBORO'	Nthmptn.		79	190	123	101	148	39	262	80	145	133	36	119	133	138	95	66	55	36	137	221	76	104	132	79	141	84	110	61	61	85	173	152	264	183	320	214	310	69	328	113	121	93	123	60	221	118	93	81	184	96
Plymouth	Devon		216	230	282	297	126	240	473	207	304	292	300	316	225	120	247	234	291	268	272	397	245	160	267	271	188	267	256	219	247	313	98	287	434	395	490	44	63	305	498	155	308	288	168	237	329	309	334	284	353	195
Poole	Dorset		106	182	227	223	60	144	399	140	245	233	202	247	96	73	190	166	187	158	162	344	136	104	216	197	65	158	198	136	173	227	27	175	376	322	433	82	175	224	440	99	243	179	121	128	282	251	250	176	299	139
Portpatrick	Wigton		419	354	247	251	410	379	176	314	217	226	335	227	480	403	268	310	394	390	475	118	418	360	257	277	459	422	261	324	293	260	460	492	81	185	133	482	577	280	89	365	230	436	352	404	346	238	275	420	162	321
Portsmouth	Hants		72	206	287	222	89	120	398	148	309	297	186	246	48	96	195	166	148	123	128	344	101	118	213	196	18	123	204	135	172	230	72	127	381	320	437	133	228	226	445	113	242	144	141	95	293	234	243	141	300	143
Preston	Lancaster		217	148	38	63	195	165	176	108	11	20	147	52	271	194	62	96	208	183	273	88	220	152	50	77	254	234	55	117	87	83	251	288	125	109	181	268	364	111	189	159	44	245	146	198	140	48	121	229	44	115
Reading	Berks		39	170	175	168	67	62	344	92	197	185	134	192	69	80	141	113	114	90	95	290	69	67	171	142	50	90	150	80	118	177	87	110	327	267	383	138	234	169	391	66	188	111	97	51	250	180	193	109	246	98
Rochdale	Lancaster		197	148	11	36	177	145	187	93	22	13	124	24	251	173	46	76	188	163	253	121	199	136	50	57	235	214	35	107	67	52	231	268	158	109	214	248	344	72	222	139	16	226	136	178	139	19	88	209	77	96
SALISBURY	Wilts		81	162	194	193	39	110	369	110	222	210	171	217	85	52	159	137	160	132	137	309	110	68	186	167	55	132	168	106	143	197	38	152	346	291	402	89	184	194	410	67	213	153	107	103	262	205	219	151	265	108
Scarborough	York		216	243	102	80	274	174	149	172	114	110	122	75	270	256	138	141	192	173	272	138	212	214	145	105	279	222	152	171	128	77	302	287	175	70	207	344	439	80	239	221	83	234	224	197	237	81	44	218	122	183
Selby	York		177	207	57	39	159	145	268	120	71	67	100	30	231	207	89	92	166	140	233	133	186	165	100	56	246	188	85	120	80	26	263	248	172	190	223	283	378	46	236	172	38	200	175	166	189	36	34	192	91	135
Sheffield	York		163	164	34	14	174	112	190	76	64	52	82	38	217	163	45	48	144	118	219	146	160	121	78	12	205	166	43	76	36	18	221	234	183	112	229	239	334	31	247	129	34	178	131	141	166	26	66	168	102	92
Shrewsbury	Salop		154	76	71	102	115	111	262	44	93	81	127	105	207	105	37	52	170	142	210	180	176	73	40	84	185	185	46	64	64	106	163	224	217	190	273	181	276	111	281	71	97	206	55	149	108	95	141	198	136	35
Southampton	Hants.		74	188	217	207	63	118	383	131	235	223	183	231	73	78	179	152	154	125	130	329	104	97	198	181	31	125	188	120	157	214	51	145	366	307	422	112	207	207	430	97	227	146	122	96	277	219	238	144	285	127
Stafford	Stafford		134	106	55	72	113	89	248	29	79	67	96	89	188	108	19	24	139	121	190	168	155	72	47	46	173	172	28	42	30	76	166	205	205	170	261	184	279	75	269	74	81	184	72	127	134	75	110	171	124	32
Stockport	Chester		179	139	7	32	162	127	200	76	30	18	109	42	233	154	30	59	170	145	235	126	181	118	40	39	218	196	18	89	49	48	214	250	163	124	219	232	327	65	227	123	30	208	119	160	132	27	97	192	82	78
Sunderland	Durham		272	270	126	111	299	228	76	201	117	129	185	96	323	288	174	174	251	226	328	69	271	246	172	138	330	274	157	200	161	111	344	340	106	13	135	364	459	131	170	253	104	287	256	249	264	108	118	276	80	208
Swansea	Glamorgan		206	66	183	214	99	176	374	124	205	193	124	217	222	86	150	150	230	208	262	292	236	98	139	180	189	254	158	139	164	216	154	278	329	302	385	162	256	209	393	89	209	264	71	197	171	207	245	260	248	106
Taunton	Somerset		146	156	208	222	49	166	399	133	230	218	226	242	150	46	172	159	218	189	202	331	174	86	194	202	120	196	182	141	173	237	40	218	367	320	422	31	128	228	432	79	234	217	94	163	255	232	262	215	282	120
Trowbridge	Wilts		99	133	173	187	10	112	368	97	195	185	174	208	113	23	138	125	166	139	155	298	129	50	161	164	85	151	148	103	140	199	55	170	334	285	390	82	178	184	398	45	200	171	71	111	233	198	225	168	244	85
Truro	Cornwall		257	250	322	336	163	280	513	247	344	332	340	356	262	160	286	273	332	303	316	445	288	200	308	316	234	300	296	255	287	351	137	328	481	434	536	85	12	342	546	194	348	331	208	277	369	346	377	326	396	234
Wakefield	York		178	176	34	10	191	139	166	100	47	42	94	14	232	187	69	72	159	134	234	124	174	145	77	36	229	182	62	100	60	20	245	249	161	88	217	263	258	40	225	153	16	194	155	165	166	13	56	186	80	115
Walsall	Stafford		115	112	74	83	100	77	259	9	95	83	102	107	172	96	37	21	133	106	171	187	140	54	66	57	153	150	46	27	33	87	154	189	224	181	280	172	367	80	288	62	103	171	61	112	152	95	115	162	143	20
Warrington	Lancaster		187	120	25	54	164	138	206	79	30	18	129	54	241	159	32	72	188	161	143	118	200	123	20	57	223	212	24	88	69	76	217	258	155	138	211	235	330	86	219	130	45	233	116	173	110	43	112	211	74	83
Warwick	Warwick		92	128	104	97	81	51	273	20	126	114	98	121	146	82	70	39	109	82	148	220	118	40	104	71	124	129	80	10	47	101	134	163	257	195	313	158	353	94	321	48	117	150	55	86	179	109	129	136	176	31
Weymouth	Dorset		128	186	244	240	65	157	416	157	250	239	217	264	122	72	198	182	205	179	184	350	158	109	220	215	91	180	213	152	191	245	8	200	389	338	444	62	157	240	452	100	256	201	124	150	284	253	265	198	302	140
Whitehaven	Cumberland		297	229	118	132	274	245	129	188	91	100	234	108	351	269	142	184	288	268	353	41	310	232	131	157	335	314	133	197	172	155	328	368	78	92	134	345	440	175	142	235	126	326	226	282	221	134	180	210	55	197
Wigan	Lancaster		199	132	25	55	176	150	194	90	19	10	134	47	253	171	44	84	195	170	255	106	207	135	33	64	236	221	36	100	74	69	229	270	143	130	199	247	342	90	207	142	39	230	128	186	122	43	111	217	62	95
WINCHESTER	Hants		62	182	205	195	62	106	370	119	223	211	171	219	73	73	167	140	143	113	118	317	92	85	186	169	33	113	176	108	145	202	59	133	354	295	410	117	212	195	418	85	215	134	113	83	265	207	226	132	273	115
Windsor	Berks		22	182	183	177	88	52	337	98	205	193	130	192	62	94	149	121	95	73	78	298	52	78	179	150	53	75	158	88	126	167	104	93	335	270	390	154	249	164	398	81	196	95	109	43	258	188	186	91	254	106
Wolverhampton	Stafford		124	106	72	89	97	83	265	14	93	81	108	105	177	92	35	29	140	114	177	185	150	56	60	63	156	155	44	33	39	93	150	194	222	187	278	168	263	85	286	58	97	176	56	118	138	95	128	168	145	16
WORCESTER	Worcester		111	97	100	115	61	80	290	26	122	110	130	136	166	61	66	53	137	111	167	216	142	25	89	89	138	159	75	42	66	119	118	183	256	213	315	137	232	112	317	27	128	180	26	114	165	124	147	166	176	14
Wrexham	Denbigh		177	87	58	90	150	133	238	70	62	50	141	85	238	136	40	70	185	167	253	149	200	105	12	80	216	217	45	88	75	110	195	248	188	171	244	213	308	109	252	104	177	234	85	173	86	76	145	217	106	64
Yarmouth	Norfolk		124	294	225	202	230	114	363	182	247	235	105	227	176	229	223	168	59	86	180	329	94	99	247	177	186	72	210	157	159	186	243	195	373	284	421	295	390	182	429	206	222	67	221	120	335	219	182	54	285	193
YORK	York		196	204	62	39	227	154	145	129	74	70	110	35	250	216	98	101	177	171	252	110	198	174	105	65	265	199	90	129	89	37	274	267	156	67	204	293	387	57	220	182	43	213	184	177	195	41	41	202	90	145

	London	Antwerp	Belfast	Boulogne	Brighton	Bristol	Brussels	Calais	Cork	Dieppe	Dover	Dublin	Edin
Antwerp	211												
Belfast	402	613											
Boulogne	101	163	503										
Brighton	52	220	454	110									
Bristol	119	330	358	220	135								
Brussels	209	32	611	161	263	328							
Calais	95	140	497	23	104	214	138						
Cork	350	561	204	451	366	231	559	445					
Dieppe	127	253	531	90	75	210	251	113	479				
Dover	71	140	473	30	80	190	138	24	421	114			
Dublin	322	533	80	423	376	278	531	417	124	451	393		
Edinburgh	393	542	170	495	448	377	602	489	374	523	464	250	
Falmouth	269	480	529	370	274	170	478	364	195	349	339	449	553
Glasgow	402	558	127	506	459	386	613	500	331	534	476	207	44
Hamburgh	448	300	733	463	500	567	332	440	798	553	400	668	662
Havre de Grace	160	313	531	150	108	186	322	158	481	45	200	451	527
Holyhead	261	475	149	365	328	209	473	359	193	403	335	63	321
Hull	171	300	313	272	225	214	380	266	372	300	242	248	242
Liverpool	205	413	197	306	259	177	414	300	241	334	276	123	212
Milford Haven	256	467	244	257	280	145	465	351	150	355	327	164	402
Newcastle-Tyne	273	419	213	371	324	289	479	365	396	399	341	272	123
Paris (by Dover)	284	177	667	164	274	384	155	187	615	100	194	587	658
Plymouth	216	427	478	317	225	120	425	311	240	300	287	398	490
Portpatrick	419	575	38	520	480	403	628	514	241	540	490	117	133
Portsmouth	72	267	441	157	48	96	281	151	327	123	127	361	437
Waterford	346	557	154	447	370	235	555	441	60	445	417	74	324
Whitehaven	297	480	85	398	351	269	506	392	254	426	368	130	134
Yarmouth	124	180	466	164	176	229	212	141	496	253	195	372	421

EX

The Compilers of the Table now submitted to th
provements upon other tables of a similar na
a portable companion, whereby may be asc
towns in ENGLAND, SCOTLAND *and* WA
they belong, from their size, &c.: o
It has been a just cause of comp
over a great mass of figures,
In the present sheet, it u
effectually succeeded
third section or squ
diately above or
on the right
WORCEST
weary
In

A TABLE,

EXHIBITING THE RECIPROCAL DISTANCE OF THE

CHIEF SEA PORTS

In the United Kingdom,

WITH OTHERS OF IMPORTANCE AS TO TRADE AND COMMUNICATION IN

France and Germany.

☞ The explanation given of the large Table is equally applicable to this.

outh.
Glasgow.
678 | Hamburgh.
535 613 | Havre de Grace.
329 647 383 | Holyhead.
258 420 333 227 | Hull.
220 551 334 105 131 | Liverpool—(*to Holyhead by sea about* 80 *miles.*)
410 724 331 166 304 209 | Milford Haven.
158 539 424 265 119 155 343 | Newcastle-upon-Tyne.
669 477 112 529 436 470 521 535 | Paris.
498 760 266 329 334 297 265 409 481 | Plymouth.
89 695 552 346 275 237 427 175 703 515 | Portpatrick.
445 663 90 293 243 244 241 334 321 177 462 | Portsmouth.
280 742 421 129 322 191 90 346 611 355 191 331 | Waterford.
142 600 426 221 180 111 301 98 562 389 159 336 204 | Whitehaven.
429 372 284 335 182 257 350 305 328 340 454 196 440 335 | Yarmouth.

RECIPROCAL Distance Table OF THE PRINCIPAL TOWNS IN ENGLAND, SCOTLAND, AND WALES:

ACCOMPANIED BY THE MOST ACCEPTED

MAIL AND COACH ROUTES,

THROUGHOUT THE

United Kingdom;

ALSO

A TABLE,

EXHIBITING THE DISTANCE OF ITS CHIEF

SEA PORTS,

FROM OTHERS OF IMPORTANCE AS TO TRADE AND COMMUNICATION IN FRANCE AND GERMANY;

And another, showing the distance from LONDON (by Chart) to the Capitals of the Principal Countries in the WORLD.

ANATORY REMARKS.

———ooo———

lic deem it necessary to offer some remarks relative to its principal features, and im- Their object has been directed to that of furnishing to the tourist and man of business ned, with tolerable precision, the distance to be travelled over between the principal The towns selected are those presumed to be the most prominent in the county to which from their locality, most appropriate to the purpose in view.

against all tables of this kind, hitherto published, that the eye is fatigued in travelling nothing to cheer or relieve, but rather confuse it, on its way to the point of information. perceived that the Publishers have done much towards removing (if they have not dicating) this inconvenience; for, by the introduction of the **black lines** *at every a person will see that the figures in horizontal line with the town must be either imme- the black line, or in the centre; and that in looking perpendicularly, the figures are of such lines, or in the middle: so that the eye may be carried over the table from to the square where is exhibited the distance* (315 *miles*) *from* Edinburgh, *without he vision or distracting the memory,—and so of any other town.*

aring the Table of Distances with the Routes, it will appear in some instances that ng discrepancies exist, the which arise from a different line of road having been taken; ut these variations (when such occur) in-nowise tend to invalidate the correctness of the table. It must here be noticed, that in constructing this table, the distances from town to town have been invariably computed along the most generally travelled Mail or Coach roads.

EXPLANATION OF THE LARGE TABLE.

To find the distance from one given town to another,

Look for the name of one town wanted in the perpendicular list, and carry your eye along the line of figures parallel with such town until it comes to the square beneath the other town sought, the figures contained in which give the distance.

EXAMPLE.

Durham *from* Canterbury *is* 311 *miles:—Having found* Durham *in the perpendicular list, conduct your eye along the* **black line** *until it arrives at that line which points upwards to* Canterbury, *where will be found the distance required. In like manner the distance of all others may be ascertained.*

——ooo——

..*T.*
F. and S.
...*W. and S.*
..............*S.*
minster. *Th. and S.*
ncaster ......*W. and S.*
Leeds ....*T. and S.*
69 | Leek ....*W.*
99 56 | Leicester ....*S.*
93 36 32 | LICHFIELD ..*T. and F.*
66 75 56 77 | LINCOLN............*F.*
77 57 109 83 117 | Liverpool........*W. and S.*
140 121 78 110 80 178 | Lyun............*T. and S.*
58 13 68 52 75 42 138 | Macclesfield......*T. and S.*
221 189 133 155 167 240 133 196 | Maidstone............*Th.*
41 32 85 71 87 36 150 19 221 | Manchester *T. W. Th. and S.*
258 226 170 192 204 277 170 239 43 258 | Margate........*W. and S.*
250 222 201 192 262 209 286 199 291 209 328 | Milford Haven ..*T. and S.*
175 114 108 82 150 156 175 124 163 139 199 126 | Monmouth ......*W. and S.*
81 12 62 30 84 53 133 21 185 36 221 177 103 | Newcastle......*M. and S.*
93 162 192 186 150 155 226 151 308 134 345 343 267 165 | Newcastle-on-Tyne. *T. and S.*
128 96 32 57 84 140 77 109 102 116 138 216 97 88 221 | Northampton..*M. F. and S.*
91 79 121 152 118 232 42 189 143 196 180 328 209 175 275 112 | NORWICH....*W. and S.*
72 44 26 40 36 102 82 61 160 69 196 229 115 55 159 57 137 | Nottingham ..*W. F. and S.*
33 36 89 76 86 43 157 23 226 7 263 216 146 43 127 121 206 73 | Oldham ....*S.*
157 117 75 77 122 169 120 129 90 144 127 195 74 108 251 43 141 100 149 | OXFORD. ......*W. and S.*
113 89 42 74 51 151 36 102 116 122 153 248 138 98 197 41 78 53 129 84 | PETERBOROUGH ..*S.*
316 255 243 223 299 297 310 277 252 282 288 265 150 244 409 219 324 267 288 189 274 | Plymouth....*M. Th. and S.*
242 195 164 156 208 239 208 206 140 226 178 218 104 188 336 135 215 188 232 88 174 124 | Poole................*Th.*
233 269 322 301 299 237 366 256 454 237 491 427 389 271 175 353 431 305 244 378 339 515 462 | Portpatrick..............
241 200 164 161 201 244 171 213 90 226 133 241 126 192 334 131 188 189 291 78 153 177 59 462 | Portsmouth ..*T. Th. and S.*
62 63 116 95 118 31 181 50 252 31 289 221 168 65 123 147 232 100 38 173 153 309 257 206 256 | Preston......*W. F. and S.*
187 147 93 107 145 190 136 159 74 174 111 218 92 138 281 61 142 122 179 30 100 184 80 408 51 202 | Reading........*W. and S.*
34 43 96 82 90 47 161 30 232 11 269 220 150 47 127 127 212 80 7 155 133 293 237 239 236 33 185 | Rochdale........*M. and S.*
212 165 133 126 177 209 179 175 116 194 153 197 82 156 305 105 197 158 202 58 144 133 30 427 46 221 50 205 | SALISBURY ..*T. and S.*
65 134 143 154 86 142 166 123 251 106 288 315 234 141 84 170 203 119 98 208 137 376 294 256 290 125 238 97 264 | Scarborough ....*Th.*
20 86 110 104 64 97 138 78 212 61 249 270 185 97 100 139 196 83 53 168 111 327 253 251 252 82 198 54 223 54 | Selby ....*M.*
33 42 66 60 47 77 119 35 198 41 235 226 141 48 126 95 167 39 38 124 89 283 209 264 208 72 154 42 179 93 44 | Sheffield ....*T. and S.*
111 46 79 40 115 58 158 54 190 70 226 143 75 34 204 95 204 79 76 105 114 225 176 298 178 92 135 81 146 176 131 88 | Shrewsbury......*W. and S.*
226 185 148 146 196 229 173 198 103 214 146 224 109 176 321 115 190 173 221 65 147 156 34 447 25 241 46 225 23 286 237 193 162 | Southampton ..*T. Th. & S.*
93 24 47 16 79 69 125 37 169 52 206 177 87 16 184 72 180 45 59 92 89 228 170 286 175 81 122 65 140 156 111 58 31 160 | Stafford ....*S.*
43 25 78 64 80 39 143 12 214 7 251 211 133 32 137 109 194 62 11 137 116 276 220 244 222 38 167 18 187 108 63 34 64 210 49 | Stockport..............*F.*
92 161 191 185 149 154 225 150 307 133 344 342 266 169 12 230 274 158 125 250 196 408 335 187 333 123 280 121 304 83 203 125 203 320 183 135 | Sunderland ....*S.*
223 171 163 138 205 157 232 166 241 182 278 66 64 146 312 160 270 157 188 136 195 206 160 410 186 204 155 193 138 290 243 198 112 164 132 176 315 | Swansea ....*W. and S.*
241 180 165 148 221 222 234 190 181 207 218 191 76 170 334 143 250 190 214 112 185 75 67 449 110 240 112 218 65 301 252 208 151 87 153 201 334 132 | Taunton........*W. and S.*
206 146 127 114 181 194 185 168 134 174 171 168 53 135 299 106 200 153 179 59 143 125 60 416 74 207 60 184 30 268 217 175 116 53 119 168 298 109 51 | Trowbridge..*T. Th. and S.*
355 294 279 262 335 336 348 304 292 321 330 303 190 284 448 257 364 304 328 226 299 51 163 559 214 354 226 332 172 415 357 322 265 164 267 315 448 246 114 165 | Truro..........*W. and S.*
9 66 90 84 58 74 132 55 213 38 250 247 165 74 102 119 183 63 30 148 105 307 233 242 232 60 178 32 203 69 24 24 108 217 82 40 101 220 233 198 343 | Wakefield..............*F.*
102 47 41 9 84 87 119 57 150 72 187 183 74 34 195 59 168 51 76 71 83 216 149 305 157 99 101 83 119 162 113 69 35 140 18 65 194 131 142 105 252 93 | Walsall................*T.*
59 36 91 65 105 18 161 23 222 18 259 191 138 35 152 123 214 84 25 143 133 279 221 236 227 30 173 29 191 124 79 55 62 211 51 21 151 167 205 175 315 56 69 | Warrington.... *W. and S.*
116 75 36 37 99 120 106 88 127 102 164 168 74 67 209 32 144 64 108 43 70 202 126 338 126 132 73 116 96 177 127 83 74 112 52 100 209 129 128 92 238 107 29 102 | Warwick ....*T. and S.*
260 198 179 169 223 250 226 210 163 228 200 210 107 190 353 151 242 206 235 106 181 103 28 468 81 262 95 239 47 310 271 229 171 59 174 223 352 162 48 63 143 253 162 225 142 | Weymouth......*T. and F.*
126 143 196 175 193 111 262 130 332 111 369 301 248 145 98 227 312 179 110 252 234 389 334 159 336 80 283 113 301 177 146 152 172 321 160 118 106 284 315 284 425 135 179 110 212 336 | Whitehaven .. *T. Th. & S.*
57 48 103 77 105 22 168 35 234 18 271 203 150 47 141 134 219 86 25 155 140 291 234 224 239 18 185 23 203 122 77 59 76 223 63 25 143 188 218 186 328 55 81 12 114 237 98 | Wigan ....*M. and F.*
214 173 136 134 184 217 171 186 97 202 134 218 103 164 309 103 178 161 209 53 144 161 44 435 25 229 34 213 24 274 225 181 150 12 148 198 308 159 92 47 196 205 128 199 100 67 309 211 | WINCHESTER, *W. & S.*
196 155 99 114 145 198 120 163 58 182 94 233 107 146 285 67 133 124 187 38 90 197 94 416 60 210 16 193 66 232 193 162 142 60 130 176 283 182 131 76 233 187 109 181 80 112 290 193 49 | Windsor........*W. and S.*
108 43 57 15 87 85 130 52 156 68 193 152 71 32 201 64 173 55 76 75 94 211 156 303 160 99 105 81 124 168 119 75 30 144 16 62 200 117 138 107 248 99 6 67 35 158 177 79 132 112 | Wolverhampton ......*W*
134 74 69 42 110 116 135 84 147 99 183 151 40 63 228 62 173 74 106 57 103 181 125 334 129 128 87 110 93 194 145 101 48 113 47 93 227 97 107 71 217 125 34 98 32 126 208 110 101 95 31 | WORCESTER *W. & S.*
92 50 92 61 122 30 170 55 212 50 249 168 106 37 184 118 212 92 57 137 134 256 208 267 210 62 166 61 178 157 112 90 32 192 45 52 184 128 182 149 292 89 67 32 92 208 143 45 174 174 62 80 | Wrexham *M. & Th.*
214 202 144 175 147 255 65 212 160 219 196 350 232 198 298 123 23 160 229 164 101 340 230 454 196 255 163 235 205 226 219 190 227 198 203 217 297 295 270 223 380 206 191 237 167 251 335 242 186 146 196 196 235 | Yarmouth *W. & S.*
25 94 109 113 76 102 151 83 232 66 268 275 194 101 81 149 200 92 58 184 122 336 252 237 201 85 214 59 232 40 14 53 136 246 111 68 81 248 262 236 372 29 122 84 136 262 145 80 234 204 128 154 117 222 | YORK ..*S.*

TABLE,

Calculated to show the DISTANCE, (as near as can be) by chart, from LONDON to the CAPITALS of the PRINCIPAL COUNTRIES in the WORLD, with the bearings from London to those Capitals, and the Latitude and Longitude from the Meridian of Greenwich.

LONDON TO	*Miles.*	*Bearings.*	*Lat.*	*Long.*	LONDON TO	*Miles.*	*Bearings.*	*Lat.*	*Long.*
Algiers.........*Africa*	900	S. by E.	36°42′N.	3°30′E.	Mexico.....*N.America*	3240	S.W. by W.	19°26′N.	90° 1′W.
Amsterdam....*Holland*	180	E. by N.	52 25 N.	4 40 E.	Milan............*Italy*	380	S.S.E.	45 28 N.	8 12 E.
Berlin.........*Prussia*	360	E. by N.	52 32 N.	13 22 E.	Morocco.........*Africa*	1200	S. by W.	30 57 N.	7 0W.
Berne......*Switzerland*	300	S.S.E.	46 57 N.	7 26 E.	Munich.......*Germany*	310	S.E. by S.	48 9 N.	11 36 E.
Bogota...*SouthAmerica*	3240	S.W.	5 24 N.	74 7 W.	Naples...........*Italy*	660	S.S.E.	40 50 N.	14 16 E.
BuenosAyres.*S.America*	4620	S.S.W.	34 35 S.	57 24 W.	Paris............*France*	227	S.½E.	48 50 N.	2 20 E.
Cairo..............*Egypt*	1320	S.S.E.	30 2 N.	31 20 E.	Pekin............*China*	3480	E.S.E.	39 55 N.	116 28 E.
Calcutta....*East Indies*	3060	S.E. by E.	22 34 N.	88 28 E.	Quebec.........*Canada*	1920	W. by S.	46 50 N.	71 10W.
Cashmire.............*Asia*	2220	S.E. by E.	34 20 N.	13 43 E.	Rio Janeiro..*S.America*	4080	S.S.W.	22 56 S.	42 2W.
Constantinople..*Turkey*	900	S.E. by S.	41 0 N.	25 56 E.	Rome............*Italy*	600	S.S.E.	41 48 N.	12 0 E.
Copenhagen...*Denmark*	480	N.E. by E.	55 41 N.	12 35 E.	St. Petersburgh..*Russia*	990	N.E.	59 57 N.	30 19 E.
Delhi.......*East Indies*	2580	S.E.	28 43 N.	77 9 E.	Samarcand.....*Tartary*	1860	E.S.E.	39 38 N.	64 9 E.
Dresden..........*Saxony*	360	E.½S.	51 3 N.	13 43 E.	Siam..........*East Indies*	3630	S.E.	12 50 N.	101 8 E.
Dublin...........*Ireland*	322	N.W. by W.	53 21 N.	6 15 W.	Stockholm......*Sweden*	720	N.E.	59 21 N.	18 4 E.
Florence...........*Italy*	480	S.S.E.	43 47 N.	11 16 E.	Stutgard........*Germany*	270	S.E.	48 46 N.	9 11 E.
Genoa..............*Italy*	420	S.S.E.	44 25 N.	8 58 E.	Tombuctoo.......*Africa*	2220	S.	17 0 N.	1 20 E.
Hamburgh. *Lwr.Saxony*	330	E.N.E.	53 33 N.	9 59 E.	Tonquin...........*China*	3540	S.E. by E.	21 0 N.	105 12 E.
Hanover........*Germany*	300	E.byN.	52 23 N.	9 43 E.	Tunis..............*Africa*	900	S.S.E.	36 44 N.	10 20 E.
Ispahan............*Persia*	1690	S.E.	32 25 N.	52 50 E.	Turin.. *Sardinia—Italy*	390	S.S.E.	45 4 N.	7 40 E.
Jedo...............*Japan*	4200	E.S.E.	36 30 N.	140 0 E.	Ummerapoora..*E.Indies*	3200	S.E. by E.	21 55 N.	96 7 E.
Lima ... *South America*	3900	S.W.	12 3 S.	77 8W.	Venice..............*Italy*	430	S.E. by S.	45 20 N.	12 21 E.
Lisbon........*Portugal*	720	S.S.W.	38 43 N.	9 9W.	Vienna.........*Austria*	420	S.E.	48 13 N.	16 23 E.
Madrid............*Spain*	660	S. by W.	40 25 N.	3 33W.	Warsaw.........*Poland*	450	E.½N.	52 14 N.	20 3 E.
Mecca...........*Arabia*	1860	S.S.E.	21 18 N.	40 15 E.	Washington.*N.America*	2280	S.W. by W.	38 58 N.	77 2W.

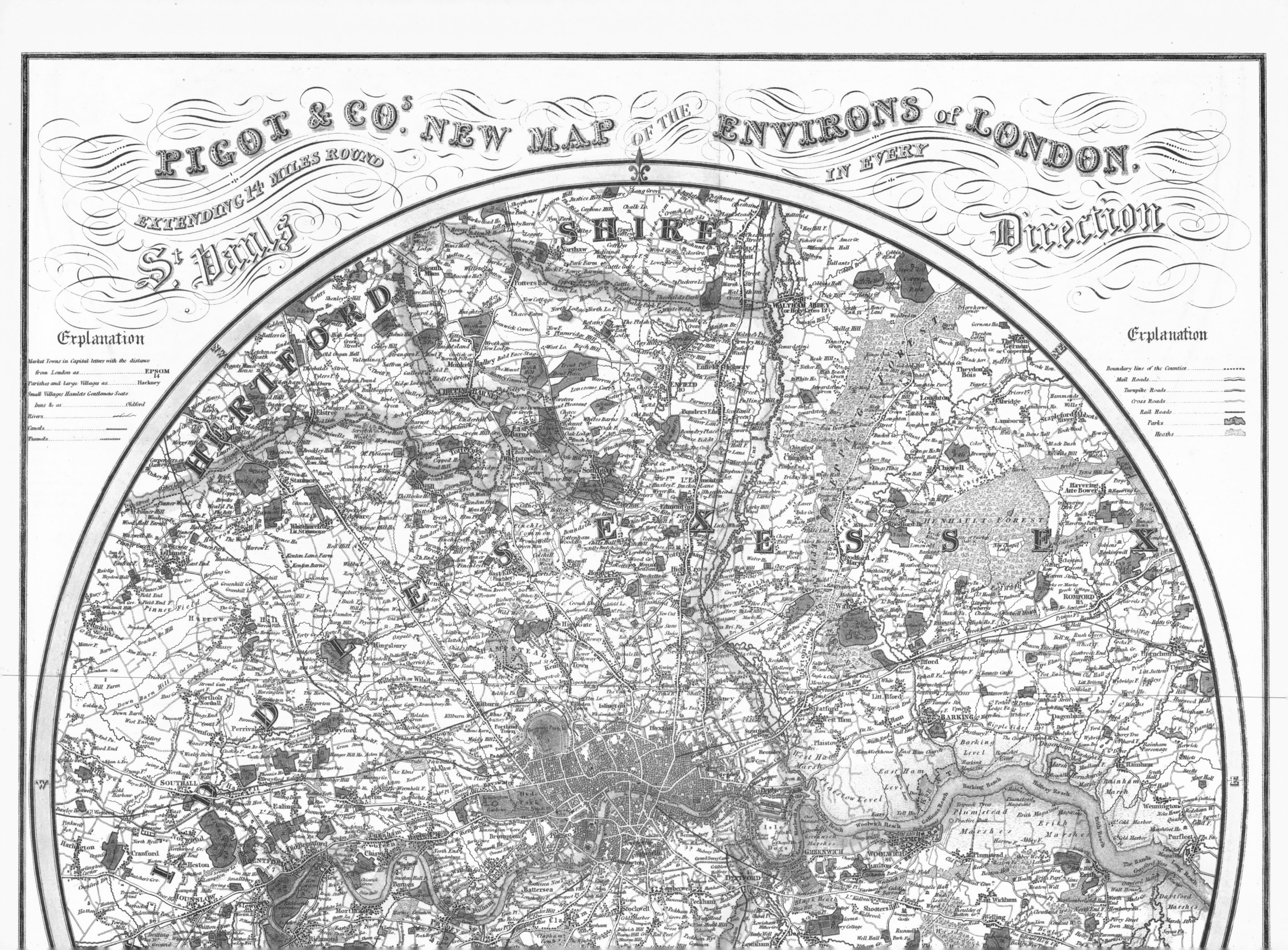
PIGOT & CO.s NEW MAP OF THE ENVIRONS of LONDON,
EXTENDING 14 MILES ROUND
St. Pauls
IN EVERY
Direction
Explanation
Market Towns in Capital letters with the distance from London as EPSOM 14
Parishes and Large Villages as Hackney
Small Villages Hamlets Gentlemans Seats Inns &c as Oldford
Rivers
Canals
Tunnels
Explanation
Boundary line of the Counties
Mail Roads
Turnpike Roads
Cross Roads
Rail Roads
Parks
Heaths
HERTFORD SHIRE
MIDDLESEX
ESSEX

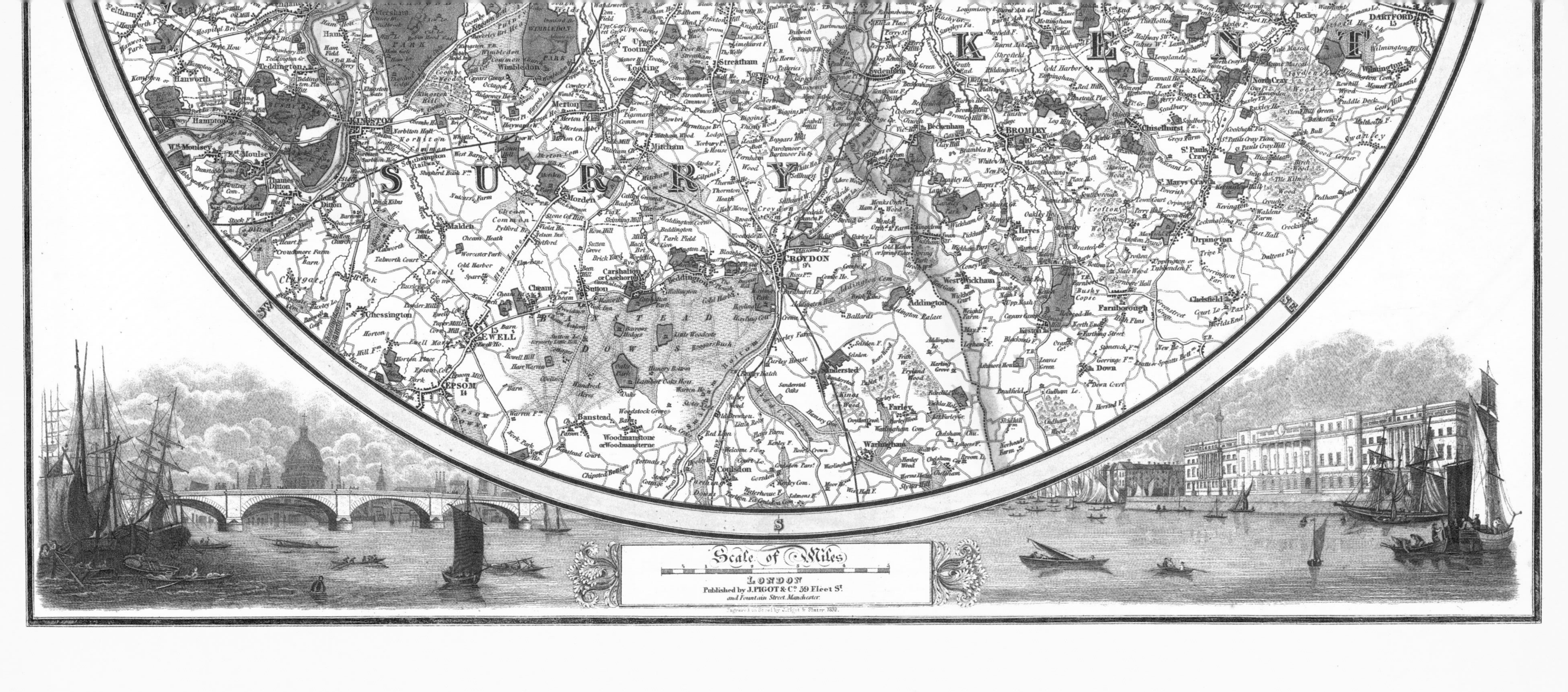
SURRY
KENT
CROYDON
BROMLEY
KINGSTON
EWELL
EPSOM
DARTFORD
Scale of Miles
LONDON
Published by J. PIGOT & Co. 59 Fleet St.
and Fountain Street Manchester.

A

Brief Topographical Sketch of the County of

BEDFORD.

BEDFORD is an inland county, bounded on the north by Huntingdonshire and Northamptonshire, on the west by Buckinghamshire, which county also, with Hertfordshire, forms its southern boundary; and its eastern extremity is met by Cambridgeshire, as well as Hertfordshire. The form of the county is oval, being about 35 miles in length, 20 broad, and its circumference 96; containing an area of 460 square statute miles.

NAME and ANCIENT HISTORY.—When the Romans landed in Britain, B. C. 55, this part of the country was included in the district inhabited by the *Catieuchlanii*, or *Cassi*, whose chief, Cassivellaunus, headed the force of the whole island against Cæsar, and the year following was totally defeated. When the Emperor Constantine divided Britain into five Roman provinces, it was included in the third division, called *Flavia Cæsariensis.* At the establishment of the kingdom of Mercia (one of the divisions of the Saxon heptarchy) it was considered as part of that kingdom, and was known as BEDICANFORD, signifying a fortress on a ford; and when Alfred divided England into counties, &c. he applied to this shire the name of *Bedeford,* hence its present appellation BEDFORDSHIRE. In this county are many remains of Roman, Saxon, and Norman antiquities, and a few Roman stations—the site of the *Magiovinum* of Antonius is at Sandy, near Potton, where many urns, coins, &c. have been dug up; another station at *Madining-bowre*, or Maiden-bower, one mile from Dunstable, called by Camden, *Magintum;* and near Biggleswade are the station *Chesterfield,* and the site of the city of *Salena,* as mentioned by Ptolemy, where are also many *tumuli.* Arlesey, near Shefford, and Leighton Buzzard, were Roman encampments, and at the latter place the Roman road, *Icknield-street,* enters the county, as does the *Watling-street* near Luton, from St. Albans; whilst another Roman causeway passes near Potton, and crosses the Ouse, on to Newport Pagnell, in Buckinghamshire.

SOIL, PRODUCE, and CLIMATE.—The surface of this county is pleasingly varied, being broken into small hills and vallies: to the south a range of chalk eminences rise to a considerable height; the extensive tract of land beneath these hills is hard and sterile, assuming a cold, dreary and uncomfortable appearance; but the aspect of this part is annually losing much of the uninviting, by the indefatigable labours of the husbandman and spirit of the agriculturist. The middle of the county, and on to the south-east corner, embraces very rich dairy ground; as does the land terminated on the north by sandy hills, the fertile tract extending in a line from the middle of the county to the south-east corner; the west side is mostly flat and sandy, yet, being well cultivated, produces great quantities of beans. The vale of Bedford is a very rich tract of land, exceedingly fruitful, and yielding heavy crops of fine wheat and barley: great quantities of turnips are also produced in this part. The land on the north side of this vale is a strong clay; that on the south, though in general lighter, is yet a good staple, and its natural fertility is much increased by the overflowing of the Ouse. On the north and north-east part the soil is a deep loam, famous from the goodness of its cultivation, and for growing crops of corn, particularly barley. The general soil of the county may be considered as possessing natural fertility, and well available to profit the agriculturist; yet, much land remains unenclosed. A number of fine woods are interspersed throughout the county, the timber of which is occasionally felled, and sent to the sea coast by the Ouse. The CLIMATE of Bedfordshire is experienced to be exceedingly healthy; the air is salubrious, and its temperature genial and invigorating.

MANUFACTURES and TRADE.—The chief manufactures of this county are the making thread lace, the platting of straw, and forming the same into hats and bonnets: the principal seat of the straw trade is Dunstable; Luton also has some considerable manufacturers, and indeed at all the principal markets great quantities of plat are brought for sale. The lace trade has much declined since machinery has been adapted to the manufacturing this article, and may be said almost to have superseded the patient labours of those who produce this beautiful texture for ornamental dress from the pillow. Bedfordshire enjoys a trade of some importance in corn, timber and seed; besides a material one derived from the extensive culture of succulent vegetables, to which the soil of whole parishes is appropriated, and the produce disseminated through the neighbouring country, while much finds its way to the Metropolitan markets. Near to Woburn that useful cleansing material fuller's earth is obtained in considerable quantities, which is conveyed upon the Grand Junction canal to different places on its line. Independent of the declension of its lace branch, this county partakes as little in the fluctuation of trade and manufactures as any other in the kingdom.

RIVERS.---The principal rivers are the OUSE and the IVEL: the former rises from two sources near Middleton Cheney, in Northamptonshire, and enters Bedfordshire a mile below Turvey; at Bedford it becomes navigable and pursuing its devious course through Huntingdonshire and Cambridgeshire, passing the city of Ely, it enters Norfolk, and falls into the wash at Lynn Regis. The Ivel rises from three sources, at Charlton, Toddington Park, and Eversholt, and flowing north-east, passes the town of Biggleswade, from whence it is navigable to its union with the Ouse at Tempsford. The Grand Junction canal passes close to Leighton Buzzard, and it is intended to form a canal communication between that town and Shefford.

CIVIL and ECCLESIASTICAL DIVISIONS.---Bedfordshire is in the Province of Canterbury and Diocese of Lincoln, and included in the Norfolk circuit: it is divided into nine hundreds, viz.:

BARFORD,	FLITT,	STODDEN,
BIGGLESWADE,	MANSHEAD,	WILLEY,
CLIFTON,	REDBORNESTOKE,	WIXAMTREE,

which collectively contain one hundred and twenty-four parishes, one county town (Bedford) and ten other market-towns. The town of Bedford returns two members to parliament, and the County two.

POPULATION.—According to the census of 1821, there were houses inhabited in the county, 15,412; uninhabited, 202; and houses building, 105. The number of families then resident in the county was 17,373; comprising 40,385 males, and 43,331 females; total, 83,716: and by a calculation made by order of government, which included persons in the army and navy, for which was added after the ratio of about one to thirty prior to the year 1811, and one to fifty for that year and the census of 1821, to the returns made from the several districts; the population of the county, in round numbers, in the year 1700, was 48,500—in 1750, 53,900—in 1801, 65,500—in 1811, 72,600—and in 1821, 85,400. The increased population in the fifty years, from the year 1700, was 5,400—from 1750 to 1801, the increase was 11,600—from 1801 to 1811, the increase was 7,100—and from 1811 to 1821, the augmented number of persons was 12,800: the grand total increase in the population of the county, from the year 1700 to the census of 1821, being about 36,900 persons.

Index of Distances from Town to Town in the County of Bedford.

THE NAMES OF THE RESPECTIVE TOWNS ARE ON THE TOP AND SIDE, AND THE SQUARE WHERE BOTH MEET GIVES THE DISTANCE.

	Ampthill	Bedford	Biggleswade	Dunstable	Harrold	Leighton Buzzard	Luton	Market Street	Potton	Shefford	Toddington	*Distance from London.*
Ampthill												45
Bedford	8											51
Biggleswade	14	11										45
Dunstable	12	20	22									33
Harrold	17	9	20	29								60
Leighton Buzzard	14	20	28	8	28							41
Luton	14	19	20	5	28	12						31
Market Street	16	22	26	4	31	12	4					29
Potton	16	12	4	26	21	26	22	30				49
Shefford	8	9	5	19	18	21	14	18	12			41
Toddington	8	15	17	5	24	8	8	9	24	12		38
Woburn	7	14	22	9	22	6	12	13	27	15	5	42

Additional information relating to the County of Bedford.

ooo

Population.—By the Census for **1831** this county contained 46,350 males, and 49,033 females—total 95,383, being an increase, since the returns made in the year 1821, of 11,667 inhabitants; and from the Census of 1801 to that of 1831 the augmentation amounted to 31,990 persons.

Under the *Reform Bill* the polling for the county members is directed to take place at Bedford, Luton, Leighton, Ampthill, Biggleswade, and Sharnbrook. The number of representatives remains the same as before the act was passed.

Railways.—The London and Birmingham passes close to *Leighton Buzzard* on the west, within six miles of *Hockliffe*, about seven from *Dunstable*, and five from *Woburn*. A line (the Eastern Junction Railway) is projected to issue from the London and Birmingham Railway (near *Newport Pagnell*) to the Eastern Counties' Railway at Ipswich; it will pass a little to the north of Bedford, and through Cambridge and Bury St. Edmunds.

A line of Railway to be called the 'London and Manchester Railway' is projected—the route proposed is through or near to the towns of St. Albans, Luton, Ampthill and Bedford—thence, by way of Leicester, to Manchester. A numerously attended meeting was held at Bedford, on the 4th August, 1840, to ascertain the opinions of the inhabitants of that town and its neighbourhood, when the liveliest interest was manifested by every one present, and the various resolutions to effect the object of the meeting were carried unanimously.

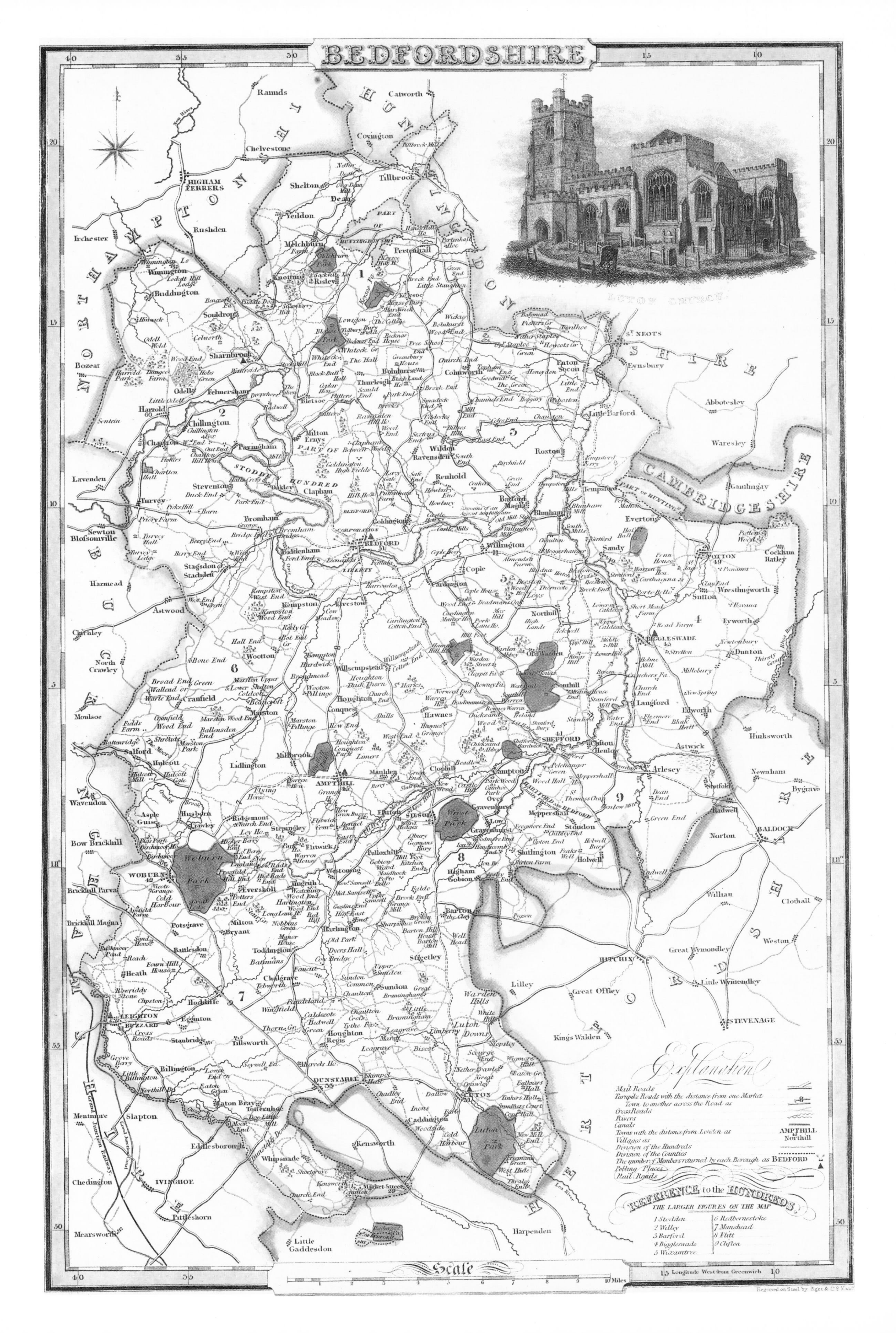
BEDFORDSHIRE
LUTON CHURCH
NORTHAMPTON
HUNTINGDON
HUNTINGDONSHIRE
CAMBRIDGESHIRE
BUCKINGHAM
HERTFORD
BEDFORD
CORPORATION
LIBERTY
STODDEN HUNDRED
HIGHAM FERRERS
ST NEOTS
AMPTHILL
BIGGLESWADE
SHEFFORD
SILSOE
WOBURN
LEIGHTON BUZZARD
DUNSTABLE
LUTON
HITCHIN
BALDOCK
STEVENAGE
IVINGHOE
POTTON
Woburn Park
Luton Park
Wrest Park
Explanation
Mail Roads
Turnpike Roads with the distance from one Market Town to another across the Road as
Cross Roads
Rivers
Canals
Towns with the distance from London as
AMPTHILL
Villages as
Northill
Division of the Hundreds
Division of the Counties
The number of Members returned by each Borough as BEDFORD
Polling Places
Rail Roads
REFERENCE to the HUNDREDS
THE LARGER FIGURES ON THE MAP
1 Stodden
2 Willey
3 Barford
4 Biggleswade
5 Wixamtree
6 Redbornestoke
7 Manshead
8 Flitt
9 Clifton
Scale
10 Miles
Longitude West from Greenwich

BERKSHIRE.

BERKSHIRE is an inland county, bounded on the north by the counties of Oxford and Buckingham, on the east by Surrey, on the south by Hampshire, and on the west by Wiltshire. It is extremely irregular in its form; in circumference, according to Roque's mensuration, it is 207 miles; but it must be presumed, that this survey takes the extreme of all the promontories, and enters into all the devious curves and windings which characterize its outward figure, for other surveyors have only stated its circumference to be about 120 miles. The Government survey states its area to comprise 756 square miles. Its greatest length, from Old Windsor to the county cross, is 42 miles; its extreme breadth, from Witham, near Oxford, to the borders of Hampshire, south of Newbury, about 28 miles; and its narrowest, from the Thames, near Reading, across to the border of Hampshire, in a direct south line, only 7 miles.

NAME and ANCIENT HISTORY.—According to Camden, this county was anciently named by the Latin writers *Bercheria;* by the Saxons *Beroc-scyre,* which appellation *Asser Menevensis,* an ancient English historian, derives from *Barroc,* a certain wood, where grew plenty of box. It is more probable, however, (observes another etymologist) that it may have been derived from the quantity of birch wood growing anciently in the county, the soil, in general, being more adapted to the growth of that wood than any other. In the reign of Alfred it was called *Berocshire.* The ancient inhabitants of a great part of this county were the *Attrebattii,* or *Attrebates,* who are supposed to have emigrated from Gaul. The south-eastern part was inhabited by a people called the *Bibroci,* or *Rhemi;* and a small portion of it, next Hampshire, by the *Segonticœ.* Under the division of Britain, by the Roman Emperor Constantine, this county was included in the BRITANNIA PRIMA; and during the Saxon heptarchy, it formed a part of the kingdom of *Wessex,* or West Saxons.—In the military history of modern times, this county is not conspicuous; the principal battles fought in it were those in 1643 and 1644, between the forces of King Charles and the Parliament, in the first of which the gallant and virtuous Lord Falkland was slain.

SOIL, PRODUCE and CLIMATE.—The agricultural appropriation of land in this county appears to be as follows: land in arable, about 250,000 acres; meadows and dairy land, 75,000; sheep walks and barren heaths, 55,000; and pasture parks, &c. 20,000. Close to the Thames, in the northern part of the county, is a fertile line of meadow, from which the land rises gently towards a range of moderately elevated hills, extending from Oxford to Faringdon; the hills being good corn land. To the south is the remarkably fertile vale of Berks, the prevailing soil of which is a strong grey calcareous loam. The greatest part of the southern side of the county consists chiefly of a gravelly loam. From Hungerford to Reading is a bed of peat, through which the river Kennet takes its course; and near Hungerford, south of the Kennet, commences a tract of poor gravel and clay. The weight of hay cut from the meadows contiguous to the river Kennet, from Hungerford to Reading, is considerable. The quantity of peat dug in the neighbourhood of Newbury, and other parts, is very great, and employs many of the labouring class. Such meadows as have peat under them, are more valuable to the landlord than the tenant;—the great value of peat arising from the demand for it as fuel, and for its ashes as manure. Numerous herds of neat cattle are grazed in this county; and the sheep, vast numbers of which are fed, are large and handsome. Swine and poultry are extremely profitable to the farmer of Berkshire, from its proximity to London. The farms are large, few being found rented under £100 a year. The county is well stocked with timber, particularly with oak and beech in the western parts, as is Windsor forest, which also abounds with wild fowl, and other game. This forest has been famous for its rural beauties, and for the pleasures of the chase, which it has afforded to a long series of our Monarchs. It was the theme of the juvenile muse of Pope, who was born within its precincts. Within the forest is contained the Great Park, covered with noble trees, and stocked with numerous herds of deer. Part of this has been greatly improved, and rendered of public utility, by the establishment of experimental farms, managed with great attention, under the particular direction of his late and present Majesty. Some of the prospects of Berkshire are of the most beautiful and animated description; the view from the magnificent Castle at Windsor, which is seated on an eminence above the Thames, is one which embraces all the various charms of a perfect landscape, and includes in the range of sight, the noble river and its windings, and parks, villas, and pleasure-grounds innumerable, scattered throughout a lovely and rich district. The CLIMATE of Berkshire is remarkably healthful, the air pure, and no endemical disease known to prevail in it.

MANUFACTURES and TRADE.—The manufactures of this county are very limited, its prosperity chiefly depending upon the export and import of commodities, by means of the Thames; an excellent general retail trade, and its agricultural and horticultural produce, joined to the rearing of all kinds of farming stock, to a great extent and profit. The malting trade is very extensive in several towns, especially at Reading, where also are manufactured, to a small extent, pins, and ribbons and other silk goods, sackings, &c. NEWBURY, formerly eminent for woollen cloths, is now the great corn mart of the county. Considerable business is done upon the banks of the Thames in timber; and the annual exportation of corn and flour to London is very great.

RIVERS and CANALS.—The principal rivers of Berkshire are, the THAMES, the KENNET, the LODDEN, the OCK, the LAMBOURN, and the ENBORNE. The FIRST of all the British streams, the Thames, enters the county at its northern extremity, about a mile south of Lechdale, and is navigable thence throughout its entire course, and in its progress waters the several towns of Abingdon, Wallingford, Reading, Henley, Maidenhead, Windsor, &c., soon afterwards flowing between the confines of Surrey and Middlesex. This noble river, which borders so large a part of this county, is a vast advantage to it, both in bestowing beauty and fertility on so many situations in it, and in affording a ready carriage by water of its commodities to the great mart of the Metropolis. The Kennet enters at Hungerford, and, flowing through Reading, unites its waters with the Thames. The Lodden enters at Swallowfield, and falls into the Thames near Wingrave. The Ock has its source near Faringdon, and is lost in the Thames near Abingdon. The Enborne, or Enburn, rises near Inkpen, and joins the Kennet at Wasing. The Lambourn has its source near the town of that name, and falls into the Kennet near Shaw. The CANALS are the WILTS and BERKS Canal, which enters the county at Hackson bridge, and the KENNET and AVON, which enters at Hungerford, and runs parallel with the Kennet river to Newbury.

CIVIL and ECCLESIASTICAL DIVISIONS.—BERKSHIRE is in the Province of Canterbury, and Diocese of Salisbury; is within the Oxford circuit, and divided into twenty hundreds, viz.:

BEYNHURST, COOKHAM, HORMER, OCK, SONNING,
BRAY, FAIRCROSS, KINTBURY-EAGLE, READING, THEALE,
CHARLTON, FARINGDON, LAMBOURN, RIPPLESMERE, WANTAGE,
COMPTON, GANFIELD, MORETON, SHRIVENHAM, WARGRAVE.

These divisions contain together 151 parishes, 12 market-towns, and one county-town (Reading.) The whole county returns nine members to parliament, viz. two each for READING, WALLINGFORD and NEW WINDSOR, one for ABINGDON, and two for the shire.

POPULATION.—According to the census of 1821, there were houses inhabited in the county, 24,705; uninhabited, 622; and houses building, 154. The number of families then resident in the county was 27,700, comprising 65,546 males, and 66,431 females; total, 131,977: and by a calculation made by order of government, which included persons in the army and navy, for which was added after the ratio of about one to thirty prior to the year 1811, and one to fifty for that year and the census of 1821, to the returns made from the several districts; the population of the county, in round numbers, in the year 1700, was 74,700—in 1750, 92,700—in 1801, 112,800—in 1811, 122,300—and in 1821, 134,700. The increased population in the fifty years, from the year 1700, was 18,000—from 1750 to 1801, the increase was 20,100—from 1801 to 1811, the increase was 9,500—and from 1811 to 1821, the augmented number of persons was 12,400: the grand total increase in the population of the county, from the year 1700 to the census of 1821, being about 60,000 persons.

Index of Distances from Town to Town in the County of Berks.

THE NAMES OF THE RESPECTIVE TOWNS ARE ON THE TOP AND SIDE, AND THE SQUARE WHERE BOTH MEET GIVES THE DISTANCE.

	Abingdon	Faringdon	Hungerford	Ilsley	Lambourn	Maidenhead	Newbury	Oakingham	Reading	Wallingford	Wantage	Windsor	*Distance from London.*
Abingdon													56
Faringdon	14												70
Hungerford	23	17											64
Ilsley, East	11	15	16										54
Lambourn	19	12	7	10									68
Maidenhead	30	40	38	29	39								26
Newbury	20	25	9	9	12	30							56
Oakingham	32	35	32	22	32	10	24						31
Reading	25	28	25	15	25	13	17	7					39
Wallingford	10	22	24	8	18	20	17	22	15				45
Wantage	10	9	14	7	8	34	15	27	20	14			60
Windsor	36	46	44	35	45	6	36	9	16	26	40		22

[See over.

Additional information relating to the County of Berks.

———ooo———

Population.—By the Census for **1831** this county contained 72,453 males, and 72,836 females—total 145,289, being an increase, since the returns made in the year 1821, of 13,312 inhabitants; and from the Census of 1801 to that of 1831 the augmentation amounted to 36,074 persons.

Representation.—Under the *Reform Bill* the borough of Wallingford is deprived of one of its members, and one is added to the county, so that the whole shire returns nine representatives as heretofore. The polling for the county members, by the late Act, is directed to take place at Abingdon, Reading, Newbury, Wantage, Wokingham, Maidenhead, Great Faringdon and East Ilsley.

Railways.—The Great Western passes close to *Maidenhead* and *Reading,* three miles to the north of *Windsor,* within three miles to the left of *Wallingford,* two north of *Wantage,* and six south of *Faringdon.* At Reading a branch is intended to join the London and Southampton Railway near Basingstoke. At Reading will also commence the projected Salisbury and Exeter Railway. The Newbury and Great Western Junction line is proposed to commence at Newbury, and proceed by Thatcham, Midgham and Woolhampton; and, crossing the London and Bath road, will proceed to Tidmarsh and Pangbourn, where it will join the Great Western Railway.

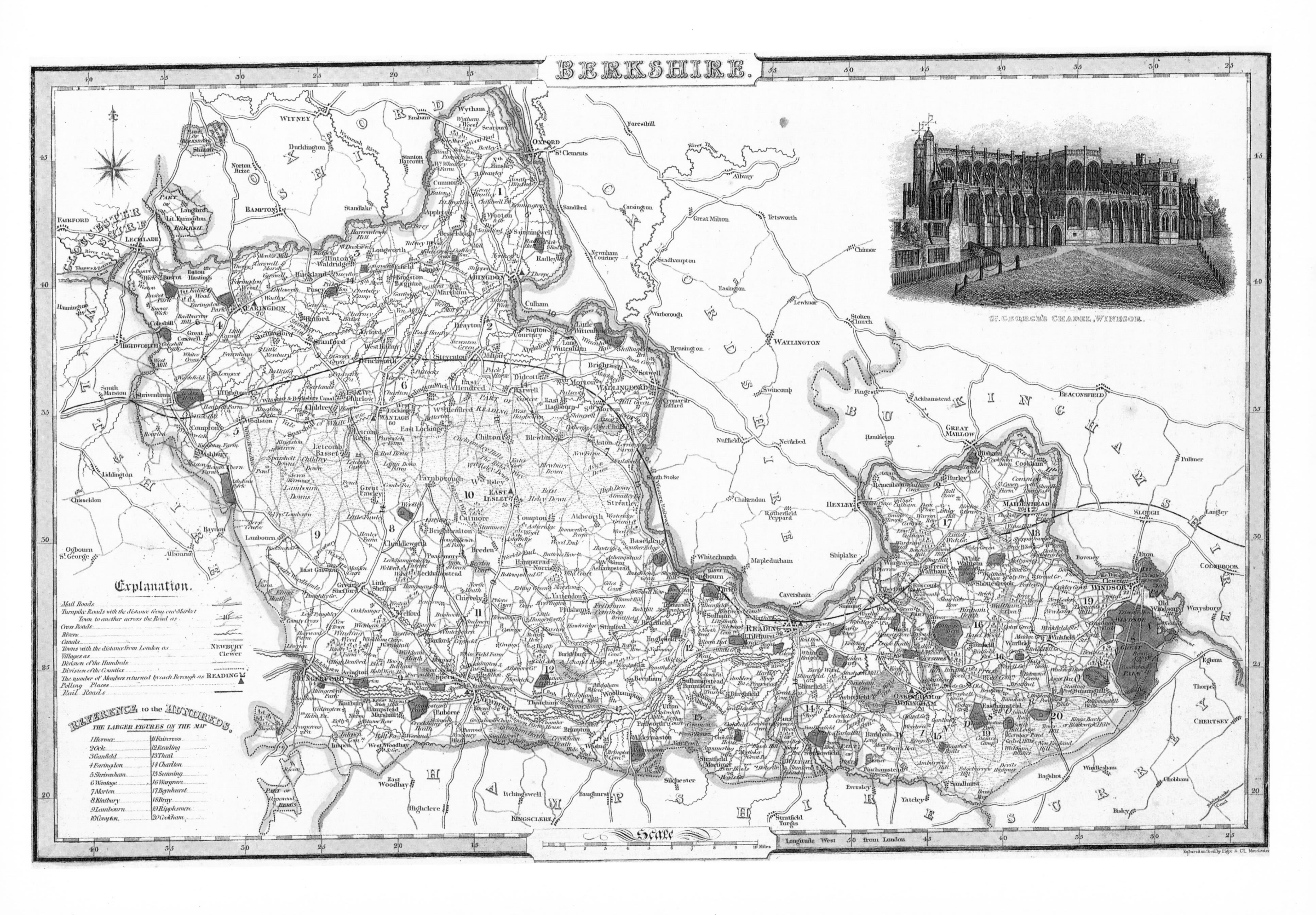

BERKSHIRE.
St. George's Chapel, Windsor.
Explanation.
Mail Roads
Turnpike Roads with the distance from one Market Town to another across the Road as
Cross Roads
Rivers
Canals
Towns with the distance from London as NEWBURY
Villages as Clewer
Division of the Hundreds
Division of the Counties
The number of Members returned by each Borough as READING
Polling Places
Rail Roads
REFERENCE to the HUNDREDS.
THE LARGER FIGURES ON THE MAP
1 Hormer.
2 Ock.
3 Ganfield.
4 Faringdon.
5 Shrivenham.
6 Wantage.
7 Morton.
8 Kintbury.
9 Lambourn.
10 Compton.
11 Faircross.
12 Reading.
13 Theal.
14 Charlton.
15 Sunning.
16 Wargrave.
17 Beynhurst.
18 Bray.
19 Ripplesmere.
20 Cookham.
Scale
10 Miles
Longitude West from London
Engraved on Steel by Fisher & Co. Manchester

BUCKINGHAMSHIRE.

BUCKINGHAMSHIRE is an inland county, bounded on the east by Bedfordshire, Hertfordshire and Middlesex, on the west by Oxfordshire and Northamptonshire, on the north by Bedfordshire and Northamptonshire, and on the south by Berkshire, and a point of Surrey. Its length, from north to south, is about 45 miles, and its greatest breadth, crossing a slip of Hertfordshire, which intersects it on the east, to the extreme of its western side, nearly 23 miles; its circumference is 138 miles, containing 740 square miles.

NAME and ANCIENT HISTORY.---The present appellation of the county was given to it by the Saxons, and is supposed to be derived from the beech trees which then grew so plentifully in these parts, and were called *Buccum;* or from the abundance of deer which were found in the woods, with which this country was covered, *Buc,* in the Saxon language, signifying a buck or hart. This part of Britain, together with the adjoining counties of Bedford and Hertford, before the invasion of Cæsar, was inhabited by the *Cattieuchlani,* who were, in the opinion of Camden, the ancient *Cassii;* and there are some remains of the name in *Cashio* hundred, and *Cashiobury,* adjoining Watford, in Hertfordshire. By the invasion of Aulus Plautius, this country became subject to the Imperial power, under Claudius Cæsar, and then formed part of BRITANNIA PRIMA; and was afterwards included in the province of 'Flavia Cæsariensis.' The Roman station, *Magiovintum,* is pretty well ascertained to have been within the limits of this county, near Fenny Stratford: its site is called *Auld* fields, where abundance of coins, and foundations of buildings, have often been discovered. The principal towns of Buckinghamshire are, Buckingham, Aylesbury, Newport Pagnell, and High Wycombe. The village of Eton, opposite to Windsor, is distinguished by its College or Public School, founded by King Henry VI, and the greatest Institution of the kind in the kingdom.

SOIL, PRODUCE and CLIMATE.---The face of the county is exceedingly varied: the southern parts are occupied by the Chilton hills, and their appendages, and are chiefly composed of chalk, intermixed with flints, and though very inferior to the northern district, with respect to richness of soil, have been rendered very productive by the great attention given to the cultivation and improvement of the land. The prolific vale of Aylesbury spreads through the middle of the county, furnishing rich pasturage to vast numbers of cattle, and supporting numerous dairy and grazing farms. The more northern parts are diversified with gentle sand hills, having also pasture and meadow land, with a small proportion of arable. The soil of this part of the county is principally composed of rich loam, strong clay, chalk, and loam upon gravel. The great weight of butter annually made on the dairy farms, is mostly purchased by the London dealers, who contract for it half-yearly; and the skim and butter milk are employed in fattening numerous herds of swine. Great attention is given to the rearing early ducks, and the suckling calves for the Metropolitan markets. The southern division of the county produces large quantities of fine beech; near a sixth part of the land between the road to Oxford and the Thames, is supposed to be covered with that wood. The application of the soil in the Chilton district is to the growth of wheat, barley, oats, beans and sainfoin. The waste lands are but inconsiderable, their extent not being more than 6,000 acres, the greater part contained in the heaths of Iver, Fulmer, Stoke and Wycombe. The CLIMATE of this county is thought to be as favourable to health and longevity as any other in the kingdom. The air on the Chilton hills is remarkably healthy; and even in the vales it is more salubrious than in the low grounds of other counties.

MANUFACTURES and TRADE.---The chief manufactures of this county are those of lace and paper, the former giving employment to a great proportion of the females belonging to the humbler class. Many very young children are also employed in this interesting branch of manufactures, who make the edgings and narrower sort of laces; and there are throughout the county many schools where the bobbins on the pillow are actively plied, to the exclusion of the works of the sempstress. But this branch has suffered severely of late years, the article produced from the machines of Nottingham having shorn it, to a great extent, of its prosperity. Besides paper and lace, the trade of the county is of a general and agricultural nature, having a tolerably prosperous traffic in grain, timber, malt, &c. The Grand Junction canal, which passes through this county, is of considerable importance to its trade, communicating with the Metropolis, and, by its navigable cuts, also with the principal towns in this and the neighbouring counties.

RIVERS and CANALS.---The principal rivers from which this county derives advantages are, the THAMES, the OUSE, and the COLNE. The Thames forms part of the boundary, dividing it from Berkshire, during a course of about thirty miles, and is navigable the whole of the way. The Ouse enters the western side of the county, and passing Water Stratford, flows in a devious course to Buckingham, thence winding to the north, through a rich tract of meadow land, pursues its way to Stony Stratford, Newport Pagnell and Olney, soon afterwards turning suddenly to the east, leaves the county near Brayfield. The Colne forms part of the eastern boundary of the county, separating it from Middlesex, and falls into the Thames between Ankerwyke and Staines. The Thames rises near to the borders of the county, in Hertfordshire, and flowing through the vale of Aylesbury, from east to west, receives the waters of several small streams, and enters Oxfordshire, near Thame, where it unites with the Isis, and both conjointly form the Thames. The only CANAL is the Grand Junction, above-mentioned, which enters this county near Wolverton, and after passing several of the principal towns, leaves it near Mansworth. There are also cuts or branches communicating with Aylesbury, Buckingham, Wendover, &c.

CIVIL and ECCLESIASTICAL DIVISIONS.----Buckinghamshire is in the Diocese of Lincoln, (with the exception of ten parishes, six of which belong to Canterbury, and four to London), and included in the Norfolk circuit: it is divided into eight hundreds, viz.:

ASHENDON,	BUCKINGHAM,	COTTESLOE,	NEWPORT,
AYLESBURY,	BURNHAM,	DESBOROUGH,	STOKE.

These divisions collectively contain about two hundred parishes, one county town (Buckingham), and fourteen other market-towns. The county sends fourteen members to parliament---two for the shire, and two each for the boroughs of AMERSHAM, AYLESBURY, BUCKINGHAM, GREAT MARLOW, WENDOVER and WYCOMBE.

POPULATION.—According to the census of 1821, there were houses inhabited in the county, 24,876; uninhabited, 549; and houses building, 148. The number of families then resident in the county was 28,867, comprising 64,867 males, and 69,201 females; total, 134,068: and by a calculation made by order of government, which included persons in the army and navy, for which was added after the ratio of about one to thirty prior to the year 1811, and one to fifty for that year and the census of 1821, to the returns made from the several districts; the population of the county, in round numbers, in the year 1700, was 80,500---in 1750, 90,700---in 1801, 111,000---in 1811, 121,600---and in 1821, 136,800. The increased population in the fifty years, from the year 1700, was 10,200---from 1750 to 1801, the increase was 20,300---from 1801 to 1811, the increase was 10,600---and from 1811 to 1821, the augmented number of persons was 15,200: the grand total increase in the population of the county, from the year 1700 to the census of 1821, being about 56,300 persons.

Index of Distances from Town to Town in the County of Bucks.

THE NAMES OF THE RESPECTIVE TOWNS ARE ON THE TOP AND SIDE, AND THE SQUARE WHERE BOTH MEET GIVES THE DISTANCE.

	Amersham	Aylesbury	Beaconsfield	Buckingham	Chesham	Fenny Stratford	Ivinghoe	Marlow	Newport Pagnell	Olney	Princes Risborough	Stony Stratford	Wendover	Winslow	Wycombe	Distance from London.
Amersham																26
Aylesbury	15															38
Beaconsfield	5	20														23
Buckingham	32	17	35													57
Chesham	3	13	8	31												28
Fenny Stratford	30	15	34	14	27											44
Ivinghoe	14	9	19	21	11	12										33
Marlow	12	22	8	36	15	33	21									31
Newport Pagnell	28	23	33	14	25	7	15	36								51
Olney	33	30	38	19	30	12	20	41	5							56
Princes Risborough	11	8	14	26	13	23	24	13	23	28						37
Stony Stratford	34	19	37	8	24	7	14	37	6	11	25					51
Wendover	10	5	13	22	9	19	8	16	21	26	4	24				35
Winslow	25	10	29	7	23	12	14	29	16	19	17	10	15			48
Wycombe, High	7	17	5	34	9	27	15	5	29	34	8	32	11	23		29

[See over.

Additional information relating to the County of Bucks.

ooo

Population.—By the Census for **1831** this county contained 71,734 males, and 74,795 females—total 146,529, being an increase, since the returns made in the year 1821, of 12,461 inhabitants; and from the Census of 1801 to that of 1831, the augmentation amounted to 39,085 persons.

Representation.—Under the *Reform Bill*, the boroughs of Amersham and Wendover are disfranchised, and one additional member is given to the county, so that the whole shire sends *eleven* representatives to Parliament instead of *fourteen*. The polling for county members is directed, by the Bill, to take place at Aylesbury, Buckingham, Newport Pagnell, and Beaconsfield.

Railways.—The London and Birmingham Railway enters this county (from Hertfordshire) near the parish of *Marsworth;* passes about a mile and a half to the west of *Ivinghoe;* pursues nearly the course of the Grand Junction canal to *Leighton Buzzard,* about half a mile from which town there is a station; and passing on to *Denbigh Hall* station, nearly a mile to the left of *Fenny Stratford,* proceeds to *Woolverton* station, about two miles from *Stony Stratford;* and, after running through the parish and near the village of *Castle Thorp,* passes into the county of Northampton, near the parish of Ashton. From *Aylesbury* a branch communicates with the main line, about a mile and a half from *Tring,* in Hertfordshire. The Great Western Railway crosses the south-eastern corner of the county, visiting the well-known village of *Slough,* where there is a station.

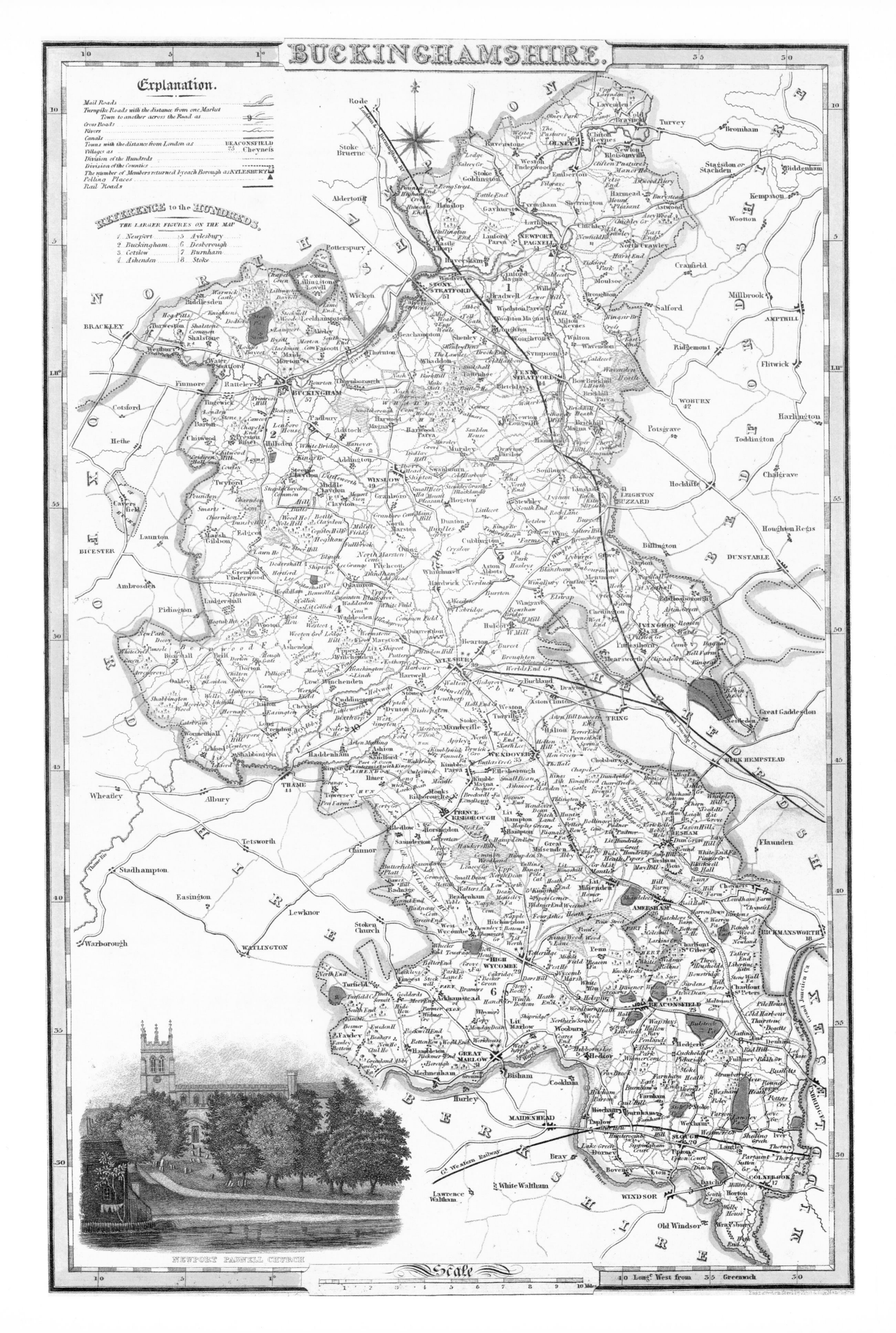
BUCKINGHAMSHIRE.
Explanation.
Mail Roads
Turnpike Roads with the distance from one Market Town to another across the Road as
Cross Roads
Rivers
Canals
Towns with the distance from London as BEACONSFIELD 23
Villages as Cheyneis
Division of the Hundreds
Division of the Counties
The number of Members returned by each Borough as AYLESBURY
Polling Places
Rail Roads
REFERENCE to the HUNDREDS.
THE LARGER FIGURES ON THE MAP
1. Newport
2. Buckingham
3. Cotslow
4. Ashenden
5. Aylesbury
6. Desborough
7. Burnham
8. Stoke
NORTHAMPTON
BEDFORD
HERTFORD
MIDDLESEX
BERKSHIRE
OXFORD
NEWPORT PAGNELL CHURCH
Scale
Miles
Long. West from Greenwich

CAMBRIDGESHIRE.

CAMBRIDGESHIRE is an inland county, bounded on the north-west by the counties of Northampton, Huntingdon and Bedford; on the south by Hertfordshire and Essex; on the east by Suffolk; on the north-east by Norfolk, and on the north by Lincolnshire. Its greatest length is nearly fifty miles, and its breadth at the south and widest extremity above twenty-five; in circumference it is one hundred and thirty miles, and contains 858 square miles. Its limits, for all the northern half, are rivers, and their communicating branches, so intermixed as with difficulty to be traced; the southern half has an indented and undistinguished boundary line on the adjacent counties. Its figure somewhat resembles that of the human ear, the county of Huntingdon cutting into its western side by a circular projection.

ANCIENT HISTORY.—During the Heptarchy this county composed part of the kingdom of *East Anglia;* the *Devil's ditch,* which runs across Newmarket heath, in a straight line for several miles, to Reach, where the fens were anciently marshy and impassable, Camden mentions to have been one of the boundaries of that kingdom: the earth that was dug out of the trench is thrown up, and forms a high bank on the east side, which is that next to the fens. Ely and its district, from its situation, has frequently held out a long time against foreign and domestic foes; and particularly was the last place in the kingdom which submitted to William the Conqueror.

SOIL, PRODUCE and CLIMATE.—Notwithstanding the immense expense and labour which have been bestowed in draining the fens, there is still a large extent in a waste and unimproved condition. In this part the application of the land is various; where the soil is preserved from the floods, or only subject to occasional inundations, it has all the fertility of water meadows; the crops of oats are particularly abundant, the produce being frequently from fifty to sixty bushels per acre. On the western side of this district, many thousand acres are laid out in pasture. The fenny country extends south of the Ouse, and runs up to the neighbourhood of Cambridge. The south-western part of the county is the most agreeable, being raised in its surface and watered by the Cam. Some very fine butter is made on the dairy farms in this district; and the vicinity of Cottenham (a village near Cambridge) is famous for a peculiar kind of new cheese, of a singularly delicious flavour. The superiority of this cheese is not ascribed to any particular mode in the management of the dairies, but solely to the nature of the herbage on the commons. In this part of the county many calves are suckled for the London markets. In some of the parishes, bordering on Essex, saffron is cultivated; and hemp and flax are produced in other parts of the county. The south-eastern division, reaching from Gogmagog hills to Newmarket, is bleak, heathy and thinly inhabited; being connected with that vast tract of land, which, extending southwards into Essex, and northward across Suffolk into Norfolk, forms one of the largest plains in the kingdom. The southern parts of the county, consisting chiefly of elevated land, exhibit a remarkable contrast to the north division, and are productive of fine wheat, barley and oats; though the heaths and commons that intersect these districts, furnish sustenance to many thousand sheep: the number kept in the county may be averaged at 153,000. The valley through which the Cam flows, from Steeple Morden to Walton, is called the 'Dairies,' from being almost wholly appropriated to dairy farms. The quantity of wood land is not very considerable, the whole extent of timber scarcely amounting to 1000 acres, and these principally scattered through widely sundered parishes.—The SOIL is diversified, consisting principally of a mixture of clay and sand, and of a strong black mould and gravel. The rich marshes in the vicinity of Wisbeach, consist of a mixture of sand and clay, or silt; in the fens, of a strong black earth or moor, lying upon gravel or turf moor, very favourable for the culture of oats and coleseed. In the uplands the soils vary, being composed of chalk, gravel loam, and tender clay, and clay upon gravel.—CLIMATE.—In general the air is pure and healthy, excepting in the more northern parts, which are rendered damp and unhealthy, by the vast tracts of fenny ground; these have, however, been considerably drained of late years, and though much remains to be done, the impurity of the air has been greatly diminished, and the climate happily and materially improved.

MANUFACTURES are scarcely known in this county, with the exception of a sort of white bricks for cleaning iron, brass, &c. and coarse pottery ware; but the general trade of some of the towns is very considerable, and the commerce arising from agricultural produce of great importance. Wisbeach possesses a valuable trade in the export of corn, and of oil from the seed mills in its neighbourhood. Cambridge may be said to be sufficiently famous by its University as to dispense with other distinctions. Newmarket, partly in this county and partly in Suffolk, is the most celebrated place in all England for horse races, for which its extensive and finely turfed heath is peculiarly adapted. Charles II. built a seat here for the sake of this diversion; and the town still derives its sole consequence and support from the attendance of nobility and gentry at the several meetings. The fleetest horses in the world are trained here for the course, and the neighbouring farmers profit considerably in the disposal of provender for their support.

RIVERS.—The principal rivers of Cambridgeshire are the OUSE and the GRANTA, or CAM. The former enters the county between Fen Drayton and Earith: thence it runs eastward through the fens; and afterwards, taking a northerly direction, passes Stretham, Ely and Littleport, and flows into Norfolk. The Cam has three branches, the chief of which rises near Ashwell, in Hertfordshire, and enters this county to the west of Guilden Morton; thence flowing to the north-east, it receives several rivulets, and near Grantchester has its current enlarged by the united waters of its sister streams; and hence taking a northerly course, the Cam glides through the walks of science, ornamenting the grounds of the principal Colleges at Cambridge, and falls into the Ouse, near Thetford.

CIVIL and ECCLESIASTICAL DIVISIONS.—Cambridgeshire is divided into two parts by the river Ouse: the most northerly is chiefly composed of the Isle of Ely, a separate district possessing a jurisdiction within itself; and in the diocese of Ely, the whole county is comprehended: it is included in the Norfolk circuit, and is divided into sixteen hundreds, viz.:

ARMINGFORD,	FLENDISH,	RADFIELD,	WETHERLEY,
CHESTERTON,	LONGSTOW,	STAPLOE,	WHITTLESFORD,
CHEVELY,	NORTHSTOW,	STAINE,	WISBEACH,
CHILFORD,	PAPWORTH,	THRIPLOW,	WITCHFORD.

It contains one city (Ely,) one county and borough town (Cambridge,) nine other market towns, and 167 parishes. It sends six members to parliament, viz.—two for the UNIVERSITY, two for the town of CAMBRIDGE, and two for the COUNTY.

POPULATION.—According to the census of 1821, there were houses inhabited in the county, 20,869; uninhabited, 247; and houses building, 217. The number of families then resident in the county was 25,603; comprising 60,301 males, and 61,608 females; total, 121,909: and by a calculation made by order of government, which included persons in the army and navy, for which was added after the ratio of about one to thirty prior to the year 1811, and one to fifty for that year and the census of 1821, to the returns made from the several districts; the population of the county, in round numbers, in the year 1700, was 72,000—in 1750, 76,000—in 1801, 92,300—in 1811, 104,500—and in 1821, 124,400. The increased population in the fifty years, from the year 1700, was 4,000—from 1750 to 1801, the increase was 16,300—from 1801 to 1811, the increase was 12,200—and from 1811 to 1821, the augmented number of persons was 19,900: the grand total increase in the population of the county from the year 1700 to the census of 1821, being about 52,400 persons.

Index of Distances from Town to Town in the County of Cambridge.

THE NAMES OF THE RESPECTIVE TOWNS ARE ON THE TOP AND SIDE, AND THE SQUARE WHERE BOTH MEET GIVES THE DISTANCE.

	Cambridge	Chatteris	Ely	Linton	March	Newmarket	Royston	Soham	Thorney	Whittlesea	Wisbeach	*Distance from London.*
Cambridge												51
Chatteris	28											71
Ely	16	12										*(by way of Cambridge)* 67
Linton	11	33	21									48
March	32	8	19	36								79
Newmarket	13	25	13	14	26							60
Royston	13	32	30	15	39	26						38
Soham	19	18	6	19	25	7	32					70
Thorney	40	18	32	50	14	45	44	39				86
Whittlesea	30	15	27	41	11	40	39	33	5			78
Wisbeach	43	19	31	50	11	39	51	33	14	19		90

[See over.

Additional information relating to the County of CAMBRIDGE.

ooo

POPULATION.—By the Census for 1831 this county contained 72,031 males, and 71,924 females—total 143,955, being an increase, since the returns made in the year 1821, of 22,046 inhabitants; and from the Census of 1801 to that of 1831 the augmentation amounted to 54,609 persons.

REPRESENTATION.—Under the *Reform Bill* one additional member is given to the county, whereby the shire returns *seven* representatives instead of *six* as heretofore. The polling for county members is directed, by the said Act, to take place at CAMBRIDGE, NEWMARKET, and ROYSTON, and for the convenience of those voters resident in the Isle of Ely, at the city of ELY, WISBEACH, and WHITTLESEA.

RAILWAYS.—The NORTHERN and EASTERN RAILWAY, for which an Act was passed in 1836, opens a communication between *Cambridge* and the *Metropolis:* it passes near *Linton, Saffron Walden, Bishops Stortford* and *Waltham Abbey.* Branches from this line are projected to Hertford and to Ware. At Cambridge commences the line of the Great Northern Railway, by way of Lincoln to York; and a branch is also projected to Norwich.

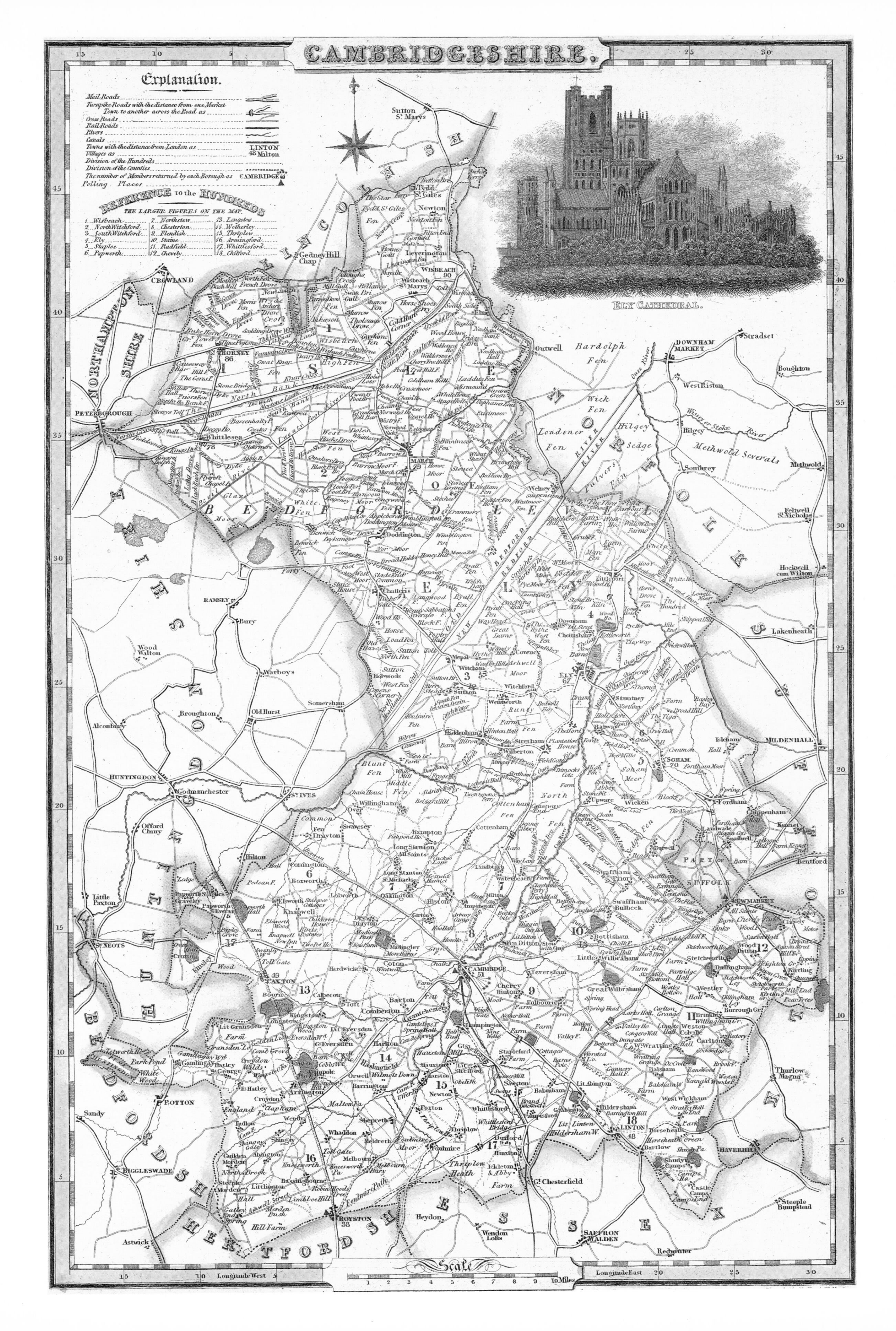
CAMBRIDGESHIRE.
Explanation.
Mail Roads
Turnpike Roads with the distance from one Market Town to another across the Road as
Cross Roads
Rail Roads
Rivers
Canals
Towns with the distance from London as
Villages as
Division of the Hundreds
Division of the Counties
The number of Members returned by each Borough as
Polling Places
LINTON
48 Milton
CAMBRIDGE
REFERENCE to the HUNDREDS
THE LARGER FIGURES ON THE MAP.
1. Wisbeach
2. North Witchford
3. South Witchford
4. Ely
5. Staploe
6. Papworth
7. Northstow
8. Chesterton
9. Flendish
10. Staine
11. Radfield
12. Chevely
13. Longstow
14. Wetherley
15. Thriplow
16. Armingford
17. Whittlesford
18. Chilford
Ely Cathedral.
LINCOLNSHIRE
NORTHAMPTONSHIRE
HUNTINGDONSHIRE
BEDFORDSHIRE
HERTFORDSHIRE
ESSEX
SUFFOLK
NORFOLK
ISLE OF ELY
BEDFORD LEVEL
PART OF SUFFOLK
CROWLAND
PETERBOROUGH
THORNEY 86
WISBEACH 90
MARCH 79
ELY 67
CAMBRIDGE 51
ROYSTON 38
LINTON 48
SAFFRON WALDEN
NEWMARKET 60
HUNTINGDON
ST. NEOTS
POTTON
BIGGLESWADE
DOWNHAM MARKET
MILDENHALL
HAVERHILL
SOHAM 70
CAXTON 49
Scale
Miles
Longitude West
Longitude East

CHESHIRE.

CHESHIRE is one of the western counties, distinguished in its figure by the two horns which project to the east and west of its northern side: it is bounded on the north by the rivers Mersey and Tame, which separate it from Lancashire; on the east by the counties of Derby and Stafford, the limits of which are marked for the most part by hills and streams; on the south by Shropshire, and a detached part of Flintshire, and the estuary of the Dee. Its length from north to south is about thirty miles; its extreme breadth from horn to horn almost sixty, but across its middle part not more than forty; its circumference is 112 miles, containing 1,052 square miles, and 673,280 statute acres.

SOIL and AGRICULTURAL PRODUCE.—The soil of this county, generally speaking, is composed of clay and sand; the former prevailing in the hundreds of Broxton, Wirral and Macclesfield, and the latter in the hundreds of Eddisbury, Northwich, Nantwich and Bucklow. Large tracts of peat moss and black moor land exhibit themselves in that part which lies upon the confines of Yorkshire and Derbyshire. Cheshire was celebrated, some centuries ago, for the great extent of its forests and heath lands. Its principal forests were those of Delamere, or *Mara and Mondram,* Wirral and Macclesfield; all of them well supplied with timber. The forest of Delamere must have been of great extent, not less than *fifty* townships being within its boundary: within the last two centuries it contained upwards of 11,000 acres, the soil consisting chiefly of gravel and white sand; 2,000 acres were inclosed, pursuant to an act of parliament passed in 1812, and the land now sustains thriving plantations of various timber. Some of the rising grounds, in the neighbourhood of the old and new pales, which have been detached by Royal grants from the forest land, are much indebted for their rising beauty to the taste and expenditure of Thomas Cholmondley, Esq. and Nicholas Ashton, Esq., whose plantations are as extensive as they are useful and adorning. The general appearance of the county is that of an extended plain, and is for the most part a flat country, whence it has obtained the name of 'the Vale Royal of England.' Although the surface of Cheshire is stated to be chiefly level, it must not be thence inferred to be deficient in varied beauty and picturesque landscape, as partial topographers have unfairly written; on the contrary, various parts of Cheshire possess high claims to the notice of the artist and the admirer of diversified scenery, and from the several prominences may be contemplated nature clothed both in magnificent and simple garbs. Wirral boasts many delightful marine views; the prospect of the Welch coast, from Parkgate and its neighbourhood, is interesting, and includes the venerable ruins of Flint Castle, the towns of Flint, Holywell, &c.; while the active scenery, produced from vessels in the coasting and coal trades continually passing to and fro, gives a lively and pleasing colouring to the picture. The vicinities of Macclesfield, Astbury, Nantwich, Sandbach, Bunhill, Kelsall-hill, and from the summit of Beeston, afford prospects extensive and luxuriant. The view from Halton is also very wide, enriched by the meanderings of the Mersey; and the eye is carried over a large district of Lancashire. From Beeston the 'Vale Royal' of the county is seen in all its beauty, highly cultivated and spotted with woods and coppices; in the distance are the towering Welch mountains, and the estuary of the Dee gives a pleasing perspective to the whole. From other elevations, besides those of Mowcop, Alderley Edge, Bucklow Hills, the hills of Shuttingslow, and at Frodsham, may be enjoyed a visual banquet of no ordinary excellence and interest. SALT and CHEESE have been considered the staple commodities of this county, both of them being exported to a great amount. The annual average weight of rock-salt for exportation, for the purpose of fish-curing, &c., sent down the Weaver during twenty years, was estimated at upwards of 55,000 tons; and the annual average of white salt, for the like period, is stated at about 140,000 tons, chiefly for exportation, the fisheries, and colonies. The principal pits are at Wheelock, Lawton, Roughwood in Leftwich, Middlewich, Anderton, Betchton, near Northwich, Nantwich, and Frodsham. These several works give employment to upwards of 3,000 hands. The quantity of cheese taken off by the London market, annually, is said to be upwards of 14,000 tons—Bristol and York, 8,000 tons—besides large quantities sent to Scotland, Ireland, &c.; added to which, the home consumption, and that of the immediate well populated neighbourhood, must take off considerable quantities. In 1827, it is stated, about 96,000 cows were kept in Cheshire; but this number is by some considered erroneous, as being insufficient to the production of the immense weight of cheese made in this county, without taking into account the consumption of milk, cream and butter. The other productions of this prolific county are potatos, (which are cultivated to much advantage), corn, millstones, timber, &c. Cheshire has ever been classed amongst the counties of England that boast a salubrious climate: not any particular disease is known to prevail in it; and, although subterranean labour employs a great number of its inhabitants, instances of extreme longevity are as numerous as in other healthful counties of a like population.

MANUFACTURES and MINERALS.—The manufactures of Cheshire are very extensive, and important in their character; the cotton trade, and the introduction of machinery, having combined in raising it to a station of consequence amongst the manufacturing counties of England. Stockport, a populous and flourishing town, participates largely in all the branches of the cotton trade; Macclesfield and Congleton have extensive silk factories; great numbers of hats are made in some of the towns, whilst in others are works for smelting copper and making brass, and the perfecting machinery of various kinds applicable to the different manufactures. The veins of metal which have been discovered and worked in this county, are those of copper and lead, at Alderley Edge, where also is found cobalt; lead and copper ore have likewise produced profit from the mines at Mottram; and those metals, as well as iron, have been found in other parts, though in veins not rich enough to inspire speculation. Coal is found in great plenty in numerous parts of the county, particularly on its north-east side, in the townships of Adlington, Bollington, Hurdsfield, Norbury, Pott-Shrigley, Poynton, Worth, &c.; these collieries supplying Manchester, Macclesfield, Stockport, &c. with this article, now so essential to manufacturing purposes.

RIVERS and CANALS.—The principal rivers of Cheshire are the DEE, the MERSEY, the WEAVER, the BOLLIN, the DANE, the WHEELOCK, the PEOVER, and the TAME. Besides these, there are other inconsiderable streams, which either rise in or wash the lands of this county, and are tributary waters to the other rivers; as, the Gowy, the Betley, the Ashbrook, the Biddle, the Birkin, the Croco, the Walwern, the Mar, the Grimsditch, and the Flookersbrook. Cheshire is also noted for its beautiful sheets of water, called meres, lakes, and pools; among these is the noble COMBERMERE, more than a mile in length, giving name to Combermere Abbey. Chapel-mere and Moss-mere are fine pieces of water, in front of Cholmondley Castle. The other meres are Bar-mere, Quoisley-mere, Rosthern-mere, Bag-mere, Pick-mere, Oakmere, Mere-pool, &c. The principal CANALS which benefit this county are, the Duke of Bridgwater's, which was commenced in 1761, the communication between Manchester and Liverpool opened in 1772, and the whole finished in 1776; the Grand Trunk Canal, the act for cutting which was passed in 1766; the Ellesmere Canal, the act obtained in 1793; the Chester and Nantwich Canal (now united with the Ellesmere) obtained its act in 1772, and was completed in 1776; and the Peak Forest canal, which obtained the sanction of Government in 1794. These grand works of labour and art afford uninterrupted and cheap intercourse between the towns of Chester, Liverpool, Manchester, &c.; besides communicating with the north of England, Staffordshire, Shropshire, and adjacent counties.

CIVIL and ECCLESIASTICAL DIVISIONS.—Cheshire is a County Palatine, having a distinct government; in the Province of Canterbury, and Diocese of Chester, which comprehends all Cheshire and Lancashire, and various parts of Westmoreland, Cumberland, Yorkshire, Denbigh, and Flintshire. It is divided into two Archdeaconries, and apportioned into seven hundreds, viz. BROXTON, BUCKLOW, EDDISBURY, MACCLESFIELD, NANTWICH, NORTHWICH, and WIRRAL; these collectively contain one city and county town (Chester), twelve other market towns, and 90 parishes. The whole county sends four representatives to parliament, viz. two for the city of Chester, and two for the shire.

POPULATION.—According to the census of 1821, there were houses inhabited in the county, 47,094; uninhabited, 1,212; and houses building, 414. The number of families then resident in the county was 52,024, comprising 132,952 males, and 137,146 females; total, 270,098: and by a calculation made by order of government, which included persons in the army and navy, for which was added after the ratio of about one to thirty prior to the year 1811, and one to fifty for that year and the census of 1821, to the returns made from the several districts; the population of the county, in round numbers, in the year 1700, was 107,000---in 1750, 131,600---in 1801, 198,100---in 1811, 234,600---and in 1821, 275,500. The increased population in the fifty years, from the year 1700, was 24,600---from 1750 to 1801, the increase was 66,500---from 1801 to 1811, the increase was 36,500---and from 1811 to 1821, the augmented number of persons was 40,900: the grand total increase in the population of the county, from the year 1700 to the census of 1821, being about 168,500 persons.

Index of Distances from Town to Town in the County of Chester.

THE NAMES OF THE RESPECTIVE TOWNS ARE ON THE TOP AND SIDE, AND THE SQUARE WHERE BOTH MEET GIVES THE DISTANCE.

Distance from Manchester.	Town	Altrincham	Chester	Congleton	Frodsham	Knutsford	Macclesfield	Malpas	Middlewich	Mottram	Nantwich	Northwich	Parkgate	Runcorn	Sandbach	Stockport	Tarporley	*Distance from London.*
8	Altrincham																	183
38	Chester	30																182
24	Congleton	21	33															162
29	Frodsham	24	10	29														192
15	Knutsford	7	25	14	17													176
19	Macclesfield	16	36	8	28	12												167
45	Malpas	37	15	30	24	33	35											169
24	Middlewich	16	20	13	18	9	18	24										167
12	Mottram	17	47	25	40	22	16	51	31									187
36	Nantwich	28	20	18	24	21	23	12	12	43								164
20	Northwich	13	18	19	12	7	20	26	6	30	17							174
48	Parkgate	36	11	42	16	31	45	26	30	53	30	28						190
28	Runcorn	24	15	36	6	16	28	30	20	41	27	14	20					188
26	Sandbach	19	25	9	23	11	17	22	5	41	10	11	35	25				162
7	Stockport	9	39	20	33	14	12	44	23	8	35	22	45	33	25			179
33	Tarporley	25	10	25	15	19	26	14	10	42	9	12	20	16	15	34		173
33	Tarvin	25	6	27	10	19	32	18	14	42	14	12	16	12	19	34	4	165

[*See over.*

Additional information relating to the County of CHESTER.

———ooo———

POPULATION.—By the Census for **1831** this county contained 164,152 males, and 170,258 females—total 334,410, being an increase, since the returns made in the year 1821, of 64,312 inhabitants; and from the Census of 1801 to that of 1831 the augmentation amounted to 142,659 persons.

REPRESENTATION.—By the *Reform Bill* the elective franchise is conferred upon MACCLESFIELD and STOCKPORT, which return two members each, besides two additional ones being given to the county, so that the whole shire returns *ten* representatives to Parliament instead of *four*, as before the passing the Act. Under the new *Boundary Act* the county is divided into two parts, respectively named the *Northern Division* and the *Southern Division;* the former includes the hundreds of Macclesfield and Bucklow, and the latter the hundreds of Broxton, Eddisbury, Nantwich, Northwich, and Wirrall, and also the city and county of the city of Chester. The election of members for the northern division is held at KNUTSFORD, and for the southern at CHESTER: besides the place of election, the polling, for the northern division, takes place at STOCKPORT, MACCLESFIELD, and RUNCORN; and for the southern (besides the place of election) at NANTWICH, NORTHWICH, SANDBACH, and BIRKENHEAD.

RAILWAYS.

The GRAND JUNCTION RAILWAY passes about two miles from *Northwich* (at the *Hartford* station), and the like distance from *Middlewich* (at the *Winsford* station). *Nantwich* is four miles from *Crewe* station on the Grand Junction line, and *Sandbach* nearly five. The BIRKENHEAD and CHESTER RAILWAY, the works for which commenced on the 3rd May, 1838, runs from *Birkenhead* (opposite *Liverpool)* to *Chester;* from that city it takes the name of the CHESTER and CREWE RAILWAY, and joins the Grand Junction at *Crewe* station. A line is proposed, and a Company formed, for extending the communication from Chester to the Orme's Head, on the Welch coast; by which means, it is said, twenty-four hours will be saved in the transmission of the mails to the inland parts of Ireland—and that the mails, by this route, may arrive in Dublin several hours before the departure of the despatches for the interior. The MANCHESTER and BIRMINGHAM RAILWAY runs from *Stockport* to *Crewe,* and also joins the Grand Junction between *Stone* and *Stafford,* from whence an extension line goes by *Tamworth* to *Rugby,* and joins the London and Birmingham; and a branch will connect *Stockport* with *Macclesfield.* At Stockport the line is carried over the river Mersey by a stupendous viaduct, the arches of which are of surprising altitude. From Macclesfield a line is projected to Derby: this, if accomplished, will give the inhabitants of Leicestershire and Derbyshire a direct Railway conveyance to Manchester and Liverpool.

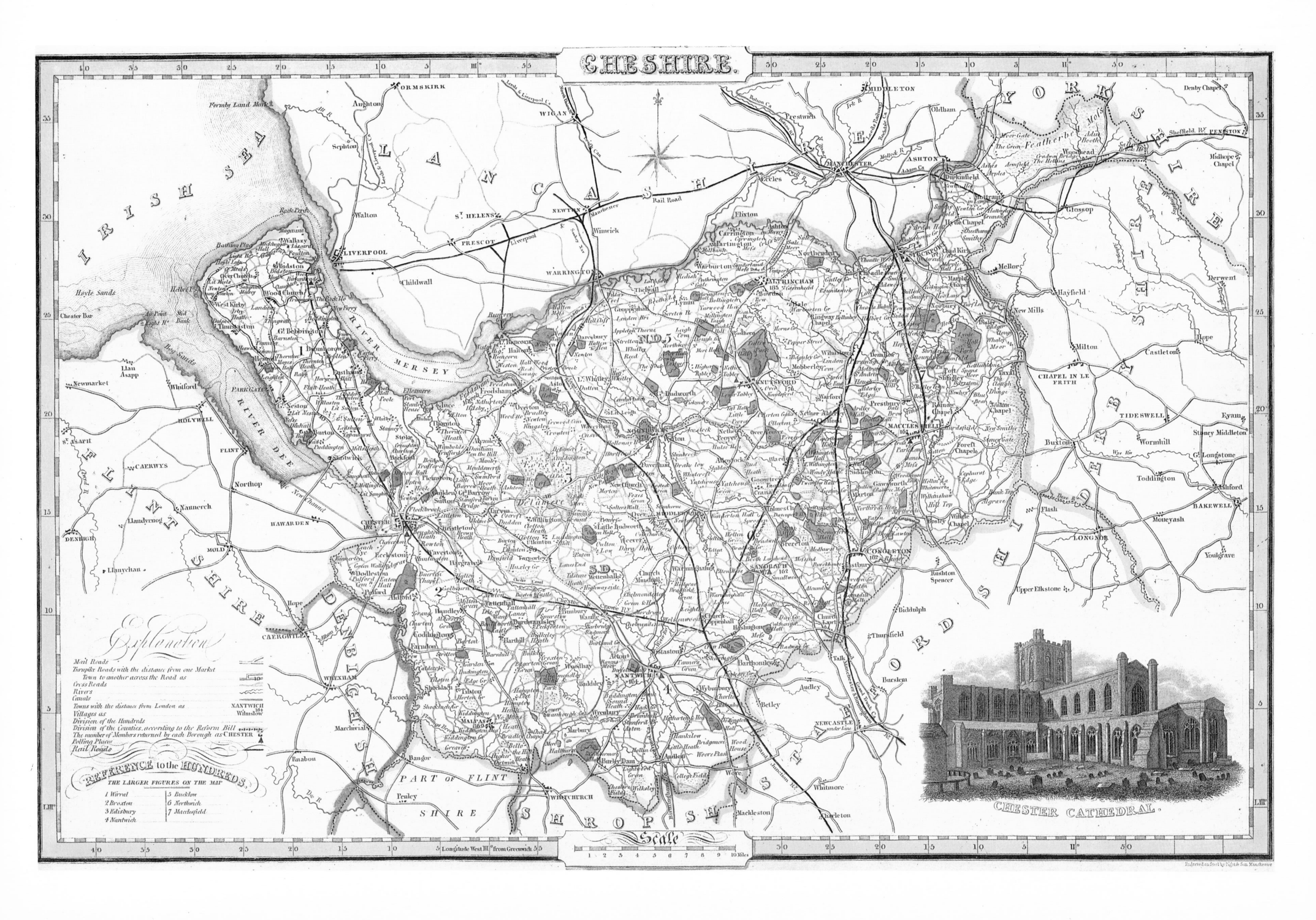

CHESHIRE.
CHESTER CATHEDRAL.
Explanation
Mail Roads
Turnpike Roads with the distance from one Market Town to another across the Road as
Cross Roads
Rivers
Canals
Towns with the distance from London as
Villages as
Division of the Hundreds
Division of the Counties according to the Reform Bill
The number of Members returned by each Borough as CHESTER
Polling Places
Rail Roads
REFERENCE to the HUNDREDS,
THE LARGER FIGURES ON THE MAP
1 Wirral
2 Broxton
3 Edisbury
4 Nantwich
5 Bucklow
6 Northwich
7 Macclesfield
Scale
IRISH SEA
RIVER MERSEY
RIVER DEE
LIVERPOOL
CHESTER
WARRINGTON
STOCKPORT
MACCLESFIELD
NANTWICH
WHITCHURCH
WREXHAM
FLINT
HOLYWELL
MOLD
HAWARDEN
BAKEWELL
LONGNOR
TIDESWELL

CORNWALL.

CORNWALL, the most westerly county in England, is almost an island, being surrounded on all sides by the sea, except towards the east, where it is bounded by the county of Devon, for the length of 43 miles from north to south. From this boundary to the westward, the land continually decreases in breadth, forming itself into a figure resembling a cornucopia; having the Bristol channel on the north, and the English channel on the south; both seas meeting in a manner in a point, at the promontory called the Land's End, on the west. Twenty miles may be regarded as its medium breadth, till approaching Mount's Bay, between which place and St. Ives it is not more than five and a half miles wide; its extreme length is 90 miles, and its circumference estimated at 200; containing 1,327 square miles. Detached as Cornwall is by situation from the west of England, it was formerly still further separated, by the use of a totally different language, a dialect of the Armorican, and related to the Welch. The names of many of the ancient towns, its castles, rivers, mountains, manors, seats and families are derived from the Cornish tongue; and most of the technical appellations in the arts of mining, husbandry and fishing may be traced to the same source; but the language itself has for two or three centuries ceased to be common, and is now utterly extirpated. The SCILLY ISLANDS are situated in a group or cluster, about nine leagues west of the Land's End; having different and chiefly modern appellations, but deriving their general name from the small isle of Scilly, which is now only a furlong in extent. In a clear day the islands may be seen from the Land's End—appearing like a cluster of cliffs, or fragments of ruined castles, round which the Atlantic rolls in a vast curve.

SOIL, CLIMATE, AGRICULTURAL PRODUCE, FISHERIES, &c.—Cornwall, from its soil, appearance and climate, is one of the least inviting of the English counties. A ridge of bare rugged hills, intermixed with bleak moors, runs through the midst of its whole length, and in the narrower parts extends from side to side. The low grounds between the hills and the sea are, in some parts, rendered sufficiently fertile by the aid of manure; the chief dependence for which is on the sea sand, and sea weeds which are collected on the coast, and carried on the backs of horses to the places where the dressing is wanted: another excellent manure is formed by the mixture of lime and earth with bruised and damaged pilchards, and the refuse salt used in curing them. The saltness of the atmosphere, and the violence of the winds, will scarcely suffer trees, or even hedges, to grow near the shore; so that nearly the whole county presents a naked and almost desolate appearance. With the many natural disadvantages to which this county is subjected, still the agriculturist, in many parts of it, finds himself well rewarded for his labours. The grain which succeeds best is barley, of which very large crops are produced on the banks of the Camel, and in its neighbourhood; potatoes also yield abundantly in some lands, and seem peculiarly calculated for the climate. Good cider is made on the east side of the county;—the dairy is but little attended to, and milch cows are principally kept for rearing the young stock. The woodlands are not numerous; but the face of the county, in this respect, has been very greatly improved of late years, as many of the resident gentlemen have embellished their estates with plantations. The cattle are chiefly of the Devonshire breed, as are the sheep, with some of the Leicestershire breed. Cornwall is indebted for its welfare, populousness, and relative importance, to its mineral treasures, and the shoals of fish upon its coast. Of the great variety of the finny tribe, none is so considerable an object of commerce as the pilchard, which appears in immense shoals during the summer and autumn; the first swarm generally arriving at the Land's End in the middle of July. Besides the great supply these fish afford to the miners and poor of Cornwall, large quantities are cured and exported, principally up the Mediterranean.—The CLIMATE of this county, though not so genial as most others in England, cannot be stated to be unwholesome. The air is made extremely moist by the surrounding body of water; and the high lands in the centre intercept the mists and clouds in their passage, so that rains or fogs are almost daily experienced: at the same time, the winds are continually shifting from one point to another; which circumstance, while it increases the mutability of the atmosphere, has a favourable effect in preventing those stagnations of damp air, which are so prejudicial to health in some wet countries. The winters are mild, and the frosts of short duration; the summers are cool, and the autumns too wet to bring some of the fruits of the earth to proper maturity.

MINES, MINERALS, &c.—From early antiquity this county has been noticed for the TIN, which it produced, and which was an object of commerce to civilized nations, while Britain was a land of barbarians. Tin-mines are dispersed throughout the greatest part of Cornwall; and the quantity procured is greater than in any other part of the world, and forms an object of considerable consequence, both in domestic and foreign commerce. Some state the number of men employed in the mines at 12,000, others at not above 9,000; but, including the streamers, who are a distinct body from the miners, the number of men, women and children employed in raising the ore, washing, stamping and carrying it, will probably amount to 16,000. The King's eldest son is born Duke of Cornwall, and derives a revenue, not only from the lands appertaining to the Dutchy, but from the mines of tin and copper: he has under him an officer, called Lord Warden of the Stannary Court, whose jurisdiction extends over the mines and miners of Cornwall and Devonshire. The revenue arising to the Duke from the tin-mines averages about £10,000. annually. Besides tin and copper, there are found here lead, lapis-calaminaris, pyrites, bismuth, zinc, antimony, cobalt, arsenic, wolfram, menachenite and molybdena; there is also abundance of iron ore in many parts of the county, but the mines of it have not been much worked. Soap rock, and clays of remarkable purity (excellent for potters' use), and fine rock crystals, are procured here.

RIVERS.—The principal rivers are the TAMAR, the LYNHER, the FOWEY, the CAMEL or ALAN, the FAL and the HEYL. There are also many smaller streams, which, after meandering in devious tracks, are absorbed in the larger waters. There are likewise several pools or lakes of some magnitude, as the Looe, the Dozmery, the Swan-pool, &c. The Tamar is one of the most considerable rivers in the west of England: its banks are richly diversified with rocks, woods and meadows; and the scenery, in various parts of its course, is extremely interesting and beautiful. This river rises in a moor near Morrinstow, and after effecting a junction with the Lyd and Tavy, and subsequently uniting with Lynher creek, forms between Devonport and Saltash the spacious basin called the Hamoaze or Plymouth harbour.

CIVIL and ECCLESIASTICAL DIVISIONS.—Cornwall is in the Province of Canterbury and Diocese of Exeter, and included in the Western Circuit. It is divided into nine hundreds, viz. EAST, KERRIER, LESNEWTH, PENRITH, POWDER, PYDER, STRATTON, TRIGG, and WEST. These divisions contain, collectively, one county town (Launceston), 27 other market towns, and 203 parishes. Cornwall possesses more Parliamentary boroughs than any other county in the kingdom, and the number of its representatives is also greater. This pre-eminence of representation is not very ancient; and appears to have arisen from the large hereditary revenue yielded by the Dutchy to the Crown, or to its immediate heir, the Prince of Wales. The whole County sends forty-two members to parliament, viz. two for the COUNTY, and two each for the following boroughs:—

BODMIN,	FOWEY,	NEWPORT,	ST. MICHAEL,
BOSSINEY,	HELSTON,	PENRYN,	SALTASH,
CALLINGTON,	LAUNCESTON,	ST. GERMAINS,	TREGONEY,
CAMELFORD,	LISKEARD,	ST. IVES,	TRURO,
EAST LOOE,	LOSTWITHIEL,	ST. MAWES,	WEST LOOE.

POPULATION.—According to the census of 1821, there were houses inhabited in the county, 43,873; uninhabited, 1,820; and houses building, 535. The number of families then resident in the county was 51,202; comprising 124,817 males, and 132,630 females; total, 257,447: and by a calculation made by order of government, which included persons in the army and navy, for which was added after the ratio of about one to thirty prior to the year 1811, and one to fifty for that year and the census of 1821, to the returns made from the several districts; the population of the county, in round numbers, in the year 1700, was 105,800—in 1750, 135,000—in 1801, 194,500—in 1811, 223,900—and in 1821, 262,600. The increased population in the fifty years, from the year 1700, was 29,200—from 1750 to 1801, the increase was 59,500—from 1801 to 1811, the increase was 29,400—and from 1811 to 1821, the augmented number of persons was 38,700: the grand total increase in the population of the county from the year 1700 to the census of 1821, being about 156,800 persons.

Index of Distances from Town to Town in the County of Cornwall.

THE NAMES OF THE RESPECTIVE TOWNS ARE ON THE TOP AND SIDE, AND THE SQUARE WHERE BOTH MEET GIVES THE DISTANCE.

Distance from Exeter	Town	Bodmin	Bossiney	Callington	Camborne	Camelford	Falmouth	Fowey	Grampound	Helston	Land's End	Launceston and Newport	Liskeard	Looe, East and West	Lostwithiel	Marazion	Padstow	Penryn	Penzance	Redruth	St. Austell	St. Columb	St. Germains	St. Ives	St. Mawes	St. Michael, or Midshall	Saltash	Stratton	Tregoney	Truro	Distance from London
62	Bodmin																														234
62	Bossiney	16																													229
40	Callington	23	25																												216
93	Camborne	32	49	55																											266
56	Camelford	12	5	19	43																										229
92	Falmouth	34	50	51	10	45																									270
59	Fowey	11	30	23	35	25	33																								239
74	Grampound	18	34	34	21	31	19	13																							250
99	Helston	40	57	60	10	52	12	30	25																						277
119	Land's End	60	76	79	24	73	35	59	45	23																					292
40	Launceston, &c.	21	17	12	53	15	53	29	38	59	80																				213
49	Liskeard	14	23	9	46	17	44	14	25	49	69	17																			225
53	Looe, East & West	20	31	15	46	25	42	9	24	48	70	26	8																		232
63	Lostwithiel	6	25	21	34	18	32	8	13	39	59	26	12	16																	236
106	Marazion	47	60	67	11	60	22	45	32	10	13	64	57	63	46																286
75	Padstow	14	16	38	32	15	33	29	16	39	56	30	29	33	21	46															243
90	Penryn	31	48	52	12	48	2	31	17	10	33	51	41	40	30	20	31														267
109	Penzance	48	61	69	14	63	25	48	35	13	10	67	60	60	49	3	46	13													282
89	Redruth	31	45	51	4	43	10	30	17	10	28	49	41	42	30	15	28	8	18												263
68	St. Austell	13	32	29	26	26	24	8	6	30	50	33	20	17	8	37	19	22	40	22											245
70	St. Columb	11	24	33	28	20	26	18	10	32	53	30	24	27	15	40	8	24	42	24	10										244
52	St. Germains	22	31	9	54	25	51	21	33	57	77	19	8	12	20	64	37	49	37	49	28	32									226
104	St. Ives	45	56	65	10	56	22	44	31	14	18	64	55	56	44	9	43	29	8	14	36	37	63								278
85	St. Mawes	30	46	42	22	43	19	25	12	27	46	50	37	36	25	33	29	17	36	18	18	25	45	33							262
65	St. Michael	15	30	38	20	28	18	20	8	24	44	35	29	38	22	31	14	16	31	16	12	7	37	30	17						248
46	Saltash	28	34	9	61	28	58	28	40	64	84	21	15	19	26	71	45	56	74	56	34	39	6	70	51	43					220
50	Stratton	30	19	30	62	18	64	41	47	70	90	16	36	44	36	77	35	62	78	62	42	43	37	77	59	46	37				223
75	Tregoney	20	36	36	21	33	19	15	3	25	45	40	27	26	15	32	18	17	35	17	7	12	35	31	10	10	42	49			253
82	Truro	22	40	43	12	35	11	21	8	17	37	42	32	31	21	24	22	9	27	9	13	15	11	21	10	7	47	52	7		255
67	Wadebridge	5	16	27	36	12	34	15	18	40	61	27	18	24	10	48	8	32	51	32	15	8	30	45	33	15	33	30	20	23	239

[See over.

Additional information relating to the County of CORNWALL.

———ooo———

POPULATION.—By the Census for **1831** this county contained 146,949 males, and 155,491 females—total 302,440, being an increase, since the returns made in the year 1821, of 44,993 inhabitants; and from the Census of 1801 to that of 1831 the augmentation amounted to 114,171 persons.

REPRESENTATION.—By the *Reform Bill* the following boroughs have been deprived of the elective franchise, namely, BOSSINEY, CALLINGTON, CAMELFORD, EAST LOOE, WEST LOOE, FOWEY, LOSTWITHIEL, NEWPORT, ST. GERMAINS, ST. MAWES, ST. MICHAEL, SALTASH, and TREGONEY; and the following boroughs have been deprived of *one* member each—HELSTON, LAUNCESTON, LISKEARD, and ST. IVES. Under the same Act two additional county members have been given, so that, now, the entire county returns *fourteen* members to Parliament instead of *forty-two* as heretofore. By the new *Boundary Act* the county is divided into two parts, respectively named the *Eastern Division* and the *Western Division:* the former includes the hundreds of East, Lesnewth, Stratton, Trigg, and West; and also the following parishes and places in the hundred of Powder—St. Austell, St. Blazey, St. Denis, St. Ewe, Fowey, Gorran, Ladock, Lanlivery, Lostwithiel, Luxulion, Mevagissey, St. Mewan, St. Michael-Carhaise, Roach, St. Sampson, St. Stephen's-in-Brannel, and Tywardreth; together with all such part of the hundred of Pyder as is not included in the western division; which said latter division includes the whole of the hundreds of Kerrier and Penwith, also such part of the hundred of Powder as is not included in the eastern division, together with the following parishes in the hundred of Pyder—St. Agnes, Crantock, Cubert, Newlyn, St. Enoder, and Perranzabuloe, and the Scilly Islands. The election of members for the eastern division of the county is held at BODMIN, and for the western at TRURO: besides the place of election the polling, for the eastern division, takes place at LAUNCESTON, LISKEARD, STRATTON, and ST. AUSTELL; and for the western division (besides the place of election) at PENZANCE, HELSTON, and REDRUTH.

RAILWAYS.—The town of *Redruth* and the port of *Hayle,* near *St. Ives,* on the Bristol channel, possesses Railway communication. A Railway is now in progress from *Exeter,* which will enter Cornwall near *Launceston,* passing near *Bodmin* to *Truro,* and thence to *Penzance.* There are several other lines proposed to intersect this county: one is projected to commence at the south-eastern corner, and to pass East Looe, St. Austell and Grampound, on to the port of Falmouth; another line to enter the county near Callington and the Tamar navigation, and, visiting Padstow, to join the Falmouth line near Tregoney; a third, the most westerly, is destined to connect the towns of Truro, Redruth and Penzance. There are various Railways connected with the mines, for the transit of tin and copper ore to the ports for embarkation; and one is about being constructed from Truro to New Quay.

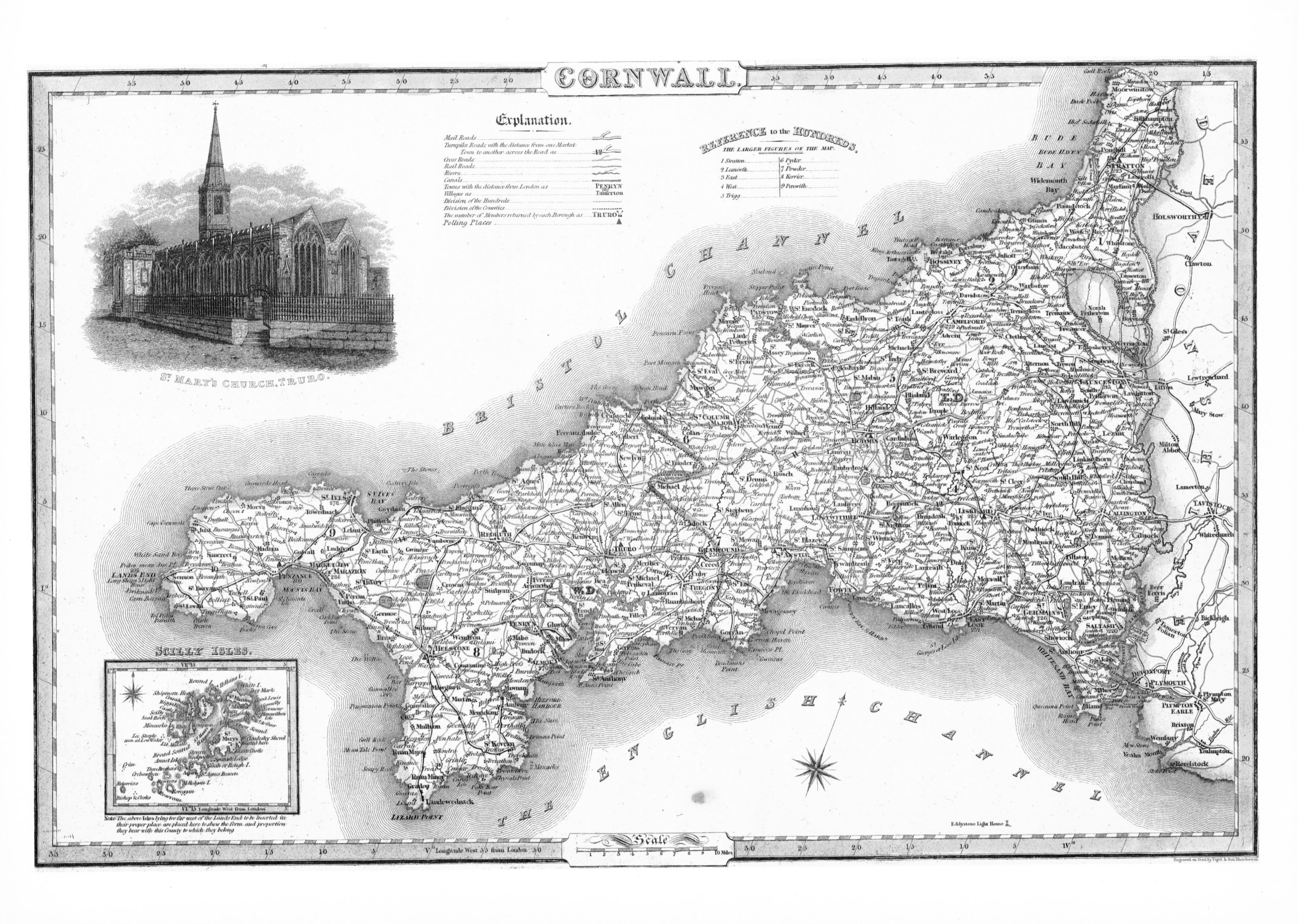
CORNWALL.
Explanation.
Mail Roads
Turnpike Roads with the distance from one Market Town to another across the Road as
Cross Roads
Rail Roads
Rivers
Canals
Towns with the distance from London as
PENRYN
Villages as
Tamerton
Division of the Hundreds
Division of the Counties
The number of Members returned by each Borough as
TRURO
Polling Places
REFERENCE to the HUNDREDS.
THE LARGER FIGURES ON THE MAP.
1 Stratton
2 Lesnewth
3 East
4 West
5 Trigg
6 Pyder
7 Powder
8 Kerrier
9 Penwith
St. MARY'S CHURCH, TRURO.
BRISTOL CHANNEL
THE ENGLISH CHANNEL
DEVON
BUDE BAY
WHITESAND BAY
MOUNTS BAY
SCILLY ISLES.
Note The above Isles lying too far west of the Lands End to be inserted in their proper place are placed here to show the form and proportion they bear with this County to which they belong
LIZARD POINT
Eddystone Light House
Scale
10 Miles
V° Longitude West 3.5 from London
Engraved on Steel by Pigot & Son Manchester.

CUMBERLAND.

CUMBERLAND is a maritime and northern county, bounded on the west by the Irish sea, on the east by the counties of Northumberland and Durham, on the south by those of Westmoreland and Lancaster, and on the north it is separated from Scotland by the waters of the Solway, the Scots' Dike, and the river Liddal. The greatest extent of the county is about 80 miles, but its mean length is not more than 60; its general breadth is 35, and its circumference 224 miles; containing 1,478 square miles.

NAME and ANCIENT HISTORY.—The ancient history of Cumberland has given much interesting employment to the antiquarian: its name is derived from the *Cimbri* or *Cumbri*, who were the aboriginal inhabitants; but who were, in common with those of Yorkshire, Lancashire, Durham and Westmoreland, called, by Ptolemy, the *Brigantes*. When Cumberland was conquered by the Saxons, it became part of the kingdom of Northumberland, and was then by its new lords first called *Lumbra-land* or *Lumer-land*, the land or county of the *Cumbri;* hence the easy transition to the present mode of spelling 'Cumberland.' A little below Carlisle was the famous 'Picts' Wall,' built in the year 121, by the Emperor Adrian, across the Island, from the German ocean to the Irish sea; about 100 miles in length, eight feet broad and twelve high, to prevent the incursions of the Picts and Scots: the remains of this wall are to this day still discernible in several places. At the time of the Norman Conquest, Cumberland was so impoverished, that William the Conqueror remitted all its taxations; for which reason it is not rated in the Domesday Book, as other counties are. At Workington, a port in this county, landed the unfortunate Mary, Queen of Scots, when she was driven to take refuge in the dominions of her insidious rival, Elizabeth; and at Burgh-upon-Sands died, in 1307, the victorious Edward I, as he was preparing for an expedition against Scotland.

SOIL and CLIMATE.—The soils are various: along the western boundary they have been classed under the divisions of fertile clays, or strong loams, which occupy but a small portion of the county, and are chiefly appropriated to the growth of wheat; dry loams and light sandy soils prevailing, with wet loam, through other parts; and black peat earth in the mountainous districts. The surface of this county is extremely irregular and broken: the districts to the south-west exhibit a gigantic combination of lofty and rugged mountains, promiscuously thrown together, but inclosing many beautiful though narrow vallies, as well as fine lakes, rivers, and some extensive woodlands; on the east side another range of hills stretches away to Scotland: along the western shore is a strip of cultivated land, from two to four miles in width; but the woodlands are inconsiderable, and the general appearance of this district is bleak and naked, presenting extensive moors. The CLIMATE varies considerably: the lower parts of the county are mild and temperate; while on the higher grounds, and upon the mountains and their vicinity, the air is cold and piercing; but all parts are healthy, though subject to great and frequent falls of rain, particularly in the autumn, which makes the harvests precarious.

MINES, MINERALS and MANUFACTURES.—The mineralogical productions of this county are rich and varied, and include lead, copper and iron ores, zinc, cobalt, antimony and black lead. The lead mines are chiefly in Alstone moor; the most considerable copper mines are near Caldbeck, at Hesket Newmarket, in Borrowdale, and at Newlands, in the neighbourhood of Keswick. At Crowgarth, in the parish of Egremont, is an iron mine, which is unrivalled for productiveness in Great Britain: in 1791-2 upwards of 20,000 tons were supplied to the Carron foundry and some other places. The famous black lead or wadd mines are situated at the head of Borrowdale, in a place difficult of access; and the richness and quality of the substance is unrivalled by any mine of the like material in the world. Valuable seams of coal are found in several parts; those about 12 miles to the east of Carlisle are productive, and of superior quality. About eight miles S. E. of this city is an immense bed of gypsum, or plaster of Paris, which is worked to great profit. The principal MANUFACTURES of Cumberland, exclusive of those derived from its mineral productions, are the spinning and manufacturing of cotton into various fabrics, and calico printing: coarse linens, checks, woollens, &c. are also produced in several of the towns, and Carlisle has been long famous for its ginghams: several paper-mills are established in different parts of the county; earthenware is manufactured near Dearham and other parts; hats are also manufactured to a considerable extent; and near Workington are iron-works, which employ several hundred workmen; and from this port a large quantity of coal is exported.

RIVERS, LAKES, &c.—The rivers and smaller streams are numerous; the principal are, the EDEN, the EAMONT, the DUDDON, the EHEN, the DARWENT, the GREATA, the COCKER, the ELLEN, the WAVER, the WAMPOOL, the CALDEW, the PETERIL, the ESK, the LIDDAL, the LINE or LEVEN, the IRTHING, and the GELT: the greater number of those rivers are not benefited in their navigation by the flowing of the tide inland, to a larger extent than from two to three miles, though the county enjoys a boundary of 67 miles of sea-coast. In 1823 a large SHIP CANAL, navigable for vessels of 100 tons burthen, was completed; it is eleven miles in length, and forms a communication between the City of Carlisle and the Solway frith. This romantic county abounds with lakes: the principal are known by the names of Ulls-water, about nine miles in length and three quarters of a mile in breadth; Thirles-mere, or Leathes-water, a narrow irregular sheet, about three miles in length, skirts the bay of Helvellyn; Derwent-water, or Keswick-lake, of an oval figure, about three miles in length and about one and a half in breadth; Bassenthwaite-water, or Broad-water, about three miles north of Keswick-lake, is four miles long and one at its greatest breadth, and is surrounded with beautiful scenery; Over-water, in a barren situation, is about half a mile in length and a quarter in breadth; Lowes-water, above Mellbreak, about a mile long and a quarter broad; Crummock-water expands its pellucid bosom beneath lofty mountains, and extends nearly four miles in length and half a mile in breadth; Buttermere-water, about a mile south of Crummock-lake, from which it is separated by a beautiful and luxuriant vale, is about a mile and a half long and half a mile broad, into which numerous torrents pour down from the mountains, one of the roaring cataracts falling between four and five hundred yards; Ennerdale-water rests beneath the mountains, near to Whitehaven, and is guarded by craggy and almost impassable heights, its length being about two miles and its breadth three quarters of a mile; Waste-water expands its crystal surface in the bosom of Waste-dale to the length of three miles and in breadth about three quarters of a mile; Burnmoor-tarn, lying among wild mountains, near Miter-dale, covers about 250 acres; Devock-water, among the hills S. E. of Ravenglass; Talkin-tarn and Tindale-tarn possess about fifty acres each; and Turnwaddling covers a hundred acres, at Armathwaite.

CIVIL and ECCLESIASTICAL DIVISIONS.—Cumberland (with the exception of the ward of Allerdale above Darwent, which is in the Diocese of Chester,) is in the Diocese of Carlisle, and in the Province of Canterbury. It is divided into five *wards*, synonimous with hundreds in other counties, but so called here from the inhabitants of each division being formerly obliged to keep watch or '*ward*' against the northern irruptions; they are respectively denominated ALLERDALE above Darwent, ALLERDALE below Darwent, CUMBERLAND, ESKDALE and LEATH: these contain one city and county town (Carlisle), 17 other market towns, and 104 parishes. The whole county returns six members to parliament, viz. two for the city of CARLISLE, two for the borough of COCKERMOUTH, and two for the COUNTY.

POPULATION.—According to the census of 1821, there were houses inhabited in the county, 27,246; uninhabited, 908; and houses building, 155. The number of families then resident in the county was 31,804, comprising 75,600 males, and 80,524 females; total, 156,124: and by a calculation made by order of government, which included persons in the army and navy, for which was added after the ratio of about one to thirty prior to the year 1811, and one to fifty for that year and the census of 1821, to the returns made from the several districts; the population of the county, in round numbers, in the year 1700, was 62,300—in 1750, 86,900—in 1801, 121,100—in 1811, 138,300—and in 1821, 159,300. The increased population in the fifty years, from the year 1700, was 24,600—from 1750 to 1801, the increase was 34,200—from 1801 to 1811, the increase was 17,200—and from 1811 to 1821, the augmented number of persons was 21,000: the grand total increase in the population of the county, from the year 1700 to the census of 1821, being about 97,000 persons.

Index of Distances from Town to Town in the County of Cumberland.

THE NAMES OF THE RESPECTIVE TOWNS ARE ON THE TOP AND SIDE, AND THE SQUARE WHERE BOTH MEET GIVES THE DISTANCE.

	Alston	Brampton	Carlisle	Cockermouth	Egremont	Hesket Newmarket	Ireby	Keswick	Kirkoswald	Longtown	Maryport	Penrith	Ravenglass	Whitehaven	Wigton	Workington	*Distance from London.*
Alston																	281
Brampton	20																310
Carlisle	29	9															301
Cockermouth	46	35	26														305
Egremont	60	50	41	15													291
Hesket Newmarket	30	22	13	16	31												296
Ireby	41	28	19	11	26	8											304
Keswick	36	41	32	12	24	14	14										293
Kirkoswald	14	15	15	32	48	16	24	24									290
Longtown	31	11	9	35	50	22	28	41	24								310
Maryport	53	37	28	7	19	21	13	19	36	37							312
Penrith	20	22	18	29	41	13	21	18	7	27	36						283
Ravenglass	62	62	50	24	11	40	35	26	50	59	31	43					280
*Whitehaven	62	50	41	14	5	30	25	26	46	50	15	43	16				320
Wigton	40	20	11	16	31	9	8	22	24	20	16	21	40	30			305
Workington	54	43	34	8	12	24	19	20	39	43	7	37	23	8	24		312

From WHITEHAVEN to LONDON, by way of COCKERMOUTH and KENDAL, the distance is 320 miles, but by way of ULVERSTON, & over the SANDS, it is only 296 miles.

Additional information relating to the County of CUMBERLAND.

———ooo———

POPULATION.—By the Census for **1831** this county contained 81,971 males, and 87,710 females—total 169,681, being an increase, since the returns made in the year 1821, of 13,557 inhabitants; and from the Census of 1801 to that of 1831 the augmentation amounted to 52,451 persons.

REPRESENTATION.—By the *Reform Bill* WHITEHAVEN has obtained the privilege of returning *one* member, and two additional ones for the county have been given; so that the whole county now sends *nine* representatives to Parliament, instead of *six*, as heretofore. The new *Boundary Act* divides the county into two parts, respectively called the *Eastern Division* and the *Western Division:* the former includes the whole of the several wards of Cumberland, Eskdale, and Leath, and the western division, the wards of Allerdale-above-Derwent and Allerdale-below-Derwent. The election of members, for the eastern division of the county, is held at CARLISLE, and for the western at COCKERMOUTH: besides the place of election, for the eastern division, the polling takes place at BRAMPTON, WIGTON, PENRITH, and ALDSTONE; and for the western division (besides the place of election) at ASPATRIA, KESWICK, BOOTLE, and EGREMONT.

RAILWAYS.—The NEWCASTLE and CARLISLE RAILWAY is a most important line, connecting as it does the Irish and North Seas. From *Carlisle* it proceeds by the route of *Brampton, Haltwhistle, Hexham* and *Corbridge*, to *Newcastle*. The entire line was opened throughout in 1838, on the anniversary of the battle of Waterloo: from Newcastle to the Canal Basin, at Carlisle, the distance is sixty-one miles. From *Carlisle* a line is forming to *Maryport:* also one from Carlisle to Lancaster, by Penrith and Shap; and another to Lancaster, over Morecambe Bay, from Maryport to Whitehaven. A line is contemplated from Carlisle to Glasgow, by Gretna, near Dumfries, which will join the Railway at Kilmarnock. Another Railway is projected between Carlisle and the mineral district of Penrith: the line, as proposed, will start from near Penrith Castle, and take very nearly the course of the Petterill river, until it joins the Newcastle and Carlisle Railway close to Carlisle.

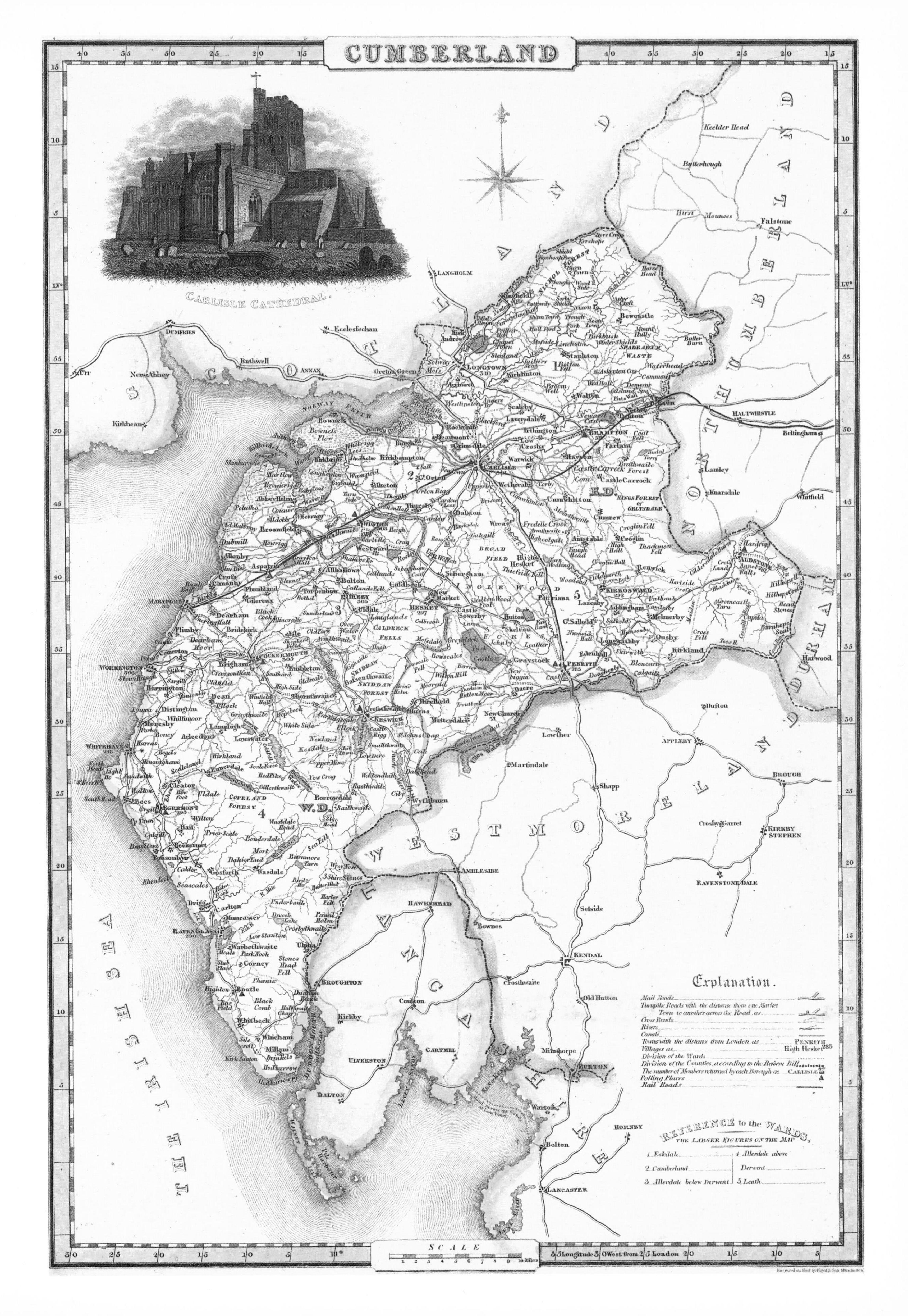
CUMBERLAND
Carlisle Cathedral.
SCOTLAND
NORTHUMBERLAND
DURHAM
WESTMORELAND
LANCASHIRE
THE IRISH SEA
SOLWAY FRITH
Keelder Head
Butterhough
Hirst
Mounces
Falstone
LANGHOLM
Ecclesfechan
DUMFRIES
Ruthwell
ANNAN
Gretna Green
New Abbey
Kirkbean
LONGTOWN 310
Bewcastle
Stapleton
Spadeadam Waste
Waterhead
HALTWHISTLE
Beltingham
BRAMPTON
Walton
Scaleby
Irthington
CARLISLE
Burgh
Bowness
Kirkbampton
Wigton
Abbey Holme
Allonby
Aspatria
MARYPORT
Dearham
Brigham
COCKERMOUTH 305
WORKINGTON
Harrington
Distington
Moresby
WHITEHAVEN
St. Bees
St. Bees Hd.
EGREMONT
Beckermet
Calder
Gosforth
Seascales
Drigg
Carlton
Muncaster
RAVENGLASS
Bootle
Whitbeck
Whicham
Millam
Hodbarrow Pt.
DUDDON MOUTH
KESWICK
Crosthwaite
Borrowdale
Wythburn
Ennerdale
Lowswater
Wasdale
COPELAND FOREST
W.D.
SKIDDAW
IREBY
Sebergham
HESKET
Dalston
Wetheral
Cumwhitton
Castle Carrock
Croglin
Kirkoswald
Renwick
Melmerby
Ousby
Kirkland
ALDSTONE
Lazonby
Gt. Salkeld
Penrith
Greystock
Dacre
Edenhall
Langwathby
Blencarn
Culgaith
Lamley
Knarsdale
Whitfield
Harwood
Dufton
APPLEBY
BROUGH
Lowther
Martindale
Shapp
Crosby Garret
KIRKBY STEPHEN
RAVENSTONE DALE
AMBLESIDE
HAWKSHEAD
Bowness
Selside
KENDAL
Crosthwaite
Old Hutton
Milnthorpe
BURTON
BROUGHTON
Coulton
Kirkby
CARTMEL
ULVERSTON
DALTON
Warton
HORNBY
Bolton
LANCASTER
Explanation.
Mail Roads
Turnpike Roads with the distance from one Market Town to another across the Road, as
Cross Roads
Rivers
Canals
Towns with the distance from London as PENRITH 283
Villages as High Hesket
Division of the Wards
Division of the Counties, according to the Reform Bill
The number of Members returned by each Borough as CARLISLE 2
Polling Places
Rail Roads
REFERENCE to the WARDS,
THE LARGER FIGURES ON THE MAP
1. Eskdale
2. Cumberland
3. Allerdale below Derwent
4. Allerdale above Derwent
5. Leath
SCALE
10 Miles
Longitude West from London

DERBYSHIRE.

DERBYSHIRE is situated nearly in the middle of the Island, at an equal distance from the east and west seas. On the north, its boundaries are Yorkshire and part of Cheshire, the river Etherow separating it from the latter; on the west, it is divided from Cheshire and Staffordshire by the Goyt, the Dove, and the Trent; on the south, it is skirted by Leicestershire; and on the east, it is bounded by Nottinghamshire, its dividing limits on this and the north side being mostly artificial. The figure of Derbyshire is extremely irregular—its sides sometimes swelling into projections, and sometimes diminishing into curves. Its greatest extent from north to south is nearly fifty-five miles; its breadth, at the northern extremity, is about thirty-three, contracting as it advances south, and when near its junction with Leicestershire narrowing almost to a point; its circumference is 130 miles, containing 1,026 square miles. The derivation of the word 'Derby,' from which the shire takes its name, has given rise to much altercation among etymologists and antiquarians. By the Saxons it is said to have been called *Northworthigie,*—which name was rejected by the Danes, who styled it *Deoraby,* of which 'Derby' appears a contraction. Some accounts state, that the site of Derby was formerly a park for deer, from whence it was called *Deer-by;* and it is attempted to support this assertion by the figure of the county arms—*a buck couchant in a park:* but this position fails when it is ascertained that it went by the name *Deoraby* long before the introduction of coat armoury into this kingdom. The most generally received opinion is, that the town derives its name from its situation on the river Derwent, and that it was originally called *Derwent-by,* which in course of time became corrupted into *Deoraby, Deroby,* and 'Derby.'

SOIL, CLIMATE, &c.—The most common soil in this county is a reddish clay or marl; the southern district is in general composed of it, having little or no stone near the surface, but interspersed with small beds of sand or gravel; and in moist situations is found land of a blackish colour and loose texture: this kind of soil is likewise seen on the north-west of the county, where extensive beds of lime-stone abound. The large tract on the east side, extending from Stanton-dale and Morley to the borders of Yorkshire, is rich in coal, which is covered with clay of various colours—black, grey, brown, and yellow, the last colour prevailing; similar soil is also met with in the north extremity of the county. In the vallies, near the banks of the larger rivers, the soil is very different from that of the adjacent parts, and has been evidently varied by the depositions from inundations. Peat bogs exist in the north parts of the county, even on the highest mountains; and in some of them trees have been found, nearly perfect. The southern part of Derbyshire is appropriated both to pasture and tillage, in nearly equal proportions; but as the dairy is as much an object of attention as the production of corn, the same land seldom remains long in tillage. The general appearance of Derbyshire is exceedingly dissimilar, its south and north parts exhibiting a striking contrast; the former not being remarkable for hills or vallies, while the latter is eminently marked by a continued succession of both. The upper and middle parts of the county are denominated the 'High Peak,' and the '*Wapentake*' or 'Low Peak;' but the south part has no particular appellation. The most considerable eminences in the tract of the High Peak are the mountains Ax-Edge and Kinder-Scout: the former is situated near Buxton, and is said to be 2,100 feet higher than the town of Derby, and 1,000 feet above the valley in which Buxton-hall stands; the latter rises near the centre of the north-west angle, and overlooks all the neighbouring eminences. The High Peak is a region of bleak barren heights; but the scenery is in many parts romantic and sublime, yet not partaking of picturesque effect, beauty being resident only in the vallies; the high grounds appearing dreary and sterile, without a tree, or verdant sward, to relieve the wearied sight of the traveller. Barren and unpleasing as these highlands are, still they are not destitute of usefulness to the contemplative lover of nature,—serving, by contrast, to heighten the beauty of the dales, vallies and streams by which they are intersected. The Low Peak abounds with eminences of various heights and extent: Brassington-moor, Alport, near Wirksworth, and Crick-cliffe, are the most elevated, and command very extensive prospects; from Alport, the Wrekin, in Shropshire, may be clearly distinguished in an open day. On the east side of the county there is also a high ridge, beginning to the south of Hardwick, and continuing to the extremity of the county, where it enters Yorkshire. The south part is in general pleasant and well cultivated, presenting no particular variety of scenery. The CLIMATE of Derbyshire may be considered healthful: the atmosphere is pure, and the higher situations generally free from epidemic diseases, though agues and fevers sometimes prevail in the vallies: one disease is, however, endemic in those parts; this is the *Bronchocele,* or 'Derby neck,' being an enlargement of the glands of the throat, and is a degree of the same disease known in the Alps and other mountainous tracts. The High Peak is peculiarly liable to violent storms, in which the rain descends in torrents, so as frequently to occasion great ravages in the lands; it is also subject to very high winds; which causes, with the elevation of the country, render it cold, so that vegetation is backward and unkindly: some kinds of grain will not grow at all in the Peak, and others seldom ripen until very late in the year.

MANUFACTURES and PRODUCE, MINES and MINERALS.—The manufactures which are carried on in this county are various and extensive. With Lancashire it partakes in the manufacture of cotton; with Nottinghamshire and Leicestershire, in the weaving stockings; with Cheshire, in the various textures of silk; with Yorkshire, in woollen cloths and iron; and to these may be added a branch in which it stands unrivalled, viz. the forming numberless beautiful ornaments of Derbyshire spar. Besides the wealth derived from these several branches of trade, the profits arising from agricultural produce are by no means inconsiderable. Upon the banks of the Dove are rich dairy-farms; many are large, and produce excellent cheese, about 2,000 tons of which are supposed to be sent annually to London. Wheat is particularly fine from many lands, but in no part more luxuriant than in the extensive fields of Chaddesden and Chelleston; barley is much cultivated in many districts, particularly in the parishes of Repton and Gresley, this sort of grain being much employed in the neighbouring town of Burton, in the brewing of ale, which has long been famous for its potency. The inclosures of Derbyshire, of a late date, have been to a wonderful extent, and this laudable system is still going on. An uncommon species of culture, as a field crop, is practised in this county, viz. camomile, upwards of 200 acres being devoted to the growth of this physical herb. The MINERAL sources of wealth in Derbyshire comprise mines of lead, copper and iron ores; antimony, alabaster, mill-stones, lime-stone, various beautiful spars peculiar to this county, and coals. The principal tract containing lead is called Kingsfield; under this denomination the whole Wapentake of Wirksworth is comprised, as well as part of the High Peak. Iron-stone is found in great abundance throughout the whole district in which coal has been discovered, the Chinley hills excepted. Calamine is obtained at Castleton, Cromford, Bonsall and Wirksworth; coal in the liberties of Norton, Alfreton and many other places. Lime-stone exists in abundance and variety; the marbles formed by it are extremely variegated and beautiful; the best are at Hopton, Money-Ash, Ashford, Matlock and Monsaldale. The flour-spar, or 'Blue John,' is obtained in a mountain to the west of Castleton; and gypsum is found at Elvaston and Chellarton.

RIVERS, CANALS and MINERAL SPRINGS.—The principal rivers of this county are the TRENT, the DOVE, the DERWENT, the WYE, the EREWASH and the ROTHER: all these rivers are enriched either by the mountain torrents, or by small rivulets, as they meander through the vales and animate the scenery, until they are lost in larger waters. The CANALS that pass through this county are the ASHBY-DE-LA-ZOUCH, the CHESTERFIELD, the CROMFORD, the DERBY, the EREWASH, the PEAK FOREST, and the TRENT AND MERSEY OR GRAND TRUNK. As might be expected in a county abounding with fossils, the MINERAL and MEDICINAL WATERS are numerous: the most celebrated warm springs are those at Matlock and Buxton; those of sulphureous property rise at Keddleston. The chalybeate waters are numerous; those in most repute are at Quarndon, about three miles from Derby. A martial vitriolic spring, the only one that has yet been found in this county, is in the liberty of Heage, about midway between Crich & Belper.

CIVIL and ECCLESIASTICAL DIVISIONS.—Derbyshire is in the Province of Canterbury and Diocese of Lichfield, and is included in the Northern Circuit. It is divided into six hundreds, viz. APPLETREE, HIGH PEAK, MORLESTON and LITCHURCH, REPTON and GRESLEY, SCARSDALE, and WIRKSWORTH; these contain two borough towns (Derby and Chesterfield), one county town (Derby), eleven other market towns, and one hundred and thirty-nine parishes.—This county sends four members to Parliament, viz. two for the Town of Derby, and two for the Shire.

POPULATION.—According to the census of 1821, there were houses inhabited in the county, 40,054; uninhabited, 1,072; and houses building, 305. The number of families then resident in the county was 42,404; comprising 105,873 males, and 107,460 females; total, 213,333: and by a calculation made by order of government, which included persons in the army and navy, for which was added after the ratio of about one to thirty prior to the year 1811, and one to fifty for that year and the census of 1821, to the returns made from the several districts; the population of the county, in round numbers, in the year 1700, was 93,800—in 1750, 109,500—in 1801, 166,500—in 1811, 191,700—and in 1821, 217,600. The increase of population in the 50 years, from the year 1700, was 15,700—from 1750 to 1801, the increase was 57,000—from 1801 to 1811, the increase was 25,200—and from 1811 to 1821, the augmented number of persons was 25,900: the grand total increase in the population of the county from the year 1700 to the census of 1821, being about 123,800 persons.

Index of Distances from Town to Town in the County of Derby.

THE NAMES OF THE RESPECTIVE TOWNS ARE ON THE TOP AND SIDE, AND THE SQUARE WHERE BOTH MEET GIVES THE DISTANCE.

Distance from Manchester.	Town	Alfreton	Ashbourn	Bakewell	Belper	Bolsover	Buxton	Castleton	Chapel-en-le-Frith	Chesterfield	Derby	Dronfield	Matlock	Tideswell	Winster	Wirksworth	*Distance from London.*
51	Alfreton																141
46	Ashbourn	17															139
32	Bakewell	15	16														153
54	Belper	7	12	16													134
53	Bolsover	11	24	18	16												145
24	Buxton	25	20	12	28	29											160
25	Castleton	24	23	10	26	26	9										164
18	Chapel-en-le-Frith	28	23	14	30	29	5	7									167
48	Chesterfield	9	22	12	16	6	24	17	23								150
59	Derby	15	13	25	8	24	33	32	34	24							126
38	Dronfield	15	25	11	22	9	23	14	20	6	29						156
42	Matlock	11	14	10	8	12	22	18	24	8	16	14					144
25	Tideswell	23	19	7	23	23	6	5	7	16	14	15	15				160
53	Winster	12	10	6	11	17	15	16	18	13	17	15	4	12			145
48	Wirksworth	9	9	11	6	16	20	21	23	14	14	16	3	17	5		140

[*See over.*

Additional information relating to the County of Derby.

———ooo———

Population.—By the Census for 1831 this county contained 117,740 males, and 119,430 females—total 237,170, being an increase, since the returns made in the year 1821, of 23,837 inhabitants; and from the Census of 1801 to that of 1831 the augmentation amounted to 76,028 persons.

Representation.—Under the *Reform Bill* two additional members for the county have been given; the whole shire, therefore, now sends *six* representatives to Parliament instead of *four*. The new *Boundary Act* divides the county into two parts, respectively called the *Northern Division,* and the *Southern Division;* the former includes the hundreds of High Peak and Scarsdale, and so much of the wapentake of Wirksworth as, by virtue of the order made at the quarter sessions for the county, held at the borough of Derby, the 28th June, 1831, is comprised in the Bakewell division, as established by such order: the southern division includes the whole of the several hundreds of Appletree, Morleston and Litchurch, and Repton and Gresley, also all such parts of the wapentake of Wirksworth as are not included in the northern division last described. The election of members for the northern division of the county is held at Bakewell, and for the southern at Derby: besides the place of election, for the northern division, the polling takes place at Chesterfield, Chapel-en-le-Frith, Alfreton, and Glossop; and for the southern division (besides the place of election) at Ashbourn, Wirksworth, Melbourn, and Belper.

RAILWAYS.

The Birmingham and Derby Railway commences at *Derby,* and joins the London and Birmingham Railway about three miles from *Birmingham,* and for London at *Hampton.* The North Midland proceeds from *Derby,* and, leaving the town of *Duffield* on the left, passes through *Belper* and *Chesterfield* to *Rotherham* and *Sheffield.* The Midland Counties' Railway also originates at *Derby,* and forms a communication with *Nottingham* by means of a branch at *Long Eaton.* From Derby a Railway is intended to be constructed to Macclesfield—which, if carried into effect, will open to the inhabitants of Leicestershire and Derbyshire a direct Railway communication with the great towns of Manchester and Liverpool. The Cromford and High Peak Railway, although the first constructed in this county, is perhaps now of the least importance: it originates a short distance to the north of *Wirksworth* and south of *Cromford,* and, pursuing a north-westerly course, joins the Peak Forest canal between three and four miles to the north-west of *Chapel-en-le-Frith.* The value of this Railway will be most materially enhanced if a line in contemplation be carried into effect: the proposal is to unite the North Midland Railway, at Duffield, with the High Peak Railway near Wirksworth—which will open a more direct communication than at present exists between the manufacturing districts of Lancashire and the Midland Counties.

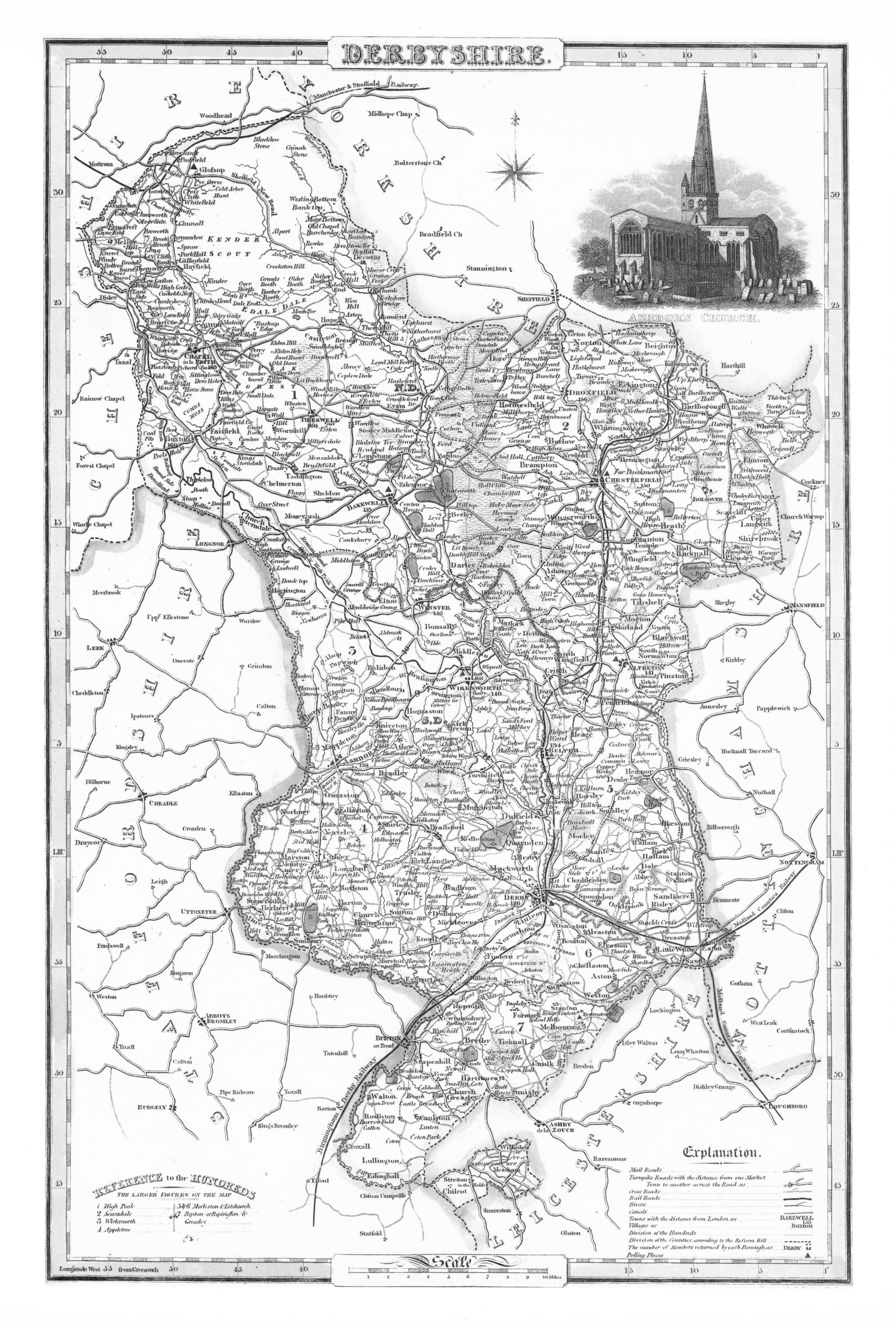
DERBYSHIRE.
ASHBORN CHURCH.
Explanation.
Mail Roads
Turnpike Roads with the distance from one Market Town to another across the Road, as
Cross Roads
Rail Roads
Rivers
Canals
Towns with the distance from London, as
BAKEWELL 153
Villages as
Buxton
Division of the Hundreds
Division of the Counties, according to the Reform Bill
The number of Members returned by each Borough, as
DERBY
Polling Places
REFERENCE to the HUNDREDS
THE LARGER FIGURES ON THE MAP
1 High Peak
2 Scarsdale
3 Wirksworth
4 Appletree
5 & 6 Morleston & Litchurch
7 Repton or Repington & Gresley
Scale
10 Miles
Longitude West 55 from Greenwich
YORKSHIRE
CHESHIRE
STAFFORDSHIRE
LEICESTERSHIRE
NOTTINGHAMSHIRE
Manchester & Sheffield Railway
Midland Counties Railway
Birmingham & Derby Railway
SHEFFIELD
CHESTERFIELD
BAKEWELL
DERBY
BELPER
ALFRETON
ASHBORN
WIRKSWORTH
MANSFIELD
NOTTINGHAM
LOUGHBORO
ASHBY DE LA ZOUCH
BURTON on Trent
UTTOXETER
CHEADLE
LEEK
LONGNOR
BUXTON
CHAPEL EN LE FRITH
GLOSSOP
TIDESWELL
DRONFIELD
BOLSOVER
WINSTER
RUDGELY
ABBOTS BROMLEY

DEVONSHIRE.

DEVONSHIRE, a maritime county, is one of the most valuable in England, and in size ranks the third, (being only exceeded by Yorkshire and Lincolnshire). It is bounded on the west and north-west by the Bristol channel, on the west by the river Tamar and a small rivulet called Marsland water; on the south and south-east by the British channel, and on the east and south-east by the counties of Dorset & Somerset, the dividing limits here being artificial. The greatest length of the county from north to south is nearly 71 miles, and from east to west about the same extent; its area comprising about 2,579 square miles. Camden, in speaking of its name, says—'The hithermost part of the county of the *Damonii* is now commonly called Devonshire; by the Cornish Britons *Deunon;* by the Welch, *Deufney* (the deep vallies), because the lower parts of it are chiefly inhabited; by the Saxons, *Deuonschire,* whence comes the Latin name *Devona,* and the common contraction *Denshire,* and not from the Danes, as the sciolists warmly maintain.'

SOIL, PRODUCE and CLIMATE.—The external aspect of Devonshire is extremely varied and irregular; and the heights in many parts, but particularly in Dartmoor and its vicinity, swell into mountains; the altitudes of the principal eminences being from 1,500 to 1,800 feet. On approaching this tract from the south and south-east, the eye is bewildered by an extensive vale, exhibiting gigantic '*tors,*' large surfaces covered with vast masses of scattered granite and immense rocks, which seem to have been precipitated from the steep declivities into the valleys. Dartmoor, and the waste called the forest of Dartmoor, occupy a great portion of the western district, which, extending from the vale of Exeter, nearly reaches to the banks of the Tamar, and includes between two and three hundred thousand acres of open and uncultivated lands; of these, Dartmoor alone is supposed to comprise 80,000. These extensive tracts, though capable of considerable improvement, at present scarcely afford more than a scanty pasturage to a few thousand sheep and cattle. The right of depasture belongs to different interests; the forest itself being the property of the King's eldest son, as parcel of the Dutchy of Cornwall. The 'Vale of Exeter' differs widely in appearance from Dartmoor: the soils in this district vary exceedingly, but the most prevalent are strong red loam, shillet or foliated clay, intersected with numerous veins of iron-stone, and a mixture of sand and gravel. Wheat, barley, beans and pease are the most general productions of the arable lands; flax is also cultivated, but in no great quantity. The pasture lands are chiefly appropriated to the supply of the dairy, but in some parts considerable attention is given to the breeding of sheep and cattle: the produce of the dairy is fine butter and the poorest skim-milk cheese. Peculiar to the dairies of Devon is that delicious and rich lacteous production, 'clotted' or 'clouted' cream; the consistence of this article is in proportion to the richness of the farm-land; instances are not unfrequent that a pan of cream, when become cold, has supported upon its surface a weight equal to two ounces, without breaking what may be called the crust; it is from this cream that the butter is made—by the hand, and not by the churn as in other counties. Where the cream is produced, its price is generally regulated by that of butter; what butter is per pound, so is cream per pint: it is also sent to all parts of England, especially to London, where it obtains a very high price, although much reduced in value, richness and consistence by its dilution with milk. The district called the 'South Hams' is frequently termed the garden of Devonshire, from its fertility; its area, including the rich vale of the Dart (which extends towards Ashburton), comprises nearly 250 square miles: the principal kind of soil is a strong red loam, with a substratum of clay; the common crops, on the arable lands, are wheat, barley, oats, turnips and potatoes,—the last-named root is cultivated in many parts of Devonshire with great success. Great quantities of cider are made in this district; and as every farm has its orchard, the general produce affords a considerable surplus for exportation, even after large deductions have been made for home consumption. The district of West Devon is beyond the Dartmoor mountains; the soil is a portion of loamy mould, mixed, in various degrees of quality, with perished slate-stone rubble, reduced by the action of the atmosphere to its original silt or mud. Nearly two-thirds of the inclosed lands of this district are employed alternately in the cultivation of grasses and raising corn; the remainder is either in tillage, or occupied by orchard-grounds. North Devon, in its most extended sense, comprehends the whole district situated between Dartmoor and the British channel; but more generally is limited to the country round Bideford, Barnstaple, South Molton and the north coast. In this tract, the ground is greatly diversified, and the scenery beautiful. The land is chiefly appropriated to the growth of wheat and oats; and the soil is generally productive, except, perhaps, on the summits of the highest hills. The established breed of sheep in this county is the middled wool class, bearing a strong resemblance to the Dorsets; the native breed of horses is very small, resembling the Welch and Highland breeds; the pack-horses used in the inclosed country are of a similar nature, but larger. Among the products of Devonshire should be noticed the great variety of fish which abound in its rivers, and on its beautiful coasts; the which, in addition to the home consumption, supply a very considerable quantity of food for the Bath and even London markets.—The CLIMATE of Devonshire is remarkably mild, particularly on the southern part of the county, where its genial influence is every where visible: vegetation suffers but little interruption here during the winter season, and the earth seems to wear a perpetual verdure; the myrtle flourishes here unsheltered. It is only on the northern coast, and north-east corner of the county, that the severity of the winter is experienced: on the higher parts of Dartmoor the air is bleak and piercing, but it is also invigorating and salubrious; and even in these elevated regions the snow seldom continues, in the most severe winters, more than ten days or a fortnight. Medical men have been long so well convinced of the advantages resulting from the mildness of the climate of the south of Devon, that they recommend it to their consumptive patients in preference to Lisbon or the south of France.

MANUFACTURES and MINERAL PRODUCTIONS.—The manufacture of coarse woollen goods has long been carried on to a great extent in this county; they consist chiefly of articles but little consumed in England, as druggets, duroys, long ells and serges; the markets for these are Italy, Spain, Germany, Holland, Portugal and France; besides this, the East India Company takes off a quantity of long ells annually. About a fourth part of these articles are shipped at Exeter, the remainder at Dartmouth and Plymouth. Several towns on the coast are materially benefited by a trade with Newfoundland, though not to the extent formerly enjoyed by them. Broad and narrow men's cloths are made in some parts, but this trade is now principally transferred to Yorkshire. Axminster stands pre-eminent in the manufacture of carpets, the most beautiful Turkey and Persia carpets being imitated with great success. At Honiton the most beautiful and the broadest cushion laces in the kingdom are made. The METALLIC SUBSTANCES of the county are the ores of tin, lead, iron and manganese; gold, silver, copper, bismuth, antimony and cobalt have also been found, but in small quantities. The tin-works were anciently numerous and valuable, but have in a great measure been abandoned, the mines of Cornwall being considerably more productive. Not many years ago some very rich lead ore was discovered, near the surface, at Coombe-Martin. Iron-stone is found in various parts of the county, but not particularly rich in metal. Native silver has been found at Coombe-Martin; and that there were formerly mines of gold appears from various grants made in the reigns of Edward III. and Richard II. The most remarkable of the inflammable substances discovered in Devonshire is the Bovey coal, of which there are two species, the stone-coal and the wood-coal: the latter is said to make as strong a fire as oaken billets, especially if set on edge; but the heat of the former is accounted the most intense. According to Kirwan, this coal consists of wood penetrated with petrol or bitumen.

RIVERS and MINERAL SPRINGS.—This county is watered by many rivers; the principal are, the EXE, the TORRIDGE, the OKE, the DART, the PLYM, the TEIGN, the OTTER, the AXE, and the LYN; the TAMAR is also considered as belonging to Devonshire. The *Isk* of the Britons, the *Isca* of the Romans, and the *Ex* or 'Exe' of the Saxons and of the moderns, rises in Exmoor, in Somersetshire; and, after receiving several streams in its progress to Topsham, where it meets the tide, falls into the British channel at Exmouth, after a course of sixty miles. The source of the Torridge is so near that of the Tamar, that its springs are supposed to be the same, and the difference in their course to arise from variation in the height of the ground where they issue: this river becomes navigable at Wear Giffard, and enters the Bristol channel at Barnstaple bay. The Taw rises in Dartmoor, and falls into the Torridge about five miles below Barnstaple. The river Dart has also its source in the mountains of Dartmoor, and from the velocity of its current is most appropriately named: it wanders through delightful valleys and between wood-capped eminences, disclosing new beauties at every curve till it makes its exit in the British channel at Dartmouth. The Plym also rises in Dartmoor, and falls into the sound a little below Plymouth. The Teign rises among the moors on the east of Dartmoor, and falls into the sea at Teignmouth. The Otter and Sid enter the county from the borders of Somersetshire; the Axe runs out of Dorsetshire; and all of them flow into the British channel. The Lyn, which rises in the forest of Exmoor, is a small but rapid river, pursuing its impetuous course over rocks of immense size, and at length rushes into the British channel.—The MINERAL WATERS are very numerous, and chiefly of the chalybeate kind: the strongest springs of this description arise at Grubb's Wall, near Cleave; at Balla marsh, near King-steington; at Islington, in the vicinity of Totnes; at Brook, near Tavistock; and at Bampton.

CIVIL and ECCLESIASTICAL DIVISIONS.—Devonshire is in the Province of Canterbury and Diocese of Exeter, and included in the Western Circuit; it is divided into thirty-two hundreds, viz.—

AXMINSTER,	COLYTON,	HAYTOR,	SHERWILL,
BAMPTON,	CREDITON,	HEMYOCK,	STANBOROUGH,
BLACK TORRINGTON,	ERMINGTON,	LIFTON,	TAVISTOCK,
BRAUNTON,	EXMINSTER,	MOLTON,	TAWTON,
BUDLEIGH EAST,	FREMINGTON,	OTTERY,	TEIGNBRIDGE,
BUDLEIGH WEST,	HALBERTON,	PLYMPTON,	TIVERTON,
CLISTON,	HARTLAND,	ROBOROUGH,	WITHERIDGE,
COLERIDGE,	HAYBRIDGE,	SHEBBEAR,	WONFORD.

These divisions contain collectively one city and county town (Exeter, which is also a county of itself,) 40 market towns, and 465 parishes. The whole county sends 26 members to Parliament, viz. two each for the towns of ASHBURTON, BARNSTAPLE, BEER-ALSTON, DARTMOUTH, EXETER, HONITON, OAKHAMPTON, PLYMOUTH, PLYMPTON, TAVISTOCK, TIVERTON, TOTNES; and two for the COUNTY.

POPULATION.—According to the census of 1821, there were houses inhabited in the county, 71,486; uninhabited, 3,082; and houses building, 756. The number of families then resident in the county was 90,714, comprising 208,229 males, and 230,811 females; total, 439,040: and by a calculation made by order of government, which included persons in the army and navy, for which was added after the ratio of about one to thirty prior to the year 1811, and one to fifty for that year and the census of 1821, to the returns made from the several districts; the population of the county, in round numbers, in the year 1700, was 248,200—in 1750, 272,200—in 1801, 354,400—in 1811, 396,100—and in 1821, 447,900. The increased population in the fifty years, from the year 1700, was 24,000—from 1750 to 1801, the increase was 82,200—from 1801 to 1811, the increase was 41,700—and from 1811 to 1821, the augmented number of persons was 51,800: the grand total increase in the population of the county, from the year 1700 to the census of 1821, being about 199,700 persons.

[*Table of Distances—see over.*]

Index of Distances from Town to Town in the County of Devon.

THE NAMES OF THE RESPECTIVE TOWNS ARE ON THE TOP AND SIDE, AND THE SQUARE WHERE BOTH MEET GIVES THE DISTANCE.

	Ashburton	Axminster	Barnstaple	Bideford	Brixham	Chudleigh	Chumleigh	Collumpton	Crediton	Dartmouth	Exeter	Exmouth	Hatherleigh	Holsworthy	Honiton	Ilfracombe	Kingsbridge	Modbury	Moreton-Hampstead	Newton Abbott and Newton Bushel	Oakhampton	Ottery St. Mary	Plymouth	Sidmouth	South Molton	Tavistock	Teignmouth	Tiverton	Torquay	Torrington	Distance from London.
Ashburton																															192
Axminster	44																														147
Barnstaple	50	57																													192
Bideford	47	64	9																												201
Brixham	18	54	68	64																											202
Chudleigh	10	34	47	44	24																										180
Chumleigh	34	45	17	14	52	30																									190
Collumpton	32	20	36	34	42	20	22																								161
Crediton	21	33	30	28	38	17	14	14																							175
Dartmouth	18	56	68	65	4	22	52	42	40																						204
Exeter	19	25	39	36	30	9	22	12	8	31																					172
Exmouth	32	26	51	55	40	22	35	22	21	41	10																				167
Hatherleigh	29	58	22	17	47	27	15	34	20	47	29	42																			201
Holsworthy	42	67	27	19	60	40	26	48	34	60	42	55	13																		214
Honiton	35	9	46	49	46	25	35	10	24	47	16	18	45	58																	156
Ilfracombe	60	66	10	18	78	57	26	46	40	78	48	61	32	37	56																202
Kingsbridge	20	60	70	67	17	26	54	47	42	12	34	44	50	52	51	80															207
Modbury	14	60	64	59	20	24	49	48	36	15	33	43	42	44	51	74	8														206
Moreton-Hampstead	12	37	39	36	30	12	23	24	12	29	12	25	19	32	28	49	31	26													184
Newton Abbott	8	40	51	48	14	6	35	27	23	16	15	28	31	44	31	61	20	20	12												188
Oakhampton	22	47	29	24	40	20	18	34	18	40	22	35	8	20	38	39	43	35	12	24											195
Ottery St. Mary	31	15	46	48	42	21	34	10	20	43	12	12	41	54	6	56	46	47	24	27	34										162
Plymouth	24	68	57	52	32	34	46	55	45	28	44	54	35	38	59	67	22	12	29	32	30	55									216
Sidmouth	34	16	52	57	45	24	37	16	23	46	15	10	44	57	9	62	49	50	27	30	37	6	58								158
South Molton	42	44	11	18	57	37	8	24	20	58	27	40	23	31	34	22	62	57	31	43	26	34	54	40							181
Tavistock	20	57	44	40	39	30	34	45	34	35	33	46	23	24	49	55	28	20	22	28	16	45	14	48	42						206
Teignmouth	15	42	56	53	18	8	39	29	23	22	15	25	36	57	32	65	27	27	20	7	29	29	39	32	42	35					189
Tiverton	33	25	31	36	44	23	22	6	12	43	15	27	32	46	16	41	48	49	24	29	30	16	58	21	19	42	30				168
Torquay	12	46	60	58	9	12	42	33	29	12	21	31	41	54	37	69	21	22	19	7	31	33	31	36	49	32	8	35			207
Torrington	40	59	10	6	58	38	14	39	28	58	36	49	12	16	49	21	61	53	28	10	18	48	16	51	16	34	47	34	49		196
Totnes	8	48	58	55	10	14	42	35	30	10	24	34	37	50	39	68	12	12	19	8	30	35	24	38	50	30	15	37	9	48	196

Additional information relating to the County of Devon.

POPULATION.—By the Census for **1831** this county contained 235,630 males, and 258,538 females—total 494,168, being an increase, since the returns made in the year 1821, of 55,128 inhabitants; and from the Census of 1801 to that of 1831 the augmentation amounted to 151,167 persons.

REPRESENTATION.—By the *Reform Bill* the boroughs of BEERALSTON, OAKHAMPTON, and PLYMPTON are deprived of the elective franchise; and ASHBURTON and DARTMOUTH send *one* member each, in place of *two*: DEVONPORT, by the same Act, has obtained the privilege of returning *two* members, and the like number, in addition, is given to the county. The whole shire, by these alterations, sends *twenty-two* representatives to Parliament, instead of *twenty-six*, as before the passing of the Bill. Under the new *Boundary Act*, the county is divided into two parts, respectively named the *Northern Division* and the *Southern Division;* the former includes the several hundreds of Bampton, Black Torrington, Braunton, Crediton, Fremington, Halberton, Hartland, Haybridge, Hemyock, North Tawton and Winkleigh, Shebbear, Sherwill, South Molton, Tiverton, Witheridge, and West Budleigh: the southern division comprises those of Axminster, Clyston, Colyton, Ottery St. Mary, East Budleigh, Lifton, Exminster, Teignbridge, Haytor, Coleridge, Stanborough, Ermington, Plympton, Roborough, and Tavistock, and also the Castle of Exeter, and the hundred of Wonford, except such parts of that hundred as are included in the limits of the City of Exeter. The election of members for the northern division is held at SOUTH MOLTON, and for the southern at EXETER: besides the place of election the northern division polls at CULLOMPTON, BARNSTAPLE, TORRINGTON, HOLSWORTHY and CREDITON; and for the southern division (besides the place of election) polling takes place at HONITON, NEWTON ABBOT, KINGSBRIDGE, PLYMOUTH, TAVISTOCK, and OAKHAMPTON.

RAILWAYS.

The BRISTOL and EXETER RAILWAY, in its route from the latter city, passes a short distance to the east of *Cullompton,* and about six miles east of *Tiverton,* to which town there will be a branch; it then runs near *Wellington* and *Taunton,* on through *Bridgwater* to *Bristol.* Beyond Bridgwater there will be branches running to the coast of the Bristol Channel, and to the coal-field near Bristol. This Railway is an elongation of the Great Western, and when completed, will be one of the most interesting and profitable in the kingdom. From Exeter will proceed the Exeter and Plymouth Railway—passing to the east of Chudleigh and Newton Bushel, and through Totnes and Modbury to Plymouth: and the Railway to *Penzance* will run by *Oakhampton,* and enter *Cornwall* near *Launceston.* Another line from Exeter, through Crediton, Chumleigh and Barnstaple, to Ilfracombe, will open a communication between the Bristol and British Channels.

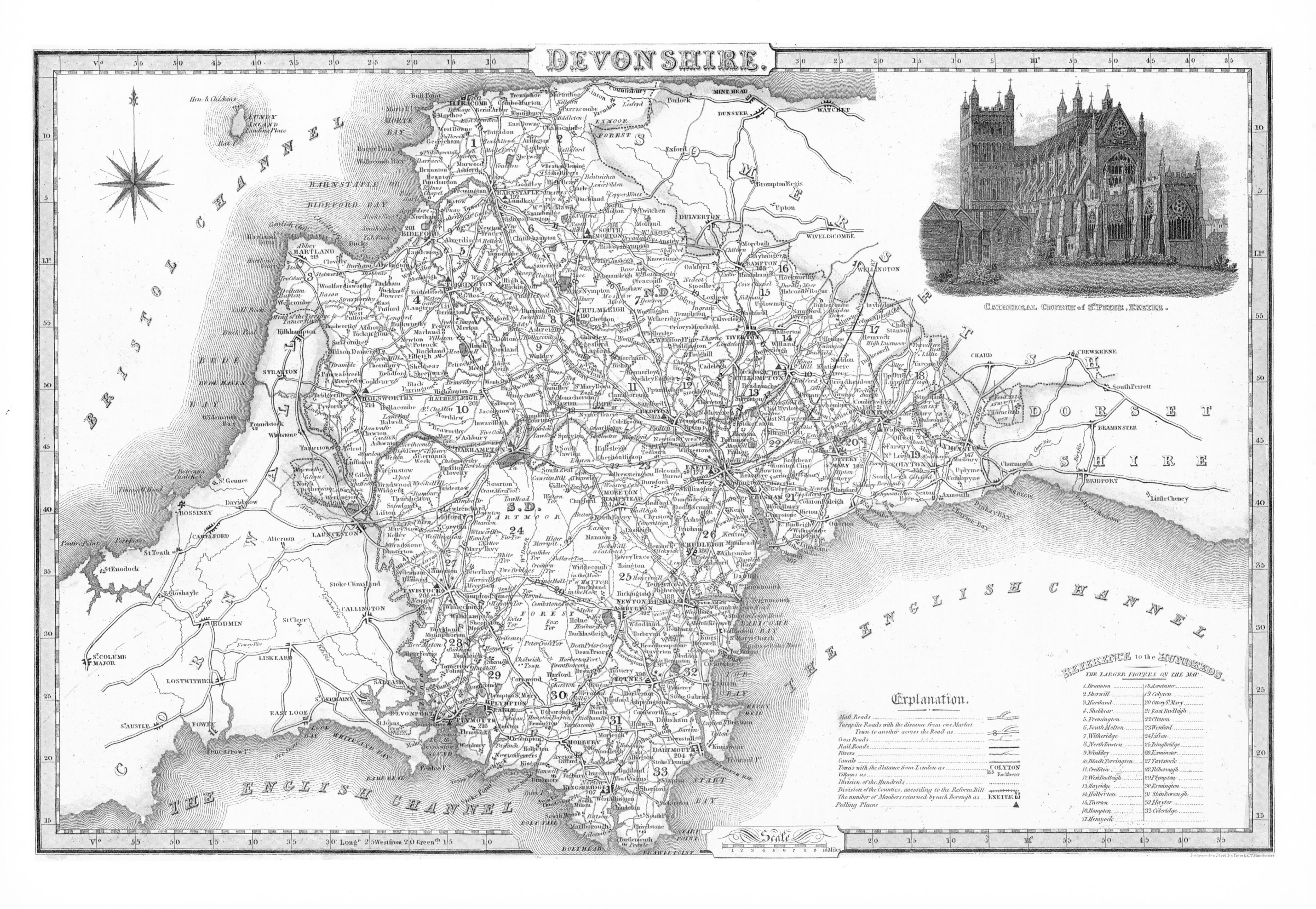

DEVONSHIRE.
CATHEDRAL CHURCH of St. PETER, EXETER.
BRISTOL CHANNEL
THE ENGLISH CHANNEL
DORSET SHIRE
SOMERSET
CORNWALL
LUNDY ISLAND
BARNSTAPLE OR BIDEFORD BAY
DARTMOOR
EXETER
PLYMOUTH
BARNSTAPLE
TIVERTON
DARTMOUTH
Explanation.
Mail Roads
Turnpike Roads with the distance from one Market Town to another across the Road as
Cross Roads
Rail Roads
Rivers
Canals
Towns with the distance from London as
COLYTON
155 Rockbear
Villages as
Division of the Hundreds
Division of the Counties, according to the Reform Bill
The number of Members returned by each Borough as
EXETER
Polling Places
REFERENCE to the HUNDREDS.
THE LARGER FIGURES ON THE MAP
1. Braunton
2. Sherwill
3. Hartland
4. Shebbear
5. Fremington
6. South Molton
7. Witheridge
8. North Tawton
9. Winkley
10. Black Torrington
11. Crediton
12. West Budleigh
13. Hayridge
14. Halberton
15. Tiverton
16. Bampton
17. Hemyock
18 Axminster
19 Colyton
20 Ottery St. Mary
21 East Budleigh
22 Cliston
23 Wonford
24 Lifton
25 Teingbridge
26 Exminster
27 Tavistock
28 Roborough
29 Plympton
30 Ermington
31 Stanborough
32 Haytor
33 Coleridge
Scale
Miles
Long. West from Greenwich

DORSETSHIRE.

DORSETSHIRE is a maritime county, situated in the south-western part of this Island; bounded on the north by Wiltshire and Somersetshire, on the east by Hampshire, on the west by Devon and part of Somersetshire, and on the south by the British channel. Its form is every where irregular: its long northern side has a considerable angular projection in the middle; the sea-shore on the south runs out into numerous points and headlands, till it stretches to the Isle of Portland; whence westward the coast is not so deeply indented, but inclines obliquely towards Devonshire. Its extent, from north to south, is about thirty-five miles; its breadth, from east to west, about fifty-five; its circumference may be estimated at nearly one hundred and sixty; and its area includes about 1,005 square miles.

NAME and ANCIENT HISTORY.—This county was anciently inhabited, according to Ptolemy, by the *Durotriges*. The Britons, according to Asser Menevensis (who was himself a Briton by birth, and flourished about the year of Christ 890), termed them *Dwr Gwr*, and the Saxons called them *Dorsettan;* the latter word signifying to dwell upon, to inhabit or be settled; and *dour* or *dwr* in British meaning 'water,' and *trig* 'an inhabitant:' hence the Britons called the *Durotriges 'Dwr Gwr,'* 'dwellers on the sea-coast.' Some are of opinion that the county took its name from *Dorchester*, as that did from King *Dorn* or *Dor*, whom they imagine to have been its founder; but this is supported by no historian of credit. Many ancient British monuments are strewed throughout the county, amongst which are, a rock idol, near Studland; a circle of stones, or *'cairn,'* near Pokeswell; a *'Cromlech,'* near Portesham; the 'Temple,' near Winterborne, with a segment of a circle of stones near it; a large groupe of *'barrows,'* near Corfe; a 'Labyrinth,' at Leigh; and, not many years ago, one of the same kind at Pimperne. A great number of the sites of Roman camps are found throughout the county; but no altar, or stone inscribed with Roman characters, has been found in these parts. The Roman *Icening-way* enters this county near Woodyates, and may still be traced through a considerable tract of country: the stations appear to have been Lyme Regis, Charmouth, Dorchester, Wimborne-Minster, Weymouth, Wareham and Poole. At Lyme landed, in 1685, the Duke of Monmouth, for the execution of his ill-judged design against James the Second, which terminated in his own destruction and that of many others.

SOIL, PRODUCE and CLIMATE.—The general appearance of this county is uneven, and in many parts very hilly. Its most striking features are the open and unenclosed parts, covered with numerous flocks of sheep, which feed on the verdant produce of the downs. In the natural division of the county, the greater proportion of the land is appropriated to pasture; the arable is estimated at one-third, and the waste at about a ninth. The principal sheep district is round Dorchester; great numbers of sheep and oxen are fed in the vale of Blackmore, which is rich pasture; and here, also, are some orchards, producing excellent cider. On the south-west side, likewise, are luxuriant vales. About Bridport, the lower lands are mostly deep rich loams; on the higher hills, throughout the western district, the soil is a sandy loam, intermixed with flint; to the north of Sherborne, which affords some of the best arable land in the county, it is a stone-brack or brash; and this is the case in the Island of Portland, and most parts of the Isle of Purbeck. The tillage, in the open parts of the county, is very much upon a chalk bottom, and, all the way towards Abbotsbury and Weymouth, is of an inferior quality: in the centre of the county the soil is good, and the land well managed; irrigation is well understood, and their watered meadows exhibit the nicest management. The flooding of meadow-land, by which an early vegetation is produced, is of such consequence to the Dorsetshire farmers, that without it their present system of managing sheep would almost be annihilated. The chief PRODUCTS of Dorset are corn, cattle, sheep, wool, timber, flax and hemp: the sheep are highly esteemed for the fineness and close texture of their wool, which is much used in the manufacture of broad-cloth. In one particular, this breed excels all others in the kingdom, which is in bringing early lambs, generally purchased by the sucklers in the neighbourhood of London, and fattened for that market. The breed of horses is not particularly regarded; oxen are chiefly those of the Devon breed; and the pigs similar to those of Hampshire but not so good. Wheat, except in some particular situations, is not in general a heavy crop; barley affords a great produce, and a large portion of malt is made for the internal consumption of the county: the strong beer is famous; the ales are also highly celebrated, and in some respects unequalled. Neither coal nor ores of any kind are found in this county; but the whole Isle of Portland seems to be one entire mass of fine freestone, and the quarries of Purbeck are well known for their valuable produce: the qualities of whiteness, solidity, durability, freely splitting in any direction, and easily working, added to its standing the water extremely well, render it one of the most valuable freestones known; several of the public and private edifices in London have been built of it, among which are Whitehall, St. Paul's church, the piers of Westminster-bridge, and the whole of Blackfriars-bridge; it is exported in large quantities to various parts of England, Ireland and France. Dorsetshire, from the mildness of its CLIMATE and the beauty of its situation, has been termed the garden of England; but it is not so mild as it used to be, or so early in its seasons,—for there were formerly large and fruitful vineyards at Sherborne and Durweston, which are not now known. The air is considered, at the present day, rather dry—more bracing and salubrious than mild and bland; and the seasons, except in spots that are peculiarly well sheltered, or that possess a very warm soil, are not nearly so forward as they are in other parts of England not so far to the south.

MANUFACTURES.—The principal manufactures are those of flax and hemp, chiefly carried on in the neighbourhood of Bridport and Beaminster; at Shaftesbury, shirt-buttons and coarse woollen cloths; at Blandford, shirt-buttons; at Stalbridge and Sherborne silk is spun; and at Wimborne many women and children are employed in knitting worsted stockings. At Poole and Abbotsbury some plain and striped cottons are wove; and at the latter place, sail-cloth, sacking, cables, ropes, large nets and cod-lines for the Newfoundland fishery, and mackarel-nets for home use are made. Beaminster participates in the manufacture of sail-cloth, and many individuals in the country around find employment in spinning the flax and preparing the materials. Taken altogether, this county holds not by any means an eminent situation as a manufacturing one: agriculture, its fisheries and stone-quarries are the main contributors to the prosperity of Dorsetshire. Some of the port towns have, however, an export trade of some consideration, especially Poole, which has long prospered in its commercial intercourse with Newfoundland, Norway, America, and various parts of Europe; besides enjoying a valuable coasting-trade. Near the mouth of Poole harbour lies a prolific oyster-bank, from which vast quantities of this fish are taken in the season, and carried by the smacks to be fattened in the Essex and Thames creeks for the London market.

RIVERS and CANALS.—The principal rivers are the FROME, the STOUR, the PIDDLE, the IVEL, and the HOOKE OR OWKE: all these rivers receive in their course a vast number of tributary streams. The Stour is the most considerable stream that waters the county; it falls into the sea near Christchurch, in Hampshire. The Frome rises in the north-west part of the county, near Evershot, and flows by Frampton and Bradford on to Dorchester; and thence passing south-east, and receiving the waters of the Winterbourne, it pursues its course to Wareham, within three miles of which it falls into Poole bay. The Ivel has its origin from several springs, at a place called Horethorne, in a hill north-east from Sherborne, from which town it flows into Somersetshire, and falls into the Parret. The Piddle rises north of Piddle Trewthyde Church, and, flowing to the south-east, it, near Keysworth, unites with the waters of Poole bay. The DORSET and SOMERSET CANAL commences at Gains' Cross, in this county; and in the course of its navigation through it benefits, besides other places, the towns of Sturminster and Stalbridge; in Somersetshire it visits many parishes and towns, and near Wedbrooke, in Wiltshire, it communicates with the Kennet and Avon canal.

CIVIL and ECCLESIASTICAL DIVISIONS.—Dorsetshire is in the Province of Canterbury and Diocese of Bristol, and included in the Western Circuit. It is apportioned into the nine divisions of BLANDFORD NORTH, BLANDFORD SOUTH, BRIDPORT, CERNE, DORCHESTER, SHASTON EAST, SHASTON WEST, SHERBORNE, and STURMINSTER: these divisions are subdivided into thirty-four hundreds and twenty-two liberties, the which collectively contain one county town (Dorchester), fourteen other market towns, and 271 parishes. The whole county returns twenty members to Parliament, viz. two each for BRIDPORT, CORFE CASTLE, DORCHESTER, LYME REGIS, MELCOMBE REGIS, POOLE, SHAFTESBURY, WAREHAM, WEYMOUTH, and two for the SHIRE.

POPULATION.—According to the census of 1821, there were houses inhabited in the county, 25,926; uninhabited, 766; and houses building, 278. The number of families then resident in the county was 30,312; comprising 68,934 males, and 75,565 females; total, 144,499: and by a calculation made by order of government, which included persons in the army and navy, for which was added after the ratio of about one to thirty prior to the year 1811, and one to fifty for that year and the census of 1821, to the returns made from the several districts; the population of the county, in round numbers, in the year 1700, was 90,000—in 1750, 96,400—in 1801, 119,100—in 1811, 128,900—and in 1821, 147,400. The increased population in the 50 years, from the year 1700, was 6,400—from 1750 to 1801, the increase was 22,700—from 1801 to 1811, the increase was 9,800—and from 1811 to 1821, the augmented number of persons was 18,500: the grand total increase in the population of the county from the year 1700 to the census of 1821, being about 57,400 persons.

Index of Distances from Town to Town in the County of Dorset.

THE NAMES OF THE RESPECTIVE TOWNS ARE ON THE TOP AND SIDE, AND THE SQUARE WHERE BOTH MEET GIVES THE DISTANCE.

	Beaminster	Blandford	Bridport	Cerne Abbas	Dorchester	Gillingham	Lyme Regis	Poole	Shaftesbury	Sherborne	Stalbridge	Sturminster	Wareham	Weymouth	Wimborne	Distance from London.
Beaminster																132
Blandford	29															104
Bridport	6	32														135
Cerne Abbas	12	17	14													120
Dorchester	18	16	15	7												120
Gillingham	30	15	36	22	25											105
Lyme Regis	12	40	9	23	24	45										143
Poole	43	16	42	31	27	32	51									106
Shaftesbury	32	12	36	22	28	4	44	28								101
Sherborne	18	18	23	11	18	12	30	35	15							117
Stalbridge	24	15	33	12	20	10	36	28	10	7						111
Sturminster	26	10	28	14	26	8	38	24	8	10	4					110
Wareham	35	16	33	26	18	31	42	10	27	33	28	24				112
Weymouth	25	24	20	16	8	33	28	28	36	26	28	28	18			128
Wimborne	39	10	37	26	22	25	46	6	22	28	24	20	10	30		101

[See over.

Additional information relating to the County of Dorset.

POPULATION.—By the Census for **1831** this county contained 76,536 males, and 82,716 females—total 159,252, being an increase, since the returns made in the year 1821, of 14,753 inhabitants; and from the Census of 1801 to that of 1831 the augmentation amounted to 43,933 persons.

REPRESENTATION.—By the *Reform Bill* the borough of CORFE CASTLE is disfranchised, and those of LYME REGIS, SHAFTESBURY, and WAREHAM are deprived of one member each; WEYMOUTH and MELCOMBE REGIS return, in conjunction, but two instead of four; and one additional member is given to the county. By these alterations the whole shire now sends *fourteen* representatives to Parliament, in place of *twenty*, as heretofore. The election of members for the county is held at DORCHESTER, and the new *Boundary Bill* directs the polling to take place, besides, at WIMBORNE, WAREHAM, BEAMINSTER, SHERBORNE, SHAFTESBURY, BLANDFORD, and CHESILTON.

RAILWAY.—The line of the projected WEYMOUTH and BATH RAILWAY will pass from the former town through or near to Dorchester, Stalbridge, Gillingham and Frome, and thence to the west of Bradford; near the latter town it will unite with the GREAT WESTERN, and by that line proceed to Bath, and thence to Bristol—at which latter city the Bristol and Exeter Railway commences.

DORSETSHIRE.
SHERBORNE CHURCH.
REFERENCE to the HUNDREDS, and Liberties,
THE LARGER FIGURES ON THE MAP.
1 Whitchurch Canonicorum H.
2 Broadwinsor L.
3 Beaminster Forum H.
4 Beaminster H.
5 Beaminster Forum & Redhone H.
6 Lothers & Bothenhampton L.
7 Godder Thorne H.
8 Lothers L.
9 Halstock L.
10 Tollerford H.
11 Poorstock L.
12 Eggerton H.
13 Ryme Intrinsica L.
14 Sherborne H.
15 Yetminster H.
16 Cerne Totcombe & Modbury H.
17 Sydling St. Nicholas L.
18 Frampton L.
19 Uggscombe H.
20 Brownshall H.
21 Buckland Newton H.
22 Alton Pancras L.
23 Whiteway H.
24 Piddletrenthide L.
25 Piddlehinton L.
26 Dewlish L.
27 George H.
28 Piddletown H.
29 Fordington L.
30 Culliford Tree H.
31 Wayhouse L.
32 Sutton Pointz L.
33 Wyke Regis & Elwall L.
34 Portland L.
35 Redlane H.
36 Gillingham L.
37 Stower Provost L.
38 Sturminster Newton Castle H.
39 Sixpenny Handley H.
40 Pimperne H.
41 Cranborne H.
42 Monckton-up-Wimborne H.
43 Wimborne St. Giles H.
44 Knowlton H.
45 Badbury H.
46 Coombs Ditch H.
47 Rushmore H.
48 Loosebarrow H.
49 Cogdean H.
50 Beer Regis H.
51 Hundredsbarrow H.
52 Bindon L.
53 Owermoigne L.
54 Winfrith H.
55 Hasilor H.
56 Rowbarrow H.
Explanation.
Mail Roads
Turnpike Roads, with the distance from one Market Town to another, across the Road, as
Cross Roads
Rail Roads
Rivers
Canals
Towns with the distance from London, as CRANBORNE 97
Villages, as Pentridge
Division of the Hundreds
Division of the Counties
The number of Members returned by each Borough, as POOLE
Polling Places
THE ENGLISH CHANNEL
WEST BAY
WEYMOUTH BAY
POOLE BAY
SWANAGE BAY
ISLE OF PURBECK
St. ALBANS HEAD
PORTLAND BILL
WILTSHIRE
SOMERSETSHIRE
DEVONSHIRE
HAMPSHIRE
DORCHESTER
SHERBORNE
SHAFTESBURY
BLANDFORD FORUM
WIMBORNE MINSTER
POOLE
WAREHAM
WEYMOUTH
MELCOMBE REGIS
BRIDPORT
LYME REGIS
BEAMINSTER
CERNE ABBAS
STALBRIDGE
CRANBORNE
SALISBURY
CHRISTCHURCH
RINGWOOD
YEOVIL
ILCHESTER
CREWKERNE
CHARD
AXMINSTER
WINCANTON
Scale
Longitude West 11°
Engraved on Steel by Pigot & Co. Manchester

DURHAM.

THE figure of this county is triangular. It is bounded on the east side, from the mouth of the river Tees to Tynemouth, by the German ocean; on the north, it is separated from Northumberland by the rivers Tyne and Derwent, and some artificial boundaries; on the west, it is divided from Cumberland and Westmoreland by the Crookburn and the Tees—the latter river also forming the whole of its south and south-east boundary. The greatest extent of the county, from Shields on the north to Sockburn on the south, is about thirty-six miles; its greatest length, from the peninsula of Hartlepool on the east to the mouth of the Crookburn on the west, at the point of union of Durham, Cumberland and Westmoreland, is about forty-five miles; its circumference is nearly one hundred and eighty, and its superficial area includes about one thousand and sixty square miles.

NAME and ANCIENT HISTORY.—Durham, the name of the city from which this county takes its title, is a corrupted term from the Saxon words *dur*, 'a hill,' and *holme*, 'a river island.' Camden says the Latins called it DVNELMVS; and, according to other authorities, it is stated to have received its appellation from the Norman word *Duresme*. This part of England was anciently inhabited by the *Brigantes*—a tribe of Britons distinguished by Tacitus as being powerful, brave and numerous, but who were subdued by the Romans, who included Durham within the division of MAXIMA CÆSARIENSIS; and the Saxons made it part of the Kingdom of Northumbria, with which it continued to be connected till the union of the Saxon States, under Egbert.

SOIL, CLIMATE & PRODUCE.—The general aspect of Durham is hilly and mountainous, particularly the west angle, which is a bleak and naked region, crossed by the ridge of hills termed the 'English Appenines,' though they do not, in this part, rise to any considerable height. The eastern and central parts include some beautitul and fertile vallies, pleasantly interspersed with hill and dale. The SOILS are various: near the river Tees, and in some spots bordering the other rivers and brooks, the soil is loamy, or a rich clay; at a further distance from the waters, the soil is of a poorer nature, commonly termed water-shaken, with spots of gravel intermixed; the hills between the sea, and an imaginary line drawn from Barnard Castle to Alansford, are, for the most part, covered with a dry loam, the fertility of which varies in proportion to its depth: from this line west, the summits as well as the sides of the hills are moorish wastes. The country possessing such diversity of soil, the produce is of course proportionably various. The woodlands are not of any considerable extent, and are chief- ..nned to the parks and seats of the Nobility; the banks of the rivers and brooks are, however, fringed with wood of long growth, particularly in the vicinity of the city. The public roads are in general good; but those off the main lines of thoroughfare are narrow and irregular; the spirit of improvement is, however, rapidly manifesting itself in the condition of the highways. Some years since, about one-third of the land of this county was supposed to be of ecclesiastical tenure; but, from the enclosure of wastes, and other circumstances of more recent date, the proportion is understood to have considerably increased.—The CLIMATE is esteemed healthy; and, although the air is sharp in the western parts, it is mild and genial towards the sea; the saline vapour from the German ocean mitigating the cold, which, in a situation so far distant from the line, would otherwise be very severe.—As an agricultural county, Durham, although not ranking with the most valuable in this Kingdom, is by no means unimportant in its productions under this head. The eastern and central parts are alternately appropriated to the growth of corn and to pasturage. Wheat, barley, oats and pease are the chief productions; but the harvests are hazardous, and the crops precarious in value. The farms are of a middling size, few exceeding two hundred acres. The cattle of Durham are in great repute—not being inferior to any in England for form, weight, quickness in fattening, or value to the dairy. The sheep are, in general, the improved Tees-water breed.

MANUFACTURES, MINES and MINERALS.—The manufactures of this county are numerous, various and important: at Chester-le-Street, Washington, Salwell, Winlaton and Lumley are extensive iron-foundries and works; and at Shortley Bridge, Derwent Coat and Blackhall Mills, manufactories of steel for sword-blades. At Durham are manufactured tammies, carpets and waistcoatings; at Darlington tammies, carpets and coarse linens, as also flax spinning, and grinding optical glasses: at South Shields are extensive salt-works; at Stockton, Sunderland and North Shields, sail-cloths, glass, and other articles; at North Shields, Sunderland and Hartlepool, are ship-building yards; and cottons are manufactured in several districts MINES and MINERALS.—The east and north-east parts of the county are famous for their extensive coal-mines; and the quantity of this important article is so great as to prohibit accurate calculation. The number of men employed in this trade, on the river Wear, are estimated as approaching near to 20,000; and it is calculated that more than 30,000 persons are supported entirely by the coal-works. In the vicinity of Wolsingham a beautiful black spotted lime-stone is procured, which is wrought into hearths, chimney-pieces, and various ornaments: fine mill-stone, and many excellent quarries of slate and fire-stone, are found in different parts of the county; and Gateshead Fell produces what are vulgarly called 'Newcastle grind-stones.' The principal lead-mines are situated in Teesdale and Weardale; but those of the former place are not so successfully worked as the latter.

RIVERS, SPRINGS, &c.—The principal rivers in this county are the TEES, the WEAR and the DERWENT. The Tees rises on the vast moor district wherein the counties of York, Cumberland, Westmoreland, Durham and Northumberland unite, and flows south-east through the romantic valley of Teesdale, for nearly thirty miles, when, suddenly turning to the north-east at Sockburn, it falls into the German sea below Stockton, and is affected as high as that town by the tide, so as to admit ships of considerable burthen. The waters forming the Wear originate from the same wild moors which give birth to the Tees; but, flowing considerably to the north of that river, it crosses the central part of the county, and loses itself in the sea, near Sunderland; it is navigable as far as Lumley Castle, from whence great quantities of coal are conveyed to the former place. The Derwent rises in the same district as the two former rivers, north of the Wear, and pursues nearly a parallel course with that river, giving animation and interest to a wild and mountainous tract on the north borders of the county, till it falls into the Tyne, near Swalwell.—At Birtley is a singular and productive SALT-SPRING, four times stronger than any sea-water; and at Butterby, near Durham, is another of the same nature, issuing from a rock in the middle of the river Wear, but only visible when that river is low: its produce is too inconsiderable to defray the expenses of working, though its quality is similar to that of Birtley

CIVIL and ECCLESIASTICAL DIVISIONS.—This county has usually been termed 'THE BISHOPRICK,' on account of the great powers formerly possessed by the Bishop of the Diocese, who was said to have all the authority in Durham, that the King exercised elsewhere. These privileges, though much abridged, are still considerable,—the Bishop acting as Lord Lieutenant of the county, and having the appointment of the High Sheriff: he is perpetual Chancellor and Justice of the Peace in his territories; all dues, amercements, and forfeited recognizances, as well as deodands, belong to him; all tenures of land originate from him, as Lord Paramount in Chief; all enclosed estates as well as moors and wastes, to which no title can be made, escheat to him; the Admiralty jurisdiction of the county belongs to him, and the conservancy of all waters within his district. Durham is reputed to be one of the best Bishopricks in England, having thirteen livings in the episcopal gift, stated at from £300. to £1,000. a year each, and which are continually augmenting in value. It is a Palatine County, in the Province of York and Diocese of Durham; and is included in the Northern Circuit. The county is apportioned into four divisions, respectively named CHESTER WARD, DARLINGTON WARD, EASINGTON WARD and STOCKTON WARD; besides the two districts of ISLANDSHIRE and NORHAMSHIRE, which are situated locally for the most part in the county of Northumberland. The two first-named wards are subdivided into three, and the two latter into two divisions, according to their local situations. These several wards and districts collectively contain one city and county town (Durham), thirteen other market towns, and, according to the returns made by command of Parliament in 1821, 75 parishes only, whilst in earlier returns the number has been stated to exceed 100: to reconcile this difference, it is conjectured that certain townships were heretofore returned as parishes, which by the last census (*i.e.* 1821) have not been so distinguished. Durham sends four members to Parliament, viz. two for the CITY and two for the COUNTY.

POPULATION.—According to the census of 1821, there were houses inhabited in the county, 32,793; uninhabited, 966; and houses building, 257. The number of families then resident in the county was 45,940, comprising 99,100 males, and 108,573 females; total, 207,673: and by a calculation made by order of government, which included persons in the army and navy, for which was added after the ratio of about one to thirty prior to the year 1811, and one to fifty for that year and the census of 1821, to the returns made from the several districts; the population of the county, in round numbers, in the year 1700, was 95,500---in 1750, 135,000---in 1801, 165,700---in 1811, 183,600---and in 1821, 211,900. The increased population in the fifty years, from the year 1700, was 39,500---from 1750 to 1801, the increase was 30,700---from 1801 to 1811, the increase was 17,900---and from 1811 to 1821, the augmented number of persons was 28,300: the grand total increase in the population of the county, from the year 1700 to the census of 1821, being about 116,400 persons.

Index of Distances from Town to Town in the County of Durham.

THE NAMES OF THE RESPECTIVE TOWNS ARE ON THE TOP AND SIDE, AND THE SQUARE WHERE BOTH MEET GIVES THE DISTANCE.

Distance from Newcastle.	Town	Barnard Castle	Bishop Auckland	Chester-le-Street	Darlington	Durham	Hartlepool	Sedgefield	South Shields	Staindrop	Stanhope	Stockton	Sunderland	*Distance from London.*
38	Barnard Castle													244
24	Bishop Auckland	14												255
8	Chester-le-Street	30	16											262
33	Darlington	16	14	25										241
14	Durham	25	10	6	18									259
30	Hartlepool	38	24	20	23	20								250
25	Sedgefield	35	21	17	20	11	12							252
8	South Shields	46	32	16	41	22	30	33						281
33	Staindrop	5	9	25	13	19	33	30	41					246
28	Stanhope	21	15	26	33	20	34	31	36	20				265
34	Stockton	29	24	27	12	20	13	9	36	24	40			242
12	Sunderland	38	23	10	31	13	21	24	9	32	33	27		272
23	Wolsingham	15	10	21	21	15	32	26	31	15	5	34	28	256

[*See over.*

Additional information relating to the County of DURHAM.

---ooo---

POPULATION.—By the Census for 1831 this county contained 121,701 males, and 132,126 females—total 253,827, being an increase, since the returns made in the year 1821, of 46,154 inhabitants; and from the Census of 1801 to that of 1831 the augmentation amounted to 93,466 persons.

REPRESENTATION.—By the *Reform Bill,* the elective franchise is conferred upon SUNDERLAND, SOUTH SHIELDS, and GATESHEAD, the former returning *two,* and the two others, *one* member each; two additional ones are also given to the county; so that the whole county now sends *ten* representatives to Parliament, instead of *four,* as heretofore. Under the new *Boundary Act,* the county is divided into two parts, respectively named the *Northern Division,* and the *Southern Division;* the former includes the wards of Chester and Easington, and the latter the wards of Darlington and Stockton. The election of members for the northern division is held at DURHAM, and for the southern at DARLINGTON: besides the place of election, the northern division polls at SUNDERLAND, LANCHESTER, WICKHAM, CHESTER-LE-STREET, and SOUTH SHIELDS; and the southern division (besides the place of election) polls at STOCKTON, BISHOP AUCKLAND, MIDDLETON-IN-TEESDALE, BARNARD CASTLE, and SEDGEFIELD.

RAILWAYS.

This county is closely intersected by Railways; the greater portion, however, are for local convenience, as connected with the workings of the numerous coal mines and the ports of shipment. The DARLINGTON and STOCKTON commences near *West Auckland,* and runs through *Darlington* to *Stockton.* The next considerable line of Railway is from *South Shields* to *Stanhope,* with a branch to *Durham.* The GREAT NORTH OF ENGLAND will connect Darlington with the city of York, passing almost close to *Northallerton* and *Thirsk,* and about five miles to the west of *Easingwold:* this line joins the York and North Midland Railway, and the Northern and Eastern from London. The Railway from *Durham* to *Newcastle,* and the projected one from the latter town to Scotland, will complete the chain of Railway communication between Edinburgh and London. The HARTLEPOOL RAILWAY connects an extensive coal field with that port. Connected with the CLARENCE RAILWAY is the BYERS GREEN branch, opened on the 31st March, 1837, for the transit of coals and merchandize.

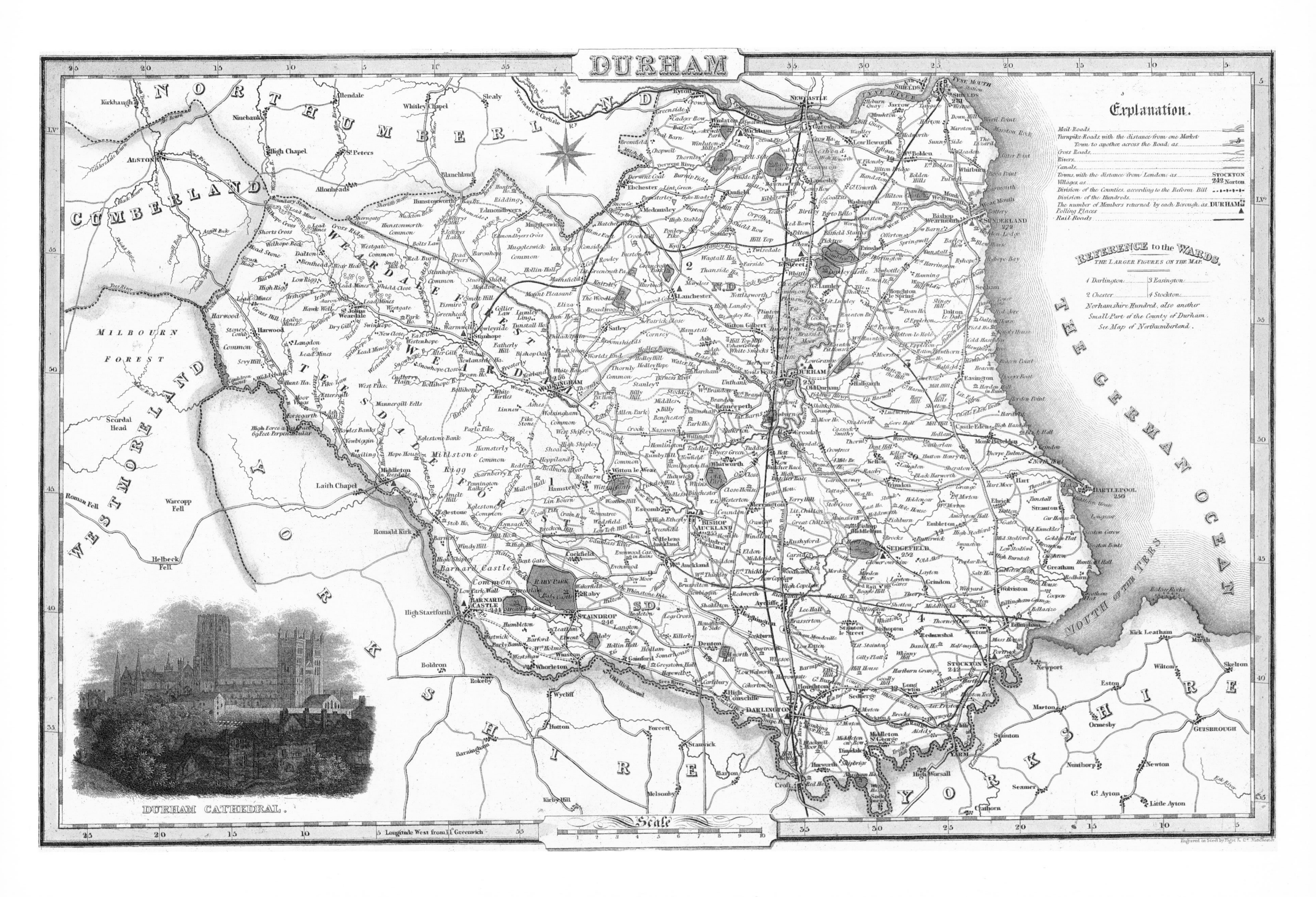

DURHAM CATHEDRAL.

ESSEX.

ESSEX is bounded by the counties of Suffolk and Cambridge on the north, by those of Hertford and Middlesex on the west, by the river Thames on the south, and by the sea on the east. Its figure on the sea-coast is irregular, being broken into a series of inlets and peninsulas, deeply cut in by arms of the sea, and exhibiting evident tokens of the force and effects of that restless element. Its extent from east to west is estimated at sixty miles, and from north to south at about fifty; its circumference is computed at 225 miles, and its area comprises about 1,530 square miles.

ANCIENT HISTORY.—At the time of the Roman invasion, Essex was inhabited by the people called *Trinobantes;* an appellation connected with the situation of their country on the borders of the broad waters, principally formed by the estuary of the Thames, at a time when its embankments were few and ill constructed. Various actions with the Danes took place in this county, as well as in many others on the east coast; one of the most memorable was fought at Assingdon (or Ashdown), near Rochford, in which King Edmund Ironside was defeated with great slaughter by the renowned Canute. In the early period of our history, the whole or greater part of this county is supposed to have been one extensive forest,—which, whilst it continued vested in the Crown, and under the local government of arbitrary foresters and stewards, was a continued fund of oppression and vexation to the subject whose estate was contiguous. This grievance was redressed by the 'Charter of Forests,' reluctantly extorted from King John, and many of these Royal districts disforested and stripped of their oppressive privileges. Previous to the dissolution, Essex contained no fewer than 47 religious houses; of these, two were mitred abbeys, six common abbeys, 22 priories, three nunneries, three colleges, two preceptories of Templars, and nine hospitals. Tilbury Fort, opposite to Gravesend, is the principal protection to the Thames: in its neighbourhood Queen Elizabeth reviewed the army she had assembled to oppose the famous Armada, in 1588. Colchester underwent a very obstinate siege in 1648, on occasion of an insurrection of the Royal adherents against the authority of the Parliament, the gallant leaders of which, on the surrender of the place, were executed.

SOIL and CLIMATE, PRODUCE and MANUFACTURES.—Essex composes part of that tract of country, on the eastern side of England, which forms the largest connected space of level ground in the whole Island,—not one lofty eminence, or rocky ridge, being found in several contiguous counties. The surface of this county is not, however, totally flat, having many gentle hills and dales; and towards the north-west, whence most of the rivers proceed, the country rises, and presents a continued inequality of surface. The most level tracts are those of the south and east hundreds; and the greater part of the county is inclosed, and rendered highly productive by the skilful management of the agriculturists. The principal productions are wheat, barley, oats, beans, pease, turnips, tares, rape, mustard, rye-grass and trefoil; many acres are also appropriated to hops, and various horticultural plants and roots, the latter being chiefly confined to the lands adjoining the Metropolis. Another product of this county is saffron, which at one period was cultivated so extensively as to bestow a second appellation on a town (*Saffron* Walden), around which it flourished abundantly: a light rich soil and dry country are particularly adapted to this plant. There is also a kind of treble crop cultivated, viz. coriander, carraway and teazle; the two former on account of their aromatic seeds; the latter for its prickly heads, used for the purpose of raising the nap on woollen cloths: these are all sown together, but come to maturity at different periods, and the succession of the whole crop lasts three or four years.—The conveniency of water carriage, and goodness of the roads throughout the county, are of great advantage in transmitting its productions, and, combined with its proximity to the metropolitan county, bestow on it a commercial superiority over many others. Almost every species of soil is to be found within the limits of Essex, from the most stubborn to the mildest loam. Its south-west part is chiefly occupied by Epping Forest and its several branches; northwards the country becomes more open and uneven; the middle of Essex is in general a fine corn country, varied with gentle inequalities of surface and sprinkled with woods. The proportion of the waste land in the whole of the county is very small, and the variety and goodness of its agricultural products are not exceeded by those of any other part of the Kingdom. Though this county is not highly celebrated for its dairies, yet those in the parish of Epping and its vicinity are famous for the richness of their cream and butter,—the latter mostly sent to London, where it bears a high character and price. Essex is proverbially distinguished for its calves, of which more are suckled or fattened here than in any other county. The marshy grounds, broken by arms of the sea into islands, and frequently inundated, afford fine pasturage for cattle. Fish are plentiful on the coast and in the various creeks of this county; some of the latter, about Colchester and the Mersey Island, are celebrated for their fine oyster beds; these afford a considerable article for exportation, and the true breed are highly valued in the Metropolis. CLIMATE.—This county lies under a proverbial imputation of being unhealthy; but this character can only apply to a small part of it, as the middle and north districts are justly noted for a fine dry soil, with a wholesome clear air. That part known by the name of the 'Hundreds of Essex,' bordering on the south coast, from its low and marshy situation, and exposure to the easterly winds and sea fogs, is certainly inimical to health, and many intermittent fevers proceed from these causes: the northern part of the coast, between the Stour and Colne, which projects further than the rest, is a more elevated and healthful country. The MANUFACTURES of Essex, of late years, have receded in consequence: at Colchester are some extensive silk-mills, and this town also retains a share of the manufacture of baize, for which it was once very famous; Bocking, Coggeshall and Braintree participate also in these trades; and in the last-named town, and its neighbourhood, many of the industrious poor are supported by the making of straw plat for the London market. The principal harbour on the Essex coast is that of Harwich; it affords an occasional shelter to the coasting fleets passing along these shores, but has not much trade of its own.

RIVERS, &c.—The principal rivers properly belonging to this County are the COLNE, the BLACKWATER (or PONT), the CHELMER, the CROUCH, the INGERBOURN, the RODING and the CAM. Besides these, Essex partakes of other rivers, which serve as natural boundaries, and irrigate and fertilize its land: these are the Thames, the Lea, the Stort and the Stour. The Colne rises on the north side of the county, and in its course passes Castle Hedingham, Halsted and Colchester; it soon afterwards expands into a wide estuary, and is navigable from the sea to within two miles of Colchester. The Blackwater has its source on the borders of Cambridgeshire, and meanders through Barking and Coggeshall; and, flowing south-east, unites with the Chelmer a little below Maldon, and then joins the waters of the ocean. The Chelmer has its original spring near Thaxted, and, after receiving several tributary brooks, joins the Blackwater (as before mentioned) near Maldon. The Crouch and Ingerbourn are small rivers, rising in the south side of the county, and slowly pass through a short course to the Thames. The Roding, a small stream, has a circuitous course in visiting Chipping Ongar, and several villages, in its progress to Wanstead, Ilford and Barking; it is made navigable to Ilford bridge. The Cam originates from three springs near Newport, and takes a different direction from any of the former rivers: it passes Audley End, Chesterton, &c., and pursues a north course to Cambridgeshire. The Lea and the Stort constitute the west boundary of the county, separating it from Middlesex and Hertfordshire; and the Stour divides it from the county of Suffolk to the north. Other smaller streams rise in Essex, and fall either into the Thames or the ocean.

CIVIL and ECCLESIASTICAL DIVISIONS.—Essex is in the Province of Canterbury and Diocese of London; is included in the Home Circuit; and divided into twenty hundreds, viz.—

BARSTABLE,	DENGIE,	HINCKFORD,	THURSTABLE,
BECONTREE,	DUNMOW,	LEXDEN,	UTTLESFORD,
CHAFFORD,	FRESHWELL,	ONGAR,	WALTHAM,
CHELMSFORD,	HARLOW,	ROCHFORD,	WINSTREE,
CLAVERING,	HAVERING,	TENDRING,	WITHAM.

These collectively contain three Archdeaconries and fifteen Deaneries; one county town (Chelmsford), fifteen other market towns, and four hundred and six parishes. The whole county sends eight members to Parliament, viz. two each for COLCHESTER, HARWICH and MALDON, and two for the SHIRE.

POPULATION.—According to the census of 1821, there were houses inhabited in the county, 49,978; uninhabited, 1,164; and houses building, 298. The number of families then resident in the county was 59,629; comprising 144,909 males, and 144,515 females; total, 289,424: and by a calculation made by order of Government, which included persons in the army and navy, for which was added after the ratio of about one to thirty prior to the year 1811, and one to fifty for that year and the census of 1821, to the returns made from the several districts; the population of the county, in round numbers, in the year 1700, was 159,200—in 1750, 167,800—in 1801, 234,000—in 1811, 260,900—and in 1821, 295,300. The increased population in the 50 years, from the year 1700, was 8,600—from 1750 to 1801, the increase was 66,200—from 1801 to 1811, the increase was 26,900—and from 1811 to 1821, the augmented number of persons was 34,000: the grand total increase in the population of the county from the year 1700 to the census of 1821, being about 136,100 persons.

Index of Distances from Town to Town in the County of Essex.

THE NAMES OF THE RESPECTIVE TOWNS ARE ON THE TOP AND SIDE, AND THE SQUARE WHERE BOTH MEET GIVES THE DISTANCE.

Town	Barking	Billericay	Braintree	Brentwood	Chelmsford	Chipping Ongar	Coggeshall	Colchester	Dunmow	Epping	Gray's Thurrock	Halsted	Harwich	Hatfield Broadoak	Ingatestone	Maldon	Manningtree	Rayleigh	Rochford	Romford	Saffron Walden	Thaxted	Waltham Abbey	Distance from London
Barking																								7
Billericay	18																							24
Braintree	35	21																						41
Brentwood	12	6	23																					18
Chelmsford	24	9	12	11																				29
Chipping Ongar	17	12	20	7	10																			21
Coggeshall	40	26	6	26	16	27																		44
Colchester	45	31	15	33	22	31	9																	51
Dunmow	31	21	9	19	13	15	15	24																40
Epping	11	18	27	12	17	7	33	39	20															17
Gray's Thurrock	14	12	33	11	21	17	36	41	30	22														21
Halsted	40	27	6	29	18	26	6	14	15	34	38													47
Harwich	66	51	36	54	42	52	30	21	45	60	62	35												72
Hatfield Broadoak	25	20	14	18	12	11	20	30	8	12	29	21	50											29
Ingatestone	17	4	18	5	6	6	21	28	18	12	15	23	48	16										23
Maldon	30	18	13	20	10	20	12	16	22	26	25	18	37	22	16									37
Manningtree	54	40	24	42	31	40	18	9	33	49	50	23	12	39	37	25								60
Rayleigh	28	10	23	16	14	23	22	30	27	28	18	29	51	26	14	14	39							35
Rochford	34	15	26	21	18	28	23	29	31	33	23	29	47	30	20	13	36	6						39
Romford	7	11	29	6	17	10	32	39	24	10	12	34	60	21	11	27	48	21	26					12
Saffron Walden	36	36	20	34	27	27	26	34	15	25	46	20	55	18	33	34	43	41	45	35				42
Thaxted	37	27	12	26	19	22	19	27	7	23	37	14	48	11	34	25	36	33	37	30	8			44
Waltham Abbey	13	20	33	18	23	13	39	44	26	6	23	40	65	18	18	32	53	33	35	12	31	33		12
Witham	32	17	7	19	9	18	7	14	17	26	30	14	35	21	15	6	23	16	18	25	27	19	32	37

Additional information relating to the County of Essex.

———ooo———

Population.—By the Census for **1831** this county contained 158,881 males, and 158,352 females—total 317,233, being an increase, since the returns made in the year 1821, of 27,809 inhabitants; and from the Census of 1801 to that of 1831 the augmentation amounted to 90,796 persons.

Representation.—By the *Reform Bill* two additional members is given to the county; and the new *Boundary Act* divides it into two parts, respectively named the *Northern Division,* and the *Southern Division;* the former includes the hundreds of Dunmow, Clavering, Freshwell, Hinckford, Lexden, Tendring, Thurstable, Uttlesford, Winstree, and Witham; and the southern includes the hundreds of Barstable, Becontree, Chafford, Chelmsford, Dengie, Harlow, Ongar, Rochford, and Waltham, and the liberty of Havering. The election of members for the northern division is held at Braintree, and for the southern at Chelmsford: besides the place of election the northern division polls at Colchester, Saffron Walden, and Thorpe; and the southern (besides the place of election) polls at Billericay, Romford, Epping, Rochford and Maldon.

Railways.—The Eastern Counties' passes to the east of *Romford* and to the west of *Billericay,* on to *Chelmsford;* thence to within a short distance of *Coggeshall, Colchester* and *Manningtree;* then, leaving the county of Norfolk, it passes a little to the west of *Ipswich,* and near *Eye* to *Norwich.*—Near Colchester a branch is projected to Harwich.

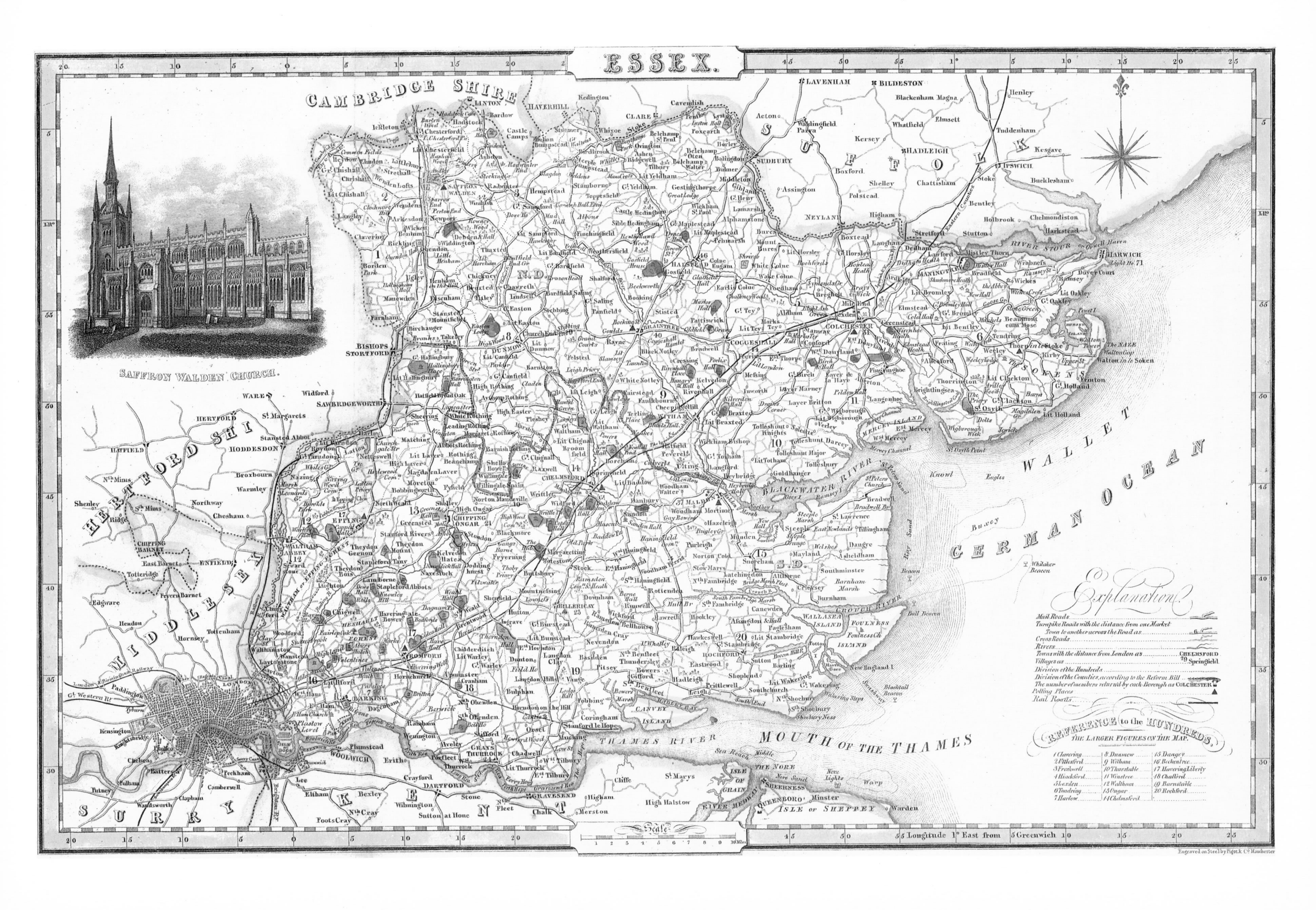
ESSEX.
CAMBRIDGE SHIRE
SUFFOLK
HERTFORD SHI
MIDDLESEX
SURRY
KENT
GERMAN OCEAN
WALLET
MOUTH OF THE THAMES
THAMES RIVER
BLACKWATER RIVER
CROUCH RIVER
RIVER STOUR or Orwell Haven
SAFFRON WALDEN CHURCH.
Explanation
Mail Roads
Turnpike Roads with the distance from one Market Town to another across the Road as 6
Cross Roads
Rivers
Towns with the distance from London as CHELMSFORD
Villages as 29 Springfield
Division of the Hundreds
Division of the Counties, according to the Reform Bill
The number of members return'd by each Borough as COLCHESTER
Polling Places
Rail Roads
REFERENCE to the HUNDREDS,
THE LARGER FIGURES ON THE MAP.
1 Clavering
2 Uttlesford
3 Freshwell
4 Hinckford
5 Lexden
6 Tendring
7 Harlow
8 Dunmow
9 Witham
10 Thurstable
11 Winstree
12 Waltham
13 Ongar
14 Chelmsford
15 Dengey
16 Beckentree
17 Havering Liberty
18 Chafford
19 Barnstable
20 Rochford
Scale
1 2 3 4 5 6 7 8 9 10 Miles
Longitude 1° East from Greenwich
Engraved on Steel by Pigot & Co. Manchester

GLOUCESTERSHIRE.

GLOUCESTERSHIRE is bounded on the north-west by Herefordshire, on the east by Oxfordshire and a small part of Berkshire, on the south by Wiltshire, and on the west by the Bristol Channel, and part of Somersetshire and Monmouthshire. It extends in length, from Clifford Chambers, on the Avon (next Warwickshire), to Clifton, near Bristol (in a south-west direction), about seventy miles; and in breadth, from Lechlade, north-west, to Preston, in the hundred of Botloe, about forty. The figure of the county is that of an ellipsis, narrow in proportion to its length; in circumference one hundred and fifty-six miles, containing 1,256 square miles.

NAME and ANCIENT HISTORY.—The county derives its name from its principal city, Gloucester; and the city from the appellation *Caer Glowe* or *Gloew,* signifying the 'Fair City,' given to it by the ancient Britons, who had the honour of founding this City; whilst a Roman station, it was called *Glevum.* During the occupation of the Island by the Romans, the south-east part of Gloucestershire was included in that division denominated BRITANNIA PRIMA, and the residue of the county BRITANNIA SECUNDA; upon a subsequent division made by Constantine, the whole county was included in the province named FLAVIA CÆSARIENSIS. It is evident, from the ruins which have been at various times excavated, that this county was much peopled by the Romans, or *Romanized* Britons: that Cirencester was the great Metropolis, or resort of pleasure and amusement; while Gloucester, and the hills about the Severn, were the great military positions. The principal Roman roads which pass through this county are the *Ikenild street,* the *Erming street,* the *Fosse way,* and the *Via Julia.* In the time of the Saxons, Gloucestershire was part of the Mercian Kingdom, and the Anglo-Saxon Monarchs are said to have had residences at Winchcombe and King's Stanley. Tewkesbury, in this county, is rendered famous in the military annals and historical records of England, from the decisive battle fought, in 1471, between the Houses of York and Lancaster, in which the latter were completely defeated; the ill-fated Prince Edward being barbarously murdered after the conflict. Tewkesbury was twice garrisoned for Charles I, but lost through cowardice and negligence. At one period it derived great consequence from its celebrated and opulent Abbey.

SOIL, PRODUCE and CLIMATE.—The general aspect of this county is greatly diversified; nature having divided it into three districts of very dissimilar character, respectively named the Hill, the Vale, and the Forest. The Hill district includes the Coteswold and the Stroudwater hills; the extent of the former hills is about thirty miles—the surface billowy, and the sides of the hills abounding with springs; the soil is generally a calcareous loam, mixed with gravel. The Stroudwater hills partake both of the Coteswold and vale character; the soil is principally a light loam, adapted to the cultivation of turnips and barley; the woodlands are chiefly beech. The Vale district is subdivided into the vales of Evesham, Gloucester and Berkeley: the soil through this district is mostly a deep and rich loam; the land appropriated to arable, meadow and pasture,—the grand objects of the husbandry being the growth of corn, breeding and fattening, and the dairy: the cattle are fattened for the London market; the swine are fed to a great weight; and the dairies, though not large, yield butter and cheese of a very superior quality. The Forest district is separated from the rest of the county by the river Severn, and is principally comprehended by the forest of Dean, which was formerly particularly valuable for the goodness and strength of its timber: the forest is divided into six walks, and has four wardens; the wood, though much decreased, still presents a thick and picturesque appearance, growing in the form of an amphitheatre on the sides of the surrounding hills; the great road through the forest is partly of Roman foundation. CLIMATE.—The air of this county is in general remarkably healthy, although of various temperature. On the Coteswold hills the air is very sharp; in the vallies it is soft and mild, even in winter.

MANUFACTURES, MINES and MINERALS.—The manufactures of Gloucestershire are more various than extensive: they embrace woollen cloths of different textures, hats, leather, wire, pins, brass, bar iron, tinned plates, edge tools, paper, &c. &c.: the staple commodities are woollen cloths and cheese; in both these articles of trade, however, the county is now somewhat on the decline; its cloth has been successfully rivalled in Yorkshire, and its cheese in North Wiltshire, Cheshire and other counties. The exports of the county comprise cheese, bacon, grain, cider, perry, fish, and some woollen cloths, &c. Of the MINERALS of Gloucestershire, the principal metallic ores are those of lead and iron: lead ore is found in various parts of the county, but not in sufficient quantity to remunerate the worker; iron ore is met with in great quantity, particularly in the forest of Dean, where, in the time of Edward I, there were seventy-two furnaces for smelting iron. Coal is found in abundance in the forests of Dean and Kingswood,—in the former it is said there are no less than 120 pits; much of this useful article is also obtained at Mangotsfield, Bitton and Bucklechurch; it abounds likewise at Syston, Iron Acton, Wick and Abston: in the latter parish, the cliffs rise perpendicularly to the height of 200 feet and upwards, and consist of a series of beds of lime-stone and petrosilex; lead ore is also found here. By the side of the road, near to Bristol, under the surface of the red soil, beautiful quartz crystals, with calcareous dog-tooth spars, are found. Excellent free-stone is obtained in several parts of the county, and many very curious fossils, especially near Gloucester and Wotton-under-Edge; at the latter place are also found singular stones, in the form of cockle and oyster-shells; and the *cornua ammonis* and *conchæ rugosæ* are very abundant. Indeed, to the geologist and mineralogist, abundant attractions are presented in most parts of this county.

RIVERS, CANALS and MINERAL SPRINGS.—There are several large rivers connected with this county; the principal are the SEVERN, the WYE, the FROME OR STROUD, and the two AVONS. The Severn, which is considered the second commercial river in England, rises on the east side of a vast mountain, called Plyn Lymmon, in the south-east part of Montgomeryshire, in Wales: in its course through the counties of Salop and Wilts, it is augmented by numerous streams; and near the city of Gloucester it divides into two channels, which soon uniting again, form the tract of land called Alney Island: when the Severn has thus re-united its two branches, it is shortly joined by the various canals from the clothing districts of the county, and, becoming considerably enlarged, swells into a broad estuary; when, studded with sails, and gliding between a range of fine pastures and villages, it grows wider gradually, till it receives the Wye, near Chepstow, and the Avon from Somersetshire—thus forming the Bristol Channel. The Frome or Stroud rises not far east of Painswick, and, running westward, falls into the Severn about five miles south of the city of Gloucester. The Upper Avon rises in Northamptonshire, and joins the Severn at Tewkesbury. The Wye rises within half a mile of the source of the Severn, and falls into that river near Chepstow.—The CANALS which pass through Gloucestershire are distinguished by the names of the 'Thames and Severn,' the 'Stroudwater,' the 'Berkeley,' and the 'Hereford and Gloucester.' The principal MINERAL SPRINGS are, 'St. Anthony's well,' in Abenhall parish; at Barrow and Maredon, in Bodington parish; at Ashchurch, near Tewkesbury; at Ambleton, near Winchcombe; at Easington, near Dursley; and at Cheltenham: the last-named town deriving its main prosperity from the medicinal waters.

CIVIL and ECCLESIASTICAL DIVISIONS.—Gloucestershire is in the Province of Canterbury and Diocese of Gloucester; is divided into twenty-eight hundreds, viz.—

BARTON-REGIS,	CLEEVE,	KIFTSGATE,	ST. BRIAVELLS,
BERKELEY,	CROWTHORNE &	LANCASTER,	SLAUGHTER,
BISLEY,	MINETY,	DUTCHY OF,	TEWKESBURY,
BLIDESLOE,	DEERHURST,	LANGLEY AND	THORNBURY,
BOTLOE,	DUDSTONE AND	SWINESHEAD,	TIBALDSTONE,
BRADLEY,	KING'S-BARTON,	LONGTREE,	WESTBURY,
BRIGHTWELLS,	GRUMBALD'S-ASH,	PUCKLE CHURCH,	WESTMINSTER,
CHELTENHAM,	HENBURY,	RAPSGATE,	WHITSTONE.

These divisions collectively contain two Cities (Bristol and Gloucester, a part of the former being in the county of Somerset), one county town (Gloucester), 24 market towns, and about 340 parishes. The whole county sends 10 members to Parliament, viz. two each for the cities of GLOUCESTER & BRISTOL, two each for CIRENCESTER & TEWKESBURY, & two for the SHIRE.

POPULATION.—According to the census of 1821, there were houses inhabited in the county, 60,881; uninhabited, 2,555; and houses building, 705. The number of families then resident in the county was 72,156, comprising 160,451 males, and 175,392 females; total, 335,843: and by a calculation made by order of government, which included persons in the army and navy, for which was added after the ratio of about one to thirty prior to the year 1811, and one to fifty for that year and the census of 1821, to the returns made from the several districts; the population of the county, in round numbers, in the year 1700, was 155,200—in 1750, 207,800—in 1801, 259,100—in 1811, 295,100—and in 1821, 342,600. The increased population in the fifty years, from the year 1700, was 52,600—from 1750 to 1801, the increase was 51,300—from 1801 to 1811, the increase was 36,000—and from 1811 to 1821, the augmented number of persons was 47,500: the grand total increase in the population of the county, from the year 1700 to the census of 1821, being about 187,400 persons.

Index of Distances from Town to Town in the County of Gloucester.

THE NAMES OF THE RESPECTIVE TOWNS ARE ON THE TOP AND SIDE, AND THE SQUARE WHERE BOTH MEET GIVES THE DISTANCE.

Town	Berkeley	Bristol	Campden	Cheltenham	Cirencester	Coleford	Dursley	Fairford	Gloucester	Lechlade	Marshfield	Minchinhampton	Mitchel Dean	Moreton-in-the-Marsh	Newent	Newnham	Northleach	Painswick	Sodbury	St. Leonard Stanley	Stow-on-the-Wold	Stroud	Tetbury	Tewkesbury	Thornbury	Wickwar	Winchcombe	Distance from London
Berkeley																												114
Bristol	18																											119
Campden	45	56																										90
Cheltenham	25	45	20																									98
Cirencester	25	27	29	15																								90
Coleford	12	30	49	29	37																							122
Dursley	5	23	44	24	20	18																						110
Fairford	31	35	27	23	8	45	25																					80
Gloucester	17	34	29	9	16	20	15	25																				106
Lechlade	37	39	30	26	12	48	28	4	28																			77
Marshfield	22	12	55	31	26	34	20	33	33	34																		103
Minchinhampton	13	29	39	20	10	25	9	18	14	21	20																	100
Mitchel Dean	15	33	40	20	28	8	19	36	11	39	37	19																114
Moreton-in-the-Marsh	46	50	7	20	23	50	36	24	30	25	49	33	41															82
Newent	20	40	38	18	26	16	24	34	8	37	42	23	7	39														113
Newnham	14	32	41	21	26	8	17	34	12	38	34	18	6	41	13													116
Northleach	34	38	20	13	11	46	28	10	22	13	36	19	33	14	31	34												80
Painswick	12	34	32	12	10	20	10	20	6	23	27	7	18	32	16	16	14											100
Sodbury (Chipping)	12	11	56	37	25	24	14	32	28	36	8	18	27	48	36	26	36	27										108
St. Leonard Stanley	9	26	39	19	15	21	3	23	12	26	22	5	15	22	21	13	24	7	20									107
Stow-on-the-Wold	37	46	12	18	19	49	33	16	25	17	44	27	37	4	35	37	9	23	45	33								84
Stroud	12	30	34	14	12	24	10	20	9	23	24	4	16	35	19	14	16	4	23	4	26							102
Tetbury	14	27	39	25	10	26	10	18	19	21	16	5	29	33	28	22	19	12	15	7	28	8						99
Tewkesbury	26	47	19	8	23	30	25	32	11	35	43	24	21	21	12	23	22	16	39	23	22	20	29					106
Thornbury	8	11	51	31	27	18	8	35	22	38	18	16	22	44	27	22	32	20	11	15	48	18	15	32				115
Wickwar	8	15	50	30	25	22	9	33	24	36	11	12	25	43	30	26	31	21	4	16	47	19	12	33	7			112
Winchcombe	33	52	13	7	20	37	32	28	17	31	39	21	28	13	26	29	14	20	44	27	13	31	26	11	39	40		95
Wotton-under-Edge	6	20	48	27	21	24	6	29	20	33	14	9	23	37	28	20	28	19	8	12	36	15	9	29	6	4	35	108

[See over.

Additional information relating to the County of Gloucester.

---ooo---

Population.—By the Census for **1831** this county contained 185,063 males, and 201,841 females—total 386,904, being an increase, since the returns made in the year 1821, of 51,061 inhabitants; and from the Census of 1801 to that of 1831 the augmentation amounted to 136,095 persons.

Representation.—By the *Reform Bill* Cheltenham and Stroud has obtained the elective franchise, the former returning one member, and the latter two; two additional ones have also been given to the county, so that the whole shire now sends *fifteen* representatives to Parliament, instead of *ten*, as heretofore. The new *Boundary Act* divides the county into two parts, respectively called the *Eastern Division* and the *Western Division;* the former includes the several hundreds of Crowthorne and Minety, Brightwell's Barrow, Bradley, Rapsgate, Bisley, Longtree, Whetstone, Kiftsgate, Westminster, Derehurst, Slaughter, Cheltenham, Cleeve, Tibaldstone, Tewkesbury, and Dudstone and King's Barton, and also the city and county of the city of Gloucester, and the borough of Cirencester; and the western division includes the several hundreds of Berkeley, Thornbury, Langley and Swineshead, Grumbald's Ash, Pucklechurch, Lancaster, Botloe, St. Briavells, Westbury, and Blidesloe; besides such parts of the hundreds of Henbury and Barton Regis as are not included in the limits of the city of Bristol. The election of members for the eastern division of the county is held at Gloucester, and for the western division at Dursley: besides the place of election the eastern division polls at Stroud, Tewkesbury, Cirencester, Campden, Northleach, and Cheltenham; and the western division (besides the place of election) polls at Wotton-under-Edge, Newent, Newnham, Coleford, Sodbury, and Thornbury.

RAILWAYS.

The Bristol and Exeter Railway, which may be considered a continuation of the Great Western Railway, commences at the former city, and, taking the route of *Bridgwater*, runs near the towns of *Taunton* and *Wellington*, through *Cullompton* to *Exeter*. The Western Union proceeds from *Gloucester* to *Stroud*, and, passing a short distance to the west of *Cirencester*, joins the Great Western Railway near *Swindon*, in Wiltshire. The Bristol and Gloucester Railway forms a communication between the two cities. The Gloucester and Birmingham Railway will go by *Cheltenham, Tewkesbury, Worcester* and *Bromsgrove* to *Birmingham;* from which latter town proceeds the Grand Junction to Manchester and Liverpool; and the Birmingham and London to the Metropolis. A Railway is projected from Cheltenham to Oxford. The proposed Gloucester and Hereford Railway will pass between these two cities by way of Ledbury. Another line (the Gloucester and South Wales), will run, by way of Newnham, Chepstow and Newport to Cardiff.

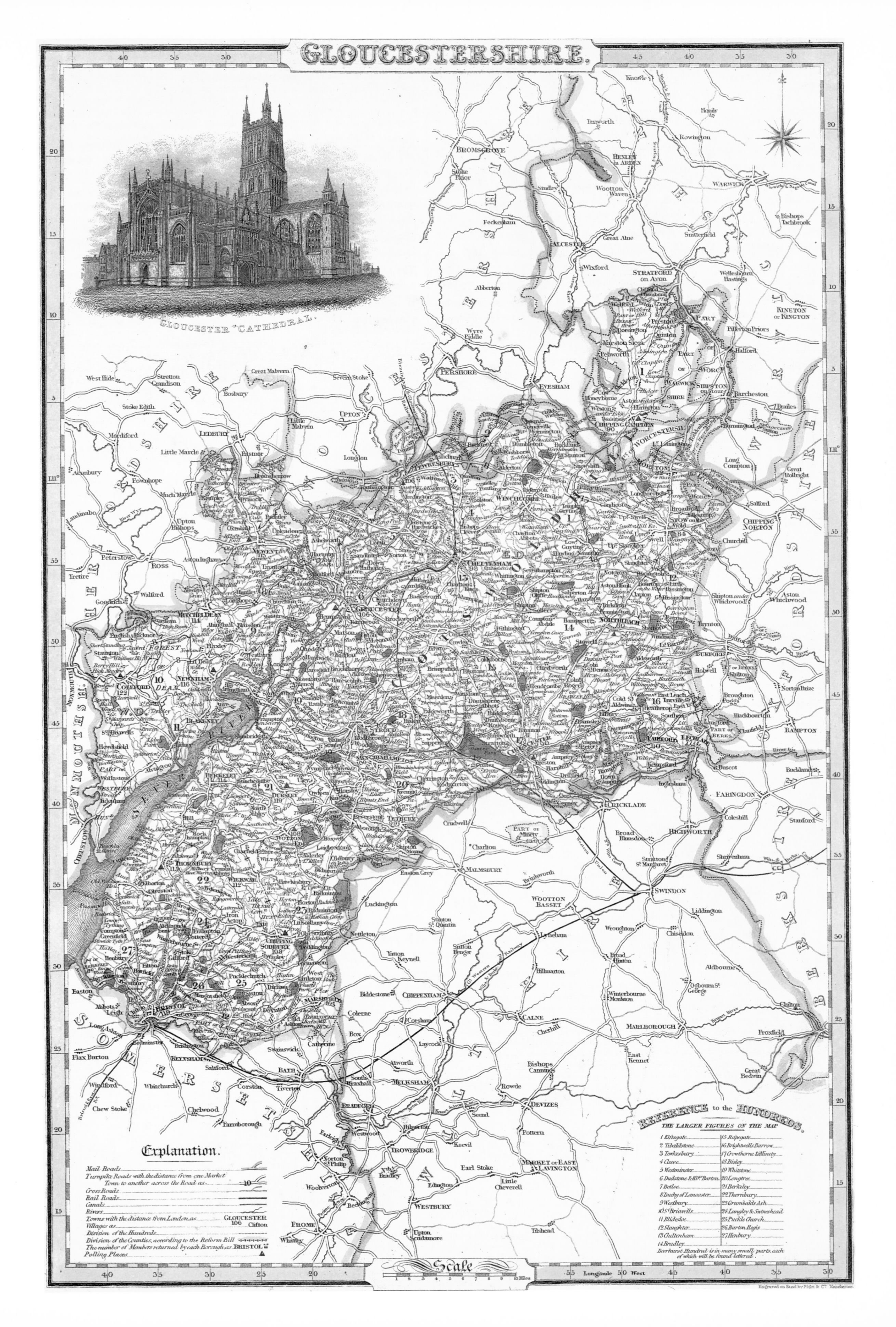

GLOUCESTERSHIRE.
GLOUCESTER CATHEDRAL.
BROMSGROVE
WARWICK
ALCESTER
STRATFORD on AVON
KINETON or KINGTON
PERSHORE
EVESHAM
CHIPPING CAMDEN
LEDBURY
UPTON
TEWKESBURY
WINCHCOMBE
MORETON
STOW on the WOLD
CHIPPING NORTON
NEWENT
ROSS
CHELTENHAM
GLOUCESTER
NORTHLEACH
MITCHELDEAN
BURFORD
COLEFORD
NEWNHAM
CIRENCESTER
FAIRFORD
LECHLADE
MINCHINHAMPTON
DURSLEY
TETBURY
CRICKLADE
FARINGDON
HIGHWORTH
MALMSBURY
THORNBURY
WICKWAR
WOTTON
SWINDON
WOOTTON BASSET
CHIPPING SODBURY
MARSHFIELD
CHIPPENHAM
CALNE
MARLBOROUGH
BRISTOL
KEYNSHAM
BATH
MELKSHAM
DEVIZES
BRADFORD
TROWBRIDGE
MARKET or EAST LAVINGTON
WESTBURY
FROME
Explanation.
Mail Roads
Turnpike Roads with the distance from one Market Town to another across the Road as
10
Cross Roads
Rail Roads
Canals
Rivers
Towns with the distance from London as
GLOUCESTER 106
Villages as
Clifton
Division of the Hundreds
Division of the Counties, according to the Reform Bill
The number of Members returned by each Borough as
BRISTOL
Polling Places
REFERENCE to the HUNDREDS.
THE LARGER FIGURES ON THE MAP
1 Kiftsgate
2 Tibaldstone
3 Tewkesbury
4 Cleeve
5 Westminster
6 Dudstone & Kg.s Barton
7 Botloe
8 Duchy of Lancaster
9 Westbury
10 St. Briavells
11 Blidesloe
12 Slaughter
13 Cheltenham
14 Bradley
15 Rapsgate
16 Brightwells Barrow
17 Crowthorne & Minety
18 Bisley
19 Whitstone
20 Longtree
21 Berkeley
22 Thornbury
23 Grumbalds Ash
24 Langley & Swineshead
25 Puckle Church
26 Barton Regis
27 Henbury
Deerhurst Hundred is in many small parts. each of which will be found lettered.
Scale
Longitude
West

HAMPSHIRE.

HAMPSHIRE, or the COUNTY OF SOUTHAMPTON, is a maritime county, situate on the southern coast of the Kingdom; bounded on the north by Berkshire, on the east by Sussex and Surrey, on the south by the English Channel and the Sound, which separates it from that part comprised within the Isle of Wight, and on the west by Wiltshire and Dorsetshire. It extends in length, from north to south, about 55 miles; in breadth, from east to west, about 40; its circumference is about 150 miles, and its area comprises 1,628 square miles. The figure of this county approaches nearest to that of a square, with a triangular projection at the south-west angle. Its limits, on the south side, are the numerous creeks and inlets formed by the sea; on the west and east, they are mostly artificial; and on the north, they are chiefly indicated by the rivers Enborn and Blackwater.

NAME and ANCIENT HISTORY.—Hampshire was called by the Britons *Gwent* or *Y Went*, and by the Saxons *Hamptuncure*, from 'Hampton,' since called Southampton. At the invasion of the Romans, a great part of the county was in possession of the *Regni* and the *Belgæ*: the former were a tribe of ancient Britons, and the latter a people of the Low Countries. This county is thought to be the first that wholly submitted to the Romans; and, though less than many others in England, it had six Roman stations, and a Roman road ran parallel to the great *Ikening* street as far as the sea-coast in Suffolk. The Belgæ kept possession of the county sixty years after the first landing of the Saxons under Hengist. The Saxons divided the country of the Belgæ into three counties, namely, Somersetshire, Wiltshire and Hampshire.

SOIL, PRODUCE, CLIMATE, &c.—The surface of Hampshire is beautifully varied with gently-rising hills and fruitful vallies; adorned with numerous seats and villages, and interspersed with extensive woodlands. The chief part of the county is enclosed; though large tracts of open heath and uncultivated land, remain in the vicinity of Christchurch, and on the borders of Dorsetshire: the aggregate extent of the waste lands, exclusive of the forests, is supposed to include nearly 100,000 acres. The soils are extremely numerous, but the far greater proportion has a tendency to chalk. In most parts the soil is deep and rich, producing heavy crops of wheat and barley, as well as other grains; and great quantities of malt are made throughout the county. The vicinity of Redbridge is distinguished for its valuable salt-marshes; a great proportion of land in the parishes eastward of Alton, and bordering on Surrey, is appropriated to the growth of hops, the plantations of which have been greatly increased of late years, through the reputation of the Farnham hops. Here is more wood than in any other county in England, especially oak; and the greatest part of the British navy has been built and repaired with the timber it has produced. Hampshire has obtained considerable repute as a breeding county, and particularly of sheep and hogs; the former has given way to the more valuable south-down breed, but the latter is proverbially famous: the bacon cured in the county is very rich and fine, and of a peculiarly pleasant flavour, similar to that of ham; very little of this bacon leaves the county, notwithstanding much is sold, in London and other places, under the inviting name of 'Hampshire bacon.'—The CLIMATE of this county, in most parts of it, is of the most healthful and invigorating nature, especially upon the downs that cross it from east to west; nor are the exhalations from the low grounds near the sea so pernicious as in other counties, and the seasons are mild and genial.

In MANUFACTURES and MINERALS, Hampshire perhaps has less claims to notice than any other English county. The former comprise a few stuff goods, as shalloons and denims; and some serges and other coarse woollens. The mineral productions are mostly confined to the cliffs on the sea-coast, particularly in the neighbourhood of Lymington, Hordwell and Christchurch. A great variety of potter's clay occurs in different parts of the county, varying in its colour from a brown to a dead white, and all convertible into a beautiful white brick. This county is famous as possessing within its boundaries several exceedingly handsome towns, and the most strongly fortified port (PORTSMOUTH) in Great Britain, where the largest ships are built, and where are docks, arsenals and storehouses of unrivalled magnitude; and at Gosport, across the mouth of the harbour, is one of the largest naval hospitals in the kingdom. Off the point of land terminating this peninsula is the noted road of Spithead, where the men of war anchor when they are prepared for and expect immediate actual service.

RIVERS and CANALS.—The principal rivers in Hampshire are, the ITCHIN, the AVON, the BOLDRE WATER, the EXE, the ANTON, and the TESE or TEST; several smaller streams rise in the north-west parts, but soon quit the county in their passage to the Thames. The Itchin has its source in the vicinity of Alresford, and falls into the Southampton water about half a mile east from that town. The Avon enters the county from Wiltshire; and, after being much increased by different rivulets which rise in the district of the New Forest, and also by the Stour below Christchurch, it falls into the sea at Christchurch bay. The Boldre water is formed by various springs rising in the New Forest, and uniting mostly above Brockenhurst; whence they, in a single stream, pass Boldre and Lymington to the sea. The Exe also has its source in the same district; and, beginning to widen near Beaulieu, opens in a broad estuary to the sea, below Exbury. The Anton rises in the north-west angle of the county; and, flowing through part of Andover, has its stream increased by the Tillhill brook, and afterwards runs into the Tese. The Tese has its origin below Whitchurch; and, after its junction with the Avon, passes Stockbridge and Romsey; and below Redbridge it opens, and forms the head of Southampton water. CANALS.—Out of the three distinct lines of canal that originate in this county, two of them terminate in the Southampton water. The Basingstoke Canal is still regarded as a valuable acquisition to the northern parts of the county, as the Redbridge and Andover Canal is to the interior, by bringing to it foreign supplies of the heaviest and most bulky kind: this, crossing Surrey, falls into the Thames below Chertsey. From Redbridge a branch of this canal connects immediately with Southampton: and a collateral branch is also navigable to Alderbury common, within two miles of Salisbury. The Winchester and Salisbury Canal is supposed to be one of the most ancient in the kingdom, the Act for making it being obtained in the reign of Charles the First.

CIVIL and ECCLESIASTICAL DIVISIONS.—Hampshire (including the Isles of Wight, Jersey, Guernsey, Alderney and Sark) is in the Province of Canterbury and Diocese of Winchester: it is apportioned into the divisions of ALTON NORTH, ALTON SOUTH, ANDOVER, BASINGSTOKE, FAWLEY, KINGSCLERE, NEW-FOREST EAST, NEW-FOREST WEST, PORTSDOWN, and ISLE OF WIGHT; these are subdivided into forty-one hundreds and nine liberties, all of which collectively contain one city (Winchester), two county towns (Winchester and Southampton, the latter being a county of itself,) twenty-seven market towns, 298 parishes, and about one thousand villages. The whole county returns twenty-six members to Parliament, viz. two each for ANDOVER, CHRISTCHURCH, LYMINGTON, NEWPORT, NEWTOWN, PETERSFIELD, PORTSMOUTH, SOUTHAMPTON, STOCKBRIDGE, WHITCHURCH, WINCHESTER, YARMOUTH, and two for the SHIRE.

POPULATION.—According to the census of 1821, there were houses inhabited in the county, 49,516; uninhabited, 1,943; and houses building, 287. The number of families then resident in the county was 57,942; comprising 138,373 males, and 144,925 females; total, 283,298 (including convicts on board the hulks in Portsmouth harbour): and by a calculation made by order of Government, which included persons in the army and navy, for which was added after the ratio of about one to thirty prior to the year 1811, and one to fifty for that year and the census of 1821, to the returns made from the several districts; the population of the county, in round numbers, in the year 1700, was 118,700—in 1750, 137,500—in 1801, 226,900—in 1811, 253,300—and in 1821, 289,000. The increased population in the 50 years, from the year 1700, was 18,800—from 1750 to 1801, the increase was 89,400—from 1801 to 1811, the increase was 26,400—and from 1811 to 1821, the augmented number of persons was 35,700: the grand total increase in the population of the county from the year 1700 to the census of 1821, being about 170,300 persons.

Index of Distances from Town to Town in the County of Hants.

THE NAMES OF THE RESPECTIVE TOWNS ARE ON THE TOP AND SIDE, AND THE SQUARE WHERE BOTH MEET GIVES THE DISTANCE.

Town	Alresford	Alton	Andover	Basingstoke	Bishop's-Waltham	Brading, Isle of Wight	Christchurch	Cowes, Isle of Wight	Fareham	Fordingbridge	Gosport	Havant	Lymington	Newport, Isle of Wight	Odiham	Petersfield	Portsmouth	Ringwood	Romsey	Ryde, Isle of Wight	Southampton	Stockbridge	Whitchurch	Winchester	Distance from London.
Alresford																									57
Alton	10																								47
Andover	18	27																							64
Basingstoke	12	12	18																						45
Bishop's-Waltham	12	18	24	25																					66
Brading, Isle of Wight	30	37	44	44	20																				82
Christchurch	42	52	41	53	37	30																			102
Cowes, Isle of Wight	30	40	38	42	22	13	29																		84
Fareham	20	25	32	33	8	15	43	17																	73
Fordingbridge	32	42	26	40	25	45	15	27	27																91
Gosport	23	30	37	36	14	9	49	12	5	32															(by Fareham 78) 74
Havant	21	25	37	36	13	13	51	21	8	35	10														66
Lymington	36	46	35	44	26	23	12	17	30	21	35	38													94
Newport, Isle of Wight	41	47	50	54	30	7	28	5	18	39	13	22	15												84
Odiham	17	8	24	8	27	43	61	51	35	49	38	34	54	51											40
Petersfield	8	12	26	24	15	22	48	30	16	39	20	12	40	31	22										55
Portsmouth	28	30	41	45	17	9	46	12	9	34	2	9	37	12	39	18									72
Ringwood	36	46	33	45	29	38	9	32	32	6	37	40	15	30	54	44	41								91
Romsey	18	28	17	29	19	30	24	20	20	14	25	30	18	25	35	34	28	18							74
Ryde, Isle of Wight	33	39	46	50	22	4	35	9	10	36	5	14	24	7	44	23	5	41	29						77
Southampton	18	29	25	30	10	22	24	12	12	15	17	20	18	17	36	24	22	20	7	21					77
Stockbridge	15	25	7	22	19	41	34	28	27	24	32	33	28	33	30	27	34	28	10	37	16				67
Whitchurch	15	17	7	11	23	45	47	37	31	33	35	36	39	42	17	23	40	41	23	25	40	7			56
Winchester	7	17	14	18	10	32	35	24	18	25	23	23	29	29	24	18	25	28	11	28	12	9	12		64
Yarmouth, Isle of Wight	41	51	40	49	31	19	18	13	30	26	25	34	5	10	59	43	25	20	23	23	19	33	44	33	98

[See over.

Additional information relating to the County of Hants.

---ooo---

POPULATION.—By the Census for **1831** this county contained 152,097 males, and 162,216 females—total 314,313, being an increase, since the returns made in the year 1821, of 31,015 inhabitants; and from the Census of 1801 to that of 1831 the augmentation amounted to 94,657 persons.

REPRESENTATION.—By the *Reform Bill* the following boroughs have been deprived of the elective franchise, namely, STOCKBRIDGE and WHITCHURCH; and NEWTOWN and YARMOUTH, in the Isle of Wight: CHRISTCHURCH and PETERSFIELD are deprived of one member each. The county has two additional members given to it, besides one other for the Isle of Wight, which, for that purpose, is separated, by the Bill, from the county of Hants. The whole shire (including the Isle of Wight) now sends *nineteen* representatives to Parliament, instead of *twenty-six,* as heretofore. The new *Boundary Act* separates the county into two parts (in neither of which is included the Isle of Wight), respectively called the *Northern Division* and the *Southern Division;* the former includes the whole of the several divisions of Alton, Andover, Basingstoke, Kingsclere, Droxford, Odiham, Petersfield, and Winchester; and the southern includes the several divisions of Fareham, Lymington, Ringwood, Romsey, and Southampton, as also the town and county of the town of Southampton. The election of members for the northern division is held at WINCHESTER, for the southern at SOUTHAMPTON, and for the Isle of Wight member at NEWPORT; besides the place of election, the northern division polls at ALTON, ANDOVER, BASINGSTOKE, KINGSCLERE, ODIHAM, PETERSFIELD, and BISHOP'S WALTHAM; the southern division (besides the place of election) polls at FAREHAM, LYMINGTON, PORTSMOUTH, RINGWOOD and ROMSEY; and the Isle of Wight (besides Newport) polls at WEST COWES.

RAILWAYS.—The LONDON and SOUTHAMPTON passes between three and four miles to the north of *Odiham,* on to *Basingstoke* and *Winchester*. From Southampton a branch is projected to Salisbury, passing Romsey. Portsmouth will be connected with the London and Southampton line by the intended Portsmouth Junction Railway.

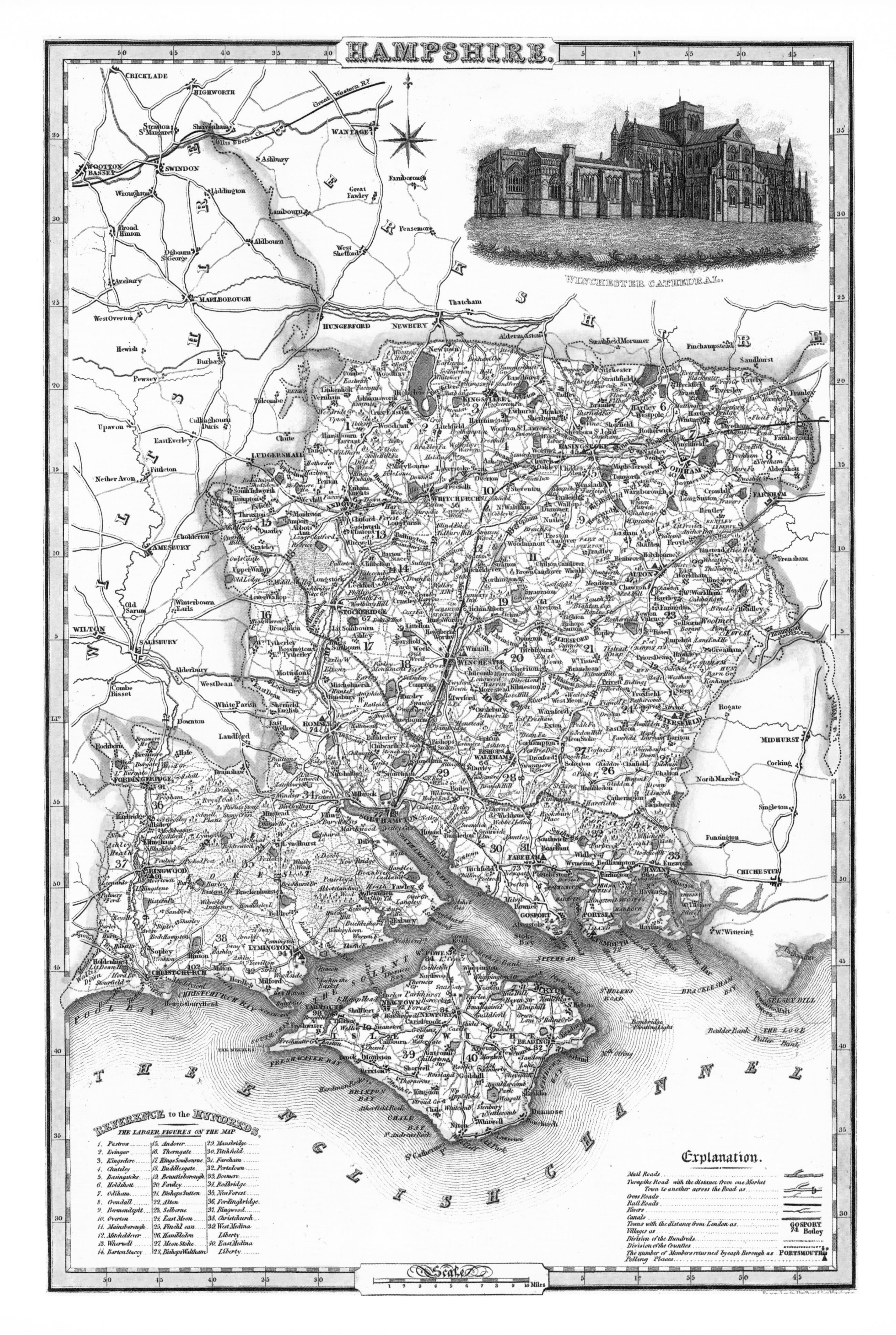
HAMPSHIRE.
WINCHESTER CATHEDRAL.
CRICKLADE
HIGHWORTH
Great Western Ry
WANTAGE
SWINDON
WOOTTON BASSET
MARLBOROUGH
HUNGERFORD
NEWBURY
Thatcham
LUDGERSHALL
AMESBURY
WILTON
SALISBURY
KINGSCLERE
BASINGSTOKE
ODIHAM
FARNHAM
WHITCHURCH
ANDOVER
STOCKBRIDGE
ALTON
WINCHESTER
ALRESFORD
PETERSFIELD
ROMSEY
BISHOPS WALTHAM
SOUTHAMPTON
FORDINGBRIDGE
RINGWOOD
LYMINGTON
CHRISTCHURCH
FAREHAM
HAVANT
GOSPORT
PORTSEA
CHICHESTER
MIDHURST
YARMOUTH
NEWPORT
NEWTOWN
BRADING
COWES
RYDE
POOL BAY
CHRISTCHURCH BAY
Hengistbury Head
THE SOLENT
SPITHEAD
St HELENS ROAD
BRACKLESHAM BAY
SELSEY BILL
Boulder Bank
THE LOOE
Pullar Bank
Bembridge Floating Light
FRESHWATER BAY
THE NEEDLES
BRIXTON BAY
CHALE BAY
St Catherine's Pt
THE ENGLISH CHANNEL
REFERENCE to the HUNDREDS.
THE LARGER FIGURES ON THE MAP
1. Pastrow
2. Evingar
3. Kingsclere
4. Chuteley
5. Basingstoke
6. Holdshott
7. Odiham
8. Crondall
9. Bermondspit
10. Overton
11. Mainsborough
12. Mitcheldever
13. Wherwell
14. Barton Stacey
15. Andover
16. Therngate
17. Kings Sombourne
18. Buddlesgate
19. Bountisborough
20. Fawley
21. Bishops Sutton
22. Alton
23. Selborne
24. East Meon
25. Finchl ean
26. Hambledon
27. Meon Stoke
28. Bishops Waltham
29. Mansbridge
30. Titchfield
31. Fareham
32. Portsdown
33. Bosmere
34. Redbridge
35. New Forest
36. Fordingbridge
37. Ringwood
38. Christchurch
39. West Medina Liberty
40. East Medina Liberty
Explanation.
Mail Roads
Turnpike Road with the distance from one Market Town to another across the Road as
Cross Roads
Rail Roads
Rivers
Canals
Towns with the distance from London as
GOSPORT 74
Villages as
Botley
Division of the Hundreds
Division of the Counties
The number of Members returned by each Borough as
PORTSMOUTH
Polling Places
Scale
10 Miles

HEREFORDSHIRE.

HEREFORDSHIRE is an inland county, bounded on the north by Shropshire, on the north-east and east by Worcestershire, on the south-east by Gloucestershire, on the south-west by Monmouthshire, on the west by Brecknockshire, and on the north-west by Radnorshire. Its form is nearly an ellipsis, but some detached parishes are situated beyond the general outline. The greatest extent of the county, from Ludford on the north, to the opposite border, near Monmouth, on the south, is thirty-eight miles; its greatest width, from Clifford on the west, to Cradley on the east, is thirty-five miles; and its circumference 180 miles; including about 860 square miles.

NAME and ANCIENT HISTORY.—This county is asserted by some to take its name from the city of Hereford, which is said to be pure Saxon, and to signify 'the *ford* of the army:' but other authorities contend that it is derived from the British name of the county, *Ereinac;* and that '*Here,*' the first part of the Saxon name, was implicitly borrowed from '*Erei,*' the first part of the British. However this may be, it is not difficult to infer that the words '*Here,*' or '*Erei,*' in conjunction with '*ford,*' by easy transition have given to the county its present appellation 'Hereford.' Herefordshire, together with Radnorshire, Brecknockshire, Monmouthshire and Glamorganshire, constitute that district which, at the period of the Roman invasion, was inhabited by the *Silures,* a brave and hardy people, who, in conjunction with the *Ordovices,* or inhabitants of North Wales, under the heroic Caractacus, for a considerable time retarded the progress of the Roman arms: at length, by the military talents of the Roman General, Julius Frontinus, the brave Britons were compelled to relinquish to the enemy the forest of Dean, and the present counties of Hereford and Monmouth, and retire into the fastnesses of Wales; from whence offering no further resistance to the Roman domination, the complete and undisturbed possession of South Britain was thus insured to the conquerors, who included Herefordshire in the district named BRITANNIA SECUNDA.

SOIL, PRODUCE, &c.—The general aspect of this county is extremely beautiful: its surface is finely diversified and broken by swelling heights, so as greatly to resemble the more central parts of Kent. From many of these elevations the prospects are uncommonly fine; but are peculiarly so from the Malvern Hills on the east, and the Hatterell or Black Mountains on the west. The fertility of the soil is very great, and the country is clothed in almost perpetual verdure: on every side a luxuriance of vegetation is exhibited, in widely extended corn-fields, teeming orchards, expansive meadows and flourishing plantations; every part seems uniformly productive, except, perhaps, on the north and west outskirts. The general character of the soil is a mixture of marl and clay, containing a large proportion of calcareous earth; deep beds of gravel are occasionally met with; fullers' earth is sometimes dug near Stoke; and red and yellow ochres, with pipe clay, are found in different parts of the county. Iron ore has been met with in the districts bordering on Gloucestershire, but none has been dug of late years; though, from the considerable quantities that have been discovered imperfectly smelted, and from the remains of hand-blomaries also found, it has been thought that iron-works were established here as early as the Roman times. Herefordshire is particularly famous as a cider county; yet this, though a favourite object of its husbandry, is by no means the only one: cattle, sheep, swine, corn, &c. have equally strong claims on the attention of the farmer. Plantations of fruit-trees are found on every aspect, and on soils of every quality, and under every culture. The particular era when the plantations of apple-trees acquired the peculiar eminence which they yet retain, was during the reign of Charles I, when, by the spirited exertions of Lord Scudamore, and other gentlemen of the county, Herefordshire became in a manner one entire orchard. An orchard is generally raised with most success in a hop-yard, the ground under this description of culture being always well tilled and manured. The annual produce of the fruit greatly varies: in a plentiful year it is almost beyond conception, as the trees are then loaden to excess, and frequently break under the weight of the apples; at these times, indeed, the branches generally receive the support of props or forked poles: this kind of excessive fruitage, however, seldom occurs oftener than once in four years; what may be named a full fruitage takes place, perhaps, once in every three years: in some of these seasons of abundance, twenty hogsheads of cider have been made from the produce of a single acre of orchard ground. The principal markets for the fruit-liquors of Herefordshire are London and Bristol, from which ports great quantities are sent to Ireland, to the East and West Indies, and to foreign markets in bottles. The principal part of the liquors is bought immediately from the press (or pound) by the country dealers who reside within the district, and who in general prefer having it in that state, that the fermentation and subsequent management may take place under their own immediate inspection. The cultivation of hops forms a considerable branch of the rural economy of this county, and is still increasing, particularly in the parts bordering on Worcestershire: they are of two kinds—the white and the red—but each kind has several varieties; the white hops are the most delicate, and have the preference with the buyers, though the red sorts are more hardy, and impart a stronger quality in brewing. Herefordshire is rich in woodland—many species of trees, in different districts, growing up spontaneously, and becoming strong and vigorous in a very short period.

RIVERS and CANALS.—The principal rivers of this county are the WYE, the LUGG, the MUNNOW, the ARROW, the FROME, the TEAM (or TEME), and the LEDDON. The Wye, which has so often been celebrated for the picturesque scenery that adorns its meandering channel, rises near the summit of the Plinlimmon hills, in Montgomeryshire; and entering Herefordshire near Clifford Castle, passes Hereford, Ross, &c.; after which, by a sinuous course, it falls into the Severn a little below Chepstow: the principal fish taken in the Wye are salmon, which are in perfection between the months of August and December only. These fish were so much more abundant formerly than at present, that in the indentures of apprenticeship at Hereford there was a clause that the apprentice should not be compelled to live on them more frequently than two days a week; their passage up the river is now, however, so much obstructed by iron-works, that unless the water is swelled far above its usual height, they cannot advance: this circumstance, together with the practice of taking the fish in an illegal manner, have rendered them much less plentiful. The Lugg rises in Radnorshire, and enters Herefordshire near Stapleton Castle; near Leominster it receives the Pinsley, and it is afterwards increased by the waters of the Arrow and the Frome, and falls into the Wye near the village of Mordisford. The Munnow rises in the Herefordshire side of the Hatterell Mountains, and, after being increased by numerous streams, is lost in the Wye below Monmouth. The Team enters this county a short distance from Brampton Bryan, and, after making singular circuits, discharges itself into the Severn in Worcestershire. The Leddon has its origin in the east side of the county, and, running to the south, gives name to the town of Ledbury; thence flowing into Gloucestershire, it falls into the Severn a few miles below Minsterwar. The Arrow enters Herefordshire from Radnorshire, and, running eastward, falls into the Lugg a little below Leominster. The Frome rises near Wolfrelow, above Bromyard; and, being joined by the Loden, is united with the Lugg above Mordisford.—The CANALS are, the 'Hereford and Gloucester Canal,' and the 'Kington & Leominster Canal;' the former begins at Hereford, and after a course of 35 miles it joins the Severn opposite the city of Gloucester; the latter canal begins at Kington, and falls into the Severn just above Stourport: the length of this canal is rather more than 45 miles,—it has two tunnels, and some trifling collateral cuts, near Tenbury.

CIVIL and ECCLESIASTICAL DIVISIONS.—Herefordshire is in the Province of Canterbury and Diocese of Hereford, and is included in the Oxford Circuit. It is divided into eleven hundreds, viz. BROXASH, EWYAS-LACY, GREYTREE, GRIMSWORTH, HUNTINGTON, RADLOW, STRETFORD, WEBTREE, WIGMORE, WOLPHY and WORMELOW; these are subdivided into two hundred and nineteen parishes, containing one City and county town (Hereford), and six other market towns. The whole county returns eight members to Parliament, namely, two for the City of HEREFORD, two each for the boroughs of LEOMINSTER and WEOBLEY, and two for the SHIRE.

POPULATION.—According to the census of 1821, there were houses inhabited in the county, 20,061; uninhabited, 804; and houses building, 132. The number of families then resident in the county was 21,917, comprising 51,552 males, and 51,691 females; total, 103,243: and by a calculation made by order of government, which included persons in the army and navy, for which was added after the ratio of about one to thirty prior to the year 1811, and one to fifty for that year and the census of 1821, to the returns made from the several districts; the population of the county, in round numbers, in the year 1700, was 60,900—in 1750, 74,100—in 1801, 92,100—in 1811, 97,300—and in 1821, 105,300. The increased population in the fifty years, from the year 1700, was 13,200—from 1750 to 1801, the increase was 18,000—from 1801 to 1811, the increase was 5,200—and from 1811 to 1821, the augmented number of persons was 8,000: the grand total increase in the population of the county, from the year 1700 to the census of 1821, being about 44,400 persons.

Index of Distances from Town to Town in the County of Hereford.

THE NAMES OF THE RESPECTIVE TOWNS ARE ON THE TOP AND SIDE, AND THE SQUARE WHERE BOTH MEET GIVES THE DISTANCE.

	Bromyard	Hereford	Kington	Ledbury	Leominster	Ross	Weobley	*Distance from London.*
Bromyard								125
Hereford	14							130
Kington	25	20						150
Ledbury	13	15	35					120
Leominster	12	13	14	24				136
Ross	26	14	33	13	27			120
Weobley	19	11	8	26	7	25		141

[*See over.*

Additional information relating to the County of HEREFORD.

ooo

POPULATION.—By the Census for **1831** this county contained 55,715 males, and 55,261 females—total 110,976, being an increase, since the returns made in the year 1821, of 7,733 inhabitants; and from the Census of 1801 to that of 1831 the augmentation amounted to 21,785 persons.

REPRESENTATION.—By the *Reform Bill* the borough of WEOBLY is disfranchised; and one additional member given to the county: the whole shire, therefore, now returns *seven* representatives to Parliament, instead of *eight,* as heretofore. The election of members for the county is held at HEREFORD, and besides that town the polls take place at LEOMINSTER, BROMYARD, LEDBURY, ROSS, and KINGTON.

RAILWAYS.—A line of Railway, from Hereford, connects that city with Abergavenny. Another line, from *Kington,* goes to *Brecon,* by *Hay.* The Hereford and Shrewsbury Railway, as proposed, will pass about seven miles to the west of Bromyard, and about two to the east of Leominster, through Ludlow; it will then run a short distance to the west of Church-Stretton, on to Shrewsbury.

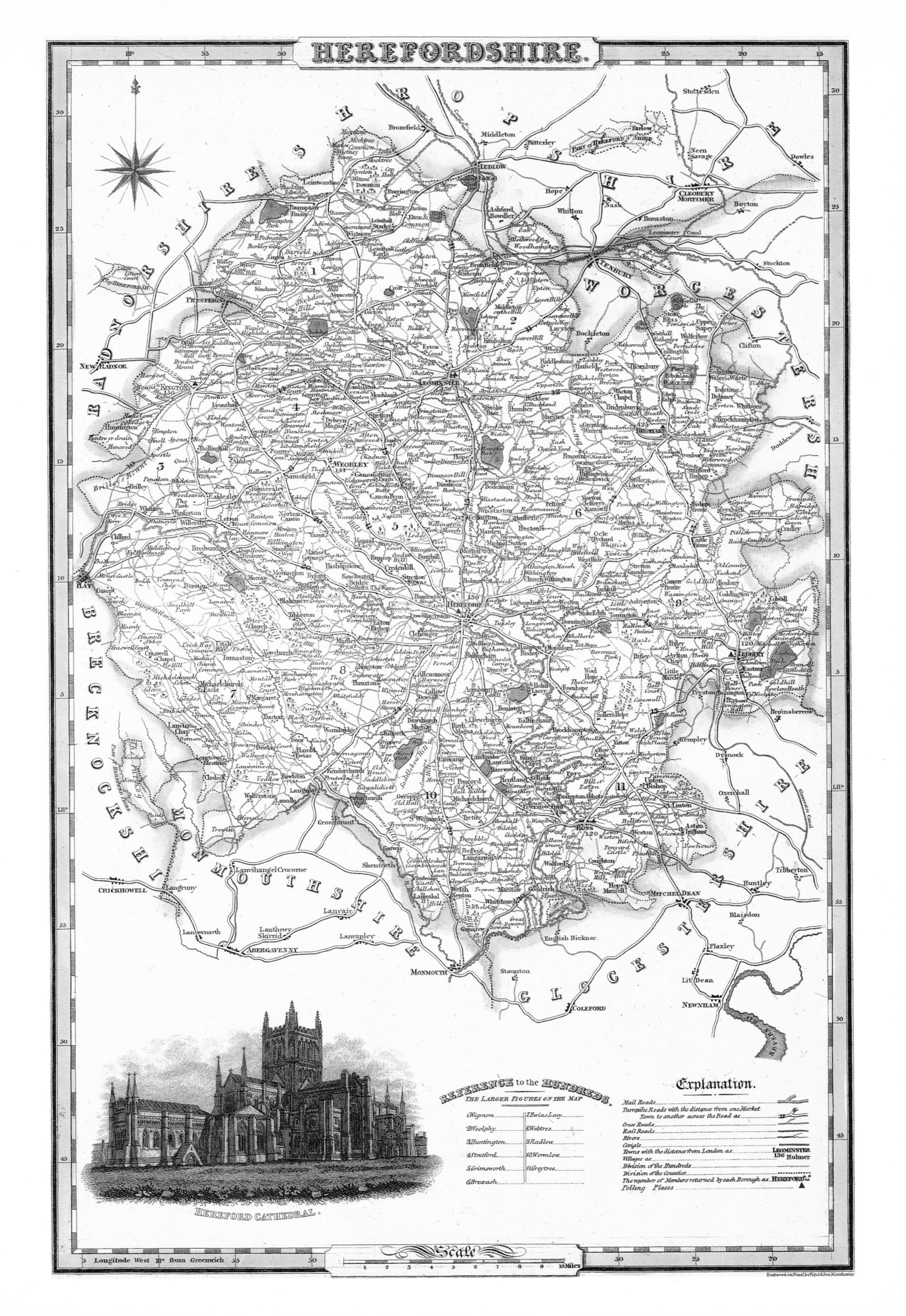

HEREFORD CATHEDRAL.

HERTFORDSHIRE.

HERTFORDSHIRE is an inland county, of an extremely irregular form, and its boundaries are of the like character. Its most distant extremities lie in a direction nearly north-east and south-west; its shortest, south-east and north-west. Upon the north it is bounded, for a few miles, by the county of Cambridge; its north-eastern angle meets the latter county and a part of Essex; whilst the southern boundary of Hertford is formed, with some considerable indentures, by Middlesex. Upon the western side are the counties of Bucks and Bedford,—the latter county also extending to, and meeting Cambridgeshire on the north. Some difficulty exists in ascertaining with precision the dimensions of this county: measured, however, from Royston, upon its N.N.E. confines, to the extremity of its most southerly indenture with Bucks, its length is about thirty-six miles; and its greatest breadth, taken in an oblique direction, from Bishop's Stortford on the east to Berkhampstead, upon the confines of Buckinghamshire, on the west, is about thirty miles: but its medium length may be grossly estimated at thirty miles, and its breadth at twenty-five miles. Its ambit is calculated at somewhat between 130 and 140 miles, and the Government returns state the area to comprise five hundred and twenty-eight square miles.

ANCIENT HISTORY.—Previous to the invasion of the Romans, Hertford, with the adjoining counties of Essex, Bedford and Buckingham, constituted the territory of the *Cassii, Trinobantes,* and *Cattieuchlatii,* over whom Cassievellaunus reigned—making, as some are inclined to think, Verulam his chief place of residence. When the Romans, under the conduct of JULIUS CÆSAR, made their first descent upon the shores of Britain from the opposite coast of conquered Gaul, the several nations (or tribes) who at that time occupied the south-eastern part of the Island summoned their forces to repel the invaders, and Casseivellaunus was unanimously chosen Commander in Chief: unavailing, however, were the desperate efforts made by these undisciplined, though gallant natives, to oppose the steady and well marshalled troops of Rome—flushed with recent triumphs, and headed by a General idolized by his soldiers; the inefficacy of further resistance was felt by the native Commander, and he was compelled to bow before the victor. Upon the final subjugation of the southern parts of the Island, and their division into districts or governments, Hertfordshire constituted a portion of one of these, to which, in compliment to the first conqueror of the country, was given the name of FLAVIA CÆSARIENSIS. When the more domestic misfortunes of Rome obliged her to withdraw her legions from the distant provinces, their domination in this country was succeeded by that of the Saxons, another race of invaders, who divided the country into a number of Kingdoms or Principalities; at which time the county of Hertford was unequally divided between the Kingdom of the East Saxons and that of Mercia, the *Ermine-street* being conjectured to have constituted the boundary.

SOIL, and CLIMATE, PRODUCE and MANUFACTURES.—The general aspect of this county is extremely pleasant; and though its eminences are not enough elevated, nor its vales sufficiently depressed and broken, to afford a decisive character of picturesque or romantic beauty, yet its surface is so diversified as to constitute a considerable display of fine scenery. The northern part is the most hilly; and a range of high ground stretches out from the neighbourhood of King's Langley towards Berkhampstead and Tring, which in many parts commands a great extent of country. Another elevated ridge commences at St. Albans, and proceeds in a north direction. The south line is also sufficiently high to include some extensive prospects. Most of the country is enclosed; and the enclosures being principally live hedges, intermixed with flourishing timber, have a verdant and pleasing effect. Independent of the wood thus distributed in hedge-rows, large quantities of very fine timber are grown in the parks and grounds belonging to the numerous seats of the nobility and gentry, which are spread over every part of the county, and give animation to almost every view. The SOILS of this county mix and run into each other in a very remarkable manner, so that they cannot be traced and named with any great certainty: the prevailing ones are loam and clay; the former is met with in almost all its gradations, and is more or less intermingled with flints, or sand. The vales through which the rivers or brooks take their course are composed of a rich sandy loam, with the exception of a small quantity of peat, or marshy moor. The principal clay district is on the north-east or Essex side; yet even here the upper surface is in general a strong wet loam. The only parts where the soils may be considered sterile are in the parishes of North Holt and North Mims, and the lower part of that of Hatfield. The chalky soil prevails generally on the northern side of the county; but indeed the basis of the whole county is chalk, either more or less pure, though the depths at which it is found are very different. By far the greatest proportion of Hertfordshire is under tillage; —as a corn country, it is considered as one of the first in England: the produce in wheat, barley and oats is very considerable; large quantities of turnips are also grown, and artificial grasses cultivated to a very great extent. The meadows are very productive in many parts, and the various streams which intersect the land are extremely favourable to irrigation. In the south-west corner of the county are many orchards; apples and cherries are their principal produce, which always finds a ready market in London. The quantity of waste lands is but inconsiderable; many acres of these are appropriated as sheep down. As the land in this county is chiefly arable, live stock has become an object of very inferior regard: the Suffolk breed is considered the best; the sheep are mostly ewes of the South Down and Wiltshire kinds. The horses are of various kinds, but the Suffolk breed appears to have the preference.—The CLIMATE of Hertfordshire is reckoned as most salubrious, and the air is generally mild; to delicate constitutions, its temperature is considered soothing and efficacious. These advantages, with the general beauty of the country, the goodness of the roads, and the almost uninterrupted fertility of the soil, have been the means of making this county a favourite residence, and attracting great numbers of wealthy persons to purchase lands for building villas, thereby causing estates to multiply in a manner unknown in the distant counties.—The chief MANUFACTURES of Hertfordshire, at one time, were cotton and silk; the former has much declined, nor is the latter carried on extensively: the principal works in these branches are (or were) situated at St. Albans, Rickmansworth and Watford. When the article was more worn than of late years, Berkhampstead employed many female hands in making black lace; but the principal employment of the labouring females, in most parts of the county, is platting straw for hats, bonnets, &c.

RIVERS, CANALS, and MINERAL SPRINGS.—The principal rivers of Hertfordshire are the LEA and the COLNE; these two are composed of many inferior streams, most of whose sources lie within the county. The Lea rises near Leagrave, in Bedfordshire; enters Hertfordshire near Bower-heath, and pursues a direction nearly from north-west to south-east, to its conflux with the Stort, about a mile east of Hoddesdon; and flowing through Broxbourn, Wormley and Cheshunt, finally quits the county near Waltham Abbey. The Colne is formed by the union of several small streams, one of which rises at Kix or Kits End, in Middlesex; these unite in the vicinity of North Mims, and flow by and give name to London-Colney, Colney Park and Colney Street; and being increased near the latter place by the Ver, Verulam, Verlam or Meuse river from St. Albans, it subsequently passes Watford and Rickmansworth, when it enters Middlesex. The names of the other chief tributary streams are the Maran, or *Mimerum,* which rises near Frogmore, and with the Beane, which originates near Cromer, joins the Lea near Hertford; the Rib, whose source is near Buntingford, and the Quin from Biggin, mingle together, and add to the waters of the Lea. From these rivers united the inhabitants of the Metropolis derive a leading necessary of life, conveyed to them by the NEW RIVER. The Ash falls into the Lea near Ware; the Stort rises in Essex, and is navigable from Bishop's Stortford to its junction with the Lea; and the Gade stream, in conjunction with another, enriches the Colne. Several of the small streams which unite to form the Rhee, (a chief branch of the Cam,) have likewise their origin in this county, in the vicinity of Ashwell. CANALS—The 'Grand Junction Canal' enters this county above Berkhampstead, and follows the course of the Gade to Rickmansworth, and from thence the course of the Colne till it leaves the county. An Act has also been obtained for the formation of another canal from St. Albans, to join the Grand Junction below Cashiobury Park.—The few MEDICINAL SPRINGS rising in this county are chiefly chalybeate: these are confined to the south part, and the principal is near the race-ground on Barnet Common: others rise on Northaw Common, and another at Cattley, in Northaw parish. Some incrustating springs have been known near Clothall, in the north part of the county.

CIVIL and ECCLESIASTICAL DIVISIONS.—Hertfordshire is in the Province of Canterbury,—part of the county is in the Diocese of Lincoln, and part of it in that of London; it is included in the Home Circuit, and divided into eight hundreds, viz. BRAUGHIN, BROADWATER, CASHIO, DACORUM, EDWINSTREE, HERTFORD, HITCHIN AND PIRTON, and ODSEY: these collectively contain one county town (Hertford), two boroughs (Hertford and St. Albans), fourteen other market towns, and one hundred and thirty-two parishes. The whole county returns six members to Parliament, viz. two each for the boroughs of HERTFORD and ST. ALBANS, and two for the SHIRE.

POPULATION.—According to the census of 1821, there were houses inhabited in the county, 23,178; uninhabited, 509; and houses building, 172. The number of families then resident in the county was 26,170; comprising 64,121 males, and 65,593 females; total, 129,714: and by a calculation made by order of Government, which included persons in the army and navy, for which was added after the ratio of about one to thirty prior to the year 1811, and one to fifty for that year and the census of 1821, to the returns made from the several districts; the population of the county, in round numbers, in the year 1700, was 70,500—in 1750, 86,500—in 1801, 100,800—in 1811, 115,400—and in 1821, 132,400. The increased population in the 50 years, from the year 1700, was 16,000—from 1750 to 1801, the increase was 14,300—from 1801 to 1811, the increase was 14,600—and from 1811 to 1821, the augmented number of persons was 17,400: the grand total increase in the population of the county from the year 1700 to the census of 1821, being about 61,900 persons.

Index of Distances from Town to Town in the County of Herts.

THE NAMES OF THE RESPECTIVE TOWNS ARE ON THE TOP AND SIDE, AND THE SQUARE WHERE BOTH MEET GIVES THE DISTANCE.

Town	Baldock	Barnet	Berkhampstead	Bishop's Stortford	Hatfield	Hemel Hempstead	Hertford	Hitchin	Hoddesdon	Redbourn	Rickmansworth	St. Albans	Stevenage	Tring	Ware	*Distance from London.*
Baldock																37
Barnet	26															11
Berkhampstead	25	18														26
Bishop's Stortford	21	26	36													30
Hatfield	18	9	17	22												19
Hemel Hempstead	22	14	4	32	11											24
Hertford	18	12	24	14	7	18										21
Hitchin	5	23	15	26	15	17	15									34
Hoddesdon	22	12	27	16	10	21	4	21								17
Redbourn	15	14	8	31	9	4	16	10	20							25
Rickmansworth	29	12	10	38	16	9	23	26	26	13						18
St. Albans	18	10	9	27	5	6	12	14	15	4	11					21
Stevenage	6	20	19	23	12	16	12	4	16	12	23	12				31
Tring	27	23	5	41	20	8	27	22	30	12	14	15	23			31
Ware	17	14	26	12	9	20	2	15	4	18	25	15	11	29		20
Watford	25	9	11	34	12	8	20	21	22	11	3	7	19	15	22	15

Additional information relating to the County of HERTS.

---ooo---

POPULATION.—By the Census for **1831** this county contained 71,395 males, and 71,946 females—total 143,341, being an increase, since the returns made in the year 1821, of 13,627 inhabitants; and from the Census of 1801 to that of 1831, the augmentation amounted to 45,764 persons.

REPRESENTATION.—By the *Reform Bill* one additional member is given to the county, the whole shire, therefore, now returns *seven* representatives to Parliament, instead of *six*, as heretofore. The election of members for the county is held at HERTFORD, and besides that town the polls take place at STEVENAGE, BUNTINGFORD, BISHOP'S STORTFORD, HODDESDON, HATFIELD, and HEMEL HEMPSTEAD.

RAILWAYS.—The NORTHERN and EASTERN RAILWAY, on its route to *Cambridge*, passes close to *Hoddesdon* and *Bishops Stortford*, about five miles to the south-east of *Hertford*, and ten east of *Ware*. Branches connecting Ware and Hertford with the main line are projected. The LONDON and BIRMINGHAM RAILWAY runs to the well-known station of *Boxmoor*, which is within a mile and a half west of *Hemel Hempstead;* then passes about four miles to the south of *St. Albans*, and one mile and a half north of *Tring:* from the latter town there is a branch to *Aylesbury*.

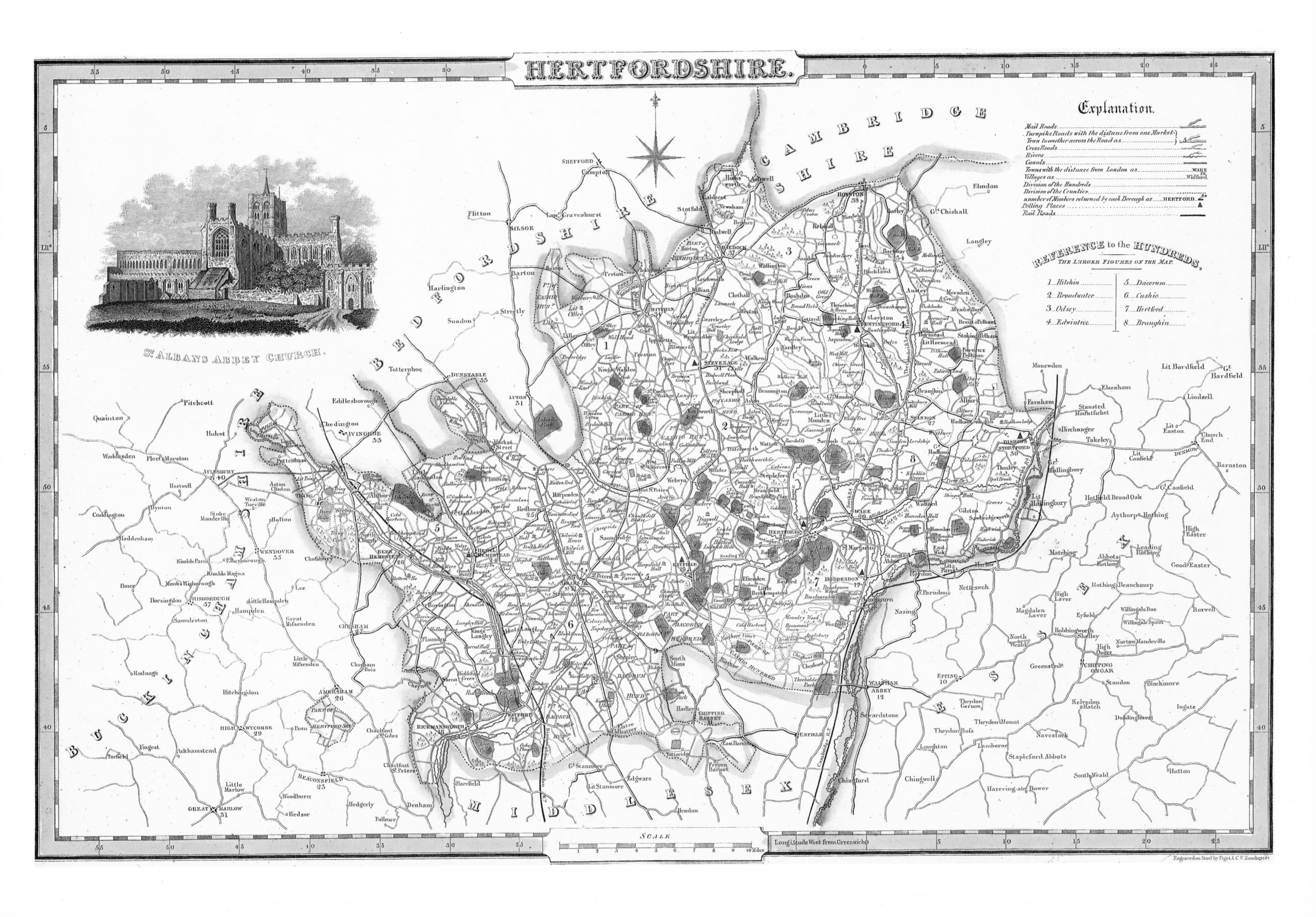

St. ALBANS ABBEY CHURCH.

HUNTINGDONSHIRE.

HUNTINGDON is an inland county, being bounded on the north by the counties of Northampton and Cambridge, on the east by Cambridgeshire, on the south by Bedfordshire, and on the west by Bedfordshire and Northamptonshire. In its general form it is an irregular square; in extent from north to south about thirty miles, from east to west twenty-three, its circumference about one hundred, and its area including 370 square miles. The limits of this county are chiefly artificial; the river Nene on the Northamptonshire border, with the Kings-delf, the Old West water and the Ouse river on the Cambridgeshire side, being the principal exceptions.

NAME and ANCIENT HISTORY.—This county takes its name from Huntingdon, its principal town, which is derived from the Saxon word *Huntedunscire*, signifying 'Hunter's Down-shire,'—this district being at that time well adapted for the sport of hunting, as it was almost one continued forest. Under the Britons this county composed a part of the extensive territory of the *Icenii*, and in the Roman division of the kingdom was included in the district named FLAVIA CÆSARIENSIS. The *Icenii* are represented by Tacitus as a brave nation; but they were subdued by the Romans in the time of Claudius, and obliged to submit to the harsh terms dictated by their conquerors. The death of Prasutagus, their King, and the impolitic arrangements of his will, by which he appointed the Emperor Nero his heir (thinking thereby to secure his kingdom from ruin), furnished the Romans with a pretext for coercive measures; and, with the most insulting rapacity, the native Chiefs were deprived of their estates—the whole kingdom of the *Icenii* was pillaged by the centurions, and the house of Prasutagus by their slaves, as if it had been taken in war; his widow, the noble Boadicea, was ignominiously scourged, and her daughters were violated by the Roman soldiers: the nation, justly inflamed to vengeance by such atrocities, flew to arms, and upwards of eighty thousand of the Romans were cut off by the intrepidity of Boadicea: success, however, did not long gild the arms of the Britons, for in a sanguinary contest the Romans obtained a complete victory over them, and the *Icenii* were unknown after this time as a separate nation; according to Tacitus, Queen Boadicea put an end to her life by poison. At the present day, the principal towns of this county are seated on the Ouse; of these, Huntingdon is the capital. At Ramsey, on the edge of the fens, was formerly a very rich Abbey, built, like that of Crowland, in the midst of a bog: the situation of these and various other religious houses (as those of Ely and Thorney) was probably chosen as well with a view to security, from the difficulty of approach, as to the plenty of fish and water-fowl inhabiting these watery retreats. Kimbolton Castle, in this county, was the place where Katherine, the divorced wife of Henry VIII, ended her days in a peaceful retirement. Huntingdon was the birth-place of Cromwell, and in the free grammar-school of that town he received his education.

SOIL, PRODUCE and CLIMATE.—The soil of this county is in general fertile, though it varies much. The east and south-east parts are of a shallow staple upon lime-stone rock, with a small intermixture of cold woodland clayey soil; the other parts of the county, however, are made up of a strong loam of red land, and of a cold woodland clay; the red land is a rich sandy loam, intermixed with keal,—iron-stone is also found amongst it; this soil is esteemed most fertile: the under stratum of the whole county, at different depths, is a very strong blue clay. From the varieties of soil here mentioned, and part of the county being enclosed and part open fields, different modes of culture are necessarily employed. The borders of the Ouse, along the south-east part of the county, consist of most fertile and beautiful meadows, of which Portsholme Mead, near Huntingdon, is particularly celebrated; the middle and western parts are fruitful in corn, and sprinkled with woods; the north-east part is composed of fens, joining those of Ely,—the fens consist of about 44,000 acres; the skirty lands bordering on them afford luxuriant grazing. The mode of management of the fen lands has been much improved of late years, and the fen men are the most expert of any in the world at ploughing. The breed of sheep is of a mixed description, nearly approaching to the Leicestershire and Lincolnshire species, with which the native breeds have been much crossed; the neat cattle are the refuse of the Lancashire, Leicestershire, and Derbyshire breeds. From the open state of the country, dairy farming is not much followed; and in the southern district the cows are used for suckling calves, to supply the London markets. The village of Stilton gives name to a very rich and delicate kind of cheese—which, however, is said *not* to be the product of its neighbourhood, but that of Melton Mowbray, in Leicestershire. No MANUFACTURES are carried on in this county, and hardly any thing bearing a reference to them, except wool-stapling and spinning the yarn: the latter is the chief business of the women and children in the winter season; in the summer they seek a more profitable employ in the fields. The brewing trade furnishes another means of employment, though to no great extent, the produce being wholly for home consumption. The CLIMATE is regarded as very healthy, considering the space occupied by the fens, and that many parts of the county are but badly supplied with pure waters, from springs or rivers.

RIVERS, &c.—The principal rivers connected with Huntingdonshire are the OUSE and the NENE (or Nen). The Ouse, which is sometimes called the Lesser Ouse, to distinguish it from another river of the same name in Yorkshire, enters the county from Bedfordshire, between St. Neots and Little Paxton; and in its course is increased by a combination of small streams from the north-west, and finally enters the Great Level of the Fens in the neighbourhood of Earith: this river is navigable along its whole line across the county. The Nene rises in Northamptonshire, and, flowing through a delightful vale, reaches Huntingdonshire near Elton, passes Yarwell and Wandsford, and, pursuing a devious course to Peterborough, slowly winds onward to the sea. Some smaller streams water the north-east side of the county, together with several large Meres, or pools of water, namely, Whittlesea Mere, Ramsey Mere, Ugg Mere, &c.: of these, the first-named lake or pool is by far the largest, and covers an area of several miles extent; it admits of agreeable sailing, and affords excellent fishing, and is in the summer season much frequented by parties of pleasure.

CIVIL and ECCLESIASTICAL DIVISIONS.—Huntingdonshire is in the Province of Canterbury and Diocese of Lincoln, and is included in the Norfolk Circuit. It is divided into the four hundreds of HURSTINGSTONE, LEIGHTONSTONE, NORMAN CROSS and TOSELAND; these are subdivided into 103 parishes, containing one county town and borough (Huntingdon), and five other market towns. The whole county returns four members to Parliament, viz. two for HUNTINGDON and two for the SHIRE.

POPULATION.—According to the census of 1821, there were houses inhabited in the county, 8,879; uninhabited, 168; and houses building, 46. The number of families then resident in the county was 10,397, comprising 24,020 males, and 24,751 females; total, 48,771: and by a calculation made by order of government, which included persons in the army and navy, for which was added after the ratio of about one to thirty prior to the year 1811, and one to fifty for that year and the census of 1821, to the returns made from the several districts; the population of the county, in round numbers, in the year 1700, was 34,700—in 1750, 32,500—in 1801, 38,800—in 1811, 43,700—and in 1821, 49,800. The increased population, from the year 1700 to 1801, was 4,100—from 1801 to 1811, the increase was 4,900—and from 1811 to 1821, the augmented number of persons was 6,100: the grand total increase in the population of the county, from the year 1700 to the census of 1821, being about 15,100 persons. *** Between the years 1700 and 1750, there occurred a *decrease* in the population of this county of 2,200 persons.

Index of Distances from Town to Town in the County of Huntingdon.

THE NAMES OF THE RESPECTIVE TOWNS ARE ON THE TOP AND SIDE, AND THE SQUARE WHERE BOTH MEET GIVES THE DISTANCE.

	Huntingdon	Kimbolton	Ramsey	St. Ives	St. Neots	Somersham	Warboys	Yaxley	*Distance from London.*
Huntingdon									59
Kimbolton	12								63
Ramsey	12	21							71
St. Ives	6	14	9						59
St. Neots	9	8	19	14					56
Somersham	10	22	9	5	18				64
Warboys	8	19	4	6	17	4			69
Yaxley	14	23	12	20	22	21	16		73

[*See over.*

Additional information relating to the County of HUNTINGDON.

———ooo———

POPULATION.—By the Census for **1831** this county contained 26,365 males, and 26,784 females—total 53,149, being an increase, since the returns made in the year 1821, of 4,378 inhabitants; and from the Census of 1801 to that of 1831 the augmentation amounted to 15,581 persons.

REPRESENTATION.—The number of representatives remains the same as before the passing of the *Reform Bill.* The election of members for the county is held at HUNTINGDON; and besides that town the polling takes place at STILTON.

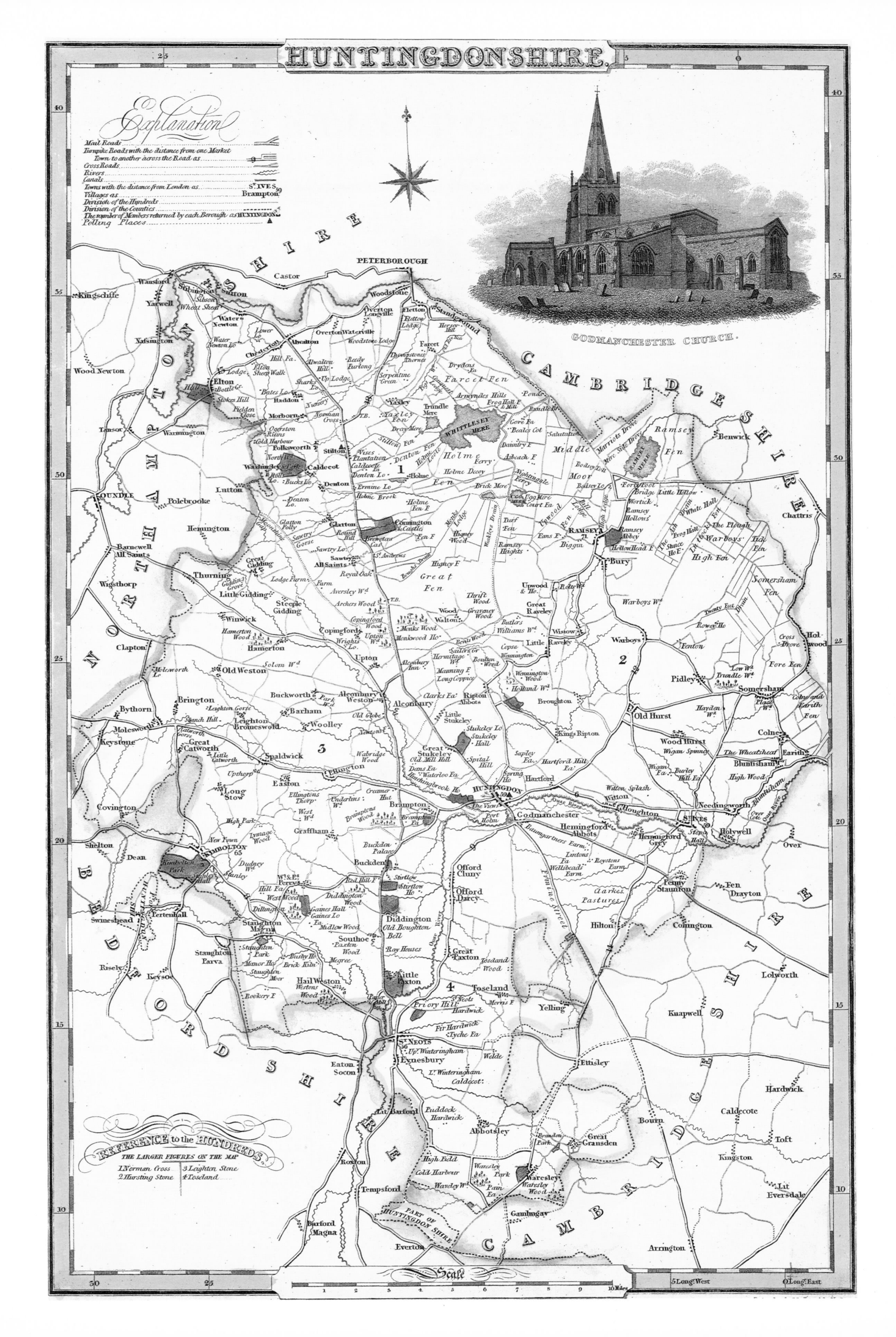
HUNTINGDONSHIRE.
Explanation
Mail Roads
Turnpike Roads with the distance from one Market Town to another across the Road as
Cross Roads
Rivers
Canals
Towns with the distance from London as St. IVES 59
Villages as Brampton
Division of the Hundreds
Division of the Counties
The number of Members returned by each Borough as HUNTINGDON
Polling Places
GODMANCHESTER CHURCH.
REFERENCE to the HUNDREDS
THE LARGER FIGURES ON THE MAP
1 Norman Cross
2 Hursting Stone
3 Leighton Stone
4 Toseland
Scale
5 Long. West
0 Long. East
NORTHAMPTONSHIRE
CAMBRIDGESHIRE
BEDFORDSHIRE
PETERBOROUGH
WHITTLESEY MERE
HUNTINGDON
KIMBOLTON
St. NEOTS
St. IVES
RAMSEY
Godmanchester
PART OF HUNTINGDON SHIRE

KENT.

KENT is a maritime county, and one of the most beautiful districts in this Island; it includes within its boundaries numerous objects replete with interest, and towns of high importance, magnitude and beauty. It is situated on the south-east extremity of Great Britain, opposite to France, from which it is distant (at its nearest point, Dover,) about twenty-four miles. Its figure is irregular, but approaches more to the trapezium than to any other. On the north it is bounded by the river Thames; on the east and part of the south sides it opens to the German Ocean and British Channel; on the remainder of the south side it is skirted by Sussex, and on the west by Surrey. It is about sixty-three miles in length from east to west (*i. e.* from the North Foreland to Deptford); and in breadth, from the point of Dungeness to the North Foreland, near forty miles; while from the central sides, it is not more than twenty-five wide. The ambit of the county is about one hundred and seventy-four miles, and its area comprises about 1,537 square miles.

NAME and ANCIENT HISTORY.—Camden observes: 'Time has not yet deprived this county of its ancient name. Cæsar, Strabo, Diodorus Siculus, Ptolemy, and others, call it CANTIUM; and the Saxons, according to Nennius, named it *Cant-guar-lantd*, which signifies *the country of the inhabitants of Kent*.' Others are of opinion that the name Kent is derived from the word '*Cainc*,' which in the British tongue signifies a *green leaf*, and was applied to this county on account of its having been formerly much shaded with woods: this is Mr. Lambard's opinion. Another learned etymologist agrees that '*Cainc*' or '*Caint*' is a British word, but insists that it is descriptive of *a country abounding in open downs*, which is the general characteristic of Kent. In Domesday Book the name of the county is written '*Chenth*.' The EARLY HISTORY of Kent involves some occurrences of high importance in the annals of the Island at large:—JULIUS CÆSAR, in the 699th year after the foundation of Rome, and fifty-five years before the birth of Christ, embarked his forces at Boulogne, and succeeded in effecting a landing near the present town of Deal, after an ineffectual opposition on the part of the Britons, who were routed. Cæsar afterwards concluded a peace with the natives, and returned in safety to the Continent. In the ensuing year, however, he returned, and with a greatly augmented force invaded the Island; he was met by the intrepid Cassievellaunus, who was invested by the natives with the chief command: after many engagements, and much bloodshed, several of the British States submitted to Cæsar, who afterwards attacked the chief town of Cassievellaunus (Verulam), and took it; when, obtaining hostages, and appointing an annual tribute to be paid by Britain, he led off his army and prisoners at two embarkations, and returned to the Continent. About ninety years after Cæsar's second invasion, the Romans, under Aulus Plautius, then Prætor in Gaul, landed in the country without opposition, on the Kent side of the Thames, where he waited the arrival of the Emperor Claudius with a considerable army,—when they together attacked the courageous, but undisciplined and unfortunate Britons, and defeated them with great slaughter. After this event, the Roman power was speedily established on a firm basis, and the southern part of Britain was included by Constantine in the division called BRITANNIA PRIMA. During the Saxon Heptarchy (of which Kent was the earliest kingdom), under the government of Egbert, it became part of the West Saxon State, and so continued until the general union of the different petty Monarchies beneath the English Crown. To the honour of this county it is mentioned, that its inhabitants were the first in England that became converts to Christianity; and by their courage and resolution retained many privileges, which the inhabitants of every other county lost, under William the Conqueror: the 'Men of Kent,' it is related, concealed by boughs of trees, met this Prince at Swanescombe, near Gravesend, and demanded and obtained the confirmation of all their rights and privileges,—particularly a tenure called *Gavel-kind*, amongst the provisions of which is one, that though the ancestor be convicted of felony or murder, the heirs shall enjoy his inheritance; hence the Kentish proverb, 'The father to the bough, and the son to the plough.'—The City of Canterbury is the principal town of Kent, and is distinguished by being the Metropolitan See of all England. Its ample and noble Cathedral has been the burial-place of many of our Kings and Princes, among whom were Henry IV., and the Black Prince; at one of its altars was murdered that turbulent and ambitious priest, the Archbishop Thomas-á-Becket. The town of Dover, which presents the nearest point of communication with France, is a bustling sea-port, and is famous for its ancient castle, perched on the summit of a stupendous cliff, that 'looks fearfully on the confused deep.' Five miles from Deal, and opposite to that town, are the dangerous Goodwin Sands; and here is the famous road for shipping, so well known over all the trading world by the name of THE DOWNS. Greenwich, a considerable town, is distinguished by its Royal Park and Observatory, and still more by its noble Hospital for maimed and decayed seamen. Several of our Monarchs, and among them Queen Elizabeth, were born in the Palace formerly situated here.

SOIL and CLIMATE, PRODUCE and MANUFACTURES.—The general aspect of Kent is very beautiful, arising from the inequality of the surface, the diversity of the scenery, and the variety of the verdure; the whole county, excepting the marshes and the Weald, is a general cluster of small hills. A great variety of soils are found in the county: its whole north side is composed chiefly of chalk and flints, as well as a large tract on the east coast; in the southern part, iron-stone and rag-stone prevail; and more westerly, clay and gravel. The Isle of Thanet is in a very high state of cultivation, and of remarkable fertility; and its soil, originally a light mould on a chalky bottom, has been greatly improved by the inexhaustible store of manure supplied by the sea. The soil of the Marshes is a stiff clay, mixed with sea-sand and small shells; the marsh lands are principally appropriated to the fattening of sheep and cattle. The upland farms of East Kent comprise different soils, of which the most prevalent are, chalk, loam, cledge, hazel mould and stiff clay: the sheep and cattle of this district are similar to those of the Isle of Thanet, namely, the former of the Romney Marsh breed, the latter mostly of the Welch kinds. The hop grounds are very extensive throughout many parts of the county, particularly in the vicinity of Canterbury, Faversham and Maidstone: the Canterbury hops are much esteemed for their strength, and the produce of the plantations all the way to Sandwich is in high repute. Besides hops, the neighbourhood of Maidstone is celebrated for its apples, cherries and filberts. In the Isle of Shepey, now as in former times, sheep are fed in great numbers in the marshes. The upland district of West Kent produces considerable quantities of timber and underwood; and on the borders of the Weald, and confines of Surrey, hops and fruit, with corn and grass, are yielded in abundance—also much timber and coppice wood. The Weald of Kent is a remarkable and considerable tract, stretching along the south side of the county from Romney Marsh to Surrey; when viewed from the adjoining hills, which command the whole extent, it exhibits a most delightful landscape, interspersed with small eminences, highly cultivated, and animated by farm houses, seats and villages, promiscuously scattered among towering oaks and other trees: the soil is principally clay, with a substratum of marl. Romney Marsh is an extensive level tract, and with Guildford Marsh, Denge Marsh, and Welland Marsh, is almost entirely appropriated to the grazing and fattening of the sheep and cattle: the marsh is defended against the violence and encroachments of the sea by an immense wall of earth, of vast strength, called 'Dunchurch Wall.' CLIMATE.— The proximity of the German Ocean and British Channel renders this county subject to cold sea-winds, which, however bracing and salutary to the animal system, are often injurious to vegetable produce, when in an infant and tender state: the prevailing winds come from the north-east and south-west; the former frequently sets in for a considerable length of time, and the air is then exceedingly keen and sharp. The south-west district is more enclosed than any other, and is the warmest part of the county—The MANUFACTURES of Kent, at one period, were of greater extent and importance than of late years. The clothing trade, which once gave employment to great numbers of its inhabitants, is now nearly forgotten in the county: at Canterbury, muslins, brocaded silks, and stockings were made; but these branches have nearly sunk into oblivion, from the variability of fashion in silks, and the migration of the others to places more distant from the Metropolis. Brawn is an article of delicacy for which Canterbury has long been, and still is celebrated. At Dartford and Crayford are iron-works; and at the latter place are extensive works for printing calicoes, and spacious bleaching grounds. At Seven Oaks are large silk-mills; and near Maidstone, and other places, paper is manufactured: the distilleries for producing the spirit called 'Maidstone Gin,' established in that town, were until of late years on a scale of great extent. The various dock-yards at Deptford, Woolwich, Chatham, &c., give employment to numerous artizans in all the different branches of naval affairs; and ship-building, sail and rope making, are carried on at other places on the sea-coast. Copperas and salt works are established at several places in the county; gunpowder is manufactured for Government near Faversham; and a beautiful kind of ornamental and toy ware, of wood, called Tonbridge ware, is made at that town. The dredging for and exportation of oysters form a profitable occupation to many persons in this county; the fish procured at Faversham and Milton are especially esteemed.

RIVERS.—The principal rivers of this county are, the THAMES, the MEDWAY, the GREATER and LESSER STOURE, the ROTHER, the DARENT, the CRAY and the RAVENSBOURNE. The Thames (the *Tamesis* of Cæsar) passes the town and Royal Hospital of Greenwich, flowing on in a bold sweep to Woolwich: between Erith and Long Reach it receives the united waters of the Cray and the Darent; and rolling onward in a semicircular course, flows between Tilbury and Gravesend, in a broad stream, nearly a mile over; thence it winds through the channel called the Hope, still increasing in width as it proceeds; and, opening due east, passes the Isle of Graine, and flows into the German ocean at the Nore, where it also mingles its stream with that of the river Medway. The Medway is formed by four streams, only one of which rises in this county: it flows through a beautiful country on towards Tonbridge (to which town it was made navigable, under an Act passed in 1740); it afterwards becomes considerably increased by other streams, and passing Rochester, Chatham, Upnor Castle and Gillingham Fort, at length enters the Thames between the Isles of Graine and Shepey. The Greater Stoure passes by Ashford, Wye and Canterbury; and proceeding to the Isle of Thanet, is joined by the Lesser Stoure; and thus increased continues its course to Sandwich, and falls into the British Channel at Pepperness. The Lesser Stoure, previous to its junction with the other Stoure, skirts Barham Downs, and passes through a beautiful country in a line nearly parallel with the latter stream. The Rother rises in Sussex, and is a boundary river of this county below Sandhurst; it empties its waters into Rye harbour. The Darent rises near Westerham; and after visiting several villages in its way to Dartford, and thence proceeding under the new appellation of Dartford Creek, and being increased by the Cray, flows onward to the Thames, which it enters at Long Reach. The Cray rises at Newell, gives name to St. Mary's Cray, Paul's Cray, Foot's Cray, North Cray, and Crayford, and falls into Dartford Creek. The Ravensbourne rises on Keston Downs, and, receiving in its progress several smaller streams, becomes navigable at Deptford, and shortly afterwards falls into the Thames.

CIVIL and ECCLESIASTICAL DIVISIONS.—Kent is in the Province of Canterbury, and the ecclesiastical jurisdiction is divided between the Archbishop of Canterbury and the Bishop of Rochester,—the former having eleven Deaneries belonging to it, and the latter four. For local purposes this county has been long divided into the two districts of East and West Kent: these together contain the five Lathes of AYLESFORD, ST. AUGUSTINE, SCRAY, SHEPWAY and SUTTON-AT-HONE; which are subdivided into sixty-two hundreds, and the Liberties of ROMNEY MARSH, and the ISLE OF SHEPEY, and the FRANCHISE AND BARONY OF BIRCHOLT. The entire county contains 411 parishes, two Cities (Canterbury and Rochester), one county town (Maidstone), and twenty-nine other market towns. The towns of Dover, New Romney, Hythe and Sandwich form members of the CINQUE PORTS,—a term bestowed on the *five* Havens that were formerly of the greatest importance among those which lie opposite to the coast of France. The original Cinque Ports were Hastings, Sandwich, Dover, Romney, and Hythe; to these have been added two other towns, Rye and Winchelsea. The freemen of the Cinque Ports are styled Barons; and in former times they enjoyed superior dignity, and had rank among the Nobility of the Kingdom: they are governed by a Lord Warden, who is also Constable of Dover Castle. Kent returns ten Representatives to the British Parliament, namely, two each for the Cities of CANTERBURY and ROCHESTER, two each for the Boroughs of MAIDSTONE and QUEENBORO', and two for the COUNTY.

POPULATION.—According to the census of 1821, there were houses inhabited in the county, 70,507; uninhabited, 3,186; and houses building, 511. The number of families then resident in the county was 85,939; comprising 209,833 males, and 216,183 females; total, 426,016: and by a calculation made by order of Government, which included persons in the army and navy, for which was added after the ratio of about one to thirty prior to the year 1811, and one to fifty for that year and the census of 1821, to the returns made from the several districts; the population of the county, in round numbers, in the year 1700, was 153,800—in 1750, 190,000—in 1801, 317,800—in 1811, 385,600—and in 1821, 434,600. The increased population in the 50 years, from the year 1700, was 36,200—from 1750 to 1801, the increase was 127,800—from 1801 to 1811, the increase was 67,800—and from 1811 to 1821, the augmented number of persons was 49,000: the grand total increase in the population of the county from the year 1700 to the census of 1821, being about 280,800 persons.

[*Table of Distances—see over.*]

Index of Distances from Town to Town in the County of Kent.

THE NAMES OF THE RESPECTIVE TOWNS ARE ON THE TOP AND SIDE, AND THE SQUARE WHERE BOTH MEET GIVES THE DISTANCE.

Town	Ashford	Bromley	Canterbury	Chatham	Cranbrook	Dartford	Deal	Deptford	Dover	Faversham	Folkestone	Gravesend	Greenwich	Hythe	Maidstone	Margate	Milton	Queenborough	Ramsgate	Rochester	Sandwich	Sheerness	Tenterden	Tunbridge	Distance from London.
Ashford																									54
Bromley	45																								10
Canterbury	15	51																							56
Chatham	27	28	25																						30
Cranbrook	19	39	32	24																					49
Dartford	41	12	41	16	36																				15
Deal	32	69	18	43	50	57																			72
Deptford	50	6	52	26	45	11	68																		4
Dover	23	68	16	41	39	56	9	67																	71
Faversham	14	42	9	16	26	32	26	43	24																47
Folkestone	16	65	16	41	35	56	16	67	7	24															71
Gravesend	36	20	33	8	31	7	50	18	49	25	50														22
Greenwich	49	6	51	25	45	10	68	1	67	42	67	17													5
Hythe	12	56	17	40	32	52	20	63	11	25	4	48	62												67
Maidstone	20	29	27	10	14	22	45	31	42	18	36	17	30	32											35
Margate	31	68	16	41	48	58	14	68	21	25	29	50	68	34	43										72
Milton	21	39	17	10	24	25	35	36	31	8	31	18	35	33	10	32									40
Queenborough	28	41	24	15	31	30	43	43	39	15	39	25	42	40	17	40	7								47
Ramsgate	31	67	17	42	48	58	12	69	20	26	27	50	68	31	43	4	33	40							73
Rochester	28	25	26	1	22	14	44	25	42	18	42	8	24	40	9	42	11	16	43						29
Sandwich	28	64	13	28	46	53	6	64	13	21	20	46	63	24	40	9	29	36	7	38					68
Sheerness	32	46	27	18	36	33	45	47	32	18	43	27	46	43	21	43	11	4	44	19	44				51
Tenterden	12	47	26	29	7	40	44	51	35	24	27	36	51	22	19	42	25	32	43	28	39	36			56
Tunbridge	34	20	41	24	19	17	59	26	56	31	50	26	26	46	14	57	24	31	57	22	53	34	27		30
Woolwich	51	7	49	24	45	8	67	4	63	40	66	15	3	63	31	63	32	39	65	23	61	42	49	27	8

Additional information relating to the County of Kent.

—ooo—

POPULATION.—By the Census for **1831** this county contained 234,572 males, and 244,583 females—total 479,155, being an increase, since the returns made in the year 1821, of 53,139 inhabitants; and from the Census of 1801 to that of 1831 the augmentation amounted to 171,531 persons.

REPRESENTATION.—By the *Reform Bill* the boroughs of NEW ROMNEY and QUEENBOROUGH have been disfranchised, and HYTHE has been deprived of one of its members. The towns of CHATHAM and GREENWICH, by the same Act, have had the right of representation conferred upon them: the former sends one member and the latter two; two additional members have been given to the county, so that Kent altogether returns *eighteen* representatives to Parliament, the same number as before the passing of the Bill. (The number (*ten* representatives) mentioned in the annexed account, is exclusive of those sent for the cinque port towns of Dover, New Romney, Hythe, and Sandwich, each of which sent two before the Reform Bill passed into law.) The new *Boundary Act* divides the county into two parts, respectively named the *Eastern Division* and the *Western Division:* the former comprises the lathes of St. Augustine and Shepway, including the liberty of Romney Marsh, and the upper division of the lathe of Scray; and the western division includes the lathes of Sutton-at-Hone and Aylesford, and the lower division of the lathe of Scray. The election of members for the eastern division is held at CANTERBURY, and for the western at MAIDSTONE: besides the place of election the eastern division polls at SITTINGBOURNE, ASHFORD, NEW ROMNEY, and RAMSGATE; and the western (besides the place of election) polls at BROMLEY, BLACKHEATH, GRAVESEND, TONBRIDGE, and CRANBROOK.

RAILWAYS.

The GREENWICH RAILWAY commences from its station at the foot of London Bridge, on the Surrey side: it was opened from *London Bridge* to *Deptford* on December 14th, 1836—and throughout, to the High-street, *Greenwich,* on the 24th December, 1838; the line is lighted with gas, and its appearance from the Old Kent road is truly brilliant. The SOUTH EASTERN opens a communication between the *Metropolis* and *Dover:* the line starts from the same station as the Greenwich (at *London Bridge*), passes *Edenbridge, Leigh, Tonbridge, Tudely, Marden, Staplehurst, Hedcorn, Ashford, Mersham, Standford* and *Folkestone:* from the last-named place it traverses the Under-Cliff, and after passing through two tunnels and a gallery, and desecrating Shakspeare Cliff, it descends to the brink of *Dover Harbour,* in a total distance of 85½ miles from London. Other lines have been projected to pass through the county by the route of Rochester, or Chatham, Faversham, Canterbury and Sandwich, and thence to Dover.

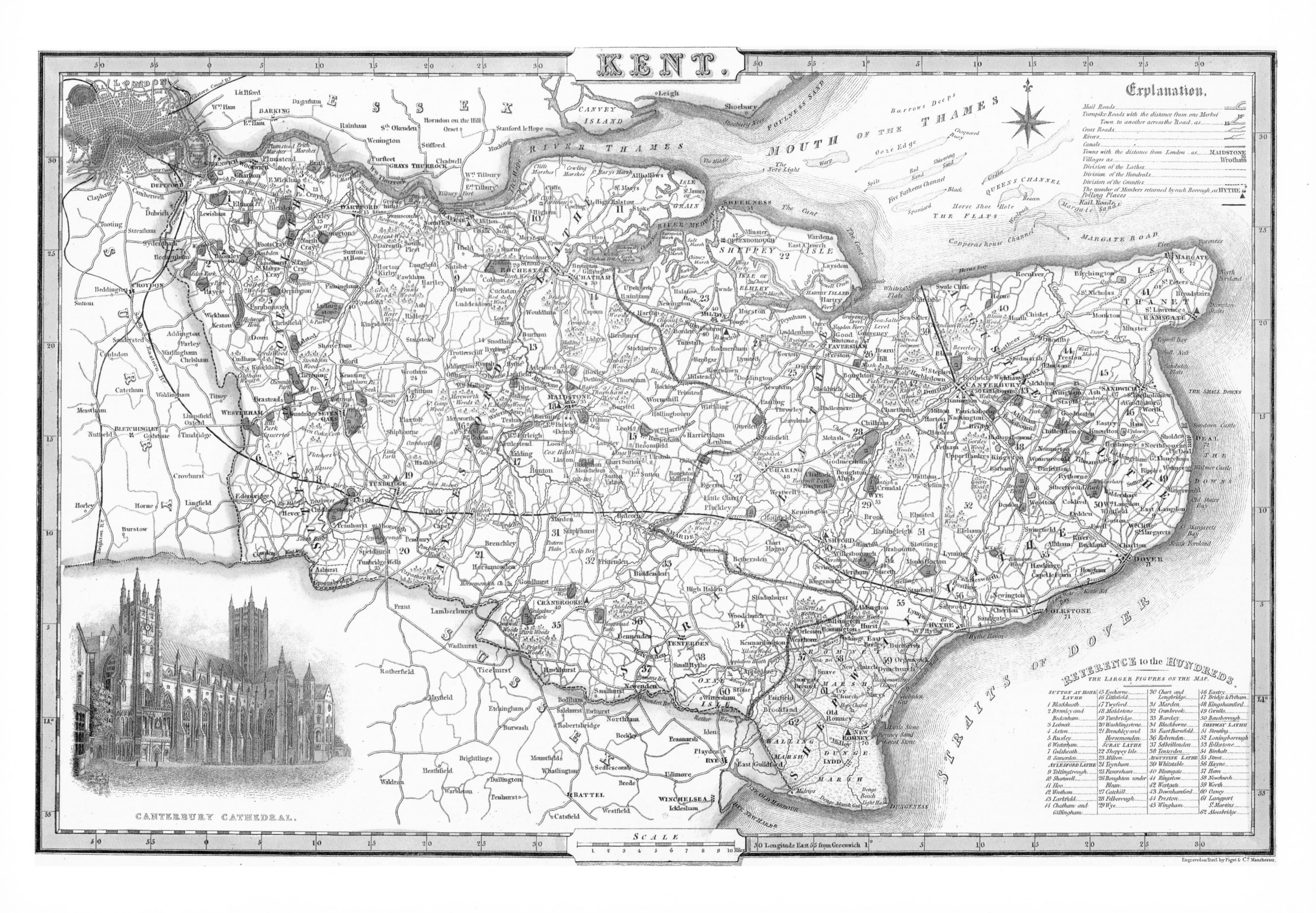

CANTERBURY CATHEDRAL.

LANCASHIRE.

LANCASHIRE, a palatine and maritime county—in consequence eminently conspicuous as regards manufactures and population, and of immeasurable importance in its value to the revenue of this Kingdom—is between 53° 20′ and 54° 25′ north latitude, and between 2° 0′ and 3° 17′ west longitude. It is bounded on the north by Cumberland and Westmoreland, on the east by Yorkshire, on the south by Cheshire and Derbyshire, and on the west by the Irish Sea. Its extreme length from north to south (including a detached hundred called Furness, which is separated on the north-west by a creek at the head of Morecambe Bay) is seventy-four miles; and its greatest breadth, which is at the southern end, about forty-five: its circumference is about 240 miles, and its area comprises 1,831 square miles.

NAME and ANCIENT HISTORY.—In the ancient history of this county we find that it was originally inhabited by the *Setantii*, or *Segantii*,—signifying 'a people dwelling in the country of the waters;' they were succeeded by the *Brigantes*, who also had a very extended tract of country. The whole of this county was denominated by the Romans, BRITANNIA SUPERIOR. The Saxons included it in Northumbria, and formed it into a separate county about 680, soon after the conquest of it by Egfrid: at this period the Roman *Alauna* (the site of which is doubtful,) was made the metropolis of the shire, and lent its appellation to the county. Soon after the introduction of Christianity, this county, along with others of the Kingdom, was divided into parishes; and about this period religious festivals were instituted by the priests, which commenced on the evening of the day dedicated to the patron saint, and hence obtained the appellation of *wakes*, which are still continued in many parts of the county, and even tolerated on the Sabbath, although the offices of religion have long ceased to form any part of the ceremonies attendant upon these popular assemblages. Previous to, and under the Norman Dynasty, this county was distinguished as an *Honour*, and was of the superior class of seigniories. The first Earl of Lancaster was Edmund Crouchback, youngest son of Henry III. In the time of the valiant John of Gaunt, fourth son of Edward, the county of Lancaster was advanced to the dignity of a Palatinate, by a Royal patent: it confers the title of Duke of Lancaster on the King, and many other high titles are derived by Nobility from this county. Lancashire has been, at a great variety of periods in history, the scene of contention and theatre of strife; and turbulent faction has at times reared its discontented head. The sanguinary conflicts between the houses of York and Lancaster, and the Royal forces of Charles I. and those of the Parliament under Cromwell, as well as the support which the Pretender received from the disaffected, have stained the fields of this county with blood: the battle of Flodden Field, of more early date, gave testimony to the prowess of the men of Lancashire, and the achievements of the heroic bowmen and billmen, from the several districts of Warrington, Wigan, Rochdale, Preston, Blackburn, Bolton, &c. A very extraordinary page in Lancashire history must not be omitted—*the Lancashire Witches:* these personages, who, in former times, used to infatuate and strike terror into the weak, are now, in these more enlightened days, deprived of the latter power, *but possess the former undiminished*, and exercise it uncontrolled over all classes, the strongest at times owning its sway; yet so little is their influence dreaded or abhorred, that the term, once opprobrious, is now adopted to express admiration. But, to go back to the age when the intellects of many individuals were darkened by this most preposterous superstition, to which even the Legislature lent its countenance, and the Judicial tribunals offered up victims,—the case of Ferdinand, fifth Earl of Derby, affords one of the most striking, and best authenticated instances on record, of the power which this delusion exercised over the mind:—On the 5th of April, 1594, he was seized with mortal sickness, (produced, probably, by poison, secretly administered,) and, after suffering great torture, he died on the 12th of the same month; he frequently cried out that the doctors laboured in vain, *because he was certainly bewitched*. In the same year, the Rev. John Darrell was an actor in this system of imposition, and a believer in the doctrine of the possession and dispossession of demoniacs; and one Hartley was executed for practising magic. In 1612 the belief in witchcraft continued to exist; and *nineteen notorious witches* were arraigned and tried at Lancaster assizes, on the 6th of August of that year; but it does not appear that any of them suffered. In 1633 other cases of demoniac agency became cognizable; and so much importance did they assume, that Charles I. in person, and his physicians, judged one of the cases; when the accused were set at liberty,—not from the discretion of the King or cunning of the council, but from the discrepancy of the witnesses, and the appearance of the fact of subornation upon the part of some of them. These are only a few of the numerous instances of fraud and credulity which exhibited themselves in this county, age after age, under the absurd delusion of witchcraft and demonology. Happily our criminal code has been freed from the reproach which once attached to it, by the removal of all the statutes relating to witchcraft.

SOIL, AGRICULTURE and CLIMATE.—The soil of Lancashire appears under several distinct heads. In Lonsdale, on the borders of the sea, it is perhaps less productive than most other parts, being of a sandy marsh nature. The elevated part of the hills is in general moory, heathy and rocky; the flat tracts are chiefly described as loam or clay,—gravel and peat being found, in various proportions, in all. The principal surface distinctions of soil are heath, moor, holme loam, clay, sand, and moss or peat; and the under strata are rock of differeut kinds, as grit or free-stone, blue-stone, lime-stone, fossil, coal, clay, marl, gravel and sand: the free-stone is of three kinds—yellow, white and red. The finest district in the county, both for situation and quality of land, is in the whole space between the Mersey and the Ribble, and between the sea-coast and the first risings of the high hills to the east. The rich grain land, called the Fylde, commences on the north bank of the Ribble, and stretches out to the south bank of the Lune. The soil of the northern part of the county is chiefly dry; the more high and mountainous tracts being principally occupied by sheep, while the various declivities and vallies in which they terminate are used for grazing. Grass land is the most prevalent in the vicinity of towns; northward, the dairy is frequently the main object; and the Fylde, the Lune, and the Low Furness districts, are those principally appropriated to the growth of grain. The principal mountains in this county are, Coniston Fell, in Furness, the highest part of which is 2,577 feet; Pendle Hill, overlooking Clithero, is 1,803 feet; Bleasdale Forest is 1,709 feet; and Rivington Pike is 1,545 feet, each above the level of the sea. The other considerable elevations are, Caton Moor, Woolfell Crag, Padiham Heights, Longridge Fell, Go Hill, Belling Hill, Hambleton Hill, Cartmel Fells and Gragrith Fell, with the ridge called Blacktone Edge, which forms the south-east boundary of the county. It is a fact worthy of remark in the annals of husbandry, that the first potatoes raised in England were grown in this county; and it is still famous for producing and cooking that valuable root.—The CLIMATE of Lancashire is humid, yet is the air generally pure and salubrious. On the north and eastern boundaries, in the elevated regions, it is of course cold and piercing; but in the lower districts, towards the south and west, it is in general mild and genial: and although the occupations of a great body of the inhabitants in the manufacturing districts may be supposed to be unfavourable to health, such is the influence of the climate, that as many old people are found in this county, in proportion to the number of inhabitants, as in most other parts of the Kingdom. With regard also to the popular error, of the county being singular as a depository of excessive rains, this is capable of the most palpable refutation, by reference to the meteorological observations of the average quantity of rain fallen in many other districts of England.

MINES and MINERALS.—The most productive and extensive of the mineralogical productions of this county is COAL, the most important of all minerals to a manufacturing community. The southern part of the county presents a very extensive coal field, furnishing an abundant supply of fuel to the manufacturing districts: its boundary may be described by a line drawn from the junction of the rivers Tame and Mersey, near Stockport, northwards towards Middleton, west of Oldham, and thence in a westerly direction to the south of Prescot, on N.W. to Ormskirk, and N.E. to Colne, on the border of Yorkshire. This valuable mineral is found more abundantly in the vicinity of Wigan, Prescot, Newton, Bolton and Oldham, than in the other parts. The principal beds on the eastern side of this grand depository are about six feet in thickness: they extend from the vicinity of Oldham to Rochdale and Bury,—but their continuity is broken by *faults*, and by deep vallies; and the general strata of Lancashire are more irregular, both in their dip and position, than those of Yorkshire. Near Wigan is obtained a beautiful species of coal, in appearance similar to black marble, of a very bituminous quality, known by the name of cannel coal. On the western and southern sides of the county are found marl and sand-stone; millstone grit is found between Colne and Blackburn, and other places; metalliferous lime-stone is the substratum between Lancaster and Kirkby Lonsdale. The mountains of Furness have valuable roofing slate and lime-stone; and near Ulverstone is produced a peculiar ore of iron, yielding the best and most ductile description of that metal, suited to the purpose of wire-drawers.

MANUFACTURES.—Under this head, unless many pages were devoted to it, justice could not be done to the vast subject; this work can only glide upon the surface, without entering into the depths of those materials, which have excited the ingenuity and contributed to the wealth of the inhabitants of Lancashire, and placed their county in so proudly prominent a position amongst the counties of England. Lancashire has prospered by all fabrics produced from the fleece, the labours of the silk-worm, and the culture of flax,—but more especially by the never-failing bounty of the cotton tree. The earth, abounding with a mineral essentially necessary to the consummation of the various works of the loom, has yielded up her riches to aid the industry of the artizan, and facilitate his labours. The cotton trade forms the staple of the county, in the manufacture of which, till the middle of the 18th century, the weavers were accustomed to throw their shuttle from hand to hand through the meshes of the work;—in 1738 the fly-shuttle was invented by Mr. John Kay. In 1767, James Hargrave, of Blackburn, constructed a spinning-jenny, that would spin twenty or thirty threads into yarn; and in this year, Thomas Highs, a reed maker, invented a machine called the water-frame throstle, for the spinning of twist by rollers. In the same year, Richard Arkwright, of Preston, then residing in Bolton, an active, enterprising and intelligent man, possessed himself of a model of Highs' spinning-frame; and this was the germ of Mr. Arkwright's future prosperity, and of the extension of the cotton trade. In 1785 the patent right of Sir Richard Arkwright's machinery was destroyed, by a decision of the Court of King's Bench, and all the accumulated improvements thrown open to the trade. In 1775 the mule was invented, by a Mr. Crompton, of Bolton; in 1787, Bolton and Watt's rotative steam-engine was introduced by Messrs. Puls, at Warrington; and in the same year the power-loom was brought into action by a Mr. Cartwright. Inkles, tapes, checks, woollens, flannels, baizes, linens, fine fabrics of cotton and hats, all rank amongst the manufactures of this county; besides silk, which of late years has increased to a prodigious importance. Calico printing, bleaching and dying are also performed on a large scale; machine making, iron founding, and paper making, claim a considerable share of consequence; and the glass and earthenware manufacturing establishments are very numerous.

RIVERS, LAKES and CANALS.—The navigable rivers of the county are, the MERSEY, the RIBBLE, the LUNE (or LOYNE), the IRWELL, the DOUGLAS, the WYRE, the KEN, the LEVEN, the DUDDEN and the CRAKE. The Mersey is the boundary of Lancashire and Cheshire in its whole course, and is formed of the waters of the Thame, the Etherow and the Goyt, which unite at Stockport, and fall into the Irish Sea a little below Liverpool. The Ribble has its source in the high moorlands of Craven, at Walton-le-Dale receives the rapid Derwent into its bosom, and finally loses itself in the Irish Sea. The Lune rises at Lune Head, in the fells of Westmoreland, receiving in its course the Leek, the Greta and the Wenning, and falls into the bay of Morecambe at Sunderland Point. The Irwell originates in two streams rising in the high moorlands of the hundred of Blackburn, the conjunction of which takes place at the head of the Royal Manor of Tottington: two miles below Bury the waters of the Irwell are augmented by those of the Roach; at Manchester it receives the Irk, and at Hulme the Medlock deposits its stream; thus increased, about nine miles below Manchester the Irwell merges in the Mersey. The moors of Anglezark give birth to the Douglas, which in its travels receives the Lostock and the Yarrow, and disappears in the estuary of the Ribble at Hesketh Bank. The confluence of two streams, at Hawthornwaite, produces the Wyre, which passes Garstang on to Poulton-in-the-Fylde; afterwards expanding into a spacious basin, called Wyre Water, at the lower part of which there is a strait, serving as a secure and natural harbour for vessels of moderate burthen. The Leven is formed by the overflow of Windermere Lake, and passes along the borders of Upper Holker into Morecambe Bay, below Ulverstone. The Dudden has its source in the '*tarns*' above Seathwaite, and, dividing Lancashire and Cumberland, falls into the Irish Sea near the Isle of Walney. The Ken, a boundary river between Lancashire and Westmoreland, giving name to the principal town (Kendal), in the latter county, washes the banks of Arnside and Cartmel, and falls into the bay of Morecambe above Lancaster Sands. The Crake takes its source from the southern extremity of Coniston Lake, and descends into the Leven near Penny Bridge. The greater number of the secondary rivers are those already named as enriching the streams of others, whose rise and course are more particularly described. The principal LAKES of this county are, Coniston Water, embosomed in the centre of Furness Fells, from five to six miles in length, and about half a mile broad in its widest part; Easthwaite Water, between Coniston and Windermere, one mile and a half in length, and rather more than a quarter of a mile in breadth; and Windermere, the largest lake in England, being twelve miles in its extreme length, and about one mile in breadth: all the islands of Windermere are in Westmoreland, and the whole lake is annexed to the Richmond fee. The CANALS in this county are numerous; to describe at full their various courses, and to dwell upon the vast facility afforded to commerce in the transition of merchandize by means of these great works of internal navigation, would much exceed the space allotted in this work for such species of information. It appears that the first complete artificial canal was planned and formed in Lancashire; this is known by the name of the 'Sankey:' the undertaking took place in 1755, under an Act of Parliament, and another Act of 1761, extending the powers and the line of the work: its length from Fiddler's Ferry to the place where it separates into three branches is nine miles and a quarter, and the whole distance from the Mersey is eleven miles and three quarters. The 'Duke of Bridgwater's Canals' were commenced in 1758-9, when Acts were passed, enabling him to carry into effect his stupendous views, aided by that wonderful self-taught genius, James Brindley. Neither rocks or hills, rivers or vallies, damped the ardour of the undertakers of these vast works; in their course at one time they are lost in immense tunnels, and at other places are carried over rivers and mountains. The most striking of all the aqueduct works is in the first canal, where it passes over the river Irwell at Barton Bridge—the aqueduct being upwards of 200 yards across the river, which runs in a valley: over the river itself it is conveyed by a stone bridge of great strength and thickness, consisting of three arches, the centre one being thirty-eight feet above the surface of the water; allowing a gratification to the spectator of beholding one vessel sailing over the top of another, with masts and sails standing. This canal extends in various directions thirty miles. Another Act was obtained by the Duke, in 1761, for his canal and navigation from Manchester to Liverpool, which was finished in five years, and is twenty-nine miles in length to its termination at Runcorn Gap. An Act, in 1795, empowered this spirited Nobleman to cut a branch from his canal at Worsley, to Leigh. The 'Trent and Mersey Communication,' the plans for which were agitated in 1755, were finally executed under the powers of an Act passed in 1766; it opened an inland communication between the great ports of Liverpool and Hull; and out of this work arose the vast idea of connecting almost all the midland counties of England with each other. The 'Leeds and Liverpool Canal' was begun in the latter end of the year 1770, when the Act was obtained; the whole length of the line of this canal, from Leeds to Liverpool, including the portion of the Lancaster canal, is upwards of 127 miles. 'Manchester, Bolton and Bury Canal,' the Act for which was obtained in 1791 is more than fifteen miles in length, commencing on the western side of Manchester, from the river Irwell. In 1792 an Act was obtained for making the 'Manchester, Ashton-under-Line and Oldham Canal,' which commences on the east side of Manchester, and is in length eleven miles,—a branch going from this canal to Stockport. The 'Rochdale Canal' obtained its Act in 1794, which authorizes a navigation from the Duke's canal, at Manchester, to the Calder navigation at Sowerby Bridge, near Halifax; its whole length being, from one extremity to the other, thirty-one miles and a half. An Act for cutting the 'Huddersfield Canal' passed in April, 1794; its eastern extremity being the Ashton-under-Line canal, and its western, Sir John Ramsden's canal, to the Calder; the length being nearly twenty miles. The 'Lancaster Canal,' for which an Act was obtained in 1792, commences at Kendal and terminates at West Houghton, being a distance of more than seventy-five miles. The 'Ulverstone Canal' is a short cut, about a mile and a half in length, communicating with the navigable channel of the bay of Morecambe and the river Leven. The 'Ellesmere Canal,' though forming no part of the inland navigation of Lancashire, opens a passage from the Mersey to the Dee, and connects the trade of this county with the Severn and North Wales. Besides these several canals, the advantages and means of inland navigation have been increased by the 'Irwell and Mersey Navigation,' the 'Weaver Navigation' and the 'Douglas Navigation;' and by a new mode of conveyance, more rapid, and (it is anticipated) more economical than water carriage, in the shape of an IRON RAILWAY between Liverpool and Manchester: the project was formed in 1822, but the measure was not immediately followed up; this stupendous work is now (1830,) however, on the eve of being completed, and sanguine expectations are entertained as to its profitable results.

CIVIL and ECCLESIASTICAL DIVISIONS.—Lancashire is in the Province of York, and partly in the Diocese of Carlisle and partly in that of Chester. It is divided into six hundreds, namely, AMOUNDERNESS, BLACKBURN, LEYLAND, LONSDALE, SALFORD and WEST DERBY; and subdivided into 70 parishes, containing one county town (Lancaster), and 29 other market towns. The whole county sends fourteen Members to Parliament, viz. two each for the Boroughs of CLITHERO, LANCASTER, LIVERPOOL, NEWTON, PRESTON and WIGAN, and two for the SHIRE.

POPULATION.—According to the census of 1821, there were houses inhabited in the county, 176,449; uninhabited, 5,759; and houses building, 1,735. The number of families then resident in the county was 203,173; comprising 512,476 males, and 540,383 females; total, 1,052,859: and by a calculation made by order of Government, which included persons in the army and navy, for which was added after the ratio of about one to thirty prior to the year 1811, and one to fifty for that year and the census of 1821, to the returns made from the several districts; the population of the county, in round numbers, in the year 1700, was 166,200—in 1750, 297,400—in 1801, 695,100—in 1811, 856,000—and in 1821, 1,074,000. The increased population in the 50 years, from the year 1700, was 131,200—from 1750 to 1801, the increase was 397,700—from 1801 to 1811, the increase was 160,900—and from 1811 to 1821, the increased number of persons was 218,000: the grand total increase in the population of the county from the year 1700 to the census of 1821, being about 907,800 persons.

Index of Distances from Town to Town in the County of Lancaster.

THE NAMES OF THE RESPECTIVE TOWNS ARE ON THE TOP AND SIDE, AND THE SQUARE WHERE BOTH MEET GIVES THE DISTANCE.

	Ashton-under-Line	Blackburn	Bolton	Burnley	Bury	Chorley	Clithero	Colne	Garstang	Haslingden	Hawkshead	Kirkham	Lancaster	Leigh	Liverpool	Manchester	Middleton	Oldham	Ormskirk	Poulton	Prescot	Preston	Rochdale	Saddleworth (York)	Stockport	Ulverstone	Warrington	*Distance from London.*
Ashton-under-Line																												187
Blackburn	31																											209
Bolton	18	12																										197
Burnley	26	11	18																									210
Bury	17	16	6	16																								195
Chorley	29	10	11	21	17																							208
Clithero	37	10	22	9	21	21																						216
Colne	32	18	25	6	22	28	9																					217
Garstang	49	21	32	28	38	20	19	28																				228
Haslingden	25	8	12	8	9	17	13	13	30																			204
Hawkshead	87	60	69	59	75	58	50	59	38	63																		266
Kirkham	47	20	29	32	35	18	29	38	10	28	48																	226
Lancaster	61	33	42	32	48	31	23	32	11	36	27	21																239
Leigh	19	19	7	25	13	16	29	34	36	19	74	35	47															197
Liverpool	43	41	33	52	39	31	51	59	42	46	80	40	53	23														205
Manchester	7	23	11	25	9	22	30	31	42	18	80	40	53	12	36													186
Middleton	8	23	13	20	7	24	29	26	43	16	82	42	55	18	42	6												192
Oldham	4	30	19	22	14	30	32	28	50	19	88	48	61	20	44	7	6											191
Ormskirk	37	25	23	36	29	15	35	42	29	35	67	27	40	19	13	30	36	38										209
Poulton	55	28	37	39	43	26	29	39	10	36	48	8	21	42	48	48	50	56	35									234
Prescot	35	33	25	46	31	23	44	52	43	40	81	42	54	13	8	28	34	36	14	49								197
Preston	38	11	20	22	26	9	20	29	11	19	49	9	22	25	31	31	33	39	18	17	32							217
Rochdale	11	18	13	15	7	24	24	21	44	10	78	42	47	20	46	11	5	7	36	50	28	33						197
Saddleworth (from Junction Inn)	8	24	19	21	13	30	30	27	50	16	84	48	53	24	48	12	10	4	42	56	40	39	6					195
Stockport (Cheshire)	8	30	18	32	16	29	37	38	49	25	87	47	60	19	39	7	13	12	37	55	31	38	18	16				179
Ulverstone	83	55	64	54	70	53	45	54	33	58	14	43	22	69	75	75	77	83	62	43	76	44	69	75	82			261
Warrington	25	30	18	32	20	21	36	39	41	26	79	39	52	10	18	18	24	26	22	47	10	30	29	30	21	74		187
Wigan	25	29	10	31	16	9	30	37	29	22	67	27	40	7	22	18	24	26	12	35	14	18	23	30	25	62	12	199

Additional information relating to the County of LANCASTER.

POPULATION.—By the Census for **1831** this county contained 650,389 males, and 686,465 females—total 1,336,854, being an increase, since the returns made in the year 1821, of 283,995 inhabitants; and from the Census of 1801 to that of 1831 the augmentation amounted to 664,123 persons.

REPRESENTATION.—By the *Reform Bill* the borough of NEWTON has been disfranchised, and CLITHEROE deprived of one of its members: the following towns have obtained the privilege of being represented, and return two members each, namely, MANCHESTER, OLDHAM, BOLTON, and BLACKBURN—SALFORD, ASHTON-UNDER-LYNE, BURY, ROCHDALE, and WARRINGTON, send one member each, and two additional ones have been given to the county: the whole shire, by these alterations, returns *twenty-six* representatives to Parliament, instead of *fourteen*, as heretofore. The new *Boundary Act* divides the county into two parts, respectively named the *Northern Division* and the *Southern Division;* the former comprises the hundreds of Lonsdale, Amounderness, Leyland, and Blackburn; and the southern includes the hundreds of Salford and West Derby. The election of members for the northern division of the county is held at LANCASTER and for the southern at NEWTON: in addition to the place of election the northern division polls at HAWKESHEAD, ULVERSTONE, POULTON, PRESTON, and BURNLEY, and for the southern division (besides the place of election) polling takes place at MANCHESTER, LIVERPOOL, WIGAN, ROCHDALE, and ORMSKIRK.

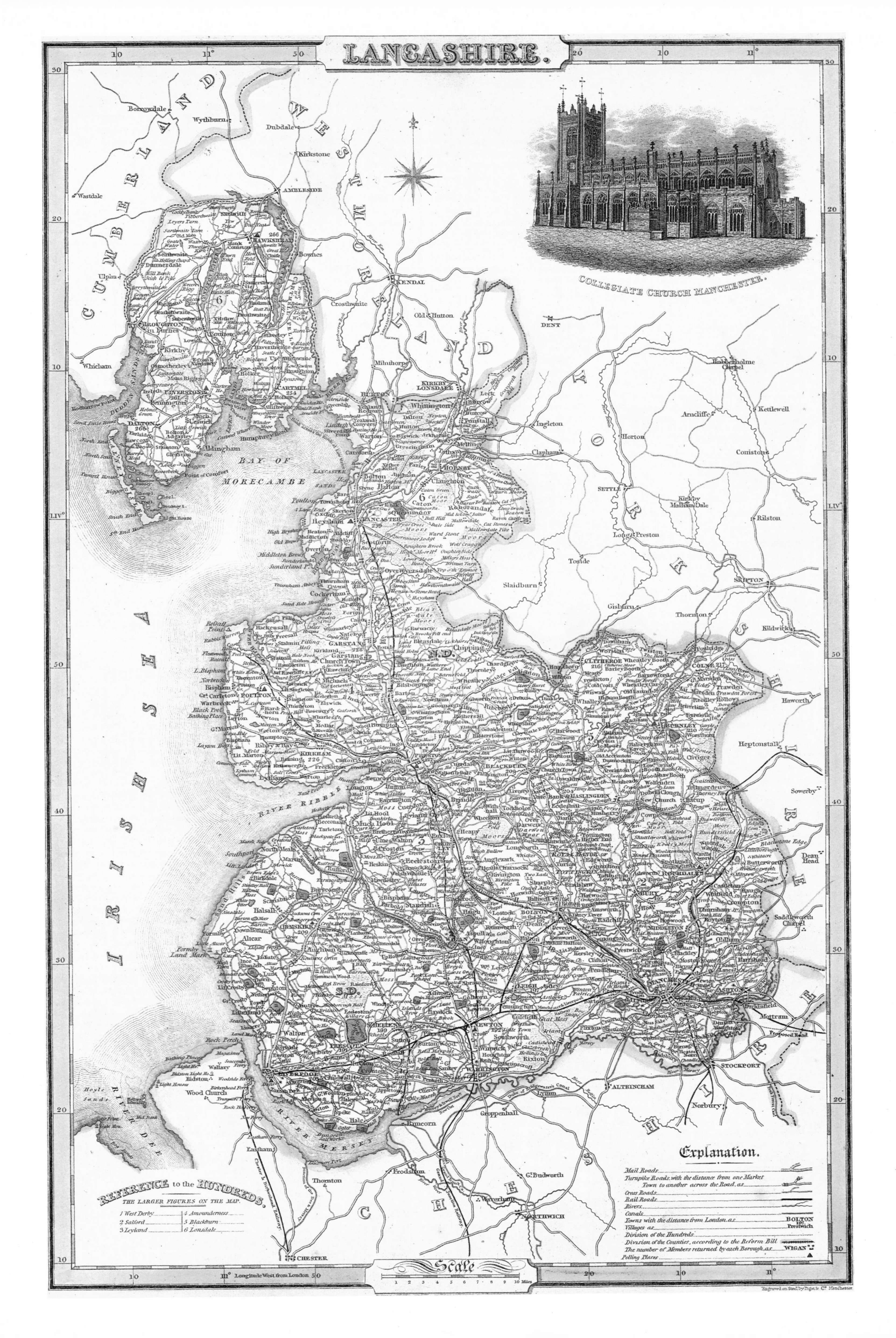
LANCASHIRE.
COLLEGIATE CHURCH MANCHESTER.
CUMBERLAND
WESTMORLAND
YORKSHIRE
CHESHIRE
IRISH SEA
BAY OF MORECAMBE
RIVER RIBBLE
RIVER MERSEY
RIVER DEE
AMBLESIDE
HAWKSHEAD
KENDAL
KIRKBY LONSDALE
ULVERSTON
CARTMEL
DALTON
LANCASTER
GARSTANG
POULTON
KIRKHAM
PRESTON
CLITHEROE
COLNE
BURNLEY
BLACKBURN
CHORLEY
WIGAN
BOLTON
BURY
ROCHDALE
ORMSKIRK
PRESCOT
LIVERPOOL
WARRINGTON
NEWTON
MANCHESTER
ASHTON
STOCKPORT
ALTRINCHAM
CHESTER
NORTHWICH
SKIPTON
SETTLE
DENT
Explanation.
Mail Roads
Turnpike Roads, with the distance from one Market Town to another across the Road, as
Cross Roads
Rail Roads
Rivers
Canals
Towns with the distance from London, as
BOLTON 197
Villages as
Prestwich
Division of the Hundreds
Division of the Counties, according to the Reform Bill
The number of Members returned by each Borough, as
WIGAN
Polling Places
REFERENCE to the HUNDREDS.
THE LARGER FIGURES ON THE MAP.
1 West Derby
2 Salford
3 Leyland
4 Amounderness
5 Blackburn
6 Lonsdale
Scale
Miles
Longitude West from London
Engraved on Steel by Pigot & Co. Manchester

RAILWAYS THROUGH LANCASHIRE.

Lancashire, as regards transit by railway, is, perhaps, one of the most, if not the most, important of the English counties—as, by parent lines and their relative branches, the traveller, at no distant period, will be enabled to transport himself from this district to the most extreme parts of England.

The Liverpool and Manchester Railway.—This well-known and justly celebrated line has established a means of rapid communication between the great manufacturing metropolis of the north—*Manchester*, and the second port in the kingdom—*Liverpool.* The Liverpool and Manchester being considered the parent railway for transit of passengers by locomotive power, claims from us a more copious notice than we have bestowed upon any other line. The project of a railway between Liverpool and Manchester was first entertained about the year 1822; so that the Darlington road, which was not opened until 1825, cannot be said to have supplied the idea. In 1824, a declaration of the inconveniences and delays of the existing modes of conveyance between the two towns was published, and signed by numerous and respectable merchants; a committee was subsequently formed, and a subscription list opened, which was soon filled. In 1825, an application was made to parliament for a bill to empower the Company to proceed with the purchase of land and the formation of the Railway: this application was met by a most strenuous opposition; the proprietors of the Duke of Bridgewater's and the Leeds and Liverpool Canals, and those of the Mersey and Irwell Navigation, combined to crush a project, the realization of which threatened to terminate their very existence; these opponents were strengthened by the Earls of Derby and Sefton. After a vigorous discussion of thirty-seven days in committee, during which the opposing counsel, in their arguments, denounced locomotive engines as *unseemly*, and the scheme altogether as pregnant with evil—profitless, wild and *visionary*—the first clauses, authorizing the operations, were negatived by a large majority, and the bill was prudently withdrawn. The Railroad Committee, undismayed, however, by their defeat, resolved to renew the application in the ensuing session; and in February, 1826, the bill was again brought before parliament, and, after considerable discussion was passed in both houses. A general meeting of subscribers was held in the May following, when Mr. Stephenson was officially appointed principal engineer to the Company. The opening of the road throughout the entire line, took place on Wednesday, the 15th of September, 1830—at which were present the Duke of Wellington, and an imposing array of nobility and gentry. Amongst the number of distinguished individuals assembled upon the occasion, was the ill-fated Mr. Huskisson, who, while in the act of shaking hands with the Duke, was struck to the ground by the *Rocket* engine, the wheels of which passed over his left leg and thigh, crushing them in a most pitiable manner: this occurred at Park Side, seventeen miles from Liverpool, where a tablet has been placed, recording the melancholy event. The unfortunate gentleman was placed in a carriage and removed to Eccles, where, though the most prompt assistance was rendered to him, he expired at nine o'clock the same evening, in the sixty-first year of his age; his remains were interred in the cemetery at Liverpool—the funeral being attended by the municipal authorities of the town, and about eleven hundred other gentlemen. From this digression we proceed to give some other particulars, more immediately concerning the line. The cost of this great undertaking amounted to about £820,000. exclusive of the great tunnel, since constructed, by which passengers are conveyed from the original station into the very heart of Liverpool. The line of railway, from the station in Lime-street, Liverpool, to that in Water-street, Manchester, was measured by order of the Directors in February, 1837, and its length ascertained to be thirty miles and three quarters and thirty-three yards. The *Sun* engine, which conveyed the seven o'clock train from Manchester to Liverpool on Friday evening, June 14th, 1838, accomplished the above distance in the short space of forty-one minutes—being at the rate of *forty-five miles per hour!* The following anecdote, as exemplifying the advantage of railway transit in business transactions, is worth recording: A gentleman left Manchester in the morning—went to Liverpool, purchased and took back with him to Manchester, on the Railroad, 150 tons of cotton. This he immediately disposed of; and the article being liked, an offer was made to take another such quantity: off he started again, and actually that evening delivered the second 150 tons—having travelled 120 miles in four separate journeys, and bought, sold and delivered 30 miles off, at two distinct consecutive deliveries, three hundred tons of goods in about 12 hours! At the expiration of the first year of travelling on the Railway, the return of the number of passengers was as follows:—416,000 persons travelled the whole distance, and about 34,000 short distances—making a total of 450,000 passengers, whose fares amounted to £99,600. The carriage of merchandise was also very considerable in that year, but we are not in possession of the amount. The sum received by the Company, from 1831 to 1836, for the traffic in passengers and goods, was £1,020,883.; and the expenses £618,108. The number of passengers carried upon the line, from July, 1835, to July, 1836, was about 780,000, or about 2,137 daily: this amounts to nearly eight times as many as the Company anticipated, by their first report, to carry—and five times as many as were travelling by coaches previous to the opening of the Railway, when there were thirty on the turnpike-road; this number is now reduced to *one!* The gross amount of receipts for the year ending June 30th, 1838, amounted to £243,659. 17*s.* 4*d.* The Liverpool and Manchester Railway has been gradually progressing in prosperity; and notwithstanding the expense of the new tunnel (which must have been enormous), and the laying down new and heavier rails, rendered necessary by the increased tonnage of goods, the dividends paying are at the rate of 10 per cent. Diverging from this Railroad there are branches to *Bolton* (exclusive of its independent line), *St. Helens* and *Runcorn Gap;* besides the North Union, which we shall notice hereafter.

At the Newton station, about midway between Liverpool and Manchester, issues the Grand Junction, opened on the 4th July, 1837. Its route is by *Warrington;* and, passing into Cheshire, it runs about two miles west of *Nantwich*, and about the same distance west of *Middlewich*, on to *Crewe*, at which station the Chester and Crewe Railway and the Manchester and Birmingham Railway joins. From Crewe the Grand Junction proceeds to *Madeley*—and, leaving *Stone*, about four miles on the left, and *Eccleshall* nearly two on the right, goes on to *Stafford;* from thence to *Penkridge*, and near to *Wolverhampton, Bilston, Wednesbury* and *Walsall;* then with a sharp curve enters *Birmingham* at the same place as the London and Birmingham Railway—by which latter the traveller can immediately start for the Metropolis. The total cost of forming this noble line has been a million and a half. The receipts for six months, ending 30th June, 1838, amounted to £125,130. 16*s.* 9*d.*; of which sum £109,902. 11*s.* 10*d.* belonged to the coaching department, and the remainder for carriage of live stock, merchandize, coal, &c. The journey from Manchester or Liverpool to Birmingham occupies, by the first class carriages, about four hours and three quarters—by the second class about five hours and a quarter.

The North Union Railway may be said to be a continuation of the Grand Junction (at Newton) in an opposite direction: it runs to *Wigan*, and thence to *Euxton* station (2½ miles from *Chorley*), on to *Preston;* from whence an elongation proceeds to the east of *Kirkham* and *Poulton.* The North Union was opened to the public on the 21st October, 1838: for the first two months the number of passengers averaged about 1,400 per day. This line, in connexion with the Grand Junction and Birmingham, opens a continued railway communication from London to Preston. The Lancaster and Preston Junction, goes by *Garstang* to *Lancaster;* from *Preston* the Railway passes on near *Kirkham* and *Poulton* to *Wyre Harbour.*

The Manchester and Bolton Railway, opened on the 29th May, 1838, runs between these towns; from the latter a line proceeds through *Chowbent* and *Leigh*, and joins the Liverpool and Manchester Railway to the east of the Newton station; a line also proceeds from *Bolton* (called the Bolton and Preston Railway), and joins the North Union near *Chorley.*

The Manchester and Sheffield Railway commences at Manchester; and passes about a mile and a half to the south or right of *Ashton*, and about two and a half from *Stalybridge;* and running to the left or north of *Glossop*, it goes to *Penistone*, where it takes rather an abrupt turn and proceeds to *Sheffield.* From the latter town a branch communicates with the North Midland Railway at Rotherham. The length of the main line, from Store-street, in Manchester, to the Cattle Market, in Sheffield, is something less than forty-one miles.

The Manchester and Leeds Railway also commences at Manchester; runs to *Rochdale*—from thence to *Littleborough, Hebden Bridge, Elland, Brighouse, Dewsbury*, and *Wakefield*, to *Normanton;* at which latter place it joins the North Midland, and by it proceeds to *Leeds.* This is a very important line, as forming a connecting link in railway communication between Liverpool and Hull, by means of the line from Leeds to Selby, and that from Selby to Hull, on the one hand, and from Manchester to Liverpool on the other.

The Manchester and Birmingham Railway, like the two preceding, starts from Manchester, and runs to *Stockport* and *Wilmslow*, with a branch beyond the latter place to *Crewe.* At Stone will commence the Extension to *Rugby*, at which place it will join the London and Birmingham Railway, and complete the communication between Manchester and London—passing through *Rugeley, Lichfield, Tamworth, Atherstone* and *Nuneaton.* The distance to Rugby by this line is 93½ miles, and to London 179—being seven miles less than the shortest turnpike road: the saving from Manchester to Wolverhampton and Birmingham is 18 miles by distance, and 8 miles by power—in all, 26 miles. An important feature in this Railway is its connexion at *Alrewas*, by a branch, with the Birmingham and Derby Railway—thus forming a valuable communication between the counties of Derby, Nottingham and Lincoln, and the manufacturing districts of Staffordshire and Lancashire.

A Railway is projected from Lancaster to Carlisle: one survey proposes that the line should pass through Kendal—another advocates Appleby—and a third mentions Shap, as a better and less expensive route than either. A survey has also been made of Morecambe Bay and the Dutton Sands, with a view of forming a Railway from Lancaster to Whitehaven: sanguine opinions have been expressed, not only of the practicability of passing over the sands, but of the land thus reclaimed being nearly equal to the whole expense of constructing the entire Railway.

LEICESTERSHIRE.

THE County of LEICESTER is situated nearly in the middle of England: bounded on the north by Nottinghamshire and Derbyshire; on the west by the latter county and Warwickshire; on the south by Northamptonshire; and on the east by the counties of Rutland and Lincoln. To the north, the Trent and Soar form part of its boundary; the famous Roman road, called *Watling Street*, and the small river Ankor (or Ankre), being its limits on the Warwickshire side; and the rivers Avon and Weyland separating it from Northamptonshire. The shape of the county is very irregular, and extends itself, from north to south, about thirty miles, and about twenty-five from east to west; being nearly one hundred miles in circumference, and its area comprising about eight hundred square miles.

NAME and ANCIENT HISTORY.—This county takes its name from its principal town, which was built long before the time of the Roman invasion; and the variations of its name proves that it has passed through a long succession of time,—its first appellation being *Caer Leon* or *Lerion;* afterwards *Lege Cestria, Leogora, Legeocester,* and in the Saxon annals *Ledcesterscyre* and *Legeocester;* whence, with some trifling alterations subsequently, its present name is derived: the Saxon word *Ledcesterscyre* having reference to the situation of the town or castle on the river *Leir* or *Liere,* now the Soar. Previous to the Roman invasion this part of the country was inhabited by the *Coritani,* but was afterwards called FLAVIA CÆSARIENSIS: in the Saxon Heptarchy it belonged to the Kingdom of Mercia. Some authors have maintained that the town of Leicester was founded by King Lear, or Leir, 850 years before the Christian era; and this personage has also had the reputation ascribed to him of erecting the great Temple of Janus, which formerly stood near the town, on the banks of the then *Leir*. This county, and especially the vicinity of its principal town, has been the arena of early and desperate contention, and more recently of civil strife: Leicester Castle was oftentimes battered down and rebuilt, but scarcely any thing remains of it now but an artificial mound or earth-work of the keep. The remains of the rich Abbey also, which had in monastic times such extensive possessions in this neighbourhood, are now nearly all levelled with the earth which covers the ashes of its ancient inhabitants: this Abbey afforded accommodation and lodgment to several of the Kings of England, on their excursions to and from the north; and it was within its walls that the great and ambitious Cardinal Wolsey died, on the 29th of November, 1530, on his journey from York to London, having just before been stripped of his dignities and ill-acquired property by his unprincipled Royal Master. It was in this county (near Market Bosworth) that the memorable 'Battle of Bosworth Field' was fought, by which the ruthless Richard the Third lost his crown and life together, fighting against the Earl of Richmond, afterwards the politic Henry the Seventh.

SOIL and CLIMATE, PRODUCE and MANUFACTURES.—The soil of this county is various, but for the most part strong and stiff, composed of clay and marl: it affords a great extent of grazing land, and is also peculiarly fitted for the culture of beans and wheat, for which it is proverbially noted: the proportion of pasture and meadow land, however, throughout the whole county, much exceeds that of arable. There are few open fields now left, and the quantity of waste ground is proportionally very small. The surface in most parts is varied and uneven: towards the north-west, the Bardon Hills rise to a considerable height; and in their neighbourhood lies Charnwood or Chorley Forest, a rough and open tract. Farther to the north-west are valuable coal-mines, which supply the country round to a great distance. The north-east part feeds vast numbers of sheep—a principal source of the wealth of the inhabitants. The Leicestershire sheep are of a very large size, without horns, and clothed with thick long flakes of soft wool, particularly suited to the worsted manufactures. The east and south-east part of the county is a rich grazing tract, which breeds numbers of cattle of large size to supply the London and other markets. This county, indeed, has long been famous for its large black horses and horned cattle, as well as its sheep; and its reputation has lately been much extended by the skill and attention of several wealthy and spirited persons of the county, who have bred every species of domestic quadruped to the utmost perfection of form and size, and as it were created new breeds of those animals in which, with perfect symmetry of shape, is united the greatest quantity of flesh with the smallest possible proportion of bone and offal. The breed of sheep called the new Leicester, has in great measure taken place of the old breed, and is dispersed through most counties in the kingdom. A considerable weight of cheese is made in the west side of the county, about Leicester forest and in some other parts. The rich kind called Stilton, is made in the villages round Melton Mowbray. This part is also a rich grazing district, and likewise much celebrated for its being the residence of many noblemen and gentlemen of distinction during the hunting season, many houses in the town are furnished solely for the accommodation of the lovers of field sports, and stabling for the reception of five hundred horses can be obtained here. The rivers supply the towns with many sorts of fish, particularly the best kind of salmon, which comes from the Trent into the Soar.—The MANUFACTURES of this county, though not so varied as those of some others, are nevertheless of great importance, and indeed commensurate with its population and extent. The manufacture of hosiery, and many other articles produced from the fleece, is very considerable, the chief seat of which is in the county town, where are also made machine net and lace to some extent, and ribbons, sewing cottons, &c. The CLIMATE is in general mild and temperate, as there are no mountains or bogs: the highest ground in the county is some of the peaks in Charnwood Forest,—these have the true mountain appearance of bare and barren rocks, projecting abruptly from the surface; the elevation of these hills is not more than nine hundred feet above the level of the sea, and consequently within a temperate region of the atmosphere: the air of the whole county may therefore be pronounced mild, temperate and healthful; and its aspect fertile and pleasing.

RIVERS and CANALS.—The principal rivers of Leicestershire are the SOAR (or SOURE), anciently the Liere, and the WREKE. The Soar rises in the south-west border, and runs to Leicester; after which it receives the Wreke, from the north-east, and then turns to Mount Soar and Loughborough—watering in its course meadows of uncommon beauty and fertility, till it falls into the Trent, not far from Cavendish Bridge. The Soar has, by recent Acts of Parliament, been made navigable from Leicester to the town of Loughborough, and from thence to its junction with the Trent; and the latter is made navigable, by an Act obtained nearly at the same period, to Melton Mowbray, where it is joined by the Oakham Canal. The western parts are watered by the two head branches of the river Ankre, which go from hence into Warwickshire. The chief communications afforded by inland navigation through this county are by the 'Leicester' and 'Loughborough' Canals, the 'Leicester and Melton Mowbray Canal,' and the 'Oakham Canal.' The Leicester Canal commences at the town of Leicester, and after running nearly two miles joins the Soar, near Belgrave; from whence, as has been observed, it is rendered navigable to the commencement of the Loughborough canal, which takes place a little below Gracedieu Brook; and the latter canal then takes a straight course to the Bushes, at Loughborough: this navigation, although so short, has been found very beneficial to the inhabitants of Loughborough, as it brings a regular supply of coal, at a cheaper rate; and by means of the Soar it enjoys an uninterrupted connection with the Trent,—and, by that river, and by the recent improved navigations to Leicester, Melton Mowbray, &c., with all the various and important canals in the interior of the Kingdom. By the Leicester and Melton Mowbray Canal, the rivers Wreke and Eye form a communication with the Soar; and the former rivers, by the addition of cuts and deviations where necessary, are made navigable to Melton Mowbray, where the Oakham Canal commences, which canal proceeds by the north side of the river Eye, and, after a course of fifteen miles, joins the town of Oakham on the north side.

CIVIL and ECCLESIASTICAL DIVISIONS.—Leicestershire is in the Province of Canterbury and Diocese of Lincoln; is included in the Midland Circuit, and divided into the six hundreds of FRAMLAND, GARTREE, GOSCOTE EAST, GOSCOTE WEST, GUTHLAXTON and SPARKENHOE; which are subdivided into two hundred and sixteen parishes, collectively containing one borough and county town (Leicester), and ten other market towns. The whole county returns four Members to Parliament, namely, two for the Borough of LEICESTER, and two for the SHIRE.

POPULATION.—According to the census of 1821, there were houses inhabited in the county, 34,775; uninhabited, 1,141; and houses building, 225. The number of families then resident in the county was 36,806, comprising 86,390 males, and 88,181 females; total, 174,571: and by a calculation made by order of government, which included persons in the army and navy, for which was added after the ratio of about one to thirty prior to the year 1811, and one to fifty for that year and the census of 1821, to the returns made from the several districts; the population of the county, in round numbers, in the year 1700, was 80,000—in 1750, 95,000—in 1801, 134,400—in 1811, 155,100—and in 1821, 178,100. The increased population in the fifty years, from the year 1700, was 15,000—from 1750 to 1801, the increase was 39,400—from 1801 to 1811, the increase was 20,700—and from 1811 to 1821, the augmented number of persons was 23,000: the grand total increase in the population of the county, from the year 1700 to the census of 1821, being about 98,100 persons.

Index of Distances from Town to Town in the County of Leicester.

THE NAMES OF THE RESPECTIVE TOWNS ARE ON THE TOP AND SIDE, AND THE SQUARE WHERE BOTH MEET GIVES THE DISTANCE.

Town	Ashby-de-la-Zouch	Billesdon	Bosworth (Market)	Hallaton	Harborough (Market)	Hinckley	Leicester	Loughborough	Lutterworth	Melton Mowbray	Mount Sorrel	*Distance from London.*
Ashby-de-la-Zouch												116
Billesdon	25											93
Bosworth (Market)	10	19										106
Hallaton	33	6	28									91
Harborough (Market)	34	9	25	7								83
Hinckley	18	21	7	28	24							99
Leicester (*by Welford* 96)	18	9	11	15	15	13						98
Loughborough	12	19	14	24	26	20	11					109
Lutterworth	27	17	17	20	13	11	12	23				89
Melton Mowbray	29	11	26	15	25	28	15	17	27			106
Mount Sorrel	15	15	15	20	22	16	7	13	19	13		105
Waltham-on-the-Wold	33	14	19	22	23	18	21	19	31	5	18	108

[*See over.*

RUTLANDSHIRE.

THE County of RUTLAND is the smallest of all the English counties, being only about eighteen miles in length, at its greatest breadth not more than sixteen, and its area comprising 149 square miles. It is bounded on the west and south-west by Leicestershire; on the south-east by Northamptonshire, from which it is separated by the river Welland; and the county of Lincoln is the boundary on its north and north-eastern sides.

SOIL and CLIMATE, PRODUCE, &c.—The soil of Rutlandshire may be in general considered rich, and it is highly productive in corn and pasture. In many parts a sort of ruddle, of a red colour, prevails—and from this soil, it has been said, the county takes its name; but this assertion is the offspring of vulgar conjecture, and unsupported by scientific etymologists, who have not hazarded opinions relative to its appellation. Rutland is beautifully varied in surface with gentle swells and depressions; the rising grounds running east and west, with vallies intervening about half a mile wide: amongst those is the rich one of Catmose, leading from the west side to the centre of the county, and comprehending the county town, Oakham. The south-western part was formerly entirely occupied by the Forest of Leafield, part of which still remains in its original state, and affords pasturage to some few deer. The AGRICULTURE of this county is good, being chiefly that pursued in Norfolk,—the turnip and sheep husbandry, in general, forming its basis; its flocks are healthy, and its corn, some of the finest in the Kingdom, is chiefly sold for seed. The AIR of this shire is considered as pure as that of any other in England. Neither in MANUFACTURES, MINES OR MINERALS has Rutland any claim to notice; and the only quarries are those of lime-stone at Ketton, which supply the adjacent country with that article. By means of the Oakham canal, which joins the Wreke at Melton Mowbray, in Leicestershire, a communication has been opened with the Trent, which has given rise to an inland trade of some consequence, particularly in the necessary article of coal.

RIVERS.—The principal rivers which either have their source in or pass through this county are, the EYE, the WELLAND, the GUASH and the CHATER. The Eye rises in Leicestershire, runs south-east and forms the boundary of the county on this side, and empties itself into the Welland. The Welland has its source near Sibbertoft, in Northamptonshire, and, running north-east, becomes the boundary of the county on this side; near Ketton it receives the waters of the Chater, and a little to the north of Stamford those of the Guash; continuing nearly the same course, it passes the towns of Market Deeping and Spalding, and flows into the sea at Fosdike Wash: this river is navigable to Stamford. The Guash and Chater both rise on the western side of the county, and running nearly parallel to each other, in an easterly course, unite with the Welland—the former on the north side, and the latter on the south side of Stamford.

CIVIL and ECCLESIASTICAL DIVISIONS and POPULATION.—Rutlandshire is in the Province of Canterbury and Diocese of Peterborough; is included in the Midland Circuit, and divided into the five hundreds of ALSTOE, EAST, MARTINSLEY, OAKHAM-SOKE and WRANDIKE: these collectively contain fifty-two parishes, one county town (Oakham), and two market towns (Oakham and Uppingham). The SHIRE is represented by two Members in Parliament. POPULATION.—According to the census of 1821, the whole county contained 3,936 families—consisting of 9,223 males, and 9,264 females; total, 18,487 inhabitants. From the year 1700 to the census of 1821, this county had only increased its population about 2,300 persons.

OAKHAM is 96 miles from London, six from Uppingham, eleven from Stamford, *(Lincolnshire)* and ten from Melton Mowbray, *(Leicestershire)*.
UPPINGHAM is 90 miles from London, eleven from Billesdon, *(Leicestershire)*, 20 from Leicester, and 22 from Peterborough, *(Northamptonshire)*.

Additional information relating to the County of RUTLAND.

ooo

POPULATION.—By the Census for **1831** this county contained 9,721 males, and 9,664 females—total 19,385, being an increase, since the returns made in the year 1821, of 898 inhabitants; and from the Census of 1801 to that of 1831 the augmentation amounted to 3,029 persons.

REPRESENTATION.—The *Reform Bill* does not interfere with the number of members returned by this county. The election is held at OAKHAM.

Additional information relating to the County of LEICESTER.

ooo

POPULATION.—By the Census for **1831** this county contained 97,556 males, and 99,447 females—total 197,003, being an increase, since the returns made in the year 1821, of 22,432 inhabitants; and from the Census of 1801 to that of 1831, the augmentation amounted to 66,922 persons.

REPRESENTATION.—By the *Reform Bill* two additional members have been given to the county, so that the whole shire returns *six* representatives to Parliament, instead of *four*, as before the passing of the Bill. The new *Boundary Act* divides the county into two parts, respectively named the *Northern Division* and the *Southern Division;* the former comprises the hundreds of West Goscote, East Goscote, and Framland, and also those two detached portions of the hundred of Gartree which are situated on the east of the hundred of East Goscote; and the southern division includes the hundred of Gartree, except as before mentioned, and the hundreds of Sparkenhoe and Guthlaxton, also the borough of Leicester and the liberties thereof. The election of members for the northern division is held at LOUGHBOROUGH, and for the southern at LEICESTER. Besides the place of election the northern division polls at MELTON MOWBRAY & ASHBY-DE-LA-ZOUCH; and the southern (besides the place of election) polls at HINCKLEY & MARKET HARBORO'.

RAILWAYS.—The MIDLAND COUNTIES' RAILWAY commences at *Derby*—runs by *Kegworth, Loughborough* and *Mount Sorrel,* passing to the east of *Leicester* and west of *Lutterworth* on to *Rugby*. This Railway forms a communication from *Derby* to *Nottingham*, and also from those towns, as well as *Leicester* and *Loughborough*, to *London* and the *South of England*. The projected Norwich and Leicester Railway will run from Leicester, by Oakham, Stamford, Peterborough and Downham, to Norwich, with an extension to Yarmouth. The LEICESTER and SWANNINGTON RAILWAY commences at the former town, and extends for a few miles beyond the latter: this Railway is mostly used for the conveyance of coal—not more than £1,000. per annum being realized by the conveyance of passengers. The BIRMINGHAM and DERBY RAILWAY runs by *Burton-upon-Trent,* six miles east from *Ashby-de-la-Zouch*, and, by *Tamworth,* six miles from *Appleby*.

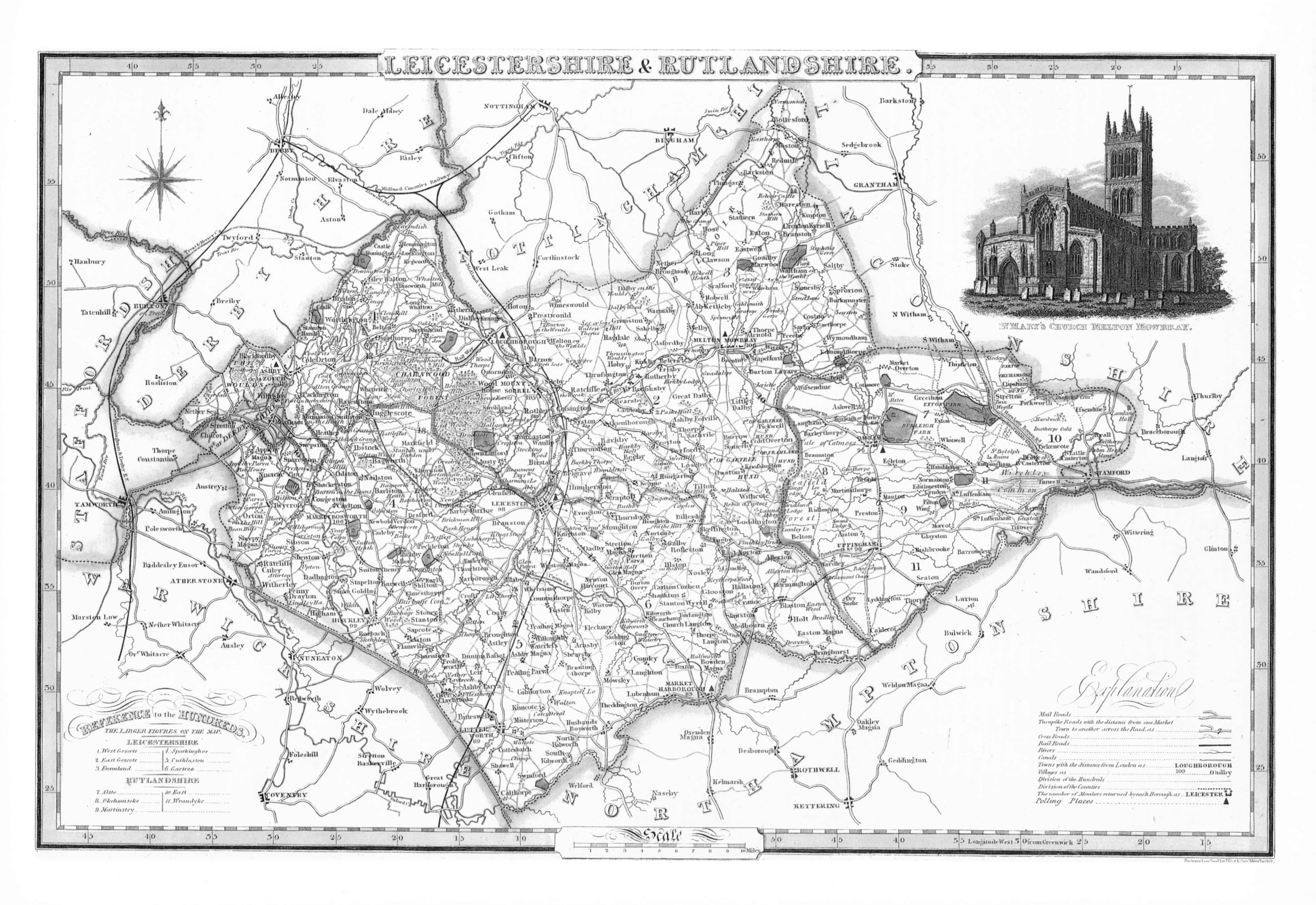
LEICESTERSHIRE & RUTLANDSHIRE.
S.T MARY'S CHURCH MELTON MOWBRAY.
NOTTINGHAMSHIRE
LINCOLNSHIRE
NORTHAMPTONSHIRE
WARWICKSHIRE
STAFFORDSHIRE
DERBYSHIRE
LEICESTER
LOUGHBOROUGH
MELTON MOWBRAY
MARKET HARBOROUGH
LUTTERWORTH
HINCKLEY
MARKET BOSWORTH
ASHBY DE LA ZOUCH
OAKHAM
UPPINGHAM
STAMFORD
NOTTINGHAM
DERBY
GRANTHAM
TAMWORTH
ATHERSTONE
NUNEATON
COVENTRY
KETTERING
ROTHWELL
BINGHAM
CHARNWOOD FOREST
Vale of Catmoss
Midland Counties Railway
Birmingham & Derby R.T.
REFERENCE to the HUNDREDS.
THE LARGER FIGURES ON THE MAP.
LEICESTERSHIRE
1. West Goscote
2. East Goscote
3. Framland
4. Sparkinghoe
5. Guthlaxton
6. Gartree
RUTLANDSHIRE
7. Alstoe
8. Okehamsoke
9. Martinsley
10. East
11. Wrandyke
Explanation
Mail Roads
Turnpike Roads with the distance from one Market Town to another across the Road, as
Cross Roads
Rail Roads
Rivers
Canals
Towns with the distance from London as LOUGHBOROUGH 109
Villages as Oadby
Division of the Hundreds
Division of the Counties
The number of Members returned by each Borough as LEICESTER
Polling Places
Scale
1 2 3 4 5 6 7 8 9 10 Miles
Longitude West 5 0 from Greenwich

LINCOLNSHIRE.

THE County of LINCOLN is a maritime one, bounded on the north by the river Humber, which separates it from Yorkshire; on the east by the German Ocean; on the south by Cambridgeshire and Northamptonshire; and on the west by the counties of Rutland, Leicester, Nottingham and York. Its form is an irregular oblong, with a bunch or bow jutting into the sea: in length, from north to south, it is seventy-five miles; in breadth, about forty-five; and its area comprises, by the most accurate survey, about 2,748 square miles.

In the ANCIENT HISTORY of this county, subsequent to its being inhabited by its original possessors (a tribe of Britons named *Coritanii),* it is recognized as being comprehended in the Roman province of FLAVIA CÆSARIENSIS. In the Heptarchy it belonged to the Kingdom of Mercia, which was then divided into two provinces, north and south; and as the river Trent was the line of separation, this county constituted a considerable part of South Mercia. From the various remains of ancient fortifications, it is fairly concluded that Lincolnshire must have been considered of great importance by the Romans, who throughout it established numerous military stations, which were connected by roads intersecting the whole county. Lincolnshire, in early times, suffered severely from the incursions of the Danes; and in the year 870 these ferocious people landed at Humberstone, and devastated the country—destroying the famous monastery of Bardney, and slaying, in the church, all the monks, without distinction or mercy; Croyland monastery also fell a sacrifice, and with it its religious inmates, none escaping the sword of the barbarians but one single youth. The skill of Alfred the Great induced the Anglo-Saxon Monarchs to lay aside their respective differences, and confederate for mutual defence; and by this policy the Danes were subdued, and the sovereignty of Mercia fell into the hands of Alfred: some places, however, were still retained by the Danes, amongst which were Lincoln and Stamford, until the year 941, when they were expelled by Edmund the Elder, and peace restored. The City of Lincoln (the *Lindum* of the Romans,) is a place of considerable importance in the ecclesiastical and military annals of the Kingdom, and was one of great extent and consequence under the Romans: it is celebrated at the present day for its Cathedral, the most prominent object of this city; it is one of the largest sacred edifices in the realm, and its architectural magnificence corresponds with its magnitude. This city has had its full share of calamity: it was once burned; afterwards besieged by King Stephen, who was here defeated and taken prisoner; pillaged by Henry VIII, under the cloak of religious zeal; and lastly suffered most severely from the fury and fanaticism of the Parliamentarian forces. Caistor, now but a small market town, is one of great antiquity, and was formerly a fortified station of the Saxons: it was built by Hengist, who, after defeating the Picts and Scots, obtained from Vortigern as much land here as he could encompass with the hide of an ox, *cut into small strips or thongs,* with which he encircled a large plot of ground, wherein he erected a fortified mansion, called by the Saxons *Thuang Castor.* Gainsborough is a very ancient town, memorable for the marriage of Alfred, and also from being near to the anchorage place of the Danish ships, when the tyrant Sweyne ravaged and laid waste many parts of this county.

SOIL, CLIMATE, PRODUCE, &c.—Every description of SOIL, from the sharpest sand and lightest moor to the strongest clay, in all the various mixtures and qualities, are found in this county, and combine the three natural features of the 'Cliffs,' the 'Wolds' and the 'Fens.' The cliffs slope towards the west into a range of rich meadow and pasture land, along which flows the Trent; those which decline to the east being a tract varied in its quality and character. The wolds are a bold range of hills, extending from Barton-on-the-Humber to Spilsby, consisting principally of sandy and flint loams, and on the western side the lower stratum is a sandy rock. The fens (a prominent tract in this county,) consist of lands which at some distant period have been recovered from the inundations of the sea, by human industry. The drainage of these fens commenced as early as William I.: through various subsequent reigns the drainage works were carried on with spirit, till the 13th year of Charles I., when an interruption took place, from the opposition of the *Gyrvii,* or 'fen-dwellers'—a rude people, enemies to improvement in lands; and from that period, till the middle of the 18th century, but little was prosecuted in the way of these useful inclosures; when Acts of Parliament were obtained, and all the tracts of fen-land were successively drained. The CLIMATE and air of Lincolnshire, upon the highest part, in point of salubrity is equal to any in the Kingdom; on the western side, along the Trent, it is very healthy; but upon the sea-coast it is not to be so much commended.—The PRODUCE of this county consists principally of sheep, neat cattle, horses and corn. The sheep are large, clothed with long thick wool, particularly serviceable for the worsted and coarse woollen manufactures, of which great quantities are annually sent into Yorkshire and other counties. The neat cattle are of a large sort; but the dairy here is little regarded, the production of fat cattle being the principal object of attention. The horses bred in Lincolnshire have long been held in high estimation, both for saddle and harness; while in the southern part excellent draught horses are produced. Large quantities of flax and hemp, rape and turnip seed, are cultivated in the Isle of Axholme; and the manufacture of canvass and sail cloths, in some towns of the county, have taken root with a considerable degree of success. In the undrained state of the fens, geese were considered the fenman's treasure; and large flocks of these birds were kept and attended, during the time of incubation, with the most assiduous care: some individuals have been known to possess 1,000 of these birds, which, on an average, would produce sevenfold in a season; they were frequently plucked, as the feathers and quills formed valuable articles of commerce. Decoys for taking wild-fowl were at one time very numerous in this county, and several remain, which still furnish the London and other markets with a tolerable supply of this delicacy.—The MINERALS and MANUFACTURES of this county are of little importance to it in the scale of trade: of the former, some variegated spotted marble, sulphurate of iron, and a sub-phosphate of iron, are all the varieties which have been yet met with. Of the latter, at Barton are manufactured starch, sacking, ropes, cables and pottery ware; at Epwall, sacking and canvass; and at Grantham, linen and paper: at Lincoln are several considerable tanneries, and some manufactories for hosiery. The trade in malt, for home consumption, and a considerable portion for exportation, is very general throughout the county.

RIVERS and CANALS.—The principal rivers which either rise in this county, pass through it, or are connected with it, are the TRENT, the ANCHOLME, the WITHAM, the WELLAND and the GLEN, besides several smaller streams. The Trent has its source in Staffordshire; and, crossing the counties of Derby and Nottingham, divides the latter from Lincolnshire on the north-west; thence flowing to Althorpe, below that place it receives the Don, and lower down the Ouse; and thus augmented falls into the Humber. The Ancholme is a small river, rising near Market Rasen; whence flowing northward to Glandford Bridge, it is navigable to the Humber. The Witham derives its source near South Witham, about ten miles north of Stamford; in its course it visits Grantham and Lincoln, and finally Boston, where it unites its waters with those of Boston Deeps. The Welland takes its rise near Sibertoft, in Northamptonshire; and, after being increased by numerous rivulets and streams, passes Market Deeping, between which town and Crowland it divides into two streams—one branching off to Wisbeach, and the other to Spalding and Surfleet; where the latter meeting the Glen, it empties itself into the Foss-dyke Wash, east of Boston.—The CANALS of this county are, the 'Grantham Canal,' which commences on the east side of that town, and joins the Trent between Holme and Radcliffe, in Nottinghamshire; the 'Louth Canal,' which runs from near the town of that name to the sea at Tetney Lock, a course of about eleven miles; and the 'Stamforth and Keadby Canal,' which passes through the fens, and at the distance of fifteen miles from its head enters the navigable Trent.

CIVIL and ECCLESIASTICAL DIVISIONS.—Lincolnshire is in the Province of Canterbury and Diocese of Lincoln, and is included in the Midland Circuit. The City of Lincoln, with four adjacent villages, form a distinct county, under the denomination of 'the City and County of the City.' The remainder is divided into three parts, viz. 'Lindsay,' 'Kesteven' and 'Holland;' these are subdivided into 33 hundreds, wapentakes, sokes, &c. which contain 629 parishes, one city and county town (Lincoln), and thirty-one other market towns. The entire county returns twelve Members to Parliament, namely, two for the City of LINCOLN, two each for BOSTON, GRANTHAM, GRIMSBY and STAMFORD, and two for the SHIRE.

POPULATION.—According to the census of 1821, there were houses inhabited in the county, 53,813; uninhabited, 979; and houses building, 302. The number of families then resident in the county was 58,760, comprising 141,570 males, and 141,488 females; total, 283,058: and by a calculation made by order of government, which included persons in the army and navy, for which was added after the ratio of about one to thirty prior to the year 1811, and one to fifty for that year and the census of 1821, to the returns made from the several districts; the population of the county, in round numbers, in the year 1700, was 180,000---in 1750, 160,200---in 1801, 215,500---in 1811, 245,900---and in 1821, 288,800. From the year 1700 to 1750, it will be seen (according to the Government returns,) that there occurred a decrease in the population of the county, of 19,800 persons, which decrease is not accounted for in the returns referred to. From 1750 to 1801, the increase was 55,300---from 1801 to 1811, the increase was 30,400---and from 1811 to 1821, the augmented number of persons was 42,900: the grand total increase in the population of the county, from the year 1700 to the census of 1821, being about 108,800 persons.

Index of Distances from Town to Town in the County of Lincoln.

THE NAMES OF THE RESPECTIVE TOWNS ARE ON THE TOP AND SIDE, AND THE SQUARE WHERE BOTH MEET GIVES THE DISTANCE.

	Alford	Barton	Boston	Bourne	Brigg	Burgh	Caistor	Crowland	Donnington	Falkingham	Gainsborough	Grantham	Grimsby	Holbeach	Horncastle	Lincoln	Louth	Market Deeping	Market Rasen	Sleaford	Spalding	Spilsby	Stamford	Tattershall	Wainfleet	Distance from London.
Alford																										140
Barton	43																									167
Boston	24	57																								116
Bourne	44	70	20																							97
Brigg	37	10	56	58																						156
Burgh	12	51	20	39	45																					131
Caistor	28	15	45	59	8	38																				157
Crowland	46	72	23	11	65	40	60																			90
Donnington	25	63	12	13	53	25	43	20																		111
Falkingham	34	61	17	9	48	38	50	20	9																	106
Gainsborough	44	28	45	53	18	50	28	63	45	45																150
Grantham	42	58	27	15	47	44	47	26	20	13	38															110
Grimsby	25	22	44	71	21	32	13	67	47	58	40	54														168
Holbeach	35	69	12	19	60	31	57	13	13	22	60	35	56													109
Horncastle	12	40	20	39	31	19	26	42	22	30	32	31	25	32												136
Lincoln	33	34	36	36	24	39	23	47	30	27	18	24	35	44	21											130
Louth	10	33	32	52	28	17	18	55	36	44	37	50	20	44	13	26										148
Market Deeping	51	77	28	8	65	43	63	10	22	16	62	24	75	20	43	43	55									90
Market Rasen	26	25	37	51	15	33	9	58	38	43	20	40	19	55	18	16	16	58								148
Sleaford	34	52	18	18	41	31	43	30	14	9	36	14	45	26	23	18	36	25	35							115
Spalding	37	74	14	11	61	32	57	8	11	14	56	27	58	8	32	38	46	13	50	21						103
Spilsby	7	48	16	33	42	4	32	39	20	31	48	41	35	29	10	31	15	44	30	27	30					133
Stamford	53	77	30	10	66	50	68	18	23	19	59	21	72	28	48	44	60	8	60	27	20	45				89
Tattershall	20	48	13	30	38	18	34	34	16	22	39	25	33	24	9	21	22	35	22	14	24	14	35			128
Wainfleet	16	56	17	35	51	4	41	37	21	33	56	42	36	28	19	40	21	43	36	30	31	9	45	18		131
Wragby	26	34	28	46	23	28	17	50	38	36	26	34	26	46	10	11	16	52	8	27	39	20	54	15	29	143

[See over.

Additional information relating to the County of Lincoln.

---ooo---

POPULATION.—By the Census for **1831** this county contained 158,717 males, and 158,527 females—total 317,244, being an increase, since the returns made in the year 1821, of 34,186 inhabitants; and from the Census of 1801 to that of 1831, the augmentation amounted to 108,687 persons.

REPRESENTATION.—By the *Reform Bill* the borough of Great Grimsby is deprived of one of its members, and two additional ones are bestowed upon the county—the whole shire returning *thirteen* members to Parliament, instead of *twelve*, as before the passing of the Bill. Under the new *Boundary Act*, two of the county members represent the parts of Lindsey, and the other two, those of Kesteven and Holland. The election of members for the former, is held at LINCOLN, and for the latter, at SLEAFORD: besides the place of election, the parts of Lindsey poll at GAINSBOROUGH, EPWORTH, BARTON, BRIGG, MARKET RASEN, GREAT GRIMSBY, LOUTH, SPILSBY and HORNCASTLE; and the parts of Kesteven and Holland (besides the place of election) poll at BOSTON, HOLBEACH, BOURN, DONINGTON, NAVENBY, SPALDING and GRANTHAM.

RAILWAYS.—A line is projected from Cambridge, to run through Huntingdonshire, passing to the west of Peterborough and east of Stamford, going near Lincoln and Gainsborough to York. There are two others contemplated, viz.:—the Hull, Nottingham and Lincoln Railway, and the Boston and Nottingham; the first will effect a communication between Nottingham and the Humber, by Newark and Lincoln; and the Boston and Nottingham line will run between those two towns, with a branch to Grantham.

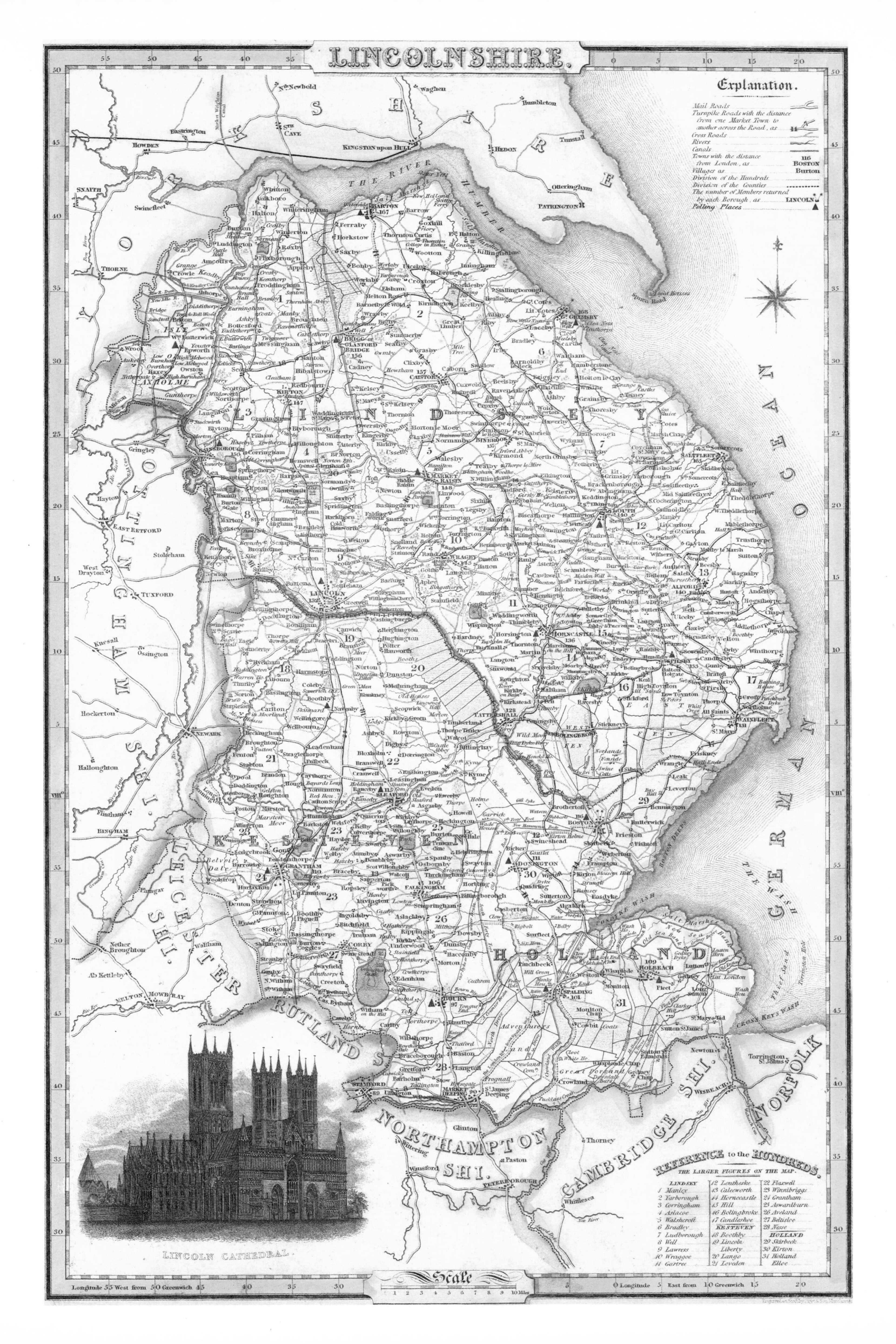

LINCOLNSHIRE.
Explanation.
Mail Roads
Turnpike Roads with the distance from one Market Town to another across the Road, as 14
Cross Roads
Rivers
Canals
Towns with the distance from London, as 116 BOSTON
Villages as Burton
Division of the Hundreds
Division of the Counties
The number of Members returned by each Borough, as LINCOLN
Polling Places
REFERENCE to the HUNDREDS.
THE LARGER FIGURES ON THE MAP.
LINDSEY
1 Manley
2 Yarborough
3 Corringham
4 Aslacoe
5 Walshcroft
6 Bradley
7 Ludborough
8 Well
9 Lawress
10 Wraggoe
11 Gartree
12 Loutheske
13 Caleeworth
14 Hornecastle
15 Hill
16 Bolingbroke
17 Candleshoe
KESTEVEN
18 Boothby
19 Lincoln Liberty
20 Lango
21 Loveden
22 Flaxwell
23 Winnibriggs
24 Grantham
25 Aswardburn
26 Aveland
27 Beltislee
28 Nesse
HOLLAND
29 Skirbeck
30 Kirton
31 Holland Elloe
LINDSEY
KESTEVEN
HOLLAND
GERMAN OCEAN
THE RIVER HUMBER
THE WASH
YORKSHIRE
NOTTINGHAMSHI.
LEICESTERSHI.
RUTLAND
NORTHAMPTON SHI.
CAMBRIDGE SHI.
NORFOLK
LINCOLN
BOSTON
GRANTHAM
STAMFORD
LOUTH
GRIMSBY
KINGSTON upon HULL
NEWARK
PETERBOROUGH
WISBEACH
Scale
Longitude West from Greenwich
Longitude East from Greenwich
LINCOLN CATHEDRAL

MIDDLESEX.

MIDDLESEX is the smallest of the counties, except one (Rutland), in England; yet is it only exceeded in its population by the largest county (York). It is one of the highest grandeur and importance in the United Kingdom, as containing the Metropolis of the British Empire, besides the City of Westminster, and being the seat of Royalty and the Legislature; as also from its having within its boundaries residences belonging to the chief Nobility of the land. It is bounded on the north by Hertfordshire; on the south by the river Thames, which separates it from the county of Surrey; on the west by Buckinghamshire, from which it is separated by the river Colne; and on the east by Essex, its boundary line at this part being the river Lea. In length from south-east to north-west it is about twenty-three miles, and in breadth it does not exceed fifteen miles; in circumference it is estimated at about 100 miles, and its area as containing 282 square miles. The shape of Middlesex is nearly quadrangular; and, were it reduced to a regular parallelogram of equal superfices, the medium length and width would be about 20 miles by 14. The whole county may be considered as a sort of demesne to the Metropolis,—being covered with its villas, intersected by the innumerable roads leading to it, and laid out in gardens, pastures, and inclosures of all descriptions for its convenience and support.

NAME and ANCIENT HISTORY.—The name MIDDLESEX is derived from the *Middle Saxons;* the people inhabiting it lying between the East, West and South Saxons, and those who were then called the Mercians. At the time of CÆSAR's invasion of Britain, the *Trinobantes* occupied this part of the Island, where, according to Cæsar, they had a very strong city: their King at that time was Imanuentius, who being murdered by Cassibelan, his son Mandrubratius saved his life by flight, and, joining Cæsar in Gaul, returned under his protection to Britain;—at the same time the *Trinobantes* applied by deputies to Cæsar to defend Mandrubratius from Cassibelan's injustice, and to send him to assume the chief authority in their State: their request being complied with, they gave forty hostages, and were the first of the Britons that submitted to the Romans. In the time of Nero, the *Trinobantes* conspired with the *Icenii* to shake off the Roman yoke; but Suetonius Paulinus suppressed this insurrection, at the expense of much Roman and torrents of British blood. On the extinction of the Roman power in this country, Vortigern, a Briton, in order to obtain his liberty from the Saxons, whose prisoner he was, gave up to them this district with others; and it was long governed by Kings of its own, but subject to those of Kent or Mercia,—of whom Sibert, in 603, first embraced Christianity, and Suthred (the last) was conquered by Egbert in 804, and left his kingdom to the West Saxons. All the Roman roads centered in this county, at a place called 'London Stone,' still to be seen in Watling-street, in the City of London. This stone seems to be preserved as the *Palladium* of the City; it is cased, like a sacred relic, within free-stone, with a hole left in the centre which discovers the original: superstitious respect has been paid to it at various times; amongst other occurrences attached to it, is that of the notorious rebel, *Jack Cade,* who, as he passed by it when he had forced his way into the city, struck his sword on '*London Stone,*' saying, '*Now is Mortimer Lord of this City,*'—as if that had been a customary ceremony of taking possession. The Royal Palaces, which at present dignify and ornament this county, are the ancient Palace of St. James, in Pall Mall; Buckingham House, in St. James's Park, originally erected by the Earl of Arlington, and lately rebuilt at a vast expense; Hampton Court, at Hampton, built by Cardinal Wolsey, and a favourite residence of William III, but now almost deserted; and Kensington Palace, chiefly remarkable for its gardens. The market towns in Middlesex afford little worthy of notice. At Brentford, where the Brent enters the Thames, King Edmund Ironside defeated the Danes, drawn off from the siege of London, and drove them across the river; to this place, also, King Charles I. advanced after the battle of Edgehill, and gave great alarm to the inhabitants of the Metropolis. In this town takes place the election of Members to represent the county in Parliament. Chelsea is distinguished by its spacious Hospital for superannuated and disabled soldiers, and by a judicious institution for the education of their children.

SOIL and AGRICULTURAL PRODUCE.—The prevailing soils in Middlesex are loam and clay, or sand and gravel more or less intermixed with loamy clay. The clay in the immediate vicinity of the Metropolis has in many parts been dug up to a considerable depth, for the purpose of brick-making; and innumerable buildings have arisen on the very spots where the land has been thus excavated. The rent per acre of good brick earth varies, according to situation, from £300. to £500., notwithstanding the very heavy duty upon bricks. The arable lands are for the most part spread out into common fields, although about 20,000 acres are now inclosed. The corn grown in this county is nearly confined to wheat and barley, rye and oats being only cultivated in small quantities. The greater part of the upland meadow and pasture lands are very productive; and in the art of hay-making, the Middlesex farmers are superior to any others in the Island. The banks of the Thames, Colne and Lea rivers, and generally of the smaller streams belonging to this county, present a series of luxuriant meadows, principally composed of a rich loamy soil; those which lie contiguous to the Thames are occupied, to an extent of many miles, by gardeners and nurserymen, who cultivate an immense quantity of fruit and vegetables for the London market. The fruit gardens, principally situated on both sides of the high road from Kensington, through the parishes of Hammersmith, Brentford, Isleworth and Twickenham, were supposed to contain, some few years since, about 3,000 acres; the kitchen gardens above 10,000 acres, and the nursery grounds 1,500 acres: but lands thus employed, near to the Metropolis, are annually diminishing in extent, and their site appropriated to the erection of buildings of different degrees of magnitude. The manures used are various, but almost all of them are procured from the Metropolis. The quantity of live stock kept in this county is probably less than in any other, in proportion to the number of acres—with the exception of cows, which are supposed to amount to between 7 and 8,000; the number of horses amounts to upwards of 30,000: neither the hogs or sheep are confined to any particular breed, although of the former vast numbers are fattened at the malt distilleries. The waste and common lands do not exceed 8,000 acres, and the woodlands and copses scarcely amount to 3,000. Middlesex, from its undulating surface, is peculiarly suited to the purposes of agriculture, being sufficiently sloping to secure a proper drainage, without having any abrupt elevations; at the same time the inequalities of the surface contribute to health, ornament and beauty, though but few parts can be considered as peculiarly picturesque. For the most part, the ground rises from the banks of the Thames towards the north; and within a few miles of London, a range of gently swelling eminences (of which Hampstead, Highgate and Muswell Hill are the chief,) protect the Metropolis from the northern blasts. These heights afford many pleasing and extensive prospects; and some equally extended may be seen from Harrow Hill, which, from rising in almost an insulated manner, forms a prominent object at the distance of several miles: this eminence is detached from a yet higher and more extensive ridge, stretching from Pinner, Stanmore, Elstree, Totteridge and Barnet to Enfield Chace. The roads throughout the county, both public and parochial, are in general good; those on the great lines of thoroughfare, for many miles around the Metropolis, are proverbially excellent, and kept in repair at a vast expense: where the flatness of the surface does not admit the advantages of draining, the roads are constructed in what is called the *barrel* form,—that is, the middle is raised as high as can be with safety to the vehicles passing on it, in order to prevent the water lying on the surface, and diminishing thereby its compactness and solidity.

MANUFACTURES, COMMERCE, &c.—The manufactures of this county are more numerous and varied than a superficial observer would believe; the principal, however, are to be found in the Metropolis, where are establishments for the manufacture of such articles of elegance and luxury as are required to be of superior workmanship, which are not only supplied to the country, but exported to all parts of the world. In the manufacture of silk goods, in all its branches, it stands unrivalled; in the drawing of wire from all the metals, and the making of pins and needles, it has long been deservedly famous; fancy articles, in worsted, silk, and gold and silver, (as laces, fringes, &c.) with beautiful and rich productions from the embroiderer's frame, are branches in which the London artizan fearlessly may court rivalship. The trade also in the Metropolis arising from the consumption of various articles of food, is immense, and influences the traffic not only of its own county, but others more distantly situated. This being the case, it may not be impertinent to notice the annual consumption of some commodities, the value of which has been pretty correctly ascertained:—The total value of cattle sold in Smithfield annually is calculated at £8,500,000.; this does not, however, give the total, as large quantities of meat in carcases, particularly pork, are daily brought from the country round the Metropolis. The consumption of wheat amounts to a million of quarters annually; of this, four-fifths are supposed to be made into bread, being a consumption of sixty-four millions of quartern loaves every year, in the Metropolis alone. The annual consumption of butter amounts to about 11,000 tons, and that of cheese to 13,000 tons. The money paid annually for milk is supposed to amount to £1,250,000, and for fruits and vegetables about a million. The consumption of poultry costs annually between 70 and £80,000. The number of rabbits sold annually it is difficult to ascertain, from the numerous itinerant hawkers of this article; but some idea may be formed, when it is known that one salesman, during a season, sold 14,000 weekly. The breweries of London are upon an immense scale, and the porter is celebrated all over Europe; the principal brewers invest in the process of its production enormous capitals, and some of the establishments employ as many as 150 horses, of great strength, beauty and value; thirteen of the chief porter breweries manufacture collectively upwards of 1,500,000 barrels of porter annually. The distilleries in London and its neighbourhood are of great magnitude, and their produce is distributed throughout the entire Kingdom. It has been computed that the total amount of property shipped and unshipped, in the port of London alone, amounts to nearly £70,000,000 yearly; and there are employed in the exports and imports about 4,000 ships, and not less than 15,000 cargoes annually enter the port: these are exclusive of about 5,000 vessels employed in the importation of coal to London alone; from this, conjecture may be assisted as to the immense quantity consumed of this essential article: the price of coals per chaldron of twelve sacks, varies according to quality and the severity or mildness of the winter, from 42*s.* to 63*s.*,—in some inclement seasons, as high as four guineas have been paid for a single chaldron. There are between 2 and 3,000 barges engaged in the inland trade; and 1,200 revenue officers are constantly doing duty in the port of London. The business of sugar refining is a branch in which upwards of eighty different firms have great capitals and numerous hands employed; their establishments are chiefly to be found at the eastern part of the Capital. Although the trade and commerce of the Metropolis are so intimately connected, in a greater or less degree, with the prosperity of Middlesex, and, indeed, the country at large, yet other places in the county have resources within themselves of high consideration. In some towns are large bleaching and calico printing works; in others, extensive iron foundries, soaperies and distilleries; immense tan-yards and rope-walks are spread through different parishes, while paper-mills, chemical works, potteries, &c., and various other manufactories of minor consequence, are occasionally met with. The entire, with the addition of its agricultural treasures, and the splendour of its two great Cities, combine to render the county of Middlesex the most important and opulent, as it is the most interesting, of all other counties in the British Empire.

RIVERS and CANALS.—The rivers of Middlesex are the THAMES, the LEA, the COLNE, the BRENT, and the NEW RIVER. The Thames (whose rise, progress, &c. have been described in the particulars of other counties,) is one of the most beautiful rivers in the world; and at London its depth is sufficient, not only for the navigation of large ships, but for making its deep capacious channel what it really is—one of the greatest ports for trade in the universe: its water is exceedingly wholesome, and fit for use in the longest voyages, during which it will work and ferment itself, till it becomes perfectly pure, clear and palatable; it abounds with a great variety of fish, and is noted for its salmon, smelts, flounders and eels. The Lea rises near Luton, in Bedfordshire, and running to Hertford and Ware, and afterwards dividing Essex from part of Hertfordshire and Middlesex, falls into the Thames below Blackwall. The Colne runs through the county of Hertford and part of Middlesex, dividing the latter county from Buckinghamshire, and falls into the Thames at Staines. The Brent, as has been mentioned, joins the Thames at Brentford. The New River is an artificial stream, brought from two springs at Chadwell and Amwell-Parva, near Ware, in Hertfordshire, for supplying the Metropolis with water. This river, with all its windings, is nearly thirty-nine miles long, has forty-three sluices, and over it upwards of two hundred bridges; it is under the management of a flourishing corporation, called 'the New River Company;' the water was brought into the basin, termed 'the New River Head,' on Michaelmas Day, 1613.—The two principal CANALS of the county are, the 'Grand Junction Canal' and the 'Paddington Canal.' The former enters Middlesex near Uxbridge; passes by Cowley and Eplingdon to the west, and Drayton, Harlington, Cranford Park, Norwood and Osterley Park to the east; where intersecting the river Brent, it falls into the Thames between Brentford and Sion House. The Paddington canal branches off from the Grand Junction near Cranford, and is continued on a level the whole way to the dock at Paddington. There is likewise a navigable canal leading from Hertfordshire along the banks of the river Lea, with which it forms a junction in the neighbourhood of Bow, from whence the united streams continue their course to Limehouse, and at that place incorporate themselves with the Thames.

CIVIL and ECCLESIASTICAL DIVISIONS.—The county of Middlesex is in the Province of Canterbury, and Diocese of London and Westminster; is included in the Home Circuit of the Judges, and divided into the six hundreds of EDMONTON, ELTHORNE, GORE, ISLEWORTH, OSSULSTONE and SPELTHORNE. The hundred of Ossultone is apportioned into four districts, respectively named Finsbury Division, Holborn Division, Kensington Division and Tower Division: these hundreds and divisions contain collectively one hundred and ninety-seven parishes, two cities (London and Westminster), and six market towns, which are, Barnet, Brentford, Edgeware, Hounslow, Staines and Uxbridge. Middlesex returns eight Members to Parliament, namely, two for the COUNTY, four for the City of LONDON, and two for WESTMINSTER.

POPULATION.—According to the census of 1821, there were houses inhabited in the county, 152,969; uninhabited, 7,327; and houses building, 2,879. The number of families then resident in the county was 261,871; comprising 533,573 males, and 610,958 females; total, 1,144,531: and by a calculation made by order of Government, which included persons in the army and navy, for which was added after the ratio of about one to thirty prior to the year 1811, and one to fifty for that year and the census of 1821, to the returns made from the several districts; the population of the county, in round numbers, in the year 1700, was 624,200—in 1750, 641,500—in 1801, 845,400—in 1811, 985,100—and in 1821, 1,167,500. The increased population in the 50 years, from the year 1700, was 17,300—from 1750 to 1801, the increase was 203,900—from 1801 to 1811, the increase was 139,700—and from 1811 to 1821, the augmented number of persons was 182,400: the grand total increase in the population of the county, from the year 1700 to the census of 1821, being about 543,300 persons.

By the above returns, the population of the City of LONDON, Within the Walls, amounted to 56,174; Without the Walls (not including any part of Southwark), 69,260; and the City of WESTMINSTER and Liberties, 182,085. The total population (including London Within the Walls, the City of Westminster and Liberties, and the Out-Parishes in Middlesex and Surrey within the London Bills of Mortality), was 1,010,049; the number in those Suburbal Parishes not within the London Bills of Mortality was 215,642. Grand Total of the Population of the BRITISH METROPOLIS and its SUBURBS, in the year 1821, 1,225,691 persons.

Index of Distances from Town to Town in the County of Middlesex.

THE NAMES OF THE RESPECTIVE TOWNS ARE ON THE TOP AND SIDE, AND THE SQUARE WHERE BOTH MEET GIVES THE DISTANCE.

	Barnet	Brentford	Edgware	Enfield	Hounslow	Southall	Staines	Uxbridge	*Distance from London.*
Barnet									11
Brentford	14								7
Edgware	4	10							8
Enfield	5	16	9						10
Hounslow	16	2	12	18					10
Southall	18	4	12	24	4				9
Staines	23	9	19	25	7	10			16
Uxbridge	15	10	11	16	9	6	9		15

Additional information relating to the County.

POPULATION.—By the Census for **1831** the county of Middlesex (including the city of London and those of its suburbs, not in the county of Surrey, and the city of Westminster) contained 631,493 males, and 727,048 females—total 1,358,541, being an increase, since the returns made in the year 1821, of 214,010 inhabitants; and from the Census of 1801 to that of 1831 the augmentation amounted to 540,412 persons.

The total population of the METROPOLIS and its suburbs (including the city of Westminster, the borough of Southwark, certain parishes without the bills of mortality, and others in the county of Surrey) by the above returns, amounted to 1,474,069 souls, being an increase, since the year 1821, of 248,378; and from the Census of 1801 to that of 1831, of 609,224 inhabitants.

REPRESENTATION.—The *Reform Bill* has created the following boroughs, and conferred upon them the right of returning two members each, namely, FINSBURY, MARYLEBONE, and the TOWER HAMLETS. The whole county, by these additions, returns *fourteen* representatives to Parliament, instead of *eight*, as heretofore. The election of members for the county is held at BRENTFORD, and besides that town, the polling takes place at ENFIELD, KING'S CROSS, or within half a mile thereof, HAMMERSMITH, BEDFONT, EDGEWARE, MILE END, and UXBRIDGE.

RAILWAYS.

This county, with that of Surrey, dividing between them the distinction of possessing within their limits the Metropolis of Great Britain, have become, in consequence, the nucleus of some of the most important Railroads that intersect the country. The LONDON and BIRMINGHAM RAILWAY has its station at *Euston-square*, near to the new church of St. Pancras; the line, however, is projected to terminate in the City. This important line received the sanction of parliament in the session of 1833, at a cost of nearly £73,000! On the 20th July, 1837, it was opened to *Boxmoor* (about 25 miles); on the 16th October following to *Tring* (31¾); April 9th, 1838, to *Denbigh Hall* (48 miles), and from *Birmingham* to *Rugby* (29 miles); and, finally, September 17th, the remaining portion between *Denbigh Hall* and *Rugby* (35½ miles): making the total length 112½ miles—the longest line and greatest Railway work completed in this kingdom at that period. The original estimate was two and a half millions, but the entire cost has considerably exceeded five millions! There are eight tunnels on the line, the longest of which (the Kilsby) is 2,398 yards; the weight of stone blocks on the whole line has been estimated at 152,460 tons, and the weight of the iron rails at 35,000 tons. This line, in connexion with the Grand Junction, affords a rapid communication between the *Metropolis* and *Birmingham, Liverpool, Manchester, Preston, Lancaster,* &c. By a connexion with other Railways, a direct means of transit is also opened to *Nottingham, Leicester, Loughborough, Leeds, York* and *Hull.* The station of the SOUTH-WESTERN or SOUTHAMPTON RAILWAY is situated at *Nine Elms*, near to *Vauxhall, Lambeth.* This line is open the whole way to *Southampton*, passing through *Basingstoke* and *Winchester.* The GREAT WESTERN line commences at *Paddington;* it was opened to *Maidenhead* on the 4th June, 1838, and to *Steventon*, within ten miles of Oxford, in May, 1840. The GREENWICH and CROYDON RAILWAYS have their *termini* at the Southwark foot of *London-bridge;* and at the latter town the DOVER and BRIGHTON lines will enter upon the Croydon rails. The EASTERN COUNTIES' RAILWAY has its chief station in *High-street, Shoreditch;* it was opened from *Mile End* to *Romford* on the 21st June, 1839, and from *Shoreditch* to *Brentwood* on the 1st July, 1840. Amongst other lines which will originate from or have their *termini* in the Metropolis are the NORTHERN and EASTERN RAILWAY, the THAMES HAVEN RAILWAY, and the LONDON and BLACKWALL RAILWAY; the last mentioned, opened from the *Minories* to *Blackwall*, on the 6th of July, 1840, passes along Goodman's-fields and Rosemary-lane. The carriages upon this Railway are attached to an 'endless' rope, whose revolutions are effected by a stationary engine of immense power.

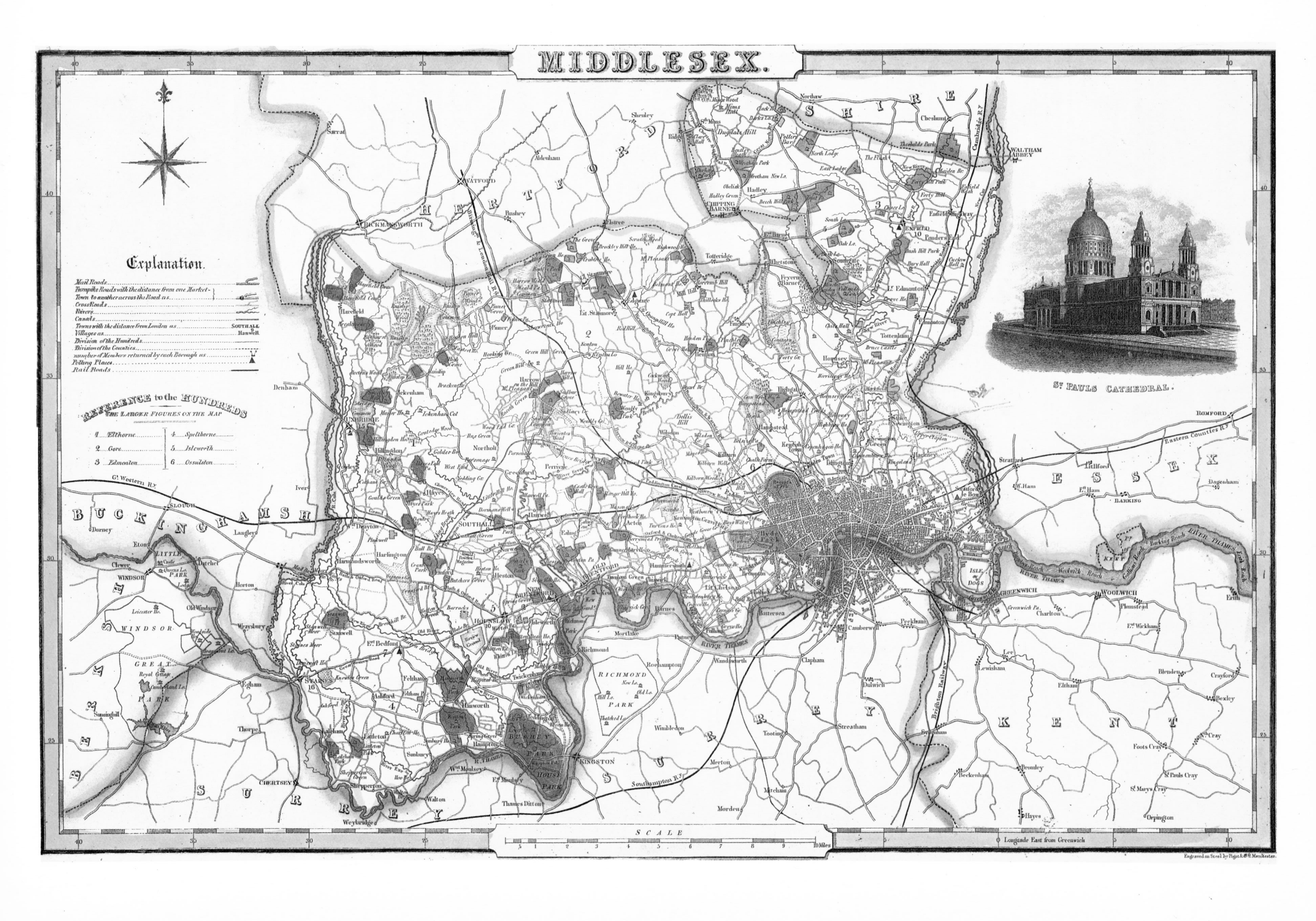
MIDDLESEX.
Explanation
Mail Roads
Turnpike Roads with the distance from one Market-Town to another across the Road as
Cross Roads
Rivers
Canals
Towns with the distance from London as
SOUTHALL
Villages as
Hanwell
Division of the Hundreds
Division of the Counties
number of Members returned by each Borough as
Polling Places
Rail Roads
REFERENCE to the HUNDREDS
THE LARGER FIGURES ON THE MAP
1 Elthorne
2 Gore
3 Edmonton
4 Spelthorne
5 Isleworth
6 Ossulston
S^T PAULS CATHEDRAL.
HERTFORDSHIRE
BUCKINGHAMSH
ESSEX
KENT
SURREY
BERKS
WATFORD
RICKMANSWORTH
UXBRIDGE
SOUTHALL
HOUNSLOW
STAINES
BRENTFORD
ENFIELD
CHIPPING BARNET
KINGSTON
CHERTSEY
WINDSOR
SLOUGH
GREENWICH
WOOLWICH
WALTHAM ABBEY
ROMFORD
BARKING
RIVER THAMES
RICHMOND PARK
Birmingm & London Rail Rd
G^t Western R^y
Eastern Counties R^y
Cambridge R^y
Southampton R^y
Brighton Railway
SCALE
10 Miles
Longitude East from Greenwich
Engraved on Steel by Pigot & Co. Manchester.

MONMOUTHSHIRE.

THE County of MONMOUTH is bounded on the south by the river Severn; on the west, by Glamorganshire and part of Brecknockshire; on the north, by part of the latter county and Herefordshire; and on the east by Gloucestershire, from which it is separated by the river Wye. Its greatest length, from north to south, is 30 miles; its breadth, from east to west, 26 miles; and its circumference about 110 miles, comprising an area of about 498 square miles. Monmouthshire was formerly reckoned one of the Welch counties; and from the names of its towns and villages, its mountainous rugged surface, as well as its situation beyond a large river, (the Wye,) which seems to form a natural boundary between England and Wales in this part, it certainly partakes most of the original character of the latter country, though it is comprehended within the civil division of the former.

NAME and ANCIENT HISTORY.—This county was formerly called *Wentsel* and *Wentsland,* and by the Britons *Gwent,* from an ancient city of that name: the modern appellation is taken from Monmouth, the county town, which Leland derives from its situation between the rivers Monnow (or Munnow) and the Wye; Camden also says it was originally called '*Mongwy*' *(Mwny).* The people inhabiting this and the neighbouring county of Hereford were the ancient *Silures;* and the early history of Monmouthshire partakes of the events which took place in the former county, and of those which happened also in Huntingdonshire. The military exploits of the Romans, and the misfortunes and final defeat of the Britons under the intrepid Caractacus and Queen Boadicea, have been before related in the annals of the counties above-mentioned. The Romans occupied the country of the *Silures,* as a conquered province, from their full establishment in the reign of Vespasian to the period of their final departure from Britain, when the colossal empire of Rome was tottering to its centre. Numerous vestiges of this nation can be traced throughout the county; fortifications, and roads, stations, &c. are well known to the antiquary; and many curious relics, comprising urns, tesselated pavements, coins, &c. have been found at different periods throughout Monmouthshire. The principal towns of this county are situated upon the banks of the Wye and the Usk. Monmouth, the county town, lies in an angle between the Wye and the Monnow: lower down the former river, the remains of Tintern Abbey, and the Castle of Chepstow, form objects highly picturesque amid the wild beauties of this tract. Beneath the Hatterell Hills are the well adapted site of a monastery, and the ruins of Ragland Castle—the latter a fortress of great strength so late as the time of Charles I., in whose favour it held out, under the Marquis of Worcester, to the very end of the civil wars.

SOIL and CLIMATE, PRODUCE and MANUFACTURES.—The surface of this county is picturesque, and particularly delightful. The eastern parts are woody, and the western mountainous,—a diversified and luxuriant scenery of hill and dale. In one part the eye is enchanted with sylvan shades, impervious woods, fields enriched with the finest corn, and meadows enamelled with flowers; from other points a scene in complete contrast may be contemplated—lofty mountains, whose summits reach the clouds, form a sublime and majestic view, awfully commanding and deeply impressive. The river Usk divides Monmouthshire into two unequal portions, of which the east and largest is, upon the whole, a tract fertile in corn and pasture, and well wooded; it abounds in lime-stone, which is burnt on the spot for the general manure of the country. The smaller western portion is mountainous, and in great part unfavourable to cultivation, whence it is devoted to the feeding of sheep: the hills feed great numbers of cattle and sheep, and some goats; and the mountains abound with coal and iron,—the latter of which constitutes the chief article of manufacture, and the coals give rise to a considerable coasting trade. The towns of Newport and Chepstow have a trade in timber and ship-building, and a very important and extensive business in coal and iron; Abergavenny has a profitable traffic in flannels; and at Pontypool and Usk is manufactured japanned ware; (this latter branch has much declined.) Near Tintern are large iron-works, at which ore, chiefly brought from Furness, in Lancashire, is smelted. Monmouth town has a respectable malt trade, and several mills for the manufacture of paper; and Chepstow partakes of the latter branch.—The CLIMATE of this county is salubrious, and friendly to convalescence and longevity: the air is pure; and if it is found in the mountainous regions of a bleak and piercing nature, yet it tends greatly to strengthen and brace the animal system, and precludes those disorders which prevail in a moist and milder atmosphere.

RIVERS and CANALS.—The county of Monmouth is abundantly watered with fine rivers, the principal of which are, the SEVERN, the WYE, the MONNOW (or MUNNOW), the RUMNEY, the USK, and the EBWY. The noble Severn, the second commercial river in the Kingdom, (of which more particular mention is made in the account of Gloucestershire,) forms the southern boundary of Monmouthshire; and receives the Wye near Chepstow, and the Avon from Somersetshire,—thus forming the Bristol Channel. The river Wye, which separates this county from Gloucestershire, is navigable for barges to Monmouth, and ships of considerable burthen come up to Chepstow, where the water rises with great violence: this river, having received two very large streams, becomes a truly noble one, and with a deep channel and full current rushes impetuously towards the sea, bearing on its surface vessels of a respectable class of tonnage. Several fine streams pass through the narrow vallies of this county, enriching the land, and beautifying the face of the country; these principally flow into the Bristol Channel. The Monnow rises in Brecknockshire, pursues its course south-east, and, dividing this county from Hereford, falls into the Wye at the town of Monmouth. The Rumney rises also in Brecknockshire, and, directing its course south-east, divides this county from Glamorganshire, and falls into the Severn. The Usk rises amidst the Black Mountains of Brecknockshire, and with a south-east direction separates this county into two unequal parts, and then falls into the Severn near Newport. The Ebwy likewise has its source in Brecknockshire, and, passing under the Beacon Mountain, flows through the wild valley of Ebwy, and falls into the Usk below Newport.—The most important source of INLAND COMMERCIAL INTERCOURSE, until a recent period, was little known in this county. The 'Monmouthshire Canal,' commenced in 1792, and completed in 1798, commences on the west side of the town of Newport, having a basin connected with the river Usk: it passes between the town and river, and crosses the Chepstow road; from thence by Malpas it pursues its route parallel to and near the river Avon, by Pontypool and Pontnewynd, being nearly eleven miles. From almost opposite Malpas a branch or canal takes its way parallel to the river Ebwy, to near Crumlin Bridge, being likewise a course of about eleven miles from the junction, and making the total length of the two canals twenty-two miles or thereabouts. From these canals several rail-roads have been constructed, leading to different iron-works, collieries and lime-kilns.

CIVIL and ECCLESIASTICAL DIVISIONS.—Monmouthshire (formerly the seat of metropolitan power) is in the Province of Canterbury, and, excepting six parishes (which are in Hereford), in the Diocese of Llandaff. It is divided into six hundreds, viz. ABERGAVENNY, CALDICOTT, RAGLAND, SKENFRETH, USK and WENTLLOOG; these are subdivided into one hundred and twenty-five parishes, containing one county town (Monmouth), and six other market towns. The whole county returns three Members to Parliament, namely, two for the SHIRE, and one for MONMOUTH borough.

POPULATION.—According to the census of 1821, there were houses inhabited in the county, 13,211; uninhabited, 520; and houses building, 166. The number of families then resident in the county was 14,122, comprising 37,278 males, and 34,555 females; total, 71,833: and by a calculation made by order of government, which included persons in the army and navy, for which was added after the ratio of about one to thirty prior to the year 1811, and one to fifty for that year and the census of 1821, to the returns made from the several districts; the population of the county, in round numbers, in the year 1700, was 39,700—in 1750, 40,600—in 1801, 47,100—in 1811, 64,200—and in 1821, 72,300. The increased population in the fifty years, from the year 1700, was 900—from 1750 to 1801, the increase was 6,500—from 1801 to 1811, the increase was 17,100—and from 1811 to 1821, the augmented number of persons was 8,100: the grand total increase in the population of the county, from the year 1700 to the census of 1821, being about 32,600 persons.

Index of Distances from Town to Town in the County of Monmouth.

THE NAMES OF THE RESPECTIVE TOWNS ARE ON THE TOP AND SIDE, AND THE SQUARE WHERE BOTH MEET GIVES THE DISTANCE.

	Abergavenny	Caerleon	Chepstow	Monmouth	Newport	Pontypool	Usk	Distance from London.
Abergavenny								144
Caerleon	16							148
Chepstow	20	14						131
Monmouth	16	21	14					127
Newport	18	3	16	23				148
Pontypool	10	8	21	21	10			148
Usk	11	7	14	13	10	7		143

[*See over.*

Additional information relating to the County of Monmouth.

POPULATION.—By the Census for **1831** this county contained 51,095 males, and 47,035 females—total 98,130, being an increase, since the returns made in the year 1821, of 26,297 inhabitants; and from the Census of 1801 to that of 1831 the augmentation amounted to 52,548 persons.

REPRESENTATION.—The *Reform Bill* does not interfere with the number of members returned by this county. The election of representatives for the county is held at MONMOUTH; and besides that town the polling takes place at ABERGAVENNY, USK, NEWPORT, & the *Rock Inn,* in the parish of BEDWELTY.

RAILWAYS.—There is a Railway from *Monmouth* to *Abergavenny;* and one is contemplated from Gloucester, by Ross, Monmouth and Brecon, to Fishguard.

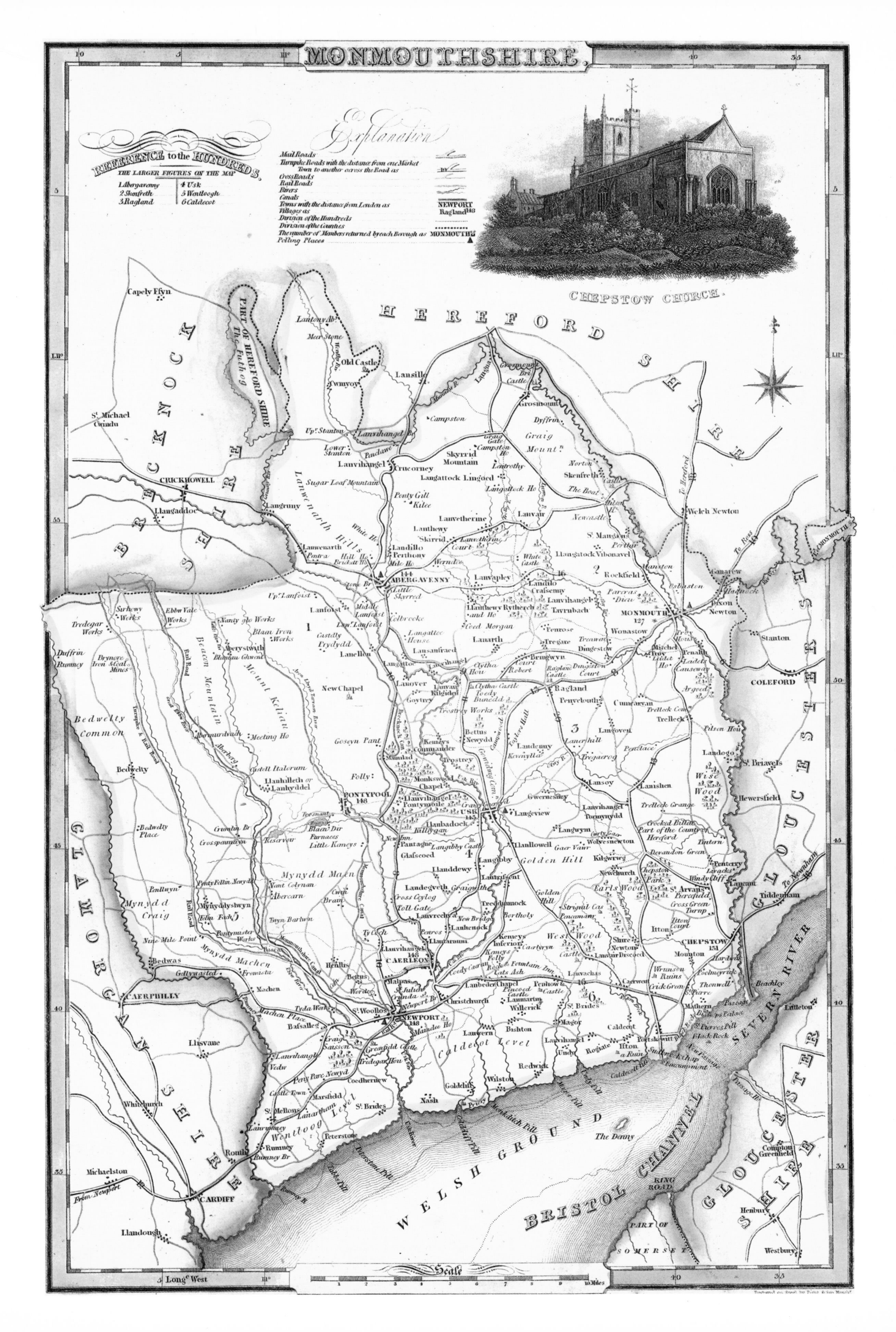
MONMOUTHSHIRE
Explanation
REFERENCE to the HUNDREDS
THE LARGER FIGURES ON THE MAP
1 Abergavenny
2 Skenfreth
3 Ragland
4 Usk
5 Wentloogh
6 Caldecot
CHEPSTOW CHURCH
HEREFORD SHIRE
BRECKNOCK SHIRE
GLAMORGAN SHIRE
GLOUCESTER SHIRE
BRISTOL CHANNEL
WELSH GROUND
SEVERN RIVER
NEWPORT
MONMOUTH
ABERGAVENNY
CHEPSTOW
PONTYPOOL
CAERLEON
USK
CARDIFF
CRICKHOWELL
COLEFORD
Scale
Long. West

NORFOLK.

THE fine and important County of NORFOLK is terminated on the north and north-east by the German Ocean; on the south and south-east by Suffolk; on the west by the Lincolnshire Washes, and by part of Lincolnshire and Cambridgeshire. It is almost entirely insulated by the sea, and by the rivers which form its internal boundary. Its figure is very compact, presenting an almost unbroken convexity to the ocean, and a curve somewhat indented to the land; thus nearly forming an oval, of which the diameter from north to south is forty-five miles, that from east to west about seventy; its circumference is about one hundred and seventy miles, and its area comprises about two thousand and ninety square miles.

NAME and ANCIENT HISTORY.—This county derives its name from the Saxons, it forming the northern district of East Anglia, and having been the residence of the '*Northern folk.*' In the time of the Romans it formed a part of that warlike kingdom of the ancient Britons, the *Iceni*. The Romans found in the aboriginal inhabitants of this county a race of heroes, who spurned at the idea of captivity; and who, with the illustrious Queen Boadicea at their head, defeated their proud invaders, and made a horrible carnage of their troops: the unfortunate sequel, with the subjugation of the ill-fated Britons, and the abandonment by them of their ancient province to their conquerors, is too well known to need narrating. The contiguity of Norfolk to Denmark laid its coast open to the barbarous incursions of the Danes; and Sweyn, King of Denmark, in consequence of the treacherous massacre of his people by Ethelred II, landed on the coast, and, marching his troops into the interior, burnt the cities of Norwich and Thetford. In the reign of Edward VI, at the era of the Reformation, a dangerous and alarming insurrection broke out in Norfolk, which was conducted by Ket, a tanner, of Norwich; the pretext for this rebellion was the dissolution of the monasteries and the alienation of the church lands: Ket acted as supreme administrator of affairs,—and, being seated under a a stately oak in the vicinity of Norwich, (since called 'the Oak of Reformation,') he issued his decrees with all the authority of a sovereign dictator. John Dudley, Earl of Warwick, afterwards Duke of Northumberland, marched against the insurgents, and succeeded in dispersing them; Robert Ket was hung in chains, on the walls of Norwich Castle. Christianity was introduced into this part of East Anglia at a very early period; Felix was constituted Bishop, and fixed his residence at Dunwich, in Suffolk: the Diocese was afterwards divided into two districts, Dunwich, and North Elmham, in Norfolk; the Episcopal See was afterwards translated from Elmham to Thetford, and from thence to Norwich, where it now remains. The first Bishop of Norwich was Herbert Lusigna, who died in 1119; the present Bishop is a Baron of the realm, and sits in the House of Peers—also as Titular Abbot of St. Bennet's, in Holme, the only Abbot now in England.

SOIL and CLIMATE, PRODUCE and MANUFACTURES.—The face of the county of Norfolk varies less than in most tracts of equal extent in the Kingdom: not a single hill of more than moderate height is to be seen, but its surface is in many parts broken into gentle undulations. The soil of the county is known to have a greater variety in it than is found in any other in England, and may be divided into five sorts or qualities:—The district round Norwich consists of a sandy loam, and also of stiff wet land, composed of a mixture of sand and clay; and to the west and north-west of the city a light sandy ground prevails: marsh-land may be considered a fifth district by itself, consisting of ooze, formed by a deposition from the sea. There are large tracts of swampy ground in the vicinity of Loddon, frequently inundated by land-floods, and producing little else but sedge and reeds; several of the western hundreds, from Thetford northwards, are open and bare, consisting of extensive heaths, having a light sandy or gravelly soil. The AGRICULTURAL PRODUCE of this county comprises all sorts of grain in abundance, and natural grasses; pease, beans, vetches or tares; cole-seed, clovers, and other artificial grasses; burnet, cocksfoot, chicary, cabbages, mangel-wurzel, lucerne, carrots and potatoes,—the latter invaluable root has but lately been adopted as a field-course. Among irregular crops may be reckoned mustard; saffron is also grown in many parts; flax is cultivated about Downham, and hemp near Old Buckenham. By the patriotic exertions and laudable example of Mr. Coke, every modern improvement in agriculture is fairly and experimentally laid open to the whole county. The fenny parts yield great quantities of butter, which is commonly sent to London under the name of 'Cambridge butter.' The sheep are a hardy, active and rather small breed, and much valued for their mutton; and innumerable Scotch and other beasts are fattened for the supply of Smithfield and its own markets. Turkies are reared here to a larger size than in any other county in England, and form a considerable object of profit to the smaller farmers; they are much esteemed in London, and fetch very great prices—particularly about the festive season of Christmas, at which period immense quantities are forwarded to the Metropolis. Rabbits are extremely numerous on the sandy heaths; and game of all kinds abounds throughout the county, especially pheasants, which are bred and preserved to such an extent as to prove a great annoyance to the farmer. The MANUFACTURES of this county, although of a most important and extensive character, are nevertheless confined to a small space; Norwich may be considered the nucleus of the prosperous trade arising from the labours of the loom. The fabrics consist chiefly of bombasins, camlets, crapes, and other articles made from worsted and silk: many diversities of shawls are likewise manufactured here, also damasks, cotton and woollen goods to a small extent, and a variety of fancy articles; the weaving of broad silks has been introduced by some spirited manufacturers; and it is anticipated that this branch must ultimately succeed to a considerable extent in this part, from the facility existing in machinery, and the number of expert artizans. Yarmouth enjoys considerable consequence, in the double capacity of a port and fishing-town; from its herring-fishery especially, and the peculiar and unrivalled method of curing that fish, it has long enjoyed great prosperity and note. Other towns in the county possess their several advantages, but no particular manufactures or trades are prominently exhibited. The CLIMATE, considering the contiguity of this county to the ocean, and its being much exposed to north and north-east winds, is more healthful, serene and mild than might be expected. The inhabitants near the coast are sometimes afflicted with ague: with the exception of this disease, which is not so prevalent in the interior of the county, the air of Norfolk is peculiarly salubrious and pleasant: the inhabitants have long been celebrated for their convalescence—an incontrovertible argument in support of the salubrity of its climate, and which tends to refute some misrepresentations that have been given of the quality of the atmosphere of Norfolk. The sea coast of Norfolk is formed either by clayey cliffs (continually a prey to the ocean), or by low sandy shores, covered with loose pebbles, and frequently rising into a kind of natural bank, composed of sand, held together by the roots of the sea reed grass; behind these sand-hills are in various parts salt marshes of considerable extent, occasionally inundated by the tides, which find entrance through the gaps between the hillocks Hunstanton Cliff, at the mouth of the Wash, is the only rocky eminence on the coast. Various small ports have been made, on the north side, by creeks and little bays; but they can only admit small vessels, and are continually filling up with sand. Banks of sand lie off at sea from the Norfolk coast in various parts, which are the dread of the coasting mariners, and occasion too frequent shipwrecks: of these, the most remarkable are the Yarmouth Sands, running parallel to Yarmouth Roads—a great resort for shipping, which ride there securely, though the entrance is both difficult and hazardous. The public roads throughout this county, in general, are excellent, and the navigation by sea, and by the different rivers, almost belt the country round.

There is not a county in England so distinguished for the native industry of its inhabitants, nor is there one superior for the beauty and neatness of the farms. The NORFOLK FARMER exhibits, both in himself and his farm, characteristic traits of excellence: industrious, economical, yet hospitable; habitually neat in his person; and presenting in his farm every thing that can evince the most sedulous attention, and comprehensive judgment, with respect to its agricultural condition. A celebrated topographer, in eulogizing Norfolk, enthusiastically yet justly says—'Whether we survey this county with respect to its climate, its population, its trade and commerce, the character of its inhabitants, the diversified beauties of prospect which embellish it, or especially with respect to the improved state of agriculture, it may with propriety be denominated THE GLORY OF ENGLAND.'

RIVERS and CANALS.—The principal rivers which have their source in this county, and others which pass through it, are, the GREAT OUSE, the LITTLE OUSE, the NEN, the WAVENEY, the WENSUM, the YARE, the BURE and the NAR. The Great Ouse rises in Huntingdonshire, and after passing Huntingdon, St. Ives and Ely, enters this county on the south-west, and, running north-east, falls into the German Ocean below Lynn Regis. The Little Ouse rises about the middle of the Suffolk border, and, separating the two counties as it flows north-west, becomes navigable from Thetford, and empties itself into the Great Ouse not far from Downham. The Nen, rising in Northamptonshire, passes the towns of Northampton, Thrapstone, Oundle, Peterborough and Wisbeach, and forms the western boundary of this county; and after communicating by several channels with the Ouse, falls into the sea at the Lincolnshire Washes. The Waveney has its source separated from that of the Little Ouse by a causeway only; and, running north-east, forms the rest of the Suffolk boundary; being navigable from Bungay to its junction with the Yare, a little above Yarmouth, where it falls into the North Sea. The Yare rises near Shipdham, in the centre of the county; and being joined by the Tase on the south, and the Wensum on the south-east of Norwich, flows on to Yarmouth, near which it receives the streams of the Waveney, Bure and Thyrne. The Bure, joined by the Thyrne and other smaller streams from the north-east, meets the Yare to the north-west of Yarmouth; it is navigable to Aylsham. The Wensum has its source at West Rudham, in this county; it environs the city of Norwich, and falls into the Yare. The Nar has its source at Nitcham; it is navigable as far as Narborough, and falls into the Greater Ouse. The smaller streams, flowing through an almost level country, are slow in their course, and frequently diffuse themselves over the lower tracts in their progress, forming shallow lakes, here called 'broads,' which are plentifully stored with fish and water-fowl; on some of them are decoys for wild-ducks. CANALS:—The inland navigation of this county at present is upon a small scale. A canal has been formed from Wisbeach, in Cambridgeshire, to Outwell Creek and Salters Load, in Norfolk, its extent being about six miles. In 1795 an Act of Parliament was obtained for cutting a navigable canal from the Eaw Bank to Lynn Regis, and in 1805 another act was passed for amending the former one; several other canals have been projected at different times, but the want of due patronage has prevented them being carried into execution.

CIVIL and ECCLESIASTICAL DIVISIONS.—Norfolk is in the Province of Canterbury and Diocese of Norwich, and gives name to a circuit. The county is divided into thirty-three hundreds, namely—

BLOFIELD,	EYNESFORD,	GREENHOE-	LODDON,
BROTHERCROSS,	FLEGG EAST,	SOUTH,	MITFORD,
CLACKCLOSE,	FLEGG WEST,	GRIMSHOE,	SHROPHAM,
CLAVERING,	FOREHOE,	GUILTCROSS,	SMITHDON,
DEPWADE,	FREEBRIDGE-LYNN,	HAPPING,	TAVERSHAM,
DISS,	FREEBRIDGE-	HENSTEAD,	TUNSTEAD,
EARSHAM,	MARSHLAND,	HOLT,	WALSHAM
ERPINGHAM NORTH,	GALLOW,	HUMBLEYARD,	AND
ERPINGHAM SOUTH,	GREENHOE NORTH,	LAUNDITCH,	WAYLAND.

These are subdivided into 731 parishes, containing one city and county town (Norwich), and 20 other market towns. The whole county returns 12 Members to Parliament, viz. 2 for the COUNTY, 2 for the City of NORWICH, and 2 each for the towns of CASTLE RISING, LYNN REGIS, THETFORD and YARMOUTH. The marine government of the county is vested in a naval officer of high jurisdiction, who is called the 'Vice-Admiral of Norfolk.'

POPULATION.—According to the census of 1821, there were houses inhabited in the county, 62,274; uninhabited, 1,269; and houses building, 525. The number of families then resident in the county was 74,498; comprising 166,892 males, and 177,476 females; total, 344,368: and by a calculation made by order of Government, which included persons in the army and navy, for which was added after the ratio of about one to thirty prior to the year 1811, and one to fifty for that year and the census of 1821, to the returns made from the several districts; the population of the county, in round numbers, in the year 1700, was 210,200—in 1750, 215,100—in 1801, 282,400—in 1811, 301,800—and in 1821, 351,300. The increased population in the 50 years, from the year 1700, was 4,900—from 1750 to 1801, the increase was 67,300—from 1801 to 1811, the increase was 19,400—and from 1811 to 1821, the augmented number of persons was 49,500: the grand total increase in the population of the county from the year 1700 to the census of 1821, being about 141,100 persons.

[*Table of Distances—See over.*

Index of Distances from Town to Town in the County of Norfolk.

THE NAMES OF THE RESPECTIVE TOWNS ARE ON THE TOP AND SIDE, AND THE SQUARE WHERE BOTH MEET GIVES THE DISTANCE.

Town	Attleburgh	Aylsham	Burnham Market	Cley	Cromer	Diss	Downham	East Dereham	Fakenham	Hingham	Holt	Lynn Regis	North Walsham	Norwich	Swaffham	Thetford	Walsingham	Watton	Wells	Wymondham	*Distance from London.*
Attleburgh																					93
Aylsham	24																				119
Burnham Market	36	27																			121
Cley	37	16	16																		123
Cromer	36	10	28	12																	130
Diss	12	30	48	50	45																91
Downham	28	38	33	43	48	42															86
East Dereham	15	17	22	22	22	28	26														101
Fakenham	27	21	10	13	22	40	34	12													117
Hingham	6	25	30	31	46	20	27	10	22												98
Holt	33	12	17	4	10	40	40	18	12	27											119
Lynn Regis	34	39	21	37	46	42	12	27	22	30	34										98
North Walsham	28	7	31	20	10	36	54	24	27	28	16	46									123
Norwich *(by Thetford)*	14	11	36	25	22	22	42	16	25	14	21	42	14								108
Swaffham	19	30	24	29	36	22	14	12	16	17	28	15	37	28							96
Thetford	15	40	42	44	50	18	24	22	34	19	40	33	43	29	18						80
Walsingham	30	20	8	10	20	45	35	16	5	26	9	25	26	28	21	43					117
Watton	10	26	33	31	33	20	20	10	22	7	27	24	35	21	9	12	30				91
Wells *(by Swaffham)*	37	22	6	9	21	50	36	22	10	32	12	28	28	32	26	44	5	35			118
Wymondham	6	20	34	34	30	18	33	12	26	6	27	37	23	9	22	20	31	12	36		100
Yarmouth	37	34	58	44	30	36	65	38	44	37	40	65	25	23	51	50	50	44	55	32	124

Additional information relating to the County of Norfolk.

---ooo---

Population.—By the Census for **1831** this county contained 189,305 males, and 200,749 females—total 390,054, being an increase, since the returns made in the year 1821, of 45,686 inhabitants; and from the Census of 1801 to that of 1831 the augmentation amounted to 116,683 persons.

Representation.—By the *Reform Bill* the borough of Castle Rising is disfranchised; but two additional members being given to the county, the nnmber of representatives *(twelve)* for the whole county is the same as before the passing of the Bill. The new *Boundary Act* divides the county into two parts, respectively named the *Eastern Division* and the *Western Division*; the former includes the hundreds of Blofield, Clavering, Depwade, Diss, Earsham, North Erpingham, South Erpingham, Eynesford, East Flegg, West Flegg, Forehoe, Happing, Henstead, Humbleyard, Loddon, Taversham, Tunstead, and Walsham; and the western division comprises the hundreds of Freebridge-Marshland, Freebridge-Lynn, Smithdon, Clackclose, Brothercross, Gallow, Holt, Launditch, South Greenhoe, North Greenhoe, Grimshoe, Wayland, Shropham, Giltcross, and Mitford. The election of members for the eastern division of the county is held at Norwich, and for the western at Swaffham: besides the place of election, the eastern division polls at Yarmouth, Reepham, North Walsham, and Long Stratton; and the western division (besides the place of election) polls at Downham, Fakenham, Lynn Regis, Thetford and East Dereham.

Railways.—The Eastern Counties' opens a communication between *Norwich* and the *Metropolis*, going by *Ipswich, Colchester, Chelmsford,* &c. Besides a branch, intended to pass, from *Norwich* to *Yarmouth*, there is a Railway projected from Norwich to Cambridge, by way of Thetford and Newmarket; and the proposed Norwich and Leicester Railway, by the route of Downham, Peterborough, Stamford and Oakham, to Leicester.

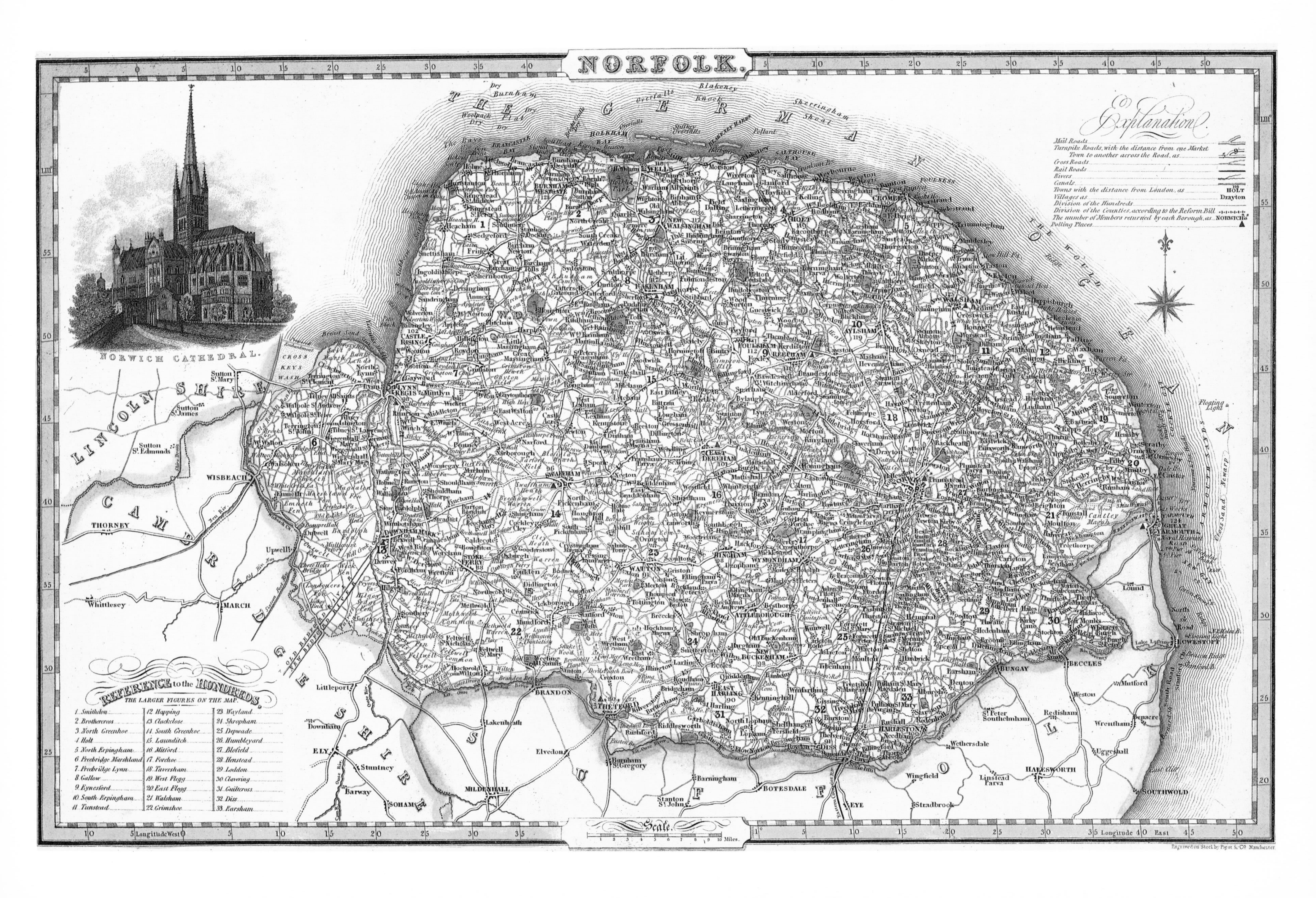
NORFOLK.
NORWICH CATHEDRAL.
Explanation
Mail Roads
Turnpike Roads, with the distance from one Market Town to another across the Road, as
Cross Roads
Rail Roads
Rivers
Canals
Towns with the distance from London, as HOLT
Villages as Drayton
Division of the Hundreds
Division of the Counties, according to the Reform Bill
The number of Members returned by each Borough, as NORWICH
Polling Places
REFERENCE to the HUNDREDS,
THE LARGER FIGURES ON THE MAP.
1 Smithdon
2 Brothercross
3 North Greenhoe
4 Holt
5 North Erpingham
6 Freebridge Marshland
7 Freebridge Lynn
8 Gallow
9 Eynesford
10 South Erpingham
11 Tunstead
12 Happing
13 Clackclose
14 South Greenhoe
15 Launditch
16 Mitford
17 Forehoe
18 Taversham
19 West Flegg
20 East Flegg
21 Walsham
22 Grimshoe
23 Wayland
24 Shropham
25 Depwade
26 Humbleyard
27 Blofield
28 Henstead
29 Loddon
30 Clavering
31 Guiltcross
32 Diss
33 Earsham
THE GERMAN OCEAN
LINCOLN SHIRE
CAMBRIDGE SHIRE
SUFFOLK
Scale
Miles
Longitude West
Longitude East
Engraved on Steel by Pigot & Co. Manchester

NORTHAMPTONSHIRE.

THE County of NORTHAMPTON lies obliquely across the middle of England, and is in contact with more surrounding ones than any other in the Kingdom. To the north and north-west it has the counties of Lincoln, Rutland and Leicester, from the two former and part of the latter of which it is separated by the river Welland; to the west it has Warwickshire; to the south, Oxfordshire and Buckinghamshire; to the east, Bedfordshire and Huntingdonshire, with a small point of Cambridgeshire. Its greatest length is sixty miles, and its breadth only about twenty-five: its circumference has been variously laid down, from 125 miles to 216; in the returns to Parliament its area is stated to comprise 1,017 square miles.

NAME and ANCIENT HISTORY.—This county takes its name from the town of Northampton; so called, it is said by some, from its situation on the north side of the river Anfona or Nen,—though others infer that it was so named in contra-distinction to Southampton. The inhabitants of this county, in the time of the Romans, were a part of the *Coritanii;* and during the Saxon Heptarchy, Northamptonshire belonged to the Kingdom of Mercia. Two Roman roads crossed this county—the 'Watling-street' in its broadest part, and a vicinal road in its narrowest. When the Danes invaded Britain, this part of the country suffered severely from the depredations of that people; and, amongst other places in the county, none experienced the effects of their wanton violence more cruelly than the city of Peterborough, which, with its rich Abbey, was destroyed by them, and continued for nearly a century in ruins,—when Ethelwald, Bishop of Winchester, with the assistance of King Edgar and his Chancellor Adulf, rebuilt the city, and restored the Monastery to its former magnificence. At the dissolution the Abbey was converted by Henry VIII. into a Cathedral, which suffered much during the civil wars; but it has subsequently been thoroughly repaired and beautified, and is now an interesting pile of building, in the Norman style of architecture. Queen Katharine of Arragon, first wife of Henry VIII, and Mary, Queen of Scots, were buried here,—the former in the year 1535, and the funeral of the unfortunate Mary was solemnized in this place in 1587: the body was brought from Fotheringay Castle, in this county (where she was beheaded), and committed, on the 31st of July, to a vault on the south side of the choir; but in the year 1612 her remains were translated to Westminster, by order of her son, King James I. In the parish of Naseby (supposed to be the centre of England,) was fought, in June 1645, the decisive battle between Charles I. and the Parliament army, commanded by Fairfax, which terminated in the total defeat and consequent ruin of the Royal party.

SOIL and CLIMATE, PRODUCE and MANUFACTURES.—Northamptonshire is almost proverbially regarded as a fine and pleasant county, interspersed with many Noblemen's and Gentlemen's seats. Its greatest defect is the scarcity of fuel; yet it still possesses some considerable remains of its old forests, particularly those of Rockingham in the north-west, and of Salcey and Whittlebury in the south. By the construction of 'the Union Canal,' coals have, however, been introduced into the county from the Trent; and they are also obtained from Lynn, in Norfolk, by means of the Nen. In the agricultural appropriation of this county, about 300,000 acres are said to be arable, 250,000 pasturage, and about 80,000 uncultivated, including the woodlands; within the latter, however, numerous deer, horses, cattle and sheep are fed; great numbers of the cattle and sheep are afterwards fattened on the rich grazing land of the county, and sent to the London markets. The prevailing system of husbandry is grazing, and several of the farmers are justly noted for their skilful management of land and stock. The surface of the county is particularly advantageous for cultivation, as it possesses neither dreary wastes nor rugged mountains, but is every where sufficiently regular for all the purposes of husbandry and tillage. The highest ground in this county is in the neighbourhood of Daventry, where the Nen and Charwell, which flow into the eastern sea, and the Leam, flowing into the western, rise within a small compass; about Towcester, in the south, the country is also hilly, and the soil intermixed with clay and a sort of gritstone. CLIMATE.—The air of Northamptonshire is esteemed equal, if not superior, to that of any county in the Kingdom; and to this is ascribed the circumstance of so many of the Nobility and Gentry having seats in it: Nordern, in his account of it, says—'so full is it of Gentry, that it may be called *the Herald's Garden.*' There is, however, a small tract of country, called 'Fenland,' about Peterborough, which is often overflowed by great falls of water from the uplands, in rainy seasons; but the inhabitants do not suffer the water to continue a sufficient time on the ground, even in winter, to affect the salubrity of the air. The PRODUCTS of Northamptonshire are in general the same with those of other farming counties: horned cattle, and other animals useful to man, are fed to extraordinary sizes; horses, of the large black breed, are also reared; and many flocks of sheep are grazed on the elevated grounds: woad, for dyers' use, is cultivated in some parts. The MANUFACTURES of this county are not by any means of importance: in some of the towns, silk stockings are wove; and in others, lace-making and wool-spinning give employment to the female working class.

RIVERS and CANALS.—In the important article of water, the county of Northampton may justly boast that it is entirely and completely independent; for, of the six rivers which flow through or intersect it, every one originates within its boundaries—and not a single brook, however insignificant, runs into it from any other district. The principal rivers are, the NEN, the WELLAND, the OUSE, the AVON, the LEAM and the CHARWELL. The northern branch of the Nen springs from Chapel Well, at Naseby; and the western from Hartwell, near Staverton; and both, uniting at Northampton, form no inconsiderable river, which, after traversing the whole length of the county, falls into the 'Lynn Deeps,' in Norfolk. The Welland rises at Sibertoft, and leaves the county after flowing the short space of four miles; it then pursues a course of nearly fifty miles, during which it becomes navigable at Stamford, and at length falls into the 'Foss-dyke Wash,' near Boston. The Ouse has its source near Brackley, and falls into the German Ocean at Lynn. The Avon, or Lesser Avon, commences its course at Avon Well, near Naseby; and, flowing in a westerly direction, passes into Warwickshire. The Leam, which rises from the village of Hellidon, is immediately joined by other rills, with which it hastens into Warwickshire; and, having given name to the two villages of Leamington, meets the Lesser Avon,—and the junction of their waters forms the celebrated AVON, which ultimately loses itself in the Severn. The Charwell springs near Charwelton, and finishes its career at the city of Oxford, where it resigns its identity to the noble Thames. CANALS.—The first artificial canal that rendered any benefit to this county was the 'Oxford,' which passes on the western verge of it, and at Braunston joins the Grand Junction canal. The Union canal proceeds north from Northampton, in its course to near Market Harborough, to which there is a cut; and, after passing the Soar, joins that river near Leicester, and thus has an easy communication with the Trent.

CIVIL and ECCLESIASTICAL DIVISIONS.—Northamptonshire is in the Province of Canterbury and Diocese of Peterborough, in the Midland Circuit. It is divided into nineteen hundreds, namely—

CHIPPING WARDEN,	GUILSBOROUGH,	NAVISFORD,	ROTHWELL,
CLELY,	HAMFORDSHOE,	NOBOTTLE-GROVE,	SPELHOE,
CORBY,	HIGHAM FERRERS,	ORLINGBURY,	TOWCESTER,
FAWSLEY,	HUXLOE,	POLEBROOK,	WILLYBROOK,
GREEN'S-NORTON,	KING'S SUTTON,		WYMERSLEY.

These are subdivided into three hundred and six parishes, collectively containing one city (Peterborough), one county town (Northampton), and eight other market towns. The whole county returns nine Members to Parliament, viz. two each for PETERBOROUGH, NORTHAMPTON, BRACKLEY, and the SHIRE, and one for HIGHAM FERRERS.

POPULATION.—According to the census of 1821, there were houses inhabited in the county, 32,503; uninhabited, 527; and houses building, 179. The number of families then resident in the county was 35,552, comprising 79,575 males, and 82,908 females; total, 162,483: and by a calculation made by order of government, which included persons in the army and navy, for which was added after the ratio of about one to thirty prior to the year 1811, and one to fifty for that year and the census of 1821, to the returns made from the several districts; the population of the county, in round numbers, in the year 1700, was 119,500—in 1750, 123,300—in 1801, 136,100—in 1811, 146,100—and in 1821, 165,800. The increased population in the fifty years, from the year 1700, was 3,800—from 1750 to 1801, the increase was 12,800—from 1801 to 1811, the increase was 10,000—and from 1811 to 1821, the augmented number of persons was 19,700: the grand total increase in the population of the county, from the year 1700 to the census of 1821, being about 46,300 persons.

Index of Distances from Town to Town in the County of Northampton.

THE NAMES OF THE RESPECTIVE TOWNS ARE ON THE TOP AND SIDE, AND THE SQUARE WHERE BOTH MEET GIVES THE DISTANCE.

	Brackley	Daventry	Higham Ferrers	Kettering	Northampton	Oundle	Peterborough	Rothwell	Thrapstone	Towcester	Wellingborough	Distance from London.
Brackley												63
Daventry	22											72
Higham Ferrers	36	27										65
Kettering	36	27	9									75
Northampton	20	12	16	15								66
Oundle	47	40	15	14	27							78
Peterborough	60	52	28	27	40	13						79
Rothwell	35	27	14	4	15	14	27					78
Thrapstone	40	33	8	9	20	8	19	12				73
Towcester	11	12	25	25	9	35	48	24	29			60
Wellingborough	30	22	5	7	10	18	30	11	10	19		67

[See over.

Additional information relating to the County of Northampton.

———ooo———

Population.—By the Census for **1831** this county contained 87,889 males, and 91,387 females—total 179,276 being an increase, since the returns made in the year 1821, of 16,793 inhabitants; and from the Census of 1801 to that of 1831, the augmentation amounted to 47,519 persons.

Representation.—By the *Reform Bill* the boroughs of Brackley and Higham Ferrers have been deprived of the elective franchise; and two additional members have been given to the county: the whole shire, therefore, now returns *eight* representatives to Parliament, instead of *nine*, as heretofore. The new *Boundary Act* divides the county into two parts, respectively called the *Northern Division* and the *Southern Division*: the former includes the liberty of Peterborough, and the several hundreds of Willybrook, Polebrook, Huxloe, Navisford, Corby, Higham Ferrers, Rothwell, Hamfordshoe, and Orlingbury; and the southern division comprises the hundreds of King's Sutton, Chipping Warden, Green's Norton, Cleley, Towcester, Fawsley, Wymersley, Spelhoe, Nobottle-Grove, and Guilsborough. The election of members for the northern division is held at Kettering, and for the southern at Northampton: besides the place of election the northern division polls at Peterborough, Oundle, Wellingborough, and Clipson; and the southern division (besides the place of election) polls at Daventry, Towcester, and Brackley.

Railways.—The London and Birmingham passes *Northampton* within about five miles, *Towcester* four miles, and *Daventry* three; the first lies on the right and the two latter on the left of the line from *London*. From the London and Birmingham line a branch will join the Midland Counties' Railway near Leicester.

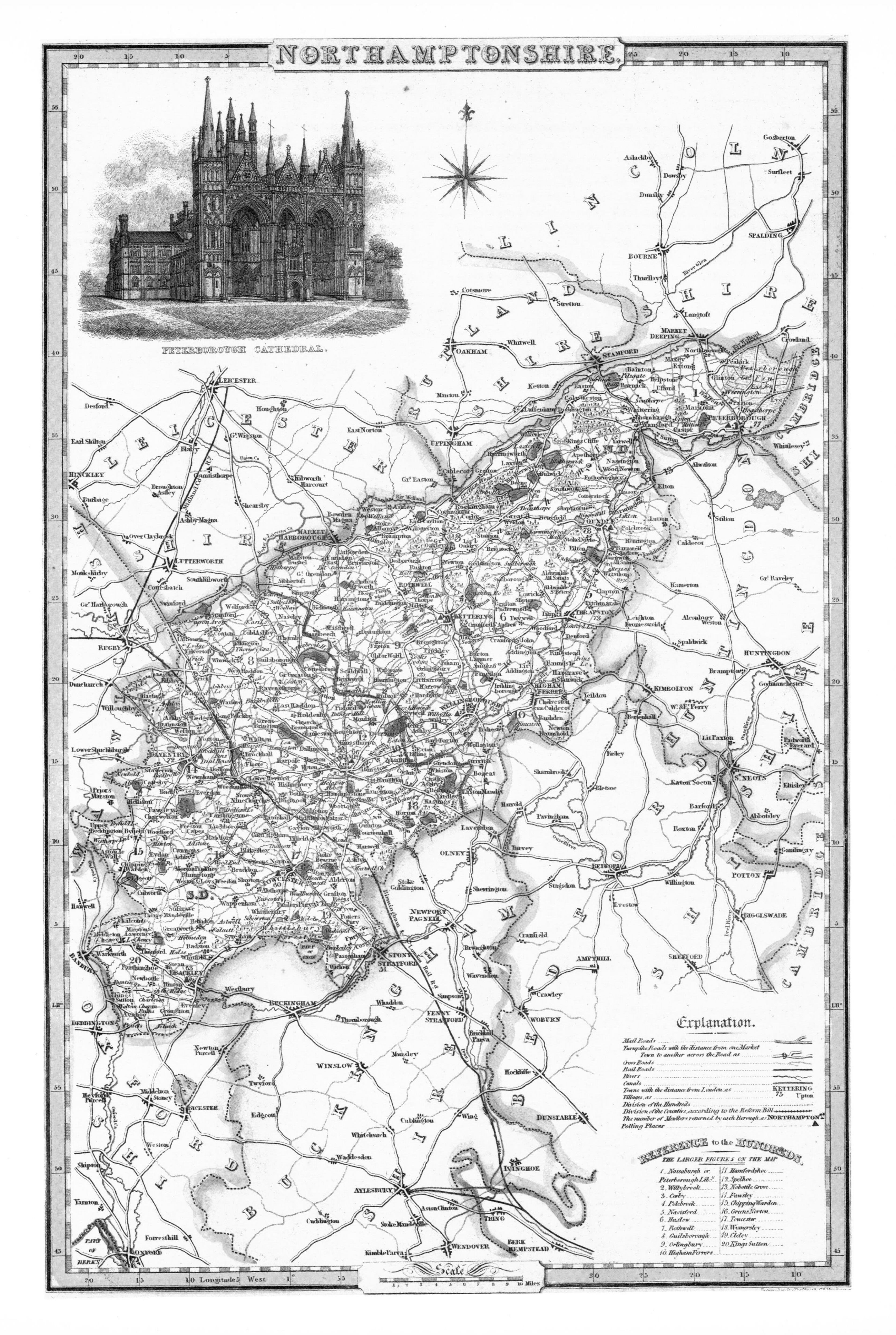
NORTHAMPTONSHIRE.
PETERBOROUGH CATHEDRAL.
Explanation.
Mail Roads
Turnpike Roads with the distance from one Market Town to another across the Road as
Cross Roads
Rail Roads
Rivers
Canals
Towns with the distance from London as
KETTERING 75
Villages, as
Upton
Division of the Hundreds
Division of the Counties, according to the Reform Bill
The number of Members returned by each Borough as NORTHAMPTON
Polling Places
REFERENCE to the HUNDREDS.
THE LARGER FIGURES ON THE MAP
1. Nassaburgh or Peterborough Lib.y
2. Willybrook
3. Corby
4. Polebrook
5. Navisford
6. Huxlow
7. Rothwell
8. Guilsborough
9. Orlingbury
10. Higham Ferrers
11. Hamfordshoe
12. Spelhoe
13. Nobottle Grove
14. Fawsley
15. Chipping Warden
16. Greens Norton
17. Towcester
18. Wymersley
19. Cleley
20. Kings Sutton
Scale
Miles
Longitude West
LINCOLNSHIRE
RUTLAND SHIRE
LEICESTERSHIRE
HUNTINGDONSHIRE
CAMBRIDGE
BEDFORDSHIRE
BUCKINGHAMSHIRE
OXFORDSHIRE
WARWICKSHIRE
STAMFORD
PETERBOROUGH
OUNDLE
KETTERING
THRAPSTON
WELLINGBOROUGH
DAVENTRY
TOWCESTER
BRACKLEY
HIGHAM FERRERS
MARKET HARBOROUGH
LEICESTER
LUTTERWORTH
RUGBY
HINCKLEY
OAKHAM
UPPINGHAM
HUNTINGDON
KIMBOLTON
S. NEOTS
BEDFORD
OLNEY
NEWPORT PAGNELL
STONY STRATFORD
BUCKINGHAM
BANBURY
DEDDINGTON
BICESTER
OXFORD
AYLESBURY
WINSLOW
FENNY STRATFORD
WOBURN
AMPTHILL
DUNSTABLE
SPALDING
BOURNE
MARKET DEEPING
POTTON
BIGGLESWADE
SHEFFORD
TRING
WENDOVER
BERK HEMPSTEAD
IVINGHOE

NORTHUMBERLAND.

THE County of NORTHUMBERLAND is a maritime one, and the most northerly of all the English counties. It is bounded on the east by the German Ocean, on the west by Scotland and Cumberland, on the north by the river Tweed and the Cheviot Hills, and its southern parts border with an irregular line on Cumberland and Durham. Its natural boundaries are in most parts mountains and rivers; and its form is a triangle, the sides of which are unequal. For size it is amongst the largest counties, its greatest length being nearly 70 miles; its breadth at the southern extremity, from east to west, about 48; and its circumference about 230 miles. Part of this county is occupied by certain hundreds in the county of Durham, viz. Norhamshire, Islandshire and Bedlingtonshire: this singularly local circumstance perhaps may account for the variance of writers in stating the square miles and acreage of the county,—some giving to it about 1,500 square miles, and 817,200 acres; others computing Northumberland to contain 1,810 square miles, and 1,157,760 acres. To reconcile these discrepancies must be, to take the lowest computation, as excluding the land of those hundreds appertaining to Durham, and the highest, as permitting it to form a part of the calculation. In the work printed by order of Parliament in 1821, containing the population returns, &c., the area of Northumberland is stated to comprise one thousand eight hundred and seventy-one square miles.

NAME and ANCIENT HISTORY.—This county received its name from the Saxons, by whom it was called *Northan-Humber-land*, signifying 'the land or county north of the Humber.' It was anciently of much greater extent than at present, comprehending Yorkshire, Durham, Lancashire, Westmoreland and Cumberland; and was a distinct Kingdom of the Saxon Heptarchy. At the time of the invasion of Britain by the Romans, this county, with several others adjoining, was inhabited by the *Ottadininii, Ottadenii*, or *Ottatinii;* a people supposed to have been so called from their situation near the river Tyne; who, being uneasy under the Roman yoke, conspired with the Caledonians, in the reign of the Emperor Severus, and emancipated themselves from his government: this Prince dying soon after, the original possessors were left masters of this province, till Theodosius, subsequently landing in England, once more reduced them. After the Romans withdrew, the Britons called in the aid of the Saxons to assist them against the Scots and Picts,—and these wily allies having vanquished their enemies, settled here themselves, and divided those parts of the Island in their possession into seven Kingdoms, of which Northumberland, afterwards called *Bernicia*, was the chief. The Roman roads passing through this county were, the *Watling Street*, entering it from Durham, and running through Corbridge on to Scotland; and a military road from Carlisle to Walwick-upon-Tyne. Near Newcastle terminated the ancient Picts' or Roman Wall, which stretched across the Island to Carlisle, for preventing the incursions of the former people and the Scots. The most memorable battles fought in this county were those of Hallidon Hill, near Berwick, in 1333,—and that of Flodden, in 1513; in both of which the Scots were defeated with great slaughter, and in the latter their valiant King, James IV, was slain. There was also fought at Hexham, in 1463, that bloody battle between the Houses of York and Lancaster, in which the latter was defeated. In former times Berwick was of great importance, on account of its very strong fortress, which was termed 'the Key of Scotland,' and was many times possessed both by the Scotch and English forces: it was here that, in 1291, the States of England and Scotland, with Edward I, assembled to determine the claims of Robert Bruce and John Baliol to the Scottish Crown,—when, after numerous conferences, on the 17th November in the following year the King appointed John Baliol successor to the Crown. The present celebrity of Berwick arises from its valuable salmon fishery. At Alnwick is one of the principal seats of the great ancient family of PERCY, Earls of Northumberland: the Castle was at a certain period reckoned one of the most impregnable fortresses in this Kingdom; at the present day it is deservedly considered one of the noblest and most magnificent models of a great Baronial Castle.

SOIL and CLIMATE, PRODUCE and MANUFACTURES.—The face of the country in this large district is various, but in the aggregate inclining to nakedness; and, although agricultural industry and perseverance have accomplished much, and overcome difficulties of magnitude, many parts still continue sterile, and to the farmer or grazier almost valueless. The mountainous parts, almost unfit for tillage, comprise nearly one-third of the land. The most fertile tracts are those on the east side, in the vales through which the rivers run in their course to the sea; and the vale of Coquet is particularly noted for its fertility. Woods are chiefly confined to the banks of rivers. The Cheviot Hills, near the north angle, are the most valuable of the mountainous tract, affording pasturage to innumerable flocks of sheep peculiar to them. The south-west angle is an extremely dreary and barren district, though rendered valuable by its lead mines. To the north of this, around the hilly regions, are some fertile dales; but the country about Redesdale is so boggy, as to be almost an impassable desert. The central part of the county stretches into melancholy wastes, on which arise a few rocky hills of no great height.—The CLIMATE of Northumberland is subject to much variation; but the air is not so cold as might be expected from its situation, so far to the north: for as it lies between the German and Irish Seas, in the narrowest part of England, it has the advantage of being warmed by the sea vapours; and hence the snow never lies long, except in the most northern parts and on the tops of lofty mountains. The air is also more salubrious than might be imagined in a country bordering on the sea; and the inhabitants are noted for their strength, robust health and longevity.—The PRODUCTS of this county are cattle, sheep, wool, corn, lead and coals, the last-named production being more prominent in consequence than any of the others: it is computed that upwards of 10,000 persons are employed in the collieries, which abound in the north-east parts, and that subsistence is given through their means to more than 20,000 souls. The principal MANUFACTURES are those chiefly depending on the collieries; such as glass works, potteries and iron foundries. A considerable source of wealth is also found in the rivers, which abound with various sorts of excellent fish, particularly trout and salmon, the Tweed being remarkable for the latter; great quantities of this fine fish are dried, and pickled for exportation: in the latter state it is in great estimation in the metropolis.

RIVERS.—This county is extremely well watered with fine rivers; of these the chief are the TWEED, the TYNE, the COQUET and the READ. The Tweed, rising in Peebles-shire, forms the boundary between Northumberland and Scotland: its general course is north-east, until it receives the waters of the Till; when, turning suddenly to the east near Loam Head, it flows past the town of Berwick, and there empties itself into the sea. The Tyne is formed by the junction of the North and South Tyne rivers: the former, rising on the borders of Scotland, passes the town of Bellingham, and a little to the north of Hexham is met by the South Tyne, which rising in Knaresdale, passes by the town of Haltwhistle: prior to its union with this river at Hexham, both rivers form the Tyne, which pursuing its course east, runs past the town of Corbridge, and about three miles west of Newcastle is further augmented by the Derwent; at the latter town it becomes navigable for large vessels, and still flowing east divides the towns of North and South Shields, emptying itself into the North Sea at Tynemouth. The Coquet rises on the western side of the county, near Museylow, on the borders of Scotland; and being joined by the Allwine at Allwineton, or Allenton, flows south-east to near Rothbury, where it receives many smaller streams, and afterwards falls into the North Sea near Warkworth—(famed in history and legendary tale for its ancient castle and hermitage.) The Read rises on the western borders of the county, and reaches the North Tyne near Bellingham.

CIVIL and ECCLESIASTICAL DIVISIONS.—Northumberland is in the Province of York and Diocese of Durham; is included in the Northern Circuit, and divided into the six wards of BAMBOROUGH, CASTLE, COQUETDALE, GLENDALE, MORPETH and TINDALE; these are subdivided into about eighty-eight parishes and parochial chapelries, containing upwards of 480 townships, one county town (Newcastle), and eleven other market towns. Northumberland returns eight Members to Parliament, namely, two each for the towns of BERWICK, MORPETH and NEWCASTLE, and two for the COUNTY.

POPULATION.—According to the census of 1821, there were houses inhabited in the county, 31,526; uninhabited, 1,166; and houses building, 190. The number of families then resident in the county was 43,128, comprising 95,354 males, and 103,611 females; total, 198,965: and by a calculation made by order of government, which included persons in the army and navy, for which was added after the ratio of about one to thirty prior to the year 1811, and one to fifty for that year and the census of 1821, to the returns made from the several districts; the population of the county, in round numbers, in the year 1700, was 118,000—in 1750, 141,700—in 1801, 162,300—in 1811, 177,900—and in 1821, 203,000. The increased population in the fifty years, from the year 1700, was 23,700—from 1750 to 1801, the increase was 20,600—from 1801 to 1811, the increase was 15,600—and from 1811 to 1821, the augmented number of persons was 25,100: the grand total increase in the population of the county, from the year 1700 to the census of 1821, being about 85,000 persons.

Index of Distances from Town to Town in the County of Northumberland.

THE NAMES OF THE RESPECTIVE TOWNS ARE ON THE TOP AND SIDE, AND THE SQUARE WHERE BOTH MEET GIVES THE DISTANCE.

Town	Allendale	Alnwick	Belford	Bellingham	Berwick-upon-Tweed	Blyth	Corbridge	Haltwhistle (by Alstone, &c.)	Hartley, or Seaton Delaval	Hexham	Morpeth	Newcastle-upon-Tyne	Rothbury	Shields (North)	Distance from London.
Allendale															283
Alnwick	51														304
Belford	65	15													322
Bellingham	24	37	50												296
Berwick-upon-Tweed	81	30	15	67											337
Blyth	40	27	42	28	57										283
Corbridge	12	42	57	18	72	28									280
Haltwhistle	15	51	67	25	82	46	18								284
Hartley	38	30	45	31	60	3	26	44							279
Hexham	10	42	57	16	72	31	4	15	29						280
Morpeth	39	19	34	25	49	8	27	40	11	30					289
Newcastle-upon-Tyne	29	34	49	30	64	13	16	36	11	20	15				273
Rothbury	38	12	27	25	42	23	30	40	26	30	15	30			303
Shields (North)	35	40	55	36	70	8	23	42	6	26	21	6	36		279
Wooler	59	20	10	45	17	40	50	61	43	50	32	47	20	54	320

[*See over.*

Additional information relating to the County of NORTHUMBERLAND.

———ooo———

POPULATION.—By the Census for **1831** this county contained 106,157 males, and 116,755 females—total 222,912, being an increase, since the returns made in the year 1821, of 23,947 inhabitants; and from the Census of 1801 to that of 1831 the augmentation amounted to 65,811 persons.

REPRESENTATION.—By the *Reform Bill* the borough of Morpeth is deprived of one of its members: the elective franchise is conferred upon TYNEMOUTH with NORTH SHIELDS, which, in conjunction, return one member; and two additional ones are given to the county: by these alterations the number of representatives now returned by the county is *ten,* instead of *eight,* as before the passing of the Bill. The new *Boundary Act* divides Northumberland into two parts, respectively named the *Northern Division* and the *Southern Division;* the former comprises the wards of Bamborough, Coquetdale, Glendale, and Morpeth, and the Berwick bounds; and the southern includes the wards of Tynedale, and Castle, and the town and county of the town of Newcastle-upon-Tyne. The election of members for the northern division is held at ALNWICK, and for the southern at HEXHAM: besides the place of election, the northern division polls at BERWICK, WOOLER, ELSDON and MORPETH; and the southern division (besides the place of election) polls at NEWCASTLE-UPON-TYNE, HALTWHISTLE, BELLINGHAM and STAMFORDHAM.

RAILWAYS.

The NEWCASTLE and CARLISLE RAILWAY passes near *Corbridge, Hexham* and *Haltwhistle,* to *Carlisle;* and there is a branch from *Newcastle* to *North Shields,* and one projected from Shields to Morpeth. The great NORTH OF ENGLAND RAILWAY will connect *Newcastle* with *Durham* and *York;* and the projected one from *Newcastle* to Scotland will complete the chain of Railway communication between *Edinburgh* and *London.* The NEWCASTLE, NORTH SHIELDS and TYNEMOUTH RAILWAY:—the works for this Railway commenced at the west end of the line about the middle of the year 1837. At *Shields* a branch passes to the steam ferry at the New Quay; and it is intended to continue the Railway in a direct line to Tynemouth Haven.

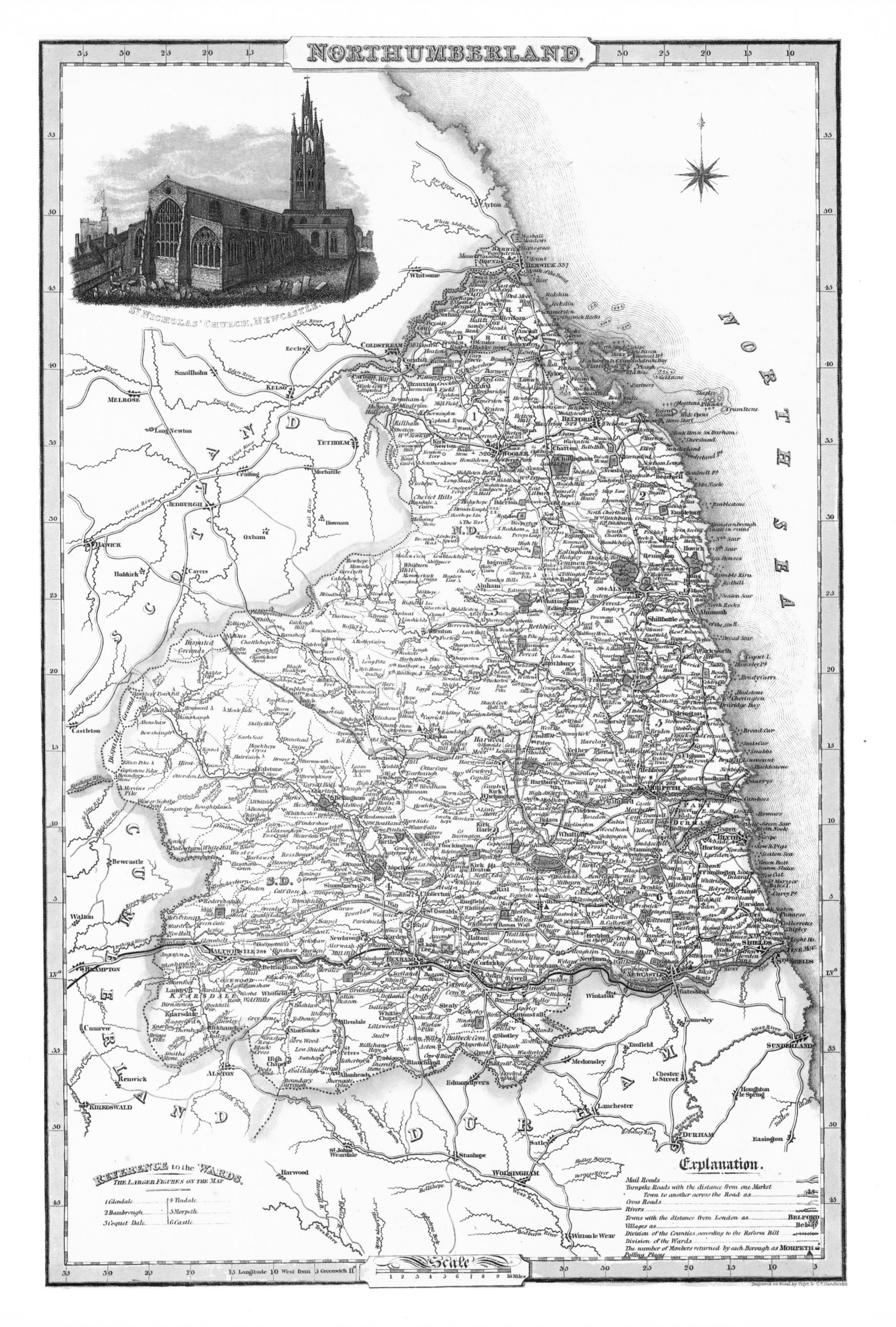
NORTHUMBERLAND.
St. NICHOLAS' CHURCH, NEWCASTLE.
NORTH SEA
SCOTLAND
CUMBERLAND
DURHAM
BERWICK 337
BELFORD 322
WOOLER 320
ALNWICK 304
MORPETH
NEWCASTLE
HEXHAM
HALTWHISTLE 288
BELLINGHAM
ROTHBURY
SHIELDS
SUNDERLAND
DURHAM
COLDSTREAM
KELSO
JEDBURGH
HAWICK
MELROSE
YETHOLM
ALSTON
KIRKOSWALD
BRAMPTON
Stanhope
Wolsingham
Lanchester
Chester le Street
Houghton le Spring
Easington
Edmondbyers
Witton le Wear
REFERENCE to the WARDS.
THE LARGER FIGURES ON THE MAP
1 Glendale
2 Bambrough
3 Coquet Dale
4 Tindale
5 Morpeth
6 Castle
Explanation.
Mail Roads
Turnpike Roads with the distance from one Market Town to another across the Road as
Cross Roads
Rivers
Towns with the distance from London as BELFORD 322
Villages as Belsay
Division of the Counties, according to the Reform Bill
Division of the Wards
The number of Members returned by each Borough as MORPETH
Polling Places
Scale
Miles
Longitude West from Greenwich
Engraved on Steel by Pigot & Co. Manchester

NOTTINGHAMSHIRE.

THE County of NOTTINGHAM is bounded on the north by Yorkshire, on the east by Lincolnshire, on the south by Leicestershire, and on the west by Derbyshire. Its form is oblong, approaching nearly to an oval—having a prominent apex on its north extremity, inserted between the counties of Lincoln and York: from this extreme point to its southern boundary, the length of the county is about fifty miles; its greatest breadth is twenty-five, and its area comprises eight hundred and thirty-seven square miles.

NAME and ANCIENT HISTORY.—This county takes its name from the town of Nottingham, called in the time of the Saxons *Snottengaham*, or *Snottingham*, which time has softened down to its present appellation. The Saxon word signified *'the dwelling of caves,'*—applicable to the principal town, as also to other parts of the county: at Nottingham especially are still existing caverns, cut with great art into apartments with chimnies, windows and other conveniences, which are supposed to have been contrived by the ancient inhabitants for places of retreat. This county was in early times inhabited by the *Coritanii;* by the Romans it was comprised in the FLAVIA CÆSARIENSIS; and during the Heptarchy it belonged to the Kingdom of Mercia. There are in Nottinghamshire vestiges of several ancient camps; the fosse-way from Devonshire to the sea-coast of Lincolnshire crossed this county; and in the time of the Romans there were three stations in it, viz. Bridgeford-on-the-Hill, Newark and Littleborough. Southwell is supposed to be the *Adpontem* of the Romans; it contains a noble and beautiful Minster, founded in the year 630 by Paulinus, the first Archbishop of York. Of the other places in the county, Nottingham is the most worthy to be noticed, considerable importance being attached to its military history:—its ancient Castle was rebuilt by the Conqueror, and repaired and strengthened by Edward IV. and Richard III.; it was never taken by storm: by Henry of Anjou it was besieged in vain; but was once surprised, in the Barons' wars, by Robert, Earl of Ferrars, who plundered the inhabitants. Here David, King of Scotland, was kept prisoner; and here Roger Mortimer, Earl of March, was seized by Edward III. and his friends, and afterwards tried and executed. At Nottingham King Charles I. set up his standard, at the commencement of the civil wars which terminated in his destruction: after the town was reduced by the Parliamentary forces, its castle was demolished.

SOIL and CLIMATE, PRODUCE and MANUFACTURES.—The soil of Nottinghamshire is various, and it assumes, in consequence, a great diversity of appearance. On the Derbyshire border, a stripe of land, extending as far south as opposite Nottingham, is the lime and coal district, and contains several woods, the land being mostly arable; a broader tract, reaching to the north-east extremity of the county, is composed chiefly of sand and gravel, including the whole of the ancient Royal 'Forest of Sherwood,' traditionally reported as the scene of the exploits of the noted outlaw, *Robin Hood,* and his associates: the greater part of this forest is now inclosed, and is the site of thriving towns, cheerful villages, and extensive parks, taken out under grants from the Crown. Norfolk husbandry has been introduced on the forest lands with the greatest success; and fine crops of barley and grasses are obtained, also some hops. Clay prevails upon the north and south borders of the Trent; these tracts are very fruitful in corn and pasture, and the neighbourhood of Retford produces fine hops, where are kept greater numbers of pigeons than even in Cambridgeshire, or any other part of the Kingdom. The fine Vale of Belvoir, lying beyond the south-east Trent bank, to the borders of Leicestershire and Lincolnshire, is a rich loamy soil, with a mixture of arable and pasture, in a high state of cultivation. The CLIMATE of this county is most genial, and perhaps the most healthful and temperate in this Island: situated as it is between the mountainous regions of Derbyshire on the one hand, and the flat or level districts of Lincolnshire on the other, it is not exposed to the keen blasts of the north, nor to a too profuse humidity, that characterizes some of the counties bordering on it. It is remarkable for its dryness, but the great fertility of the land argues that it is not so excessive as to affect the prosperity derived from agriculture; and, that it is one of the pleasantest counties in England, is evidenced by the uncommon number of elegant seats scattered over it. The PRODUCTS of this county are, coals, lead, wool, cattle, fowls, abundance of fresh-water fish, liquorice, grain of all sorts, hops and weld. The principal MANUFACTURES are, hosiery in all its branches, lace, glass & earthenware; considerable breweries, malting concerns, and tanneries, are also spread throughout the county. The trade of Nottingham is of an exceedingly high, extensive and important character; whether considered as relative to the beauty of the articles produced as embellishments of dress, or viewed as national benefits by the extensive exports. The trade consists in the making, to a vast extent, silk, cotton and woollen hosiery; and the manufacture parallel in consequence, if not stretching beyond it, is the beautiful article of bobbin net and various qualities of laces,—some of which, for their fineness, richness, or delicacy of pattern and durability, are not surpassed by the lace tediously produced by the hand upon the pillow, in this country, France or Germany. The immense number of persons, male and female, dependent upon this interesting, modern and peculiar branch, is truly astonishing; exclusive of those in the hosiery trade, which likewise gives support to a large population. The throwing and dying of silk are also important branches here; the establishments in these trades are of the first order of respectability. A great malting trade is carried on at Worksop and at Nottingham, and the ale of the latter town has long been justly and generally celebrated for its excellence. Newark, also, partakes largely in the malt trade, and it enjoys a good proportion of the weaving of coarse linens; at Mansfield are several cotton factories, and a great number of malting establishments.

RIVERS and CANALS.—The principal rivers that water this county are the TRENT, the IDLE and the ERWASH. The first-named rises in the north-west of Staffordshire, passes in its course the towns of Stone and Burton, enters this county near Thrumpton (in its course touching Nottingham and Newark), unites with the Ouse near Alkborough, and with it forms the Humber. The Idle is formed by several considerable streams rising in this county, passes the towns of East Retford and Bawtry, and empties itself into the Trent at West Stockwith. The Erwash forms the division of Derbyshire from this county, descending from the coal countries near Alfreton, and falls into the Trent a little below the Derwent.—The NAVIGABLE CANALS are the 'Chesterfield,' the 'Grantham' and the 'Cromford.' The first-named canal begins at Chesterfield, and is in length about forty-five miles to its junction with the Trent, near Stockwith. The Grantham commences on the east side of the same named town, is thirty miles in length, and joins the Trent near Crosswell Bishop. The Cromford begins at Cromford, and is in length fourteen miles to its junction with the Erwash canal, at Langley Bridge.

CIVIL AND ECCLESIASTICAL DIVISIONS.—Nottinghamshire is in the Province and Diocese of York, and included in the Midland Circuit. It is divided into the six hundreds of BASSETLAW, BINGHAM, BROXTON, NEWARK, RUSHCLIFFE and THURGARTON: these, except Bassetlaw, are apportioned into north and south divisions,—the latter hundred being separated into three portions, respectively denominated Hatfield Division, North Clay Division and South Clay Division. There is also another district called the LIBERTY OF SOUTHWELL and SCROOBY. All these collectively, contain 212 parishes, one county town (Nottingham), and eight other market towns. The whole county returns eight Members to Parliament, namely, two each for NOTTINGHAM and NEWARK, and four for the SHIRE. Until the general election in 1826, East Retford sent representatives, when petitions were presented against the return, upon charges of corruption in the borough; and in the Sessions of Parliament in 1830 a Bill was passed, transferring the elective franchise from East Retford to the hundred of Bassetlaw.

POPULATION.—According to the census of 1821, there were houses inhabited in the county, 35,022; uninhabited, 859; and houses building, 288. The number of families then resident in the county was 38,603; comprising 91,491 males, and 95,382 females; total, 186,873: and by a calculation made by order of Government, which included persons in the army and navy, for which was added after the ratio of about one to thirty prior to the year 1811, and one to fifty for that year and the census of 1821, to the returns made from the several districts; the population of the county, in round numbers, in the year 1700, was 65,200—in 1750, 77,600—in 1801, 145,000—in 1811, 168,400—and in 1821, 190,700. The increased population in the 50 years, from the year 1700, was 12,400—from 1750 to 1801, the increase was 67,400—from 1801 to 1811, the increase was 23,400—and from 1811 to 1821, the augmented number of persons was 22,300: the grand total increase in the population of the county from the year 1700 to the census of 1821, being about 125,500 persons.

Index of Distances from Town to Town in the County of Nottingham.

THE NAMES OF THE RESPECTIVE TOWNS ARE ON THE TOP AND SIDE, AND THE SQUARE WHERE BOTH MEET GIVES THE DISTANCE.

Town	Bawtry	Bingham	Blyth	Mansfield	Newark	Nottingham	Ollerton	Retford East	Southwell	Tuxford	*Distance from London.*
Bawtry											152
Bingham	37										118
Blyth	3	35									149
Mansfield	22	22	18								138
Newark	28	11	25	20							124
Nottingham	36	10	32	14	18						124
Ollerton	21	19	17	8	14	18					137
Retford East	9	28	6	18	19	29	11				144
Southwell	30	10	26	12	8	13	9	20			132
Tuxford	16	21	13	16	12	28	6	7	15		137
Worksop	10	27	6	12	21	26	8	7	17	13	146

[*See over.*

Additional information relating to the County of Nottingham.

—ooo—

Population.—By the Census for 1831 this county contained 110,443 males, and 114,877 females—total 225,320, being an increase, since the returns made in the year 1821, of 38,447 inhabitants; and from the Census of 1801 to that of 1831 the augmentation amounted to 84,970 persons.

Representation.—By the *Reform Bill* two additional members are given to the county, so that the whole shire returns *ten* representatives to Parliament (including those for the hundred of Bassetlaw, which comprises the borough of East Retford). The new *Boundary Act* divides the county into two parts, respectively called the *Northern Division* and the *Southern Division*; the former consists of the hundreds of Bassetlaw and Broxtow; and the southern division those of Rushcliffe, Bingham, Newark, and Thurgarton. The election of members for the northern division of the county is held at Nottingham and for the southern at Newark: besides the place of election, the northern division polls at Mansfield, and East Retford; and the southern (besides the place of election) polls at Bingham and Southwell.

Railways.—The town of *Nottingham* communicates with the Midland Counties' Railway, and by means of that line, with the London and Birmingham Railway. The projected lines, as connected with this county, are the Nottingham and Boston Railway, and one which will open a communication between Nottingham and the Humber and Hull, by way of Lincoln.

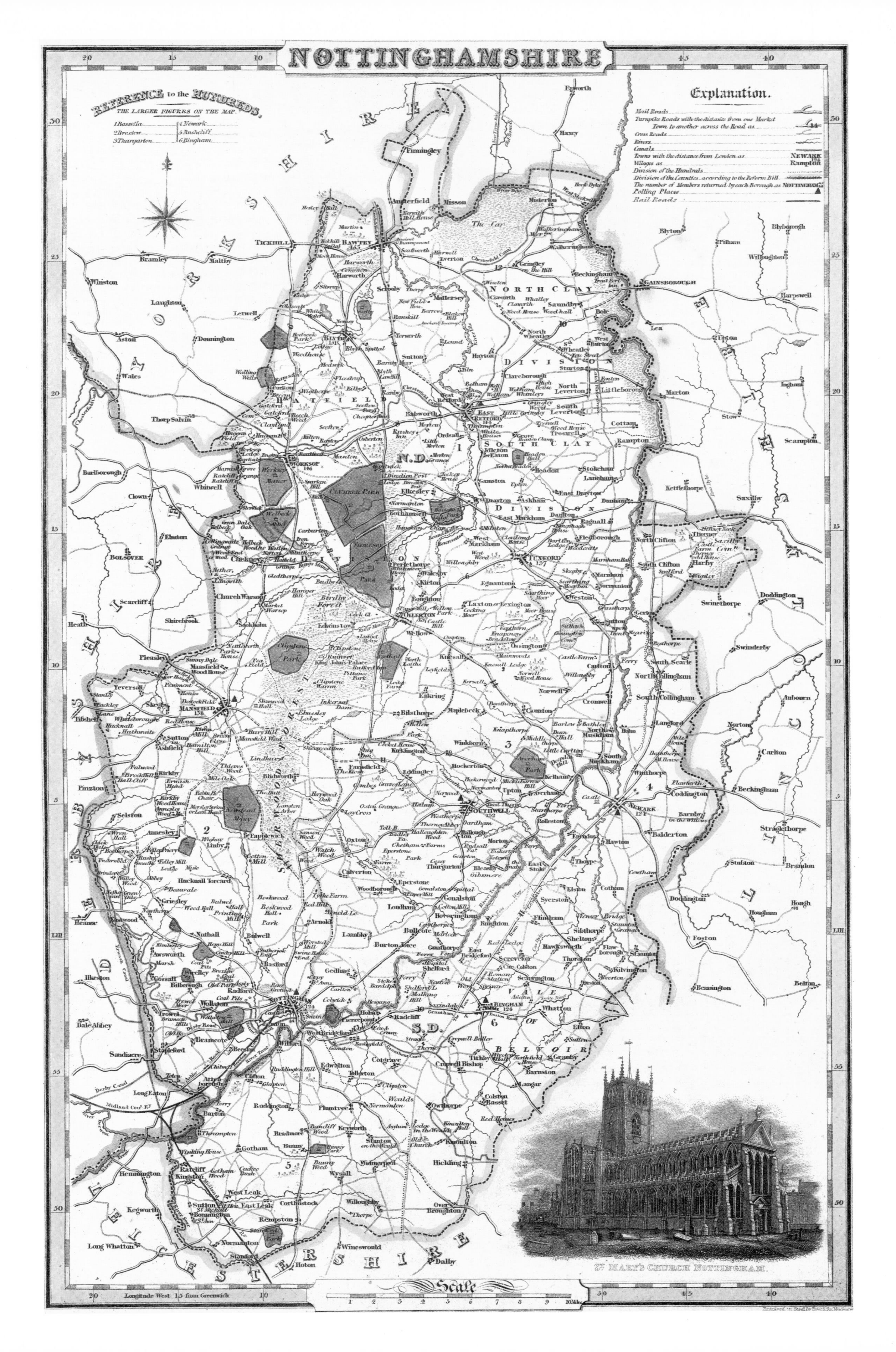
NOTTINGHAMSHIRE
REFERENCE to the HUNDREDS,
THE LARGER FIGURES ON THE MAP.
1 Bassetla
2 Broxtow
3 Thurgarton
4 Newark
5 Rushcliff
6 Bingham
Explanation.
Mail Roads
Turnpike Roads with the distance from one Market Town to another across the Road as
Cross Roads
Rivers
Canals
Towns with the distance from London as
NEWARK
Villages as
Rampton
Division of the Hundreds
Division of the Counties, according to the Reform Bill
The number of Members returned by each Borough as
NOTTINGHAM
Polling Places
Rail Roads
YORKSHIRE
LINCOLNSHIRE
LEICESTERSHIRE
DERBYSHIRE
NORTH CLAY
SOUTH CLAY
HATFIELD
N.D.
S.D.
VALE OF BELVOIR
SHERWOOD FOREST
Clumber Park
Clipstone Park
Thoresby Park
Newstead Abbey
Worksop Manor
Welbeck Abbey
The Car
Epworth
Bawtry
Tickhill
Misterton
Gainsborough
Blyth
East Retford
Worksop
Tuxford
Ollerton
Mansfield
Southwell
Newark
Nottingham
Bingham
Bolsover
Chesterfield Canal
Midland Coun. Ry.
Derby Canal
Erewash Canal
Long Eaton
Sandiacre
Ilkeston
Kegworth
Long Whatton
Hoton
Dalby
St. Mary's Church Nottingham.
Scale
1 2 3 4 5 6 7 8 9 10 Miles
Longitude West 1.5 from Greenwich
20 15 10 50 45 40
Engraved on Steel by Pigot & Co. Manchester

OXFORDSHIRE.

THE County of OXFORD is situated inland, being bounded on the north by Warwickshire and Northamptonshire, on the east by Buckinghamshire, on the south by Berkshire, and on the west by Gloucestershire. The river Charwell separates Oxfordshire from Northamptonshire on the north-east, while the county of Warwick lies contiguous to the north-west. This county is of a very irregular figure: near the centre, it is not more than seven miles across; yet in the more northern part, at no great distance, its diameter is thirty-eight miles; proceeding northwards, it assumes the resemblance of a cone, and terminates at what is called the 'Three-shire Stone' in a complete point or apex. Its greatest length is forty-eight miles, and its circumference about one hundred and thirty, containing about 750 square miles.

NAME and ANCIENT HISTORY.—This county receives its name from the city of Oxford, generally supposed to have been derived from the Saxon word *Oxenford*, a ford or passage for oxen over the river here; some writers, however, have supposed the name of the city was *Ousford*, 'a ford over the Ouse.' Oxfordshire was anciently inhabited by the *Dobunii;* but on the invasion of Britain by the Romans, it became a part of the province termed BRITANNIA PRIMA. During the Heptarchy it belonged to Mercia, and suffered greatly from the Danes; and the most memorable battles recorded in the annals of this county are those which were fought between that people and the English, in 914, at Hooknorton (or Hogsnorton), in which the latter were entirely defeated—and between the Yorkists and Lancastrians, in 1469, in which Edward IV. was made prisoner by the Earl of Warwick. A Roman military way leads into this county, pointing towards Ulchester; and the present village of Dorchester is built on the site of the station DUROCORNOVIUM. The most admired object of attraction in this county, besides its University, is the magnificent seat of Blenheim—a gift of the British Parliament to the great Duke of Marlborough, on account of his signal victory over the French at Blenheim, in Germany. The principal town in the county is the City of Oxford, renowned alike as a seat of Royalty as of erudition. The history of its famed University is involved in much obscurity—an undeniable proof of its great antiquity. Alfred, who resided here with his three sons, is said to have founded three schools at this place, for philosophy, grammar and divinity; it is, however, supposed to have been a seminary of learning even prior to the time of Alfred, although it owed its revival and its augmented consequence to his liberal patronage; and it certainly was a place of study at the Norman invasion. Some writers assert that the City was first built by Memphric, a King of ancient Britain, a thousand years before the Christian era: it was once well fortified with walls, and defended by a strong castle; the tower of the latter now forms part of the county gaol. Oxford, in common with other places in the county, suffered severely under the incursions of the Danes, who burnt the city four different times. On the western side of the town are some remains of a palace, erected by Henry I; in this palace was born Richard, surnamed *Cœur de Lion.* Many of our Kings resided here for a time, and Parliaments were summoned hither. The unfortunate Charles I. held his Court in this city during the whole civil war, whence it became a sort of centre of various military exploits, in this and the surrounding counties: one of these, the skirmish at Chalgrave, near Watlington, in 1643, deserves to be commemorated, as having cost the life of that undaunted patriot, JOHN HAMPDEN, whose firm resistance to the arbitrary measures of the Court was a principal cause of the war.—WOODSTOCK, in this county, has been the residence of several English Monarchs. Henry I. took great delight in the Palace here; in it Henry II. resided when Rice, Prince of Wales, came (in 1163,) to do homage to him. But what rendered Woodstock most famous was a Labyrinth, said to have been built by Henry, called 'Rosamond's Bower,' with a house in it, to secrete his mistress, Rosamond Clifford, from Eleanor his Queen. No traces of the Palace or Bower now remain; but Woodstock to this day is a place of considerable interest and curiosity in many points of view, and more particularly as having contiguous to it the superb Palace of Blenheim before mentioned.

SOIL and CLIMATE, PRODUCE and MANUFACTURES.—The soil of Oxfordshire may be considered, for the most part, extremely fertile, yielding abundant crops of corn and grass; it is naturally dry, and entirely exempt from fens, bogs and stagnant waters. The north corner is chiefly strong deep land, partly arable and partly pasture; the south-west contains the forest of Whichwood, a great part of which is woodland; about Oxford the soil is various,—some parts of it being light and sandy, and others deep and rich; on the banks of the Thames the soil is chiefly in pasture. There are not any high hills in this county, except the 'Chiltern' hills; the rest are only gentle eminences, which tend to vary the landscape without obstructing tillage. The system of agriculture is in general good; the Norfolk husbandry is well understood, and is in prevalent practice. On the grass-farms much cheese is made, of a good quality, though in general of the thin kind called 'toasting' cheese. The cows are principally of the old Gloucester kind, and the South Down sheep are now beginning to exclude the long-woolled breed; many boars are fed for the purpose of making brawn and sausages, which form a considerable article of trade at Oxford and other parts of the county. The PRODUCTS of Oxfordshire are chiefly those common to midland counties; the hills yield ochre, pipe clay, and some other useful earths. The MANUFACTURES are those of blankets (in a flourishing state) at Witney; paper, at Burford and other places; plush, or shag, at Banbury, and an article of pastry for which it has been long famous, called 'Banbury cakes.' The malting trade is carried on extensively, in several towns; and at Woodstock are manufactured gloves, and articles of polished steel: the former branch still flourishes; but the latter is almost lost, in consequence of the cheapness of the Birmingham and Sheffield wares. The price at one time obtained for some specimens of the Woodstock steel will convey an idea of the labour and skill bestowed: a chain, weighing only two ounces, was sold in France for £170. sterling; a box, in which the freedom of the borough was presented to Lord Cliefden, cost 30 guineas; and for a garter star, made for his late Grace the Duke of Marlborough, 50 guineas were paid. The employment of the female poor, on the south side of the county, is lace making; and on the north, spinning wool. The CLIMATE of this county is reckoned as healthy as that of any other in England, and the quick and limpid streams render the air clear and wholesome. It is colder upon and near the Chiltern hills than in other parts; but not more severe than is conducive to health, and to the invigorating and bracing the system.

RIVERS and CANALS.—The rivers of Oxfordshire form the most pleasing features of it; natural historians have stated their number at not less than *three score and ten:* each valley of length has its stream, and no district in England is better watered than this. The THAME, the ISIS, the CHARWELL, the EVENLODE and the WINDRUSH claim the first rank; but the great pride of the county is that confluence of the former two which constitutes the magnificent THAMES. The Charwell rises in Northamptonshire, enters Oxfordshire near Claydon, and falls into the Thames or Isis a little below Oxford. The Evenlode rises in the north-east part of Worcestershire, enters Oxfordshire near the 'Shires' Stone,' and falls into the Thames about four miles below Oxford. The Windrush rises in the Cotswold Hills, in Gloucestershire; enters Oxfordshire near Burford, and, passing Witney, falls into the Thames five miles to the west of Oxford. The Thame rises near Tring, in Hertfordshire; and, crossing Buckinghamshire, touches the borders of Oxfordshire at Thame. CANALS.—The Birmingham canal is of immense importance to Oxfordshire, immediately connecting London, through Oxford, with Birmingham, Manchester, Liverpool, and the Wednesbury collieries: this canal commences at Longford, in the northern extremity of Warwickshire, on the edge of the Coventry canal, and joins the Isis at Oxford.

CIVIL and ECCLESIASTICAL DIVISIONS.—Oxfordshire is in the Province of Canterbury and Diocese of Oxford; it gives name to a Circuit of the Judges. The whole county is divided into the hundreds of BAMPTON, BANBURY, BINFIELD, BLOXHAM, BULLINGTON, CHADLINGTON, DORCHESTER, EWELME, LANGTREE, LEWKNOR, PIRTON, PLOUGHLEY, THAME, and WOOTTON; these are subdivided into two hundred and seventeen parishes, which collectively contain one city and county town (Oxford), and eleven other market towns. The entire county returns nine Members to Parliament, viz. two for the CITY OF OXFORD, two for the UNIVERSITY, two for the borough of WOODSTOCK, one for BANBURY, and two for the SHIRE.

POPULATION.—According to the census of 1821, there were houses inhabited in the county, 25,594; uninhabited, 531; and houses building, 245. The number of families then resident in the county was 28,841, comprising 68,817 males, and 68,154 females; total, 136,971: and by a calculation made by order of government, which included persons in the army and navy, for which was added after the ratio of about one to thirty prior to the year 1811, and one to fifty for that year and the census of 1821, to the returns made from the several districts; the population of the county, in round numbers, in the year 1700, was 79,000—in 1750, 92,400—in 1801, 113,200—in 1811, 123,200—and in 1821, 139,800. The increased population in the fifty years, from the year 1700, was 13,400—from 1750 to 1801, the increase was 20,800—from 1801 to 1811, the increase was 10,000—and from 1811 to 1821, the augmented number of persons was 16,600: the grand total increase in the population of the county, from the year 1700 to the census of 1821, being about 60,800 persons.

Index of Distances from Town to Town in the County of Oxford.

THE NAMES OF THE RESPECTIVE TOWNS ARE ON THE TOP AND SIDE, AND THE SQUARE WHERE BOTH MEET GIVES THE DISTANCE.

Town	Bampton	Banbury	Bicester	Burford	Chipping Norton	Deddington	Henley	Oxford	Thame	Watlington	Witney	Woodstock	Distance from London.
Bampton													71
Banbury	28												75
Bicester	22	15											55
Burford	7	24	23										72
Chipping Norton	16	13	19	11									74
Deddington	23	6	10	20	10								70
Henley	36	46	31	38	41	40							35
Oxford	13	22	12	18	18	16	23						54
Thame	26	28	15	30	31	25	16	13					44
Watlington	27	37	22	31	32	31	10	18	8				45
Witney	6	21	17	7	16	17	33	11	24	25			65
Woodstock	13	16	11	14	11	10	30	8	20	22	8		62

[See over.

Additional information relating to the County of Oxford.

POPULATION.—By the Census for **1831** this county contained 76,055 males, and 75,671 females—total 151,726, being an increase, since the returns made in the year 1821, of 14,755 inhabitants; and from the Census of 1801 to that of 1831, the augmentation amounted to 42,106 persons.

REPRESENTATION.—By the *Reform Bill* the borough of WOODSTOCK is deprived of one of its members; and an additional one is given to the county, so that the whole shire sends the same number (*nine*) of representatives to Parliament as before the passing of the Bill. The election of members for the county is held at OXFORD, and the other polling places, besides that city, are DEDDINGTON, WITNEY and NETTLEBED.

RAILWAYS.—There is a branch of Railway projected from Oxford, to join the GREAT WESTERN, near *Wallingford*, in Berkshire; and a branch is open from the LONDON and BIRMINGHAM line at *Tring*, to *Aylesbury*, in Buckinghamshire.

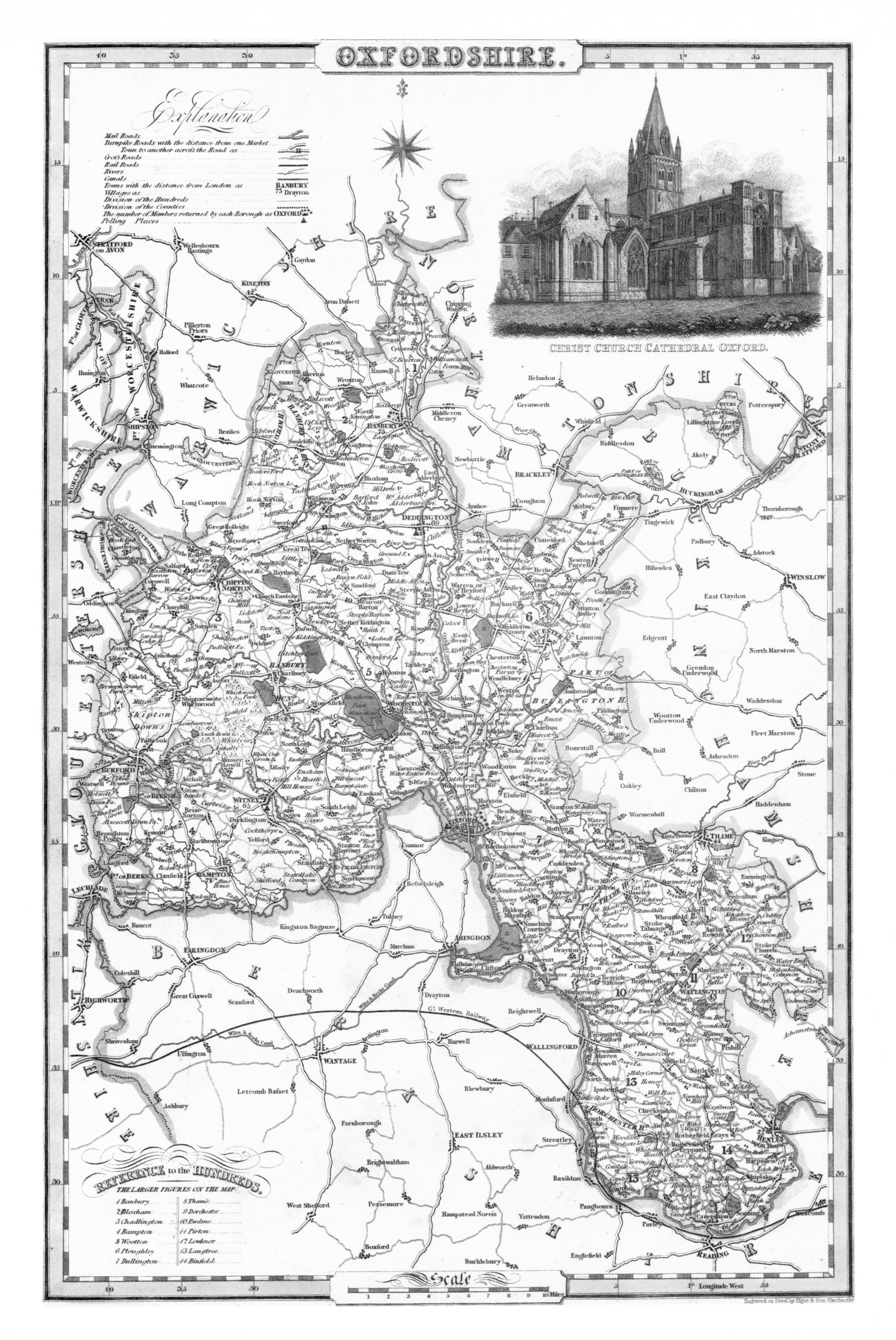
OXFORDSHIRE.
Explanation
Mail Roads
Turnpike Roads with the distance from one Market Town to another across the Road as
Cross Roads
Rail Roads
Rivers
Canals
Towns with the distance from London as
BANBURY 75
Villages as
Drayton
Division of the Hundreds
Division of the Counties
The number of Members returned by each Borough as
OXFORD
Polling Places
CHRIST CHURCH CATHEDRAL OXFORD.
REFERENCE to the HUNDREDS.
THE LARGER FIGURES ON THE MAP.
1 Banbury
2 Bloxham
3 Chadlington
4 Bampton
5 Wootton
6 Ploughley
7 Bullington
8 Thame
9 Dorchester
10 Ewelme
11 Pirton
12 Lewknor
13 Langtree
14 Binfield
Scale
10 Miles
Longitude West
Engraved on Steel by Pigot & Son Manchester
WARWICKSHIRE
NORTHAMPTONSHIRE
BUCKINGHAMSHIRE
GLOUCESTERSHIRE
BERKSHIRE
STRATFORD on AVON
BANBURY
DEDDINGTON
CHIPPING NORTON
WOODSTOCK
BICESTER
BURFORD
WITNEY
OXFORD
BAMPTON
THAME
WATLINGTON
HENLEY
ABINGDON
FARINGDON
WANTAGE
WALLINGFORD
EAST ILSLEY
READING
BUCKINGHAM
BRACKLEY
WINSLOW
LECHLADE
HIGHWORTH
KINETON
Gt. Western Railway

SHROPSHIRE.

SALOP is an inland county, bounded on the north by Cheshire and part of Flintshire; on the east by Staffordshire; on the south by the counties of Radnor, Hereford and Worcester; and on the west by those of Denbigh and Montgomery. In length, from north to south, it is about forty-five miles; & its extreme breadth about thirty-five: its circumference is computed at one hundred and sixty miles, and its area to comprise about 1,340 square miles.

NAME and ANCIENT HISTORY.—The derivation of the name of Salop, or Shropshire, has not been with any degree of certainty established; indeed, so vague and various are the opinions of writers upon this subject, that to attempt to dispel the obscurity which enwraps its etymology, by analyzing conflicting speculations, would be to assume a task more critical than useful, and unattended by the hope of arriving at a result either interesting or satisfactory. This part of the Island was originally inhabited by the Celtic tribe *Cornavii;* and their chief city (which was situated not far from the site of the present town of Shrewsbury), after its conquest by the Romans became a station of the latter people, called VRICONIUM, and was fortified by them, to secure the passage of the Severn: the walls which surrounded the town appear to have been three miles in circumference, and nine feet thick. Shrewsbury is the principal, as it is the county town of Salop; yet, although no doubt can be entertained of its high antiquity, there is no authentic record of its origin: probable conjecture has, however, assigned that event to the fifth century, when the Britons were forced by the Saxons to abandon all the country eastward of the river Severn. About Shrewsbury was esteemed the most important position on the Marches of Wales; and a strong fortress at this point continued for several centuries to be one of the principal places of rendezvous for the English armies, and hence was often visited by its successive Monarchs of the Saxon and Norman dynasties. Ludlow is a town of considerable antiquity and interest: its ancient British name was *Dinan Llys Twysog*, or 'the Prince's Palace,'—and is supposed to have been the residence of some Prince of this part of the country, prior to the subjugation of Wales by Edward I. At present it is principally indebted for its celebrity to the magnificent remains of its noble Castle, which was founded by Roger de Montmorency, and was in the days of its amplitude one of the most extensive and superb Baronial fortresses in Europe. In the military events connected with this county, Shrewsbury appears to have been a large participator: in the reigns of John and of Henry III. it was taken by storm, being defended on the latter occasion by the adherents of the Empress Maude; and in the same Henry's reign it was partly burnt by the Welch. In the reign of Edward I. a Parliament was holden here, and David, the last of the Welch Princes, beheaded. In this neighbourhood was fought a bloody battle between the army of Henry IV, commanded by his renowned son, and the forces of the fiery Henry Percy (surnamed 'Hotspur'), in which the latter was slain; and after his interment his body was taken from the grave, and beheaded, as was his uncle, the Earl of Worcester. Richard, Duke of York, and George Plantagenet, sons of Edward IV, were born in Shrewsbury. Oswestry (corrupted from *Oswaldstree*) was conspicuous as a border town, and was frequently the scene of contest—first between the Saxons and Britons, and afterwards between the latter and the Normans: the remains of its ancient Castle, even in their present dilapidated state, are fully sufficient to indicate its former prodigious strength. This town was twice burnt: first by King John, in his wars with the Barons; and not long afterwards (in the year 1233,) by the Welch Prince, Llewellin the Great.

SOIL, CLIMATE, and AGRICULTURAL PRODUCE.—Few counties are possessed of a greater variety of soil, or are more diversified in appearance: divided into nearly two equal parts by the Severn, its south portion assumes the mountainous character exhibited by the counties of Montgomery and Denbigh; whilst the north half approaches the resemblance of a level, agreeably relieved by a few single hills and romantic vallies, finely wooded. The meadows on the side of the Severn are extremely fertile, being frequently enriched by the overflowing of that river, which is navigable in its whole course. The CLIMATE is considered highly salubrious; the air is pure, although in many parts sharp and piercing. The PRODUCTIONS of this county are various and valuable: the breed of cows and sheep deserve particular notice,—the former giving large quantities of milk, and much of the cheese sold under the denomination of 'Cheshire' is produced from the dairies here; it is acknowledged that the sheep fed upon its hilly tracts afford some of the finest fleeces in the Kingdom. The whole county is in general well cultivated, yielding great quantities of grain; its southern borden producing excellent hops, and agreeably varied with fine healthy orchards.

MINERALS and MANUFACTURES.—Rich as this county is in the productions of the field, the treasures extracted from its bowels are not of minor importance: lead, iron, lime-stone, free-stone, pipe-clay and coals are found in great abundance; and in the hundred of North Bradford are salt springs; whilst on the eastern side of the county are a number of extensive iron-works, that give employment to some hundreds of hands. The chief MANUFACTURES are porcelain and flannel: the former is of great excellence, and in proportionate demand; the latter, though it has somewhat receded from its former high importance, is by no means reduced to insignificance. The principal manufacturing towns are Shrewsbury and Oswestry, for flannels; in the neighbourhood of the former town are large iron foundries, and it was here where the noble Menai Bridge was cast. In the parish of Madeley are also immense iron-works; the stupendous iron bridge that bestrides the Severn at this place was constructed from the furnaces here. At Coalport are china manufactories, of great extent and celebrity; at Bridgnorth, carpets and porcelain are manufactured; at Broseley, various descriptions of pottery ware; at Hales Owen, nails and pearl buttons; and Ludlow and its vicinity derive considerable prosperity from its extensive malting trade.

RIVERS and CANALS.—The principal rivers of this county are the SEVERN, the TERN and the RODAN; the smaller ones are the Teme, the Colun, the Ouy, the Warren and the Rea, besides several considerable brooks. The source and progress of the Severn, till it falls into the Bristol Channel, has been noticed in other counties; it enters Shropshire at Melverley, about eleven miles from Shrewsbury—flows past the latter town, and, after visiting Coalbrook-Dale, Madeley and Bridgnorth, enters Worcestershire at Bewdley. The Tern rises in the north part of this county, and, after receiving the waters of the Rodan, runs into the Severn near Brompton Ferry. The Rodan also has its source in the north of the county, and joins the Tern near Walcott.—The CANALS which pass through Shropshire are, the ELLESMERE, the SHREWSBURY, the KINGTON, the DONNINGTON WOOD, and the DUDLEY EXTENSION; all in a greater or less degree important, and perhaps essential to the carrying trade of the county.

CIVIL and ECCLESIASTICAL DIVISIONS.—Shropshire is in the Province of Canterbury, and Dioceses of Hereford, and Lichfield & Coventry; is included in the Oxford Circuit, and divided into twelve hundreds, viz.:—

BRADFORD NORTH,	CONDOVER,	OVERS,
BRADFORD SOUTH,	FORD,	PIMHILL,
BRIMSTREY,	MUNSLOW,	PURSLOW,
CHIRBURY,	OSWESTRY,	STODDESDEN.

These are subdivided into 216 parishes, collectively containing one county town (Shrewsbury), and 16 other market towns. The whole county returns twelve Members to Parliament, namely, two each for BISHOP'S CASTLE, BRIDGNORTH, LUDLOW, SHREWSBURY and WENLOCK, and two for the SHIRE.

POPULATION.—According to the census of 1821, there were houses inhabited in the county, 38,663; uninhabited, 1,012; and houses building, 179. The number of families then resident in the county was 41,636; comprising 102,056 males, and 104,097 females; total, 206,153: and by a calculation made by order of Government, which included persons in the army and navy, for which was added after the ratio of about one to thirty prior to the year 1811, and one to fifty for that year and the census of 1821, to the returns made from the several districts; the population of the county, in round numbers, in the year 1700, was 101,600—in 1750, 130,300—in 1801, 172,200—in 1811, 200,800—and in 1821, 210,300. The increased population in the 50 years, from the year 1700, was 28,700—from 1750 to 1801, the increase was 41,900—from 1801 to 1811, the increase was 28,600—and from 1811 to 1821, the augmented number of persons was 9,500: the grand total increase in the population of the county from the year 1700 to the census of 1821, being about 108,700 persons.

Index of Distances from Town to Town in the County of Salop.

THE NAMES OF THE RESPECTIVE TOWNS ARE ON THE TOP AND SIDE, AND THE SQUARE WHERE BOTH MEET GIVES THE DISTANCE.

	Bishop's Castle	Bridgnorth	Church Stretton	Cleobury Mortimer	Drayton	Ellesmere	Hales Owen	Ludlow	Madeley	Newport	Oswestry	Shiffnall	Shrewsbury	Wellington	Wem	Wenlock	Whitchurch	Distance from London.
Bishop's Castle																		158
Bridgnorth	36																	138
Church Stretton	15	19																153
Cleobury Mortimer	33	13	27															132
Drayton	40	31	32	40														151
Ellesmere	37	39	29	52	23													174
Hales Owen	51	15	34	23	43	51												117
Ludlow	20	20	16	11	48	45	34											150
Madeley	34	8	18	23	22	31	23	26										147
Newport	37	18	26	32	11	32	31	37	13									139
Oswestry	32	38	31	51	30	8	53	47	33	34								178
Shiffnall	39	11	22	25	20	34	25	30	5	8	36							136
Shrewsbury	20	20	13	33	19	16	35	29	14	15	18	18						154
Wellington	32	13	20	27	16	28	29	31	6	9	29	7	11					144
Wem	31	30	23	43	13	10	45	39	25	22	18	28	10	21				164
Wenlock	26	8	13	20	31	28	23	20	6	20	30	12	12	11	23			148
Whitchurch	41	35	33	53	13	11	57	49	28	21	20	28	20	22	10	32		161

[*See over.*

Additional information relating to the County of Salop.

Population.—By the Census for **1831** this county contained 110,788 males, and 111,715 females—total 222,503, being an increase, since the returns made in the year 1821, of 16,350 inhabitants; and from the Census of 1801 to that of 1831, the augmentation amounted to 54,864 persons.

Representation.—By the *Reform Bill* the borough of Bishop's Castle has been deprived of its elective privilege, and two additional members have been bestowed upon the county; so that the number of representatives (*twelve*) for the whole shire is the same as previous to the passing the Bill. The new *Boundary Act* divides Shropshire into two parts, respectively named the *Northern Division* and the *Southern Division;* the former comprises the hundreds of Oswestry, Pimhill, North Bradford, and South Bradford, and the liberty of Shrewsbury; and the southern division includes the hundreds of Brimstrey, Cherbury, Condover, Ford, Manslow, Overs, Purslow, including Clun, and Stoddesdon, and the franchise of Wenlock. The election of Members for the northern division of the county is held at Shrewsbury, and for the southern at Church Stretton: besides the place of election, the northern division polls at Oswestry, Whitchurch, and Wellington; and the southern division (besides the place of election) polls at Bridgnorth, Ludlow, Bishop's Castle, and Wenlock.

Railways.—The projected Shrewsbury and Birmingham Railway is intended to originate at *Shrewsbury,* and join the Grand Junction Railway at or near *Wolverhampton.* This work, if accomplished, will open a direct Railway communication between the county of Salop and *Birmingham* and *London;* and westward with Worcester, Gloucester and the Great Western. A Railway is also contemplated to port Dinllynn, in Carnarvonshire, from Wolverhampton, through Shrewsbury, and by Llangollen and Bala.

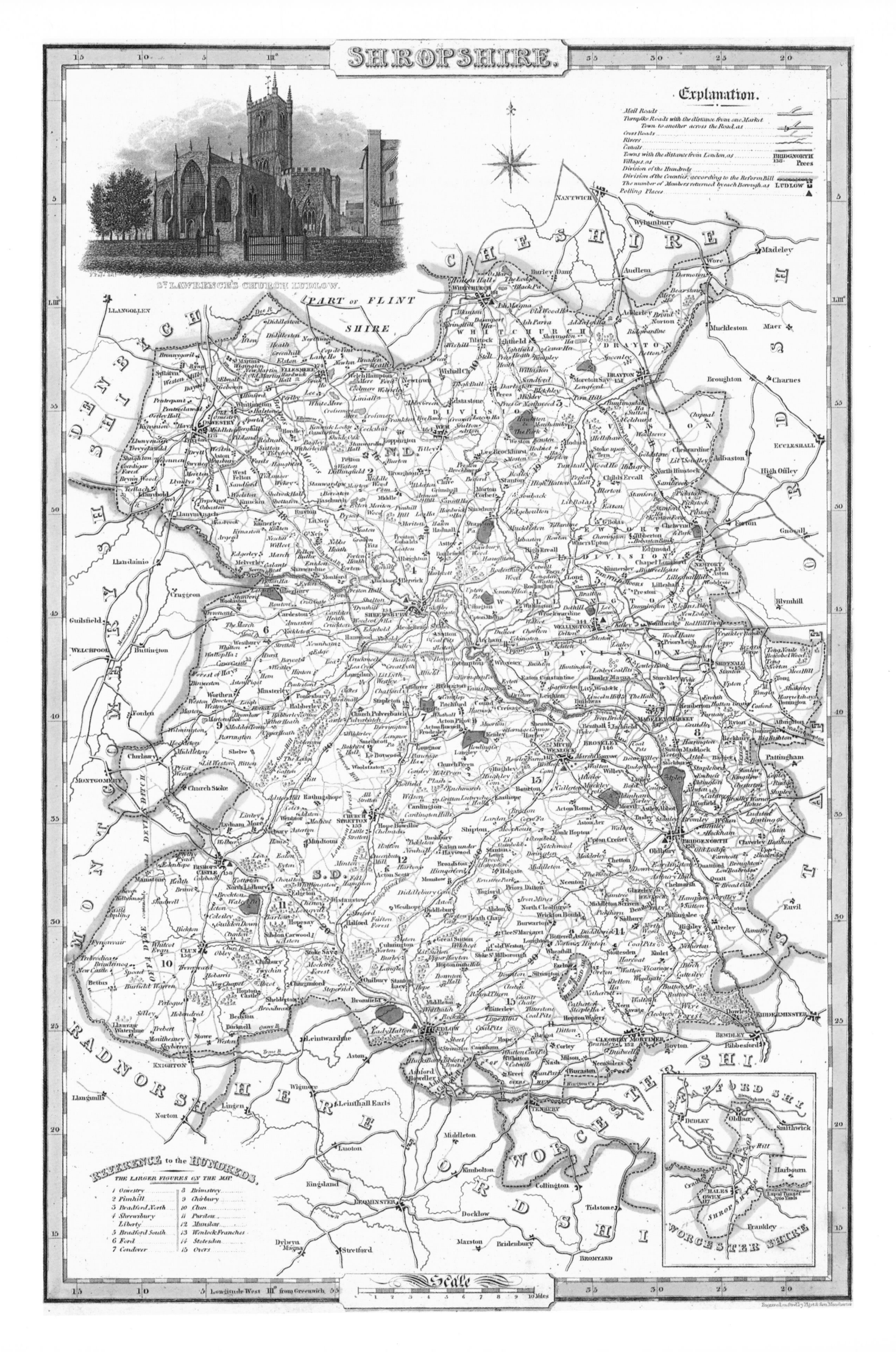
SHROPSHIRE.
St. LAWRENCE'S CHURCH LUDLOW.
Explanation.
Mail Roads
Turnpike Roads with the distance from one Market Town to another across the Road, as
Cross Roads
Rivers
Canals
Towns with the distance from London, as
BRIDGNORTH 138
Villages, as
Prees
Division of the Hundreds
Division of the Counties, according to the Reform Bill
The number of Members returned by each Borough, as
LUDLOW
Polling Places
CHESHIRE
PART OF FLINT SHIRE
DENBIGH SHIRE
MONTGOMERY SHIRE
RADNORSHIRE
HEREFORDSHIRE
WORCESTERSHIRE
STAFFORDSHIRE
NANTWICH
WHITCHURCH
ELLESMERE
OSWESTRY
WEM
DRAYTON
NEWPORT
SHREWSBURY
WELLINGTON
SHIFFNALL
MUCH WENLOCK
BROSELEY
MADELEY MARKET
BRIDGENORTH
CHURCH STRETTON
BISHOPS CASTLE
CLUN
LUDLOW
CLEOBURY MORTIMER
BEWDLEY
KIDDERMINSTER
TENBURY
LEOMINSTER
KNIGHTON
WELCHPOOL
MONTGOMERY
LLANGOLLEN
REFERENCE to the HUNDREDS,
THE LARGER FIGURES ON THE MAP.
1 Oswestry
2 Pimhill
3 Bradford North
4 Shrewsbury Liberty
5 Bradford South
6 Ford
7 Condover
8 Brimstrey
9 Chirbury
10 Clun
11 Purslow
12 Munslow
13 Wenlock Franches
14 Stotesdon
15 Overs
Longitude West III from Greenwich
Scale
Miles

SOMERSETSHIRE.

SOMERSET is a maritime county, in the south-west part of England; having the Bristol Channel on the west, Gloucestershire on the north, Wiltshire on the east, Dorsetshire on the south-east, and Devonshire on the south and south-west. Its form is oblong—being in length, from north-east to south-west, upwards of eighty miles; in breadth, from east to west, about thirty-six; and in circumference two hundred miles; its area comprehending about one thousand six hundred and forty-two square miles.

ANCIENT HISTORY.—This part of the Kingdom was in ancient times inhabited by the *Belgæ*, a warlike people, of Celtic origin, who emigrated into this country from Gaul about 350 years before the birth of Christ, and soon became possessed of a very considerable tract of territory, including the counties of Somerset, Dorset, Devon, part of Cornwall, Wilts, Hants, Sussex and part of Middlesex; in all which they established colonies, into which they willingly admitted the Britons, the Aborigines of the Island. The emigrators were occasionally assisted by Divitiacus, the most powerful Prince in Gaul, in extending the line of their possessions; and a large and deep fosse or dike was thrown up, to define the boundaries of either people, called, from the circumstance of its division, '*Wansdike*,' which to this day exists in many places About forty years after the Christian era, the Romans arrived in Britain in considerable force, having already annihilated the *Cangii*, a posthumous clan of those *Belgæ* who last migrated into this country under the protection of Divitiacus. During the stay of the Romans in this region, they founded the cities of AQUA SOLIS (Bath,) and ISCALIS or IVELCHESTER, and many other towns: their principal road was the *Fosse*, extending in a south-west direction from Bath to Perry Street, on the borders of Devonshire; another road ran nearly parallel to it, from the forest of Exmoor to Portishead or Portshut, on the Bristol Channel; and a Vicinal way extended from the *Fosse* through Stoke-under-Hamden. Under the dominion of the Saxons, who succeeded the Romans in their possession of the country, this county became a part of their Kingdom of Wessex, or of the West Saxons. In the year of our Lord 878, this county, with Wilts and Hants, became the theatre of exterminating conflict with the Danes, who had already desolated almost every other province of Britain,—and the good King Alfred was constrained to seek an asylum in the fens of Athelney; from whence, however, he soon afterwards emerged, and completely defeated the ruthless barbarians in a signal battle at Edington.

SOIL & CLIMATE, PRODUCE & MANUFACTURES, MINES & MINERALS.—Few counties contain a greater variety of soil than this: the north-east quarter is in general stony; towards its centre are fens and marshy moors of great extent; on the west side are hills, downs and open heaths; in the north-west corner lies the barren region of Exmoor; and the south part, towards Dorsetshire, is high, but well cultivated. The vallies are in general very rich; and many of the hills, a few years since undisturbed by the plough, are now well cultivated, and produce large crops of grain. Hemp, flax, teazels and woad are cultivated in considerable quantities; the dairies produce some of the finest cheese in the Kingdom. The sheep indigenous to the county are the Mendip breed, but lately every other improved system has been introduced by its eminent and spirited cultivators. The cattle are nearly the same as those of Devon, and the teams of the opulent farmers may vie with those of any other county. The Mendip Hills, which may be called the Alps of Somersetshire, lie in the north-east quarter, and abound in lead, lapis calaminaris, copper, and various spars and crystals; the Quantack Hills, on the west side, also produce lead and copper; the Broadfield Downs, and other wilds, have their mines of calamine, and iron ore has been found in various parts of the county The coal-mines in the north part are valuable treasures to the neighbourhood, and supply great part of the cities of Bath and Bristol with excellent fuel: the former city is mostly constructed with the free-stone of its neighbouring quarries, and the blue Kinton stone is admirable for paving. The rocks on the coast contain marble, gypsum and talc, and those in the inland parts are mostly composed of lime-stone; & ochres, both yellow & red, are found in plenty The principal MANUFACTURES of this county are broad and narrow fine woollen cloths, and a variety of coarse woollen goods; with coarse linens, comprising dowlases, tickings, &c.: at Chard and Taunton fine and broad laces, of great excellence, are made; and the latter town also partakes in the manufacture of silk. A considerable coasting business is carried on from some of the ports, and others have an extensive trade with Ireland. The making of brick and tiles, and the brass and iron foundries, employ a great number of hands; whilst many others procure subsistence from the fisheries. The CLIMATE of this county is various: near the sea-coast, winter is scarcely felt; and from Minehead and Dulverton on the west, to Milborne Port and Wincanton on the east (excepting on some of the eminences), it is mild and temperate: approaching the northern district it becomes more cold and boisterous, and upon the summits of the Mendip Hills, which are of great altitude, visiting tourists find themselves comparatively in the climate of Lapland.

RIVERS, CANALS, and MEDICINAL SPRINGS.—The principal rivers in this county are, the AVON (also called the West Avon), the PARRET, the AX, and the BREW or Brue; there are several other rivers and tributary streams—inconsiderable in a navigable point of view, but which, however, greatly add to the beauty of the county and the advantage of its inhabitants. The Avon rises in Wiltshire, and enters this county about four miles from Bath; passes that city, and from thence becoming navigable, pursues its course through Bristol, and reaches the Severn sea at Kingroad. The Parret, anciently called the *Pedred*, rises at South Parret, in Dorsetshire, and enters this county at North Parret, both which villages receive their name from it; near Michelny it receives the Ile, and near Langport the Yeo or Ivel, and thus increased it passes Yeovil and Ilchester; it afterwards receives other streams, and, after visiting the towns of Wiveliscombe and Taunton, reaches the port of Bridgwater, and falls into the sea at Start Point. The Ax has its source in the remarkable cavern of Wokey Hole; and, after being enriched by the Chedder water, passes Axbridge, and is lost in the sea near the village of Uphill. The Brew or Brue (and sometimes also called the *Brent*,) rises near the borders of Wilts, runs by Lydford and Glastonbury, and, crossing the moors, at length discharges itself into the Bristol Channel at Burnham. There are the following CANALS, which either commence in or pass through this county:—'The Somerset Coal Canal,' which has two branches,—one commencing at Bolton, the other at Bradstock, and both communicating with the 'Kennet and Avon Canal.' The 'Dorset and Somerset Canal' commences near Nettlebridge, and extends through Frome to the county of Dorset. The 'Ilchester and Langport Canal' is continued to the river Parret, below Great Bow-bridge, in the parish of Langport. A canal from the Mendip collieries passes through the town of Frome, and, dividing into two branches, one joins the Kennet and Avon canal near Bradford, and the other extends itself through Wincanton to the borders of Dorsetshire.—The MEDICINAL SPRINGS of this county may be considered as one of its most important features, having been the means of bringing into celebrity and sustaining the splendour of BATH—the most fashionable and beautiful city, next the Metropolis, in the Kingdom. The water of these wonderful hot springs is only equalled in its transparency by its abundance: after the water is let off from the baths for the purpose of cleansing them, it may be seen boiling up from the earth, to the astonishment of every stranger visiting these health restoring founts. The water is of a pleasant flavour—of a strengthening, attenuating, opening nature, and very grateful to the stomach. The pump rooms and baths are the most elegant and convenient that can be imagined.

CIVIL and ECCLESIASTICAL DIVISIONS.—The county of Somerset is in the Province of Canterbury, in the Diocese of Bath and Wells, and in the Western Circuit. It is divided into the three Archdeaconries of Bath, Wells and Taunton; and into two divisions, Eastern and Western: these contain forty hundreds and seven liberties, in which are four hundred and seventy-five parishes, the entire of two cities (Bath and Wells), part of the city of Bristol, and twenty-two other market towns. The whole county returns sixteen Members to Parliament, namely, two for the SHIRE, two each for the cities of BATH and WELLS, and two each for the towns of BRIDGWATER, ILCHESTER, MILBORNE PORT, MINEHEAD and TAUNTON. BRISTOL being noticed as belonging partly to this county, it must be observed that it also returns two Representatives to the Imperial Legislsture.

POPULATION.—According to the census of 1821, there were houses inhabited in the county, 61,852; uninhabited, 1,974; and houses building, 850. The number of families then resident in the county was 73,537, comprising 170,199 males, and 185,115 females; total, 355,314: and by a calculation made by order of government, which included persons in the army and navy, for which was added after the ratio of about one to thirty prior to the year 1811, and one to fifty for that year and the census of 1821, to the returns made from the several districts; the population of the county, in round numbers, in the year 1700, was 195,900---in 1750, 224,500---in 1801, 282,800---in 1811, 313,300---and in 1821, 362,500. The increased population in the fifty years, from the year 1700, was 28,600—from 1750 to 1801, the increase was 58,300---from 1801 to 1811, the increase was 30,500---and from 1811 to 1821, the augmented number of persons was 49,200: the grand total increase in the population of the county, from the year 1700 to the census of 1821, being about 166,600 persons.---By the returns above referred to, the City of BATH contained 36,811 inhabitants: the City of BRISTOL and its suburbs (not included in the above returns,) contained a population of 87,779 persons—of which number, it is stated, 52,889 were resident in the parishes situated within that City.

Index of Distances from Town to Town in the County of Somerset.

THE NAMES OF THE RESPECTIVE TOWNS ARE ON THE TOP AND SIDE, AND THE SQUARE WHERE BOTH MEET GIVES THE DISTANCE.

Town	Axbridge	Bath	Bridgwater	Bristol	Bruton	Castle Cary	Chard	Crewkerne	Dulverton	Dunster	Frome	Glastonbury	Ilchester	Ilminster	Langport	Milborne Port	Milverton	Minehead	Pensford	Petherton, South	Shepton Mallet	Somerton	Taunton	Wellington	Wells	Wincanton	Wiveliscombe	Distance from London
Axbridge																												130
Bath	28																											107
Bridgwater	17	40																										148
Bristol	18	13	34																									119
Bruton	21	24	27	27																								109
Castle Cary	23	26	24	27	3																							116
Chard	44	50	23	52	30	27																						140
Crewkerne	37	42	30	45	23	23	7																					132
Dulverton	46	67	30	64	54	51	32	40																				166
Dunster	41	63	23	58	50	47	37	40	14																			158
Frome	26	13	36	25	10	15	40	34	64	59																		108
Glastonbury	15	24	15	25	17	14	29	22	43	38	20																	127
Ilchester	27	33	20	35	15	11	17	10	48	43	24	12																125
Ilminster	39	48	25	48	27	24	5	7	34	33	36	24	12															135
Langport	28	36	12	38	18	15	15	15	36	35	29	13	8	10														132
Milborne Port	33	36	31	38	10	10	26	18	50	54	25	22	12	24	20													115
Milverton	33	55	15	50	41	38	18	26	15	18	51	30	32	20	20	43												148
Minehead	43	65	25	60	52	48	35	45	17	3	61	41	45	35	37	56	20											162
Pensford	16	10	34	6	21	22	46	39	62	57	18	20	29	41	32	32	49	59										116
Petherton, South	34	40	17	42	22	19	10	5	38	40	33	19	6	5	8	18	25	42	39									130
Shepton Mallet	14	18	27	20	8	7	32	25	54	50	12	11	15	27	18	18	41	52	14	22								115
Somerton	23	31	17	33	13	10	20	14	41	40	24	8	5	16	5	14	25	42	27	11	13							123
Taunton	29	50	11	45	30	30	16	20	25	21	45	28	24	12	13	35	8	23	47	17	33	17						146
Wellington	36	57	18	53	39	37	14	22	18	23	52	33	31	19	22	42	4	21	52	24	40	27	7					152
Wells	11	19	21	20	12	13	34	27	49	44	15	5	18	29	18	23	36	46	14	24	5	13	32	39				127
Wincanton	27	29	30	32	5	6	32	24	57	53	17	20	13	25	21	8	44	55	26	24	12	16	36	42	17			108
Wiveliscombe	34	56	16	50	43	41	23	30	15	16	52	32	35	23	26	46	3	18	50	28	44	31	11	7	37	46		154
Yeovil	32	38	25	40	15	12	17	9	47	49	28	17	5	14	14	9	34	50	34	9	19	9	20	33	22	15	37	122

[See over.

Additional information relating to the County of Somerset.

———ooo———

Population.—By the Census for 1831 this county contained 194,169 males, and 209,739 females—total 403,908, being an increase, since the returns made in the year 1821, of 48,594 inhabitants; and from the Census of 1801 to that of 1831 the augmentation amounted to 130,158 persons.

Representation.—By the *Reform Bill* the boroughs of Ilchester, Milborne Port, and Minehead are deprived of the elective franchise. By the same Act Frome has obtained the privilege of sending one member to Parliament, and two additional ones are given to the county; by these alterations the whole shire returns *thirteen* representatives to Parliament, instead of *sixteen*, as before the passing of the Bill. The new *Boundary Act* divides the county into two parts, respectively called the *Eastern Division* and the *Western Division*; the former comprises the several hundreds or liberties of Bath Forum, Bempstone, Brent and Wrington, Bruton, Catsash, Chew and Chewton, Morton Ferris, Frome, Glaston-twelve-hides, Hampton and Claverton, Horethrone, Keynsham, Kilmersdon, Mells and Leigh, Portbury, Wellow, Wells Forum, Whitstone, Winterstoke, Witham Friary, also the hundred of Hartcliffe with Bedminster, except such parts of that hundred as are within the limits of the city of Bristol: the western division includes the hundreds of Abdick and Bulstone, Andersfield, Cannington, Carhampton, Crewkerne, North Curry, Houndsborough, Berwick and Coker, Huntspill and Puriton, East Kingsbury, West Kingsbury, Martock, Milverton, North Petherton, South Petherton, Pitney, Somerton, Stone, Taunton and Taunton Dean, Tintinhull, Whitley, and Williton and Freemanors. The election of members for the eastern division of the county is held at Wells, and for the western at Taunton: besides the place of election, the eastern division polls at Bath, Shepton Mallet, Bedminster, Axbridge, and Wincanton; and the western division (besides the place of election) polls at Bridgwater, Ilchester, and Williton.

Railways.—The Bristol and Exeter passes about seven miles to the west of *Axbridge*—then through *Bridgwater;* and, leaving *Taunton* to the left or east, runs on close to *Wellington.* This line may be considered as a continuation of the Great Western, by a different proprietary; and will effect an entire line of Railway communication between London and the Metropolis of the West. From Bath the projected Bath and Weymouth Railway will commence—passing near Frome, Gillingham and Stalbridge, to Dorchester and Weymouth.

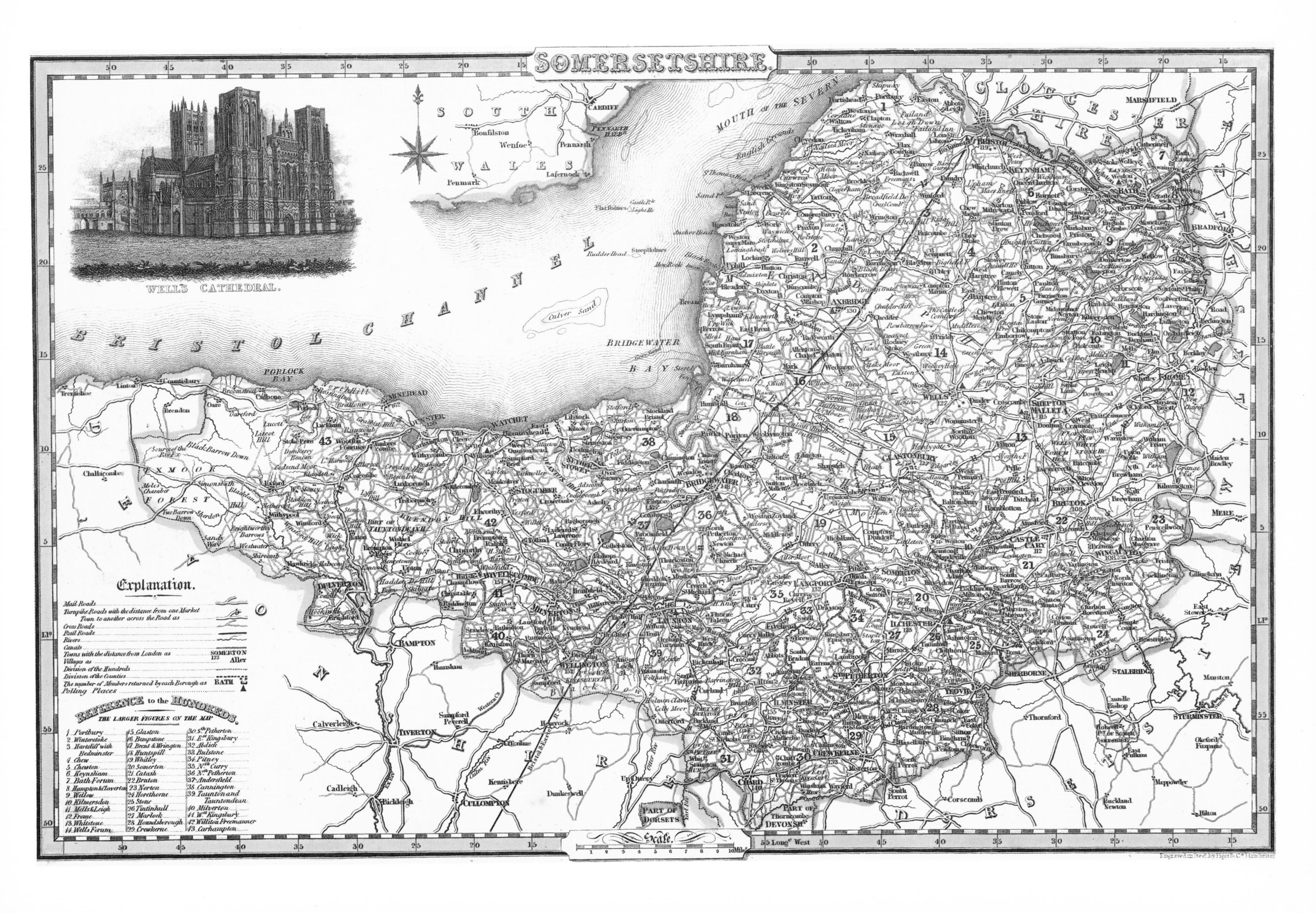
SOMERSETSHIRE
WELLS CATHEDRAL.
BRISTOL CHANNEL
MOUTH OF THE SEVERN
BRIDGEWATER BAY
PORLOCK BAY
SOUTH WALES
GLOUCESTERSHIRE
EXMOOR FOREST
DEVONSHIRE
DORSETSHIRE
PART OF DORSETS
PART OF DEVONSH
BRISTOL
BATH
WELLS
BRIDGEWATER
TAUNTON
FROME
YEOVIL
Explanation.
Mail Roads
Turnpike Roads with the distance from one Market Town to another across the Road as
Cross Roads
Rail Roads
Rivers
Canals
Towns with the distance from London as
SOMERTON 123
Villages as
Aller
Division of the Hundreds
Division of the Counties
The number of Members returned by each Borough as
BATH
Polling Places
REFERENCE to the HUNDREDS.
THE LARGER FIGURES ON THE MAP
1 Portbury
2 Winterstoke
3 Hartcliff with Bedminster
4 Chew
5 Chewton
6 Keynsham
7 Bath Forum
8 Hampton & Claverton
9 Wellow
10 Kilmersdon
11 Mells & Leigh
12 Frome
13 Whitstone
14 Wells Forum
15 Glaston
16 Bempstone
17 Brent & Wrington
18 Huntspill
19 Whitley
20 Somerton
21 Catash
22 Bruton
23 Norton
24 Horethorne
25 Stone
26 Tintinhull
27 Marlock
28 Houndsborough
29 Crewkerne
30 Sth Petherton
31 Est Kingsbury
32 Abdick
33 Bulstone
34 Pitney
35 Nth Curry
36 Nth Petherton
37 Andersfield
38 Cannington
39 Taunton and Tauntondean
40 Milverton
41 Wst Kingsbury
42 Williton Freemanner
43 Carhampton
Scale.
55 Longe West
Engraved on Steel by Pigot & Co. Manchester

STAFFORDSHIRE.

THE County of STAFFORD is situated near the centre of the Kingdom: bounded on the north-west by Cheshire, from which county it is separated by the river Dane; on the north and north-east by Derbyshire, the Dove dividing it from that county; on the south-east by Worcestershire & Warwickshire; and on the west by Shropshire. It is fifty-five miles in length, at its extreme points from north to south-west; its greatest breadth is about thirty-three miles, and its circumference about one hundred and fifty; its area containing about eleven hundred and forty-eight square miles.

NAME and ANCIENT HISTORY.—This county obtained its appellation from Stafford, the county town; but how that name originated has not been stated with sufficient perspicuity to authorise implicit credence to attach to the opinions upon the subject: it is said by some to have been derived from the river Sow having in former times been *forded* at this place by means of a *staff*. At the time of the Conquest the town of Stafford was one of some importance; for in Domesday-book it is termed a 'City,' in which the King had eighteen burgesses belonging to him; and there were twenty mansions of the Honour of the Earl of Mercia. The ancient and small city of Lichfield is famous for its beautiful Cathedral, adorned with rich painted windows—its finely sculptured western front exhibiting all the majesty of the pointed order: Dr. Wilkes dates the foundation of this noble edifice as far back as the year 657; but the origin of the city has occasioned much learned controversy, and a great difference of opinion among antiquaries: Bede, one of our most ancient writers, calls it *Lich-field*—that is, *'the field of the dead,'* from a tradition that a thousand British Christians suffered martyrdom here in the time of the Emperor Dioclesian; other controversialists say it was named by the Saxons *Licet-feld*, from its then marshy situation. But, whatever may have been the origin of the city, it derived its first importance from the Mercian Kings, and was erected into a Bishoprick by Oswy in the year 665; Offa, King of Mercia, in 785, exalting it to an Archiepiscopal See. Tamworth is a town possessing some interest, and is one of considerable antiquity; it was almost totally destroyed by the Danes about the commencement of the tenth century; but Ethelfleda, daughter of Alfred the Great, having been successful against these invaders in 914, and driven them out of the country, rebuilt the town, and erected a strong castle: this castle, with the adjacent territory, was granted by William the Conqueror to Robert Marmion, Lord of Fontenoy, in Normandy. The chief military transactions connected with the history of this county occurred at Blore Heath, near Drayton, and at Hopton Heath, near Stafford: in the former, the Lancastrians were defeated by the Yorkists; and in the latter, the Royalists defeated the Parliamentary forces, in the reign of Charles I.

SOIL and CLIMATE, PRODUCE and MANUFACTURES.—The northern part, called 'the Moorlands,' is hilly, much resembling the adjacent districts of Derbyshire; and is a bleak, wild and dreary tract, in some parts of an elevation of fifteen hundred feet above the Trent—the soil being thin, and yielding but a scanty pasture. The valley along the Trent is mostly very fertile, adorned with seats and plantations, and affords a variety of beautiful prospects. The middle and southern parts of this county are generally level, or with only gentle eminences, agreeably diversified with wood, pasture and arable land (the latter portion greatly predominating), and have a depth of rich loamy soil. The great forest of Cannock, near the centre, once covered with oaks, has long been dismantled of its wood, and is now a naked expanse. At the southern extremity, the Clent Hills, Hagley and its neighbourhood, are well known for the romantic beauties they possess.—The CLIMATE of Staffordshire is considered not unhealthy, though it may be deemed inclining to wet, especially in the northern part of the county; probably arising from a ridge of mountainous land lying to the west, which attracts the clouds in their passage. The air of the county is sharp, and more severely cold than in many other counties.—The AGRICULTURE and FARMING STOCK of Staffordshire have, within the last half century, undergone material improvement; whilst, on the rich lands bordering on the Trent, the dairy has become a source of considerable profit, and much good cheese and butter are made in that district. Although agricultural produce is a valuable auxiliary in promoting the prosperity of this county, yet its subterranean riches are of still higher importance to its welfare, as being the grand *materiel* employed in its principal manufactures. Coal is abundant in many parts, supplying the numerous iron works and manufactories, while the Moorlands contain beneath, besides coal, a store of mineral wealth, yielding lead, copper, iron, marble, alabaster, mill-stones and salt: fullers' earth is also found in this county,—pipe clay, and red and yellow ochres, in various parts; besides a blue clay, of great tenacity, and fire-proof, suited for the composition of pots for glass-houses; and potters' clay for more common purposes, in different districts, particularly Newcastle-under-Lyme. Lime-stone and iron ore are common in several places; copper and lead ore, varying greatly in purity and worth, occasionally also appears. Quarries of marble, different in colour, strength and beauty, and of various other kinds of stone of great value and utility, are plenteous.—The MANUFACTURES of this county are various; but its principal one, and for which it has long been deservedly celebrated, is its POTTERY. The chief station at which this branch of industry is carried on is in the neighbourhood of Newcastle, where it is almost the sole employment of a line of populous villages, extending ten miles: these are situated in a country full of coal, and nearly in the heart of England, with every part of which they have a navigable communication. These manufactures give employment to perhaps twenty thousand people in the county; and the operations of digging and collecting the clay, flint, *terra porcellana*, &c., in Kent, Sussex, Hampshire, Dorsetshire, Devonshire and Cornwall, and conveying them to the adjacent ports, are supposed to employ nearly forty thousand more, besides upwards of sixty thousand tons of shipping. Here are likewise iron works; and, in the southern extremity of the county, Walsall, Wolverhampton, Wednesbury, Darlaston, &c. &c. participate with Birmingham in the manufacture of different descriptions of hardware. The town of Stafford has long been famed for its manufacture of shoes, which employs a great number of hands: at Rugeley and Newcastle hats are manufactured, and at Leek various articles in the silk trade; at Fazeley are cotton spinning factories, and extensive bleaching works,—the woollen trade likewise thrives here; at Tipton and West Bromwich are inexhaustible coal mines and iron works, with blast furnaces of great magnitude.

RIVERS and CANALS.—The principal rivers of Staffordshire are the TRENT, the DOVE, the BLYTHE, the SOW, the PENK, the CHURNET, the TAME and the STOUR; there are also some other smaller streams that water the county, as the Hamps or Hanse, the Ilet and the Smetstall. The Trent rises in the north-west part of the county, and passes the town of Stone; at Great Haywood it receives the waters of the Sow, at Kings Bromley those of the Blythe, and at Wichnor it is further augmented by the Tame; it then flows past the town of Burton, about two miles beyond which it receives the Dove, when it leaves the county. The Dove rises on the borders of Derbyshire, and unites with the Trent near Newton Solney, being in its whole course a boundary between this county and Derbyshire. The Blythe has its origin about five miles north-west from Cheadle, in this county, and joins the Trent near Kings Bromley. The Sow has its source three miles south-west from Newcastle, and, after visiting the county town, is augmented by the Penk, and falls into the Trent opposite Great Haywood. The Penk rises about five miles from Rugeley, and after passing Penkridge is lost in the Sow, a little below Stafford. The Churnet springs about four miles north-west from Leek, and falls into the Dove near Doveridge, in Derbyshire. The Tame enters this county at Tamworth, and running north falls into the Trent at Wichnor. The Stour rises in Shropshire, and runs through the south angle of this county in its course to join the Severn in Worcestershire. The CANALS intersecting the county are very numerous; they are, the 'Trent and Mersey,' the 'Staffordshire and Worcestershire,' the 'Stourbridge,' the 'Birmingham Canal Navigation,' the 'Dudley Canal' and 'Dudley Extension,' the 'Wyrley and Easington,' the 'Fazeley,' 'Sir Nigel B. Gresley's,' the 'Newcastle-under-Lyme,' and the 'Caldon Branch.'

CIVIL and ECCLESIASTICAL DIVISIONS.—Staffordshire is in the Province of Canterbury, and Diocese of Lichfield and Coventry; is included in the Oxford Circuit, and divided into five hundreds, viz. CUTTLESTON, OFFLOW, PIREHILL, SEISDON and TOTMONSLOW; these are subdivided into one hundred and forty-five parishes, containing collectively one city (Lichfield), one county town (Stafford), and eighteen other market towns. The whole county returns ten Members to Parliament, viz. two each for LICHFIELD, NEWCASTLE-UNDER-LYME, STAFFORD, TAMWORTH, and two for the SHIRE.

POPULATION.—According to the census of 1821, there were houses inhabited in the county, 63,319; uninhabited, 2,326; and houses building, 429. The number of families then resident in the county was 68,780; comprising 171,668 males, and 169,372 females; total, 341,040: and by a calculation made by order of Government, which included persons in the army and navy, for which was added after the ratio of about one to thirty prior to the year 1811, and one to fifty for that year and the census of 1821, to the returns made from the several districts; the population of the county, in round numbers, in the year 1700, was 117,200—in 1750, 160,000—in 1801, 247,100—in 1811, 304,000—and in 1821, 347,900. The increased population in the 50 years, from the year 1700, was 42,800—from 1750 to 1801, the increase was 87,100—from 1801 to 1811, the increase was 56,900—and from 1811 to 1821, the augmented number of persons was 43,900: the grand total increase in the population of the county from the year 1700 to the census of 1821, being about 230,700 persons.

Index of Distances from Town to Town in the County of Stafford.

THE NAMES OF THE RESPECTIVE TOWNS ARE ON THE TOP AND SIDE, AND THE SQUARE WHERE BOTH MEET GIVES THE DISTANCE.

Distance from Manchester	Town	Abbots Bromley	Bilston	Brewood	Burslem	Burton-on-Trent	Cheadle	Eccleshall	Fazeley	Hanley	Lane End	Leek	Lichfield	Newcastle-under-Lyme	Penkridge	Rugeley	Stafford	Stoke	Stone	Tamworth	Uttoxeter	Walsall	Wednesbury	Distance from London
58	Abbots Bromley																							129
70	Bilston	24																						127
63	Brewood	16	9																					129
35	Burslem	28	36	30																				152
66	Burton	11	27	30	30																			125
42	Cheadle	17	32	27	10	25																		149
50	Eccleshall	19	23	14	14	31	16																	142
76	Fazeley	14	15	22	40	16	31	31																114
37	Hanley	27	35	29	2	35	10	16	39															150
40	Lane End	24	32	25	5	32	7	14	36	3														147
32	Leek	27	42	37	10	35	10	24	46	10	13													154
67	Lichfield	11	13	16	32	13	28	23	8	31	28	38												120
36	Newcastle	27	44	27	3	36	12	12	38	2	5	12	30											149
58	Penkridge	13	12	5	25	27	22	13	21	23	20	30	13	22										129
59	Rugeley	7	29	16	25	15	23	16	15	26	21	34	7	23	9									126
52	Stafford	11	18	11	19	24	15	7	25	18	14	24	16	16	6	9								144
37	Stoke	26	34	34	2	23	9	15	36	1	2	11	30	2	22	23	16							149
45	Stone	14	25	18	11	25	10	6	29	10	7	17	22	9	13	14	7	9						140
74	Tamworth	13	17	21	39	15	30	30	2	38	35	45	7	37	20	14	23	37	28					116
51	Uttoxeter	7	31	27	20	15	10	22	26	20	17	20	17	19	21	15	14	19	14	25				135
76	Walsall	26	4	12	37	22	37	25	14	36	28	47	9	34	13	16	18	34	25	16	27			115
73	Wednesbury	23	3	12	40	25	40	28	17	39	31	48	12	37	15	19	21	37	28	19	30	3		118
68	Wolverhampton	23	2	7	34	29	32	23	20	34	30	43	16	32	10	20	16	32	24	22	31	6	5	124

[See over.

Additional information relating to the County of STAFFORD.

POPULATION.—By the Census for **1831** this county contained 206,897 males, and 203,588 females—total 410,485, being an increase, since the returns made in the year 1821, of 69,445 inhabitants; and from the Census of 1801 to that of 1831, the augmentation amounted to 171,332 persons.

REPRESENTATION.—By the *Reform Bill* the towns of STOKE-UPON-TRENT and WOLVERHAMPTON have obtained the right of representation, and return two members each, WALSALL, by the same Act, sends one member, and two others, additional, are given to the county: the whole shire, now, returns *seventeen* representatives to Parliament, instead of *ten*, as heretofore. The new *Boundary Act* divides the county into two parts, respectively named the *Northern Division* and the *Southern Division:* the former comprises the hundreds of Pirehill, Totmonslow, and North Offlow; and the latter includes the hundreds of South Offlow, Seisdon, and Cuttlestone. The election of members for the northern division of the county is held at STAFFORD, and for the southern at LICHFIELD: besides the place of election, the northern division polls at LEEK, NEWCASTLE-UNDER-LYME, CHEADLE, & ABBOT'S BROMLEY; and the southern division (besides the place of election) polls at WALSALL, WOLVERHAMPTON, PENKRIDGE, and KING'S SWINFORD.

RAILWAYS.

The GRAND JUNCTION RAILWAY, in proceeding from *Crewe,* goes through *Madeley* (about five miles west by south from *Newcastle*): then through *Whitmore;* passes *Stone* (on the left) and *Eccleshall* (on the right), to *Stafford;* thence to *Penkridge,* and near to *Brewood, Wolverhampton, Bilston, Wednesbury* and *Walsall,* on to *Birmingham,* where it meets the London and Birmingham Railway, by which the traveller is conveyed to the Metropolis. The MANCHESTER and BIRMINGHAM RAILWAY will pass by *Stockport* (from whence there is a branch to *Macclesfield*): from *Alderley* it will pass by *Holmes' Chapel,* and join the Grand Junction at *Crewe;* from Alderley also this line will, as intended, go through *Congleton* and the *Potteries,* on to *Stone,* where will commence the extension to *Rugby,* at which place it will join the London and Birmingham Railway. From *Stone* the line takes the name of the TRENT VALLEY RAILWAY—passing through *Rugeley* and *Lichfield* to *Tamworth;* thence taking the name of the TAMWORTH and RUGBY RAILWAY, it will run by *Atherstone* and *Nuneaton* to *Rugby.* A branch is projected to issue from the Trent Valley line, near Rugeley, which will pass King's Bromley and Alrewas; and about two miles and a half from the latter place will unite with the Birmingham and Derby Railway. In the account of the Lancashire Railways we have given other particulars relating to the Grand Junction and the Manchester and Birmingham lines.

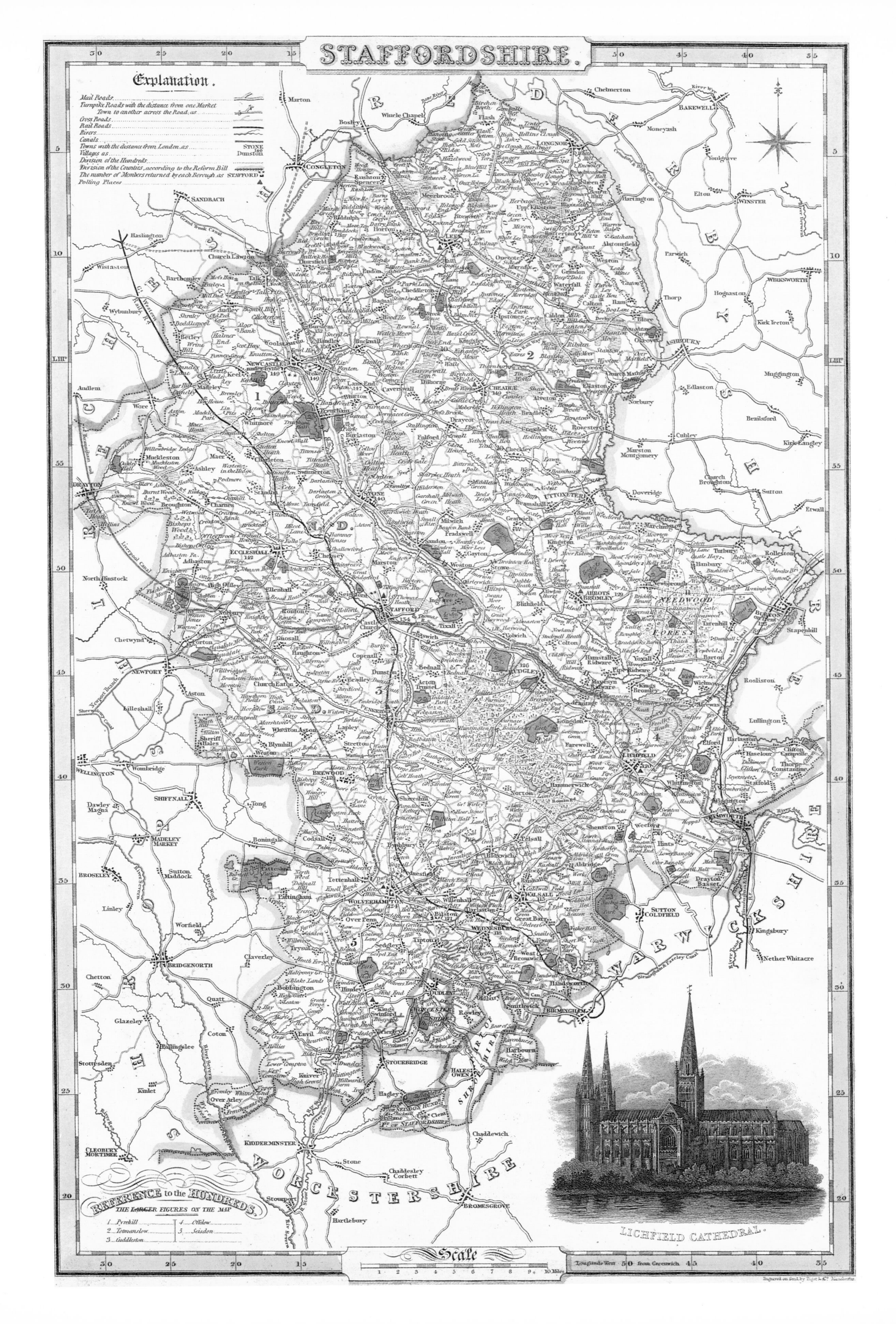
STAFFORDSHIRE.
Explanation.
Mail Roads
Turnpike Roads with the distance from one Market Town to another across the Road, as
Cross Roads
Rail Roads
Rivers
Canals
Towns with the distance from London, as STONE 140
Villages as Dunston
Division of the Hundreds
Division of the Counties, according to the Reform Bill
The number of Members returned by each Borough as STAFFORD
Polling Places
REFERENCE to the HUNDREDS,
THE LARGER FIGURES ON THE MAP
1 Pyrehill
2 Totmanslow
3 Cuddleston
4 Offlow
5 Seisdon
Scale
1 2 3 4 5 6 7 8 9 10 Miles
Longitude West 50 from Greenwich 45
DERBYSHIRE
CHESHIRE
SHROPSHIRE
WORCESTERSHIRE
WARWICKSHIRE
STAFFORD
NEWCASTLE under Lyme
LICHFIELD
WOLVERHAMPTON
WALSALL
STONE
UTTOXETER
LEEK
CHEADLE
ECCLESHALL
ABBOTS BROMLEY
RUGELEY
PENKRIDGE
BURTON
TAMWORTH
STOURBRIDGE
DUDLEY
BIRMINGHAM
KIDDERMINSTER
BROMESGROVE
NEWPORT
CONGLETON
ASHBOURN
NEEDWOOD FOREST
LICHFIELD CATHEDRAL.

SUFFOLK.

SUFFOLK is a maritime county, bounded on the north by Norfolk, from which it is separated by the Little Ouse and the Waveney rivers; on the south by Essex, from which it is divided by the river Stour; on the east by the German Ocean, and on the west by Cambridgeshire. Its figure is an irregular oblong, of about forty-seven miles in length, from Aldborough on the east, to Newmarket, on the borders of Cambridgeshire, on the west; and about twenty-seven miles from north to south: its circumference has been estimated at 144 miles, and its area to comprise 1,512 square miles.

NAME and ANCIENT HISTORY.—In the time of the Romans the inhabitants of this part of the country were called the *Iceni* or *Cenomannii*, and by them it was included in the province of FLAVIA CÆSARIENSIS. Under the Saxons it formed a part of the kingdom of East Anglia, and was called Suffolk from *Sud-folk*—literally 'southern folk' or 'people.' The precise period of Uffa's monarchy cannot be accurately ascertained, but it is certain that he died in 578. The whole of this and some of the adjacent counties knew little of respite from foreign and domestic depredators till some time after the death of Edward the Confessor: this county in particular suffered much from Sweyne, King of Denmark, who spared neither towns nor churches, unless redeemed by the people with large sums of money; though, to compensate in some measure for this cruelty, Canute, his son and successor, shewed it particular kindness. When William the Conqueror was settled on the throne of the Kingdom, he divided the manors of Suffolk among his officers. Some of the towns of this county are of great antiquity, and the remains of its once massy castles possess high interest with the antiquary. During the intestine broils between King Stephen and the Barons, Bungay Castle, erected by the Bigods, Earls of Norfolk, was so strongly fortified by Hugh Bigod (a turbulent Nobleman,) against his Sovereign, as to be rendered almost impregnable; its ruins are still to be seen, as are those of a Benedictine Nunnery, founded by Robert de Glanville in 1640. Bury St. Edmunds is supposed by some to have been the *Villa Faustinii*, or 'the seat of Faustinius;' by the Saxons it was called *Beoderic Weord*, or 'the Court of Beodericus.' This town is famous for its Abbey, which, when in its splendour, is said to have exceeded in magnificence all other establishments of the kind in England, Glastonbury excepted. Ipswich (or, as it is written in Domesday-book, *Gyppeswiz,)* was originally fortified, and inclosed by a rampart and ditch, which were broken down by the Danes when they pillaged the town in the years 991 and 1000: these defences were afterwards renewed by King John, parts of which are still remaining. Dunwich, now an inconsiderable village, was once a most important Roman station: in 630 it was an Episcopal See; and tradition records that it had once *fifty-two Churches and Monasteries*, all of which (except All Saints) have been swallowed up by the sea.

SOIL and CLIMATE, PRODUCE and MANUFACTURES.—There is in this county a very considerable variety of soil, nor is the diversity any where more distinctly marked; the whole, however, may be conveniently divided into four sorts—clay, sand, loam and fen. The first description of soil comprehends the whole midland part of the county, through nearly its whole extent from east to west, and forms about two-thirds of the land; the district over which this soil prevails is called 'High Suffolk.' The next sort of soil consists chiefly of sand, and lies in opposite sides of the county—some in the maritime part; much of this district is highly cultivated, and is one of the most profitable; the rest of the sand district lies on the western side of the county, and comprises nearly the whole of the north-western angle; it contains a few spots of such rich sand-lands as are found on the coast, but abounds with warrens and poor sheep-walks; towards the borders of Norfolk it is very light and blowing. The third district, that of loam, forms but a small portion of the county, and is not so clearly discriminated as the others; it is composed of a vein of friable, putrid, vegetable mould, of extraordinary fertility. The fen division is merely the north-west corner; its surface to some depth is common peat-bog, and is in different places under water, though much expense has been incurred for draining. The roads in every part of Suffolk are excellent, the late improvements in them being almost inconceivable. Many modern inclosures have been made by Acts of Parliament, which examples, in favourable times, will no doubt be followed, the success having been such as to encourage the practice; and as to landed property, there is no estate in Suffolk that can be considered as overgrown. The agriculture of this county approaches more nearly to perfection than, perhaps, any other in the kingdom: in the lighter lands, the Norfolk system is pursued; and in the heavier, beans and wheat, cabbages and other vegetables, are grown in rotation. The farming stock is highly valued; the cows being excellent milkers, and the horses strong, active, and capable of vast exertions. By a spirited cultivation, and the free use of clay, much valuable land has been reclaimed in the N.W. part of the county. The woods of Suffolk hardly deserve mentioning, except for the fact that they pay in general but indifferently; and nothing but the expense and trouble of grubbing prevents large tracts of land, thus occupied, from being applied much more beneficially. Hemp is cultivated in the district extending from Eye to Beccles, spreading to the breadth of about ten miles,—which oblong part of the country may be considered as its seat: land for the growth of this useful article is in the hands of both farmers and cottagers, but it is very rare to see more than five or six acres in the occupation of any one person; it is singular that no weeding is ever given to it, the hemp destroying every other plant. The fabrics wrought in this county from its own hemp have great merit.—The CLIMATE of this county has long been noticed as the driest in the Kingdom; the frosts, also, are severe; and the north-east winds, which prevail in spring, are generally sharp. But though, like the western extremity of this Island, Suffolk is not calculated to favour the weak and consumptive stranger, it is upon the whole extremely healthy, which has been proved by calculating the average mortality of the county for ten years.—The MANUFACTURES of this county are not extensive or various; light stuffs, buntings, crapes and yarns being the principal under this head, with hempen cloth for home consumption. The sea-ports depend much on the exportation of malt and corn; some are noted for making fine salt, burning lime from fossil shells, &c.; and other maritime towns derive considerable advantage from the mackarel and herring fisheries. The curing of fish employs great numbers in several towns on the coast, especially Lowestoft, upon which branch the prosperity of this town may be said to almost entirely depend.

RIVERS.—Water is very plentiful all over this county; for there are not only rivers in every part, but a great number of fine springs and rivulets. The principal rivers are, the STOUR, the LESSER OUSE, the WAVENEY, the ORWELL, the ALDE, the BLYTHE, the DEBEN and the GIPPING. The Stour rises from two sources, at Great Bradley and at Wethersfield; it passes Haverhill, Clare and Sudbury,—at the latter town it becomes navigable; thence pursuing its course to Nayland, and afterwards meeting the Orwell at Harwich, it falls into the German Ocean: during its whole course, the Stour forms the south boundary of the county. The Lesser Ouse rises on the north boundary of the county, near the source of the Waveney, from which it is separated only by a causeway; it passes the towns of Thetford and Brandon, and forms in its course the north-west boundary of the county, till it empties itself into the Great Ouse. The Waveney pursues a north-east direction, and is the boundary on that side of Suffolk; it waters the towns of Harleston, Bungay and Beccles, meets the Breedon water near Yarmouth, below which town the German Ocean receives the united streams. The Orwell rises at Broad Green, and, flowing east, becomes navigable at Stowmarket; and after visiting Needham and Ipswich, joins the Stour at Harwich. The Alde has its spring at Brundish, and, flowing past Aldborough, falls into the German Ocean at Orford Bay. The Blythe is formed of several springs; thus united passes Halesworth, and mingles with the Ocean at Southwold. The Deben rises above Debenham, flows past Wickham and Woodbridge, and unites with the sea near Felixstow. The Gipping is a river of this county, which empties itself into the Orwell between Stowmarket and Ipswich.

CIVIL and ECCLESIASTICAL DIVISIONS.—Suffolk is in the Province of Canterbury and Diocese of Norwich, and is included in the Norfolk Circuit. The most general division of the county is into two parts: the first called 'the Franchise or Liberty of St. Edmund;' and the second called 'Gildable Land,' containing the eastern part: each portion furnishes a distinct Grand Jury at the county assizes. There are two other general divisions of the county, into 'High Suffolk' and 'Low Suffolk;' and it is further divided into twenty-one hundreds, and subdivided into five hundred and ten parishes: these contain one county town (Ipswich), and nineteen other market towns. Suffolk returns sixteen Members to Parliament, namely, two each for the boroughs of ALDBOROUGH, BURY ST. EDMUNDS, DUNWICH, EYE, IPSWICH, ORFORD and SUDBURY, and two for the COUNTY.

POPULATION.—According to the census of 1821, there were houses inhabited in the county, 42,773; uninhabited, 656; and houses building, 270. The number of families then resident in the county was 55,064, comprising 132,410 males, and 138,132 females; total, 270,542: and by a calculation made by order of government, which included persons in the army and navy, for which was added after the ratio of about one to thirty prior to the year 1811, and one to fifty for that year and the census of 1821, to the returns made from the several districts; the population of the county, in round numbers, in the year 1700, was 152,700—in 1750, 156,800—in 1801, 217,400—in 1811, 242,900—and in 1821, 276,000. The increased population in the fifty years, from the year 1700, was 4,100—from 1750 to 1801, the increase was 60,600—from 1801 to 1811, the increase was 25,500—and from 1811 to 1821, the augmented number of persons was 33,100: the grand total increase in the population of the county, from the year 1700 to the census of 1821, being about 123,300 persons.

Index of Distances from Town to Town in the County of Suffolk.

THE NAMES OF THE RESPECTIVE TOWNS ARE ON THE TOP AND SIDE, AND THE SQUARE WHERE BOTH MEET GIVES THE DISTANCE.

	Aldborough	Beccles	Bildeston	Botesdale	Brandon	Bungay	Bury St. Edmunds	Clare	Debenham	Eye	Framlingham	Hadleigh	Halesworth	Haverhill	Ipswich	Ixworth	Lavenham	Lowestoft	Mendlesham	Mildenhall	Nayland	Needham Market	Orford	Saxmundham	Southwold	Stowmarket	Sudbury	Distance from London
Aldborough																												94
Beccles	22																											108
Bildeston	36	46																										63
Botesdale	38	28	20																									88
Brandon	59	49	30	21																								80
Bungay	25	6	41	21	38																							108
Bury St. Edmunds	50	43	15	16	15	38																						72
Clare	50	55	10	30	31	51	18																					56
Debenham	25	31	20	15	33	20	22	29																				83
Eye	30	23	23	8	29	17	19	34	7																			90
Framlingham	16	23	25	21	41	22	30	35	8	14																		87
Hadleigh	34	48	5	28	36	43	20	20	19	27	28																	64
Halesworth	16	10	38	26	47	9	42	50	20	19	13	39																100
Haverhill	58	62	22	33	32	55	18	7	37	40	43	25	56															59
Ipswich	24	40	11	27	41	40	26	26	13	20	18	9	31	34														69
Ixworth	52	37	16	9	15	30	7	23	18	16	30	20	36	25	24													79
Lavenham	40	49	5	22	26	49	10	10	24	26	30	10	43	17	16	16												63
Lowestoft	31	10	54	37	59	16	52	64	36	33	30	54	18	72	45	46	59											114
Mendlesham	32	31	13	9	30	24	18	27	6	7	13	18	20	33	15	11	20	38										81
Mildenhall	62	52	27	24	9	45	12	22	35	31	41	32	50	22	38	16	22	61	30									72
Nayland	42	56	11	32	38	47	22	16	26	35	33	8	46	22	16	28	12	60	26	41								57
Needham	32	43	8	16	30	31	18	21	12	16	15	10	28	29	9	15	12	44	8	29	18							71
Orford	5	32	30	33	54	31	43	44	19	25	14	29	21	52	19	37	36	34	24	55	36	25						88
Saxmundham	5	20	31	28	48	19	37	44	12	20	7	30	11	51	21	31	35	24	18	48	37	21	10					89
Southwold	18	12	46	33	53	18	46	52	25	27	21	46	10	60	36	42	48	13	32	57	50	34	24	14				105
Stowmarket	36	36	9	14	26	31	14	20	10	12	17	14	30	26	12	12	13	46	7	26	22	3	30	23	35			75
Sudbury	46	60	12	29	32	54	16	7	27	32	35	12	47	14	22	23	8	65	24	27	9	15	40	42	55	19		55
Woodbridge	16	32	19	28	49	31	34	34	13	21	11	18	24	41	8	31	25	37	18	46	24	16	12	13	28	20	29	77

[See over.

Additional information relating to the County of SUFFOLK.

———ooo———

POPULATION.—By the Census for **1831** this county contained 145,761 males, and 150,543 females—total 296,304, being an increase, since the returns made in the year 1821, of 25,762 inhabitants; and from the Census of 1801 to that of 1831, the augmentation amounted to 85,873 persons.

REPRESENTATION.—By the *Reform Bill* the boroughs of ALDBOROUGH, DUNWICH, and ORFORD are disfranchised, EYE is deprived of one of its members, and two additional ones are given to the county; so that the number of representatives, now, for the whole county is *eleven*, instead of *sixteen*, as before the passing of the Bill. The new *Boundary Act* divides Suffolk into two parts, respectively named the *Eastern Division* and the *Western Division*; the latter includes the liberty of Bury St. Edmunds, and the hundreds of Hartesmere and Stow, and the eastern division comprises all such parts of the county as are not included in the liberty of Bury St. Edmunds or either of the hundreds before mentioned. The election of members for the eastern division of the county is held at IPSWICH, and for the western at BURY ST. EDMUNDS: besides the place of election, the eastern division polls at NEEDHAM, WOODBRIDGE, FRAMLINGHAM, SAXMUNDHAM, HALESWORTH, and BECCLES; and the western division (besides the place of election) polls at WICKHAM BROOK, LAVENHAM, STOWMARKET, BOTESDALE, MILDENHALL, and HADLEIGH.

RAILWAYS.—The Eastern Counties' is intended to pass through Ipswich, run to within two or three miles to the west (or left) of Debenham, and thence through Eye on to Norwich. From Ipswich, on the south, it will run to Colchester, on to the west of Witham, through Chelmsford, to the west of Billericay and east of Romford, to London. From Ipswich a Railway is projected to join the London and Birmingham: it will run near to Stowmarket, through Bury St. Edmunds and Cambridge—and, passing a little to the south of Bedford, will join the London and Birmingham line near Newport Pagnell.

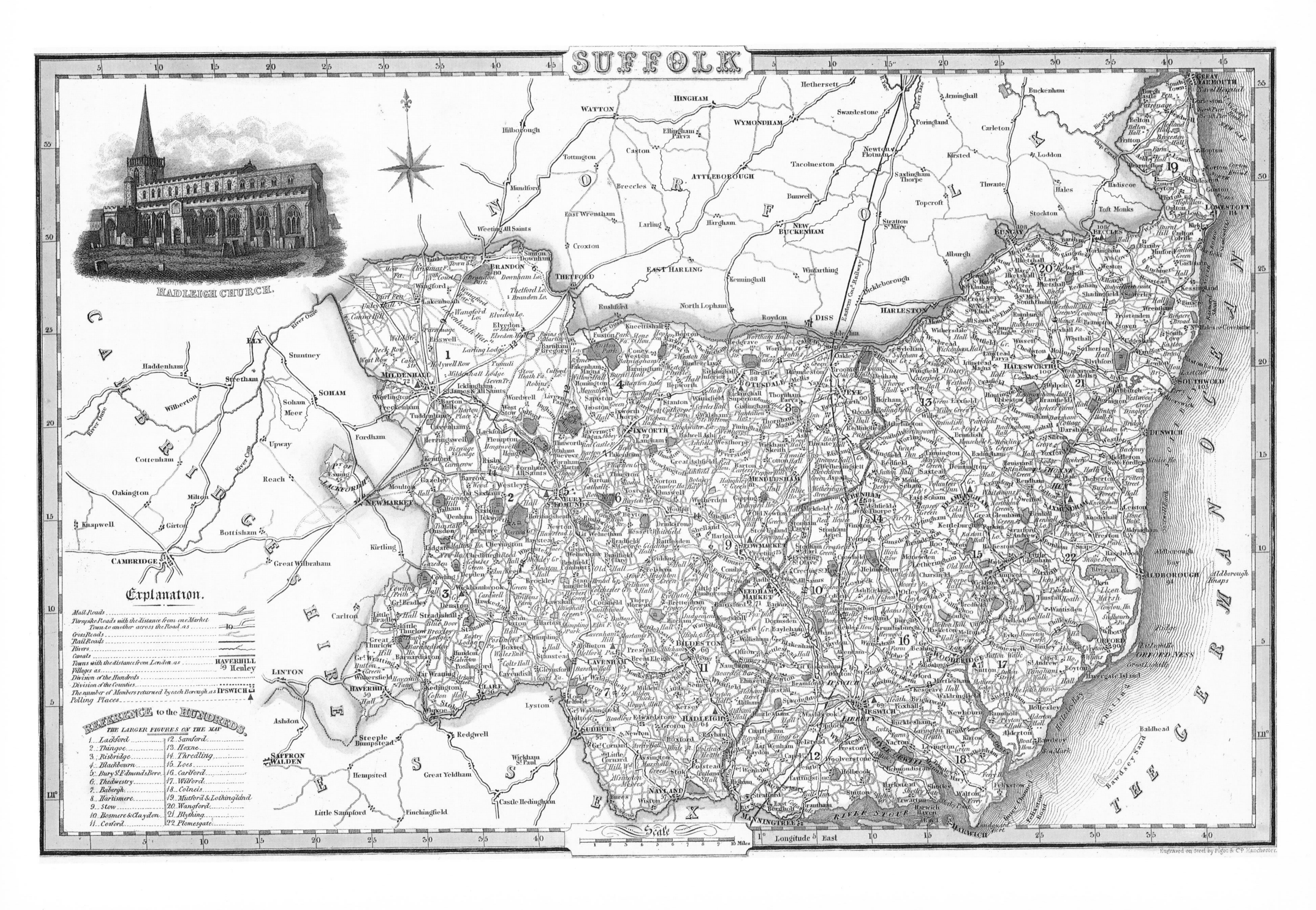
SUFFOLK
HADLEIGH CHURCH
NORFOLK
CAMBRIDGESHIRE
ESSEX
THE GERMAN OCEAN
Explanation
Mail Roads
Turnpike Roads with the distance from one Market Town to another across the Road as
Cross Roads
Rail Roads
Rivers
Canals
Towns with the distance from London as HAVERHILL 59
Villages as Henley
Division of the Hundreds
Division of the Counties
The number of Members returned by each Borough as IPSWICH
Polling Places
REFERENCE to the HUNDREDS
THE LARGER FIGURES ON THE MAP
1. Lackford
2. Thingoe
3. Risbridge
4. Blackbourn
5. Bury St Edmunds Boro.
6. Thedwestry
7. Babergh
8. Hartismere
9. Stow
10. Bosmere & Claydon
11. Cosford
12. Samford
13. Hoxne
14. Thredling
15. Loes
16. Carlford
17. Wilford
18. Colneis
19. Mutford & Lothingland
20. Wangford
21. Blything
22. Plomesgate
Scale
10 Miles
Longitude East
Engraved on Steel by Pigot & Co. Manchester.

SURREY.

THE County of SURREY is situated in the south-eastern part of the Kingdom; bounded on the north by Middlesex and a very small point of Buckinghamshire, on the west by Berkshire and Hampshire, on the south by Sussex, and on the east by Kent. In form it presents a greater regularity than any other county of England; and were it not that its northern side is marked by considerable indentions, produced by the windings of the Thames, its shape would exhibit that of almost a perfect square. In length, from Haslemere on the south, to the Thames, its boundary on the north, it is about forty miles; from east to west, it measures about thirty-five miles; and its area comprises seven hundred and fifty-eight square miles.

NAME and ANCIENT HISTORY.—On the division of this Kingdom into shires, this district, from its situation on the south of the Thames, received the name of *Suthrea*—from *Suth*, 'south,' and *Rea*, a 'river' or 'water.' The aboriginal inhabitants were the *Legentiacii*, or *Belgæ*. After the Romans had gained possession of this Island, this portion was part of the province named BRITANNIA PRIMA. During the Saxon Heptarchy, it formed, with Sussex, a distinct State, under the South Saxons: this was founded by Ella, about the year 491; and had its own Monarchs till 725, when it was subdued by Ina, King of Wessex. The most memorable incident that occurred in this county was the signing MAGNA CHARTA by King John, in 1215, at Runnymede, close to the present town of Egham. Lambeth is celebrated as containing the ancient Palace of the Archbishops of Canterbury, erected in 1188: it became the first object of popular violence in the commotions between Charles I. and the Parliament, when it was made a prison; and in it were confined, amongst other obnoxious personages, the Earls of Chesterfield and Derby. Dulwich is noted for its College, founded in 1619 by Edward Alleyn, an actor: to this day it is an object of great attraction, and its valuable library and picture gallery well merit the attention of the scientific visitor; the master of this establishment is Lord of the Manor to a considerable extent, and enjoys the affluence and ease of the Prior of a Monastery. At Guildford, the county town, are the extensive ruins of an old castle, which in Saxon times was a Royal Villa, where many of our Monarchs passed their festivals. At Farnham, also, is a castle, which is a noble building, situated on a lofty and commanding height, in a fine park: it was originally built by Henry of Blois, brother of King Stephen and Bishop of Winchester. It was seized by Louis the Dauphin and the rebellious Barons, in 1216; some years after, it was levelled to the ground by Henry III; but was afterwards re-erected in a more magnificent style, with a deep moat, a strong wall and towers. In the civil wars it was garrisoned for Charles, and it is now the Palace of the Bishops of Winchester. Amongst other places in this county which are deserving of notice from their antiquity or beauty of situation, Richmond (formerly *Sheen,)* possesses superior claims to distinction—whether as a seat of Royalty in times past, or, as it is at the present period, one of the most beautiful villages in this Kingdom,—environed by scenery of the most enchanting and diversified character, over which are spread elegant villas, and the most tastefully laid out pleasure-grounds that the imagination can picture. The ancient Royal Palace here was the favourite residence of several of our Monarchs, particularly of Edwards I, II. and III., Richard II. and Henry V.—Edward III. closed a long and victorious reign at his Palace here, in 1377; and Queen Anne, his successor's consort, died in the same Royal mansion in 1394; this Palace having been destroyed by fire in 1497, was rebuilt by order of Henry VII, who then changed the name of the town from Sheen to Richmond, in honour of the title he had borne previous to his accession to the throne; Henry died at this, his favourite Palace, April 21, 1509. Henry VIII. resided here, as did his favourite, Cardinal Wolsey; and here the Princess Elizabeth was confined by her sister, Queen Mary: upon the accession of the former Princess, she chose it for an occasional residence, and in this Palace she closed her illustrious career. In 1603, the Court was removed to Richmond, on account of the plague, and again, for a short time, in 1625. In 1630 the Palace and grounds were sold by order of Parliament, and the Royal edifice pulled down.

SOIL and CLIMATE, PRODUCE and MANUFACTURES.—The SOIL of this county, although extremely various, may be reduced to the four general heads of clay, loam, chalk and heath. The most extensive tract of uniform soil is that which extends along the whole southern border of the county, and forms what is called 'the Weald of Surrey.' Northward, a district of sandy loam stretches entirely across the county. A very large portion of the west side of Surrey is occupied by heaths, the soil of which is very indifferent. The under soil is of different strata, but principally composed of chalk and gravel. The woods, of which there are but few, are flourishing. That part of the county skirted by the Thames is remarkable for the fertility of its meadows, for the excellence of its cultivation, and for the number of its elegant villas. The south-west angle of the county is noted for growing some of the finest hops in the Kingdom. The south border is well watered, and finely varied with wood, arable and pasture; and the south-east side is a rough woody district, called 'Holmsdale,' extending into Kent. The agriculture of Surrey is by no means of the first order; but, by its vicinity to the Metropolis, the farmers and gardeners can always command a market. The waste lands are computed at about a fifth part of the whole county. House-lamb suckling forms one of the most lucrative branches of the Surrey farmer's avocations; the grain of the meat is sound and healthy, and its flavour very fine.—The CLIMATE of this county, though upon the whole salubrious, is almost as varied as the soil and surface. The southern border is moist and damp, from its flatness; as are the low parts, near the Thames. On the other hand, the atmosphere, where the chalk soils prevail, and on the whole west side, is dry, keen and bracing. The spring is in general early, and the summers are usually dry and warm.—The MANUFACTURES of the county consist of starch, tobacco, snuff, gunpowder, paper, vinegar, pottery-ware, and hats; of the latter, immense quantities are made in the borough of Southwark. There are also some extensive distilleries and breweries, bleaching and printing works; and leather dressing and wax bleaching establishments are distributed throughout the county.

RIVERS and CANALS.—The principal rivers which pass through or bound this county are the THAMES, the WEY, the WANDAL (or Vandal,) and the MOLE. The Thames, in its advance towards the sea, forms the entire northern boundary of Surrey, separating it from the counties of Buckingham and Middlesex. The river Wey enters the county near Farnham, and near Godalming it becomes navigable to the Thames at Weybridge: by its means, a considerable portion of the county is supplied with various necessaries, particularly coals, from London; and it is worthy of remark, that the first navigation locks that were constructed in this Kingdom were erected upon this river by Sir Richard Weston, of Sutton, near Guildford, who brought this contrivance over with him from the Netherlands. The Wandal rises near Croydon turnpike; and being increased by the waters of other springs at the back of the town, is joined afterwards by a small river at Wallington; thus augmented, it forms, in the centre of Carshalton, that beautiful sheet of water for which this village is celebrated; it thence passes Mitcham and Merton, on to Wandsworth, where it empties itself into the Thames. The river Mole springs on the south-east side of the county, sinks into the 'Swallows' at the foot of Box Hill, and works its way under ground (like the animal of its name,) until it emerges at Leatherhead; and, thence pursuing a northward course, joins the Thames at Moulsey.—Under the head of CANALS, besides the Wey navigation, there is a canal from Basingstoke to the Thames, which enters this county near Dradbrook; but the 'GRAND SURREY CANAL' is a work of the greatest magnitude and consequence of the kind in the county: by its many cuts, a communication is formed with various parts of the interior of Surrey, to which it is of almost inconceivable advantage. The dock of this truly noble work, at Rotherhithe, will contain one hundred sail of square-rigged vessels, at any draught of water that may be requisite for their approach to the Pool.

CIVIL and ECCLESIASTICAL DIVISIONS.—Surrey is in the Province of Canterbury and Diocese of Winchester; it is included in the Home Circuit, and divided into fourteen hundreds, which are subdivided into one hundred and forty-two parishes, containing one county town (Guildford), and nine other market towns. The whole county returns 14 Members to Parliament, namely, two each for BLETCHINGLY, GATTON, GUILDFORD, HASLEMERE and REIGATE; two also for the Borough of SOUTHWARK, and two for the COUNTY.

POPULATION.—According to the census of 1821, there were houses inhabited in the county, 64,790; uninhabited, 2,741; and houses building, 1,096. The number of families then resident in the county, was 88,806; comprising 189,871 males, and 208,787 females: total, 398,658. And by a calculation made by order of Government, which included persons in the army and navy, for which was added after the ratio of about one to thirty prior to the year 1811, and one to fifty for that year and the census of 1821, to the returns made from the several districts, the population of the county, in round numbers, in the year 1700, was 154,900—in 1750, 207,100—in 1801, 278,000—in 1811, 334,700—and in 1821, 406,700. The increased population in the fifty years, from the year 1700, was 52,200—from 1750 to 1801, the increase was 70,900—from 1801 to 1811, the increase was 56,700—and from 1811 to 1821, the augmented number of persons was 72,000: the grand total increase in the population of the county, from the year 1700 to the census of 1821, being about 251,800 persons. Of the 398,658 inhabitants in the county in 1821, 85,905 were returned for the Borough of Southwark.

Index of Distances from Town to Town in the County of Surrey.

THE NAMES OF THE RESPECTIVE TOWNS ARE ON THE TOP AND SIDE, AND THE SQUARE WHERE BOTH MEET GIVES THE DISTANCE.

	Blechingly	Chertsey	Croydon	Dorking	Epsom	Ewell	Farnham	Godalming	Guildford	Haslemere	Kingston	Reigate	Distance from London.
Blechingly													21
Chertsey	20												21
Croydon	11	19											9
Dorking	12	13	14										23
Epsom	9	13	7	9									14
Ewell	10	14	6	10	1								13
Farnham	34	17	34	22	26	27							38
Godalming	23	11	27	13	20	21	9						33
Guildford	24	10	24	12	16	17	10	4					29
Haslemere	29	23	36	22	30	31	11	19	13				42
Kingston	15	10	8	16	7	6	28	22	18	30			10
Reigate	5	16	11	6	8	9	28	19	18	24	15		20

[See over.

Additional information relating to the County of Surrey.

---ooo---

Population.—By the Census for **1831** this county contained 230,855 males, and 255,471 females—total 486,326, being an increase, since the returns made in the year 1821, of 87,668 inhabitants; and from the Census of 1801 to that of 1831, the augmentation amounted to 217,283 persons.

Representation.—By the *Reform Bill* the boroughs of Bletchingley, Gatton and Haslemere have been disfranchised, and one member taken from Reigate: by the same Act, Lambeth has obtained the right of returning two members, and the like number, in addition, has been given to the county; so that the whole county, now, sends *eleven* representatives to Parliament, instead of *fourteen*, as before the passing of the Bill. The new *Boundary Act* divides the county into two parts, respectively named the *Eastern Division* and the *Western Division:* the former includes the hundreds of Brixton, Kingston, Reigate, Taudridge, and Wallington; and the western division comprises the hundreds of Blackheath, Copthorne, Effingham, Elmbridge, Farnham, Godalming, Godley and Chertsey, Woking, and Watton. The election of members for the eastern division is held at Croydon, and for the western at Guildford: besides the place of election, the eastern division polls at Reigate, Camberwell, and Kingston; and the western division (besides the place of election) polls at Dorking, and Chertsey.

Railways.—The London and Southampton (the station for which is at *Vauxhall)* runs by *Wandsworth* and *Kingston*—passes between five and six miles to the north of *Guildford,* and about seven to the north of *Farnham;* then, by way of *Basingstoke* and *Winchester,* to *Southampton.* A branch from the Company's station at Woking is intended to be laid to Guildford. The London and Greenwich Railway (more particularly alluded to under Kent) commences in Surrey, its station being close to the southern foot of London-bridge. This is also the station of the Brighton, the Dover, and of the Croydon Railways; the latter line forms a junction with the Greenwich one at *New Cross.* The London and Brighton, after passing *Croydon,* and nearly two miles to the east of *Reigate,* runs about two miles to the east of *Crawley* and *Cuckfield,* to *Brighton.* The Dover, or South Eastern line branches off from the Brighton between *Reigate* and *Nutfield,* about two miles east from the former and a less distance west from the latter.

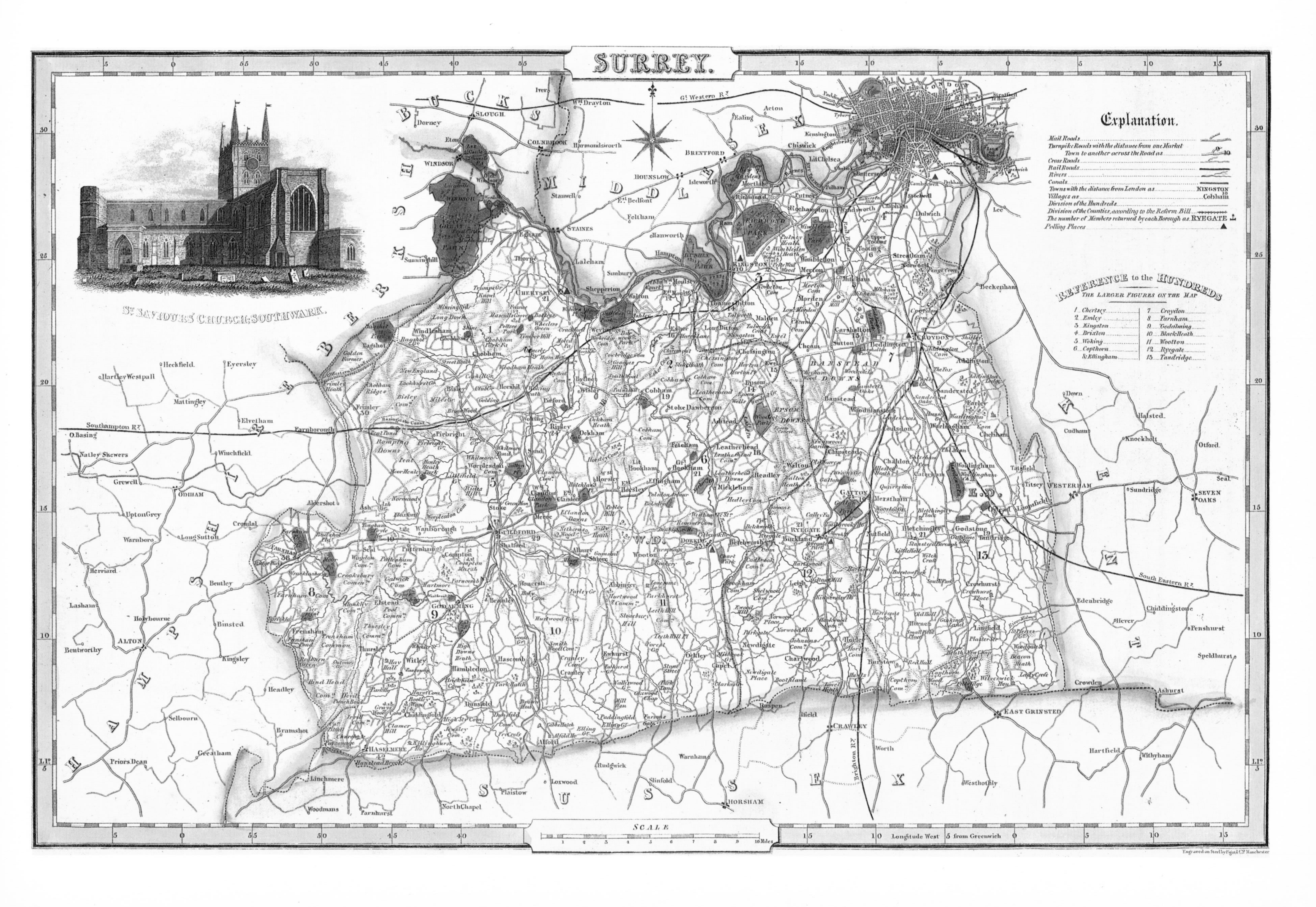
SURREY.
Explanation.
Mail Roads
Turnpike Roads with the distance from one Market Town to another across the Road as
Cross Roads
Rail Roads
Rivers
Canals
Towns with the distance from London as KINGSTON
Villages as Cobham
Division of the Hundreds
Division of the Counties, according to the Reform Bill
The number of Members returned by each Borough as RYEGATE
Polling Places
REFERENCE to the HUNDREDS
THE LARGER FIGURES ON THE MAP
1. Chertsey
2. Emley
3. Kingston
4. Brixton
5. Woking
6. Copthorn & Effingham
7. Croydon
8. Farnham
9. Godalming
10. Blackheath
11. Wootton
12. Ryegate
13. Tandridge
St. Saviours' Church, Southwark.
SCALE
10 Miles
Longitude West 5 from Greenwich
Engraved on Steel by Pigot & Co. Manchester

SUSSEX.

THE County of SUSSEX is a maritime one, being bounded on its whole southern side by the British Channel; the counties of Surrey and Kent bound it on the north; on the north-east and east is also the latter county; and on the west it is bounded by Hampshire. In length, from Emsworth, on the borders of Hampshire, on the west, to Kent Ditch on the east, it is seventy-five miles; its greatest breadth, from Beachy Head on the south-east, to Groom Bridge, near Tunbridge Wells, on the north, is twenty-eight miles; and its area comprehends one thousand four hundred and sixty square miles.

NAME and ANCIENT HISTORY.—At the time of the invasion of this country by the Romans, this part of it was inhabited by the *Regnii*. In the year 1731, one of the oldest inscriptions, in Latin, in England, was dug up from under the place where the now Council House in Chichester was erected. The translation is to the following effect: "For the preservation of the Imperial Family, this Temple was dedicated to Neptune and Minerva, by the College of Artificers belonging to King Cogidubnus, the Lieutenant of Augustus in Britain; and by those who officiated as Priests, or were honoured in it, at their own expense: the ground being given by Pudeno, the son of Pudentinus." This interesting piece of antiquity is possessed by his Grace the Duke of Richmond. Camden says, that Cogidubnus, above mentioned, was King of the *Regnii*,—that is, of all Sussex, part of Surrey, and Hampshire; and that he resided in the city now called Chichester; but that he held his crown in subordination to the Court of Rome: and it is supposed that this part of the country continued in the hands of the Romans until their final departure from Britain, in 446. After this, the Britons were hard pressed by the Scots and Picts, and Vortigern was pitched upon as their commander, who called in the Saxons to aid him in repelling the invaders; but by his weakness, or knavery, he betrayed his country into the power of those whose assistance he had solicited, and married Rowenna, a Saxon Lady. After many terrible conflicts between the Britons and Saxons, the former were driven from their native province, and forced to seek an asylum beyond the Severn, among the mountains of Wales, where their descendants remain to this day. The South Saxon (or Sussex) Monarchy lasted about 320 years, during which the most remarkable occurrence was the conversion of King Adelwach to Christianity, (who took the baptismal name of Wilfrid, and was the first Bishop of Sussex,) in the year 650. In the year 800, Egbert, King of Wessex, united the Crown of Sussex to his own; and a few years afterwards was crowned, at Winchester, King of England. Subsequent to the above events, the most memorable incidents occurring in Sussex were the two great battles: the first fought near Battle, in 1066, between William, Duke of Normandy, and Harold, King of England,—the former by his victory obtaining the Crown, and the appellation of 'the Conqueror;' and the last near Lewes, in 1263, between the Barons and King Henry III, in which that Monarch was defeated and taken prisoner.—The towns of chief note in the county are, the City of Chichester, famous for its noble Cathedral; Brighton, raised from a small fishing village to almost metropolitan consequence by the countenance of Royalty, and celebrated for its splendid Pavilion, for many years the favourite residence of his late Majesty, George IV.; and Arundel, where is the noble castle and principal seat of the Dukes of Norfolk.

SOIL and CLIMATE, PRODUCE and MANUFACTURES.—All the various SOILS of chalk, clay, sand, loam and gravel, are to be found in Sussex: chalk being the universal soil of the South Downs; clay, that of the Weald; sand, of the north part of the county; loam prevails on the south side of the hills; and gravel lies between the rich loam on the coast, and the chalk on the elevated grounds. The surface of the county is varied by several considerable hills, commencing on the borders of Hampshire, on the north-west, and extending to Beachy Head, on the south-east: that part running from Lewes to the sea is distinguished by the name of the 'South Downs,' and is noted for feeding innumerable sheep, celebrated for the fineness of their wool and the goodness of their mutton. The more north-west parts of this ridge abound in iron ore, for the smelting of which Sussex was formerly famed; but the works are now almost abandoned, owing to the too great consumption of wood, the only species of fuel natural to the county. The north and middle part of the county is well furnished with timber, growing on a strong clayey soil, of the same nature as that of the Weald of Kent. The western part of the coast is a stripe of arable land, of uncommon fertility; and the east side is a strong, well cultivated soil, intermixed with rich pasture.—Sussex is highly extolled for its FARMING STOCK, particularly its cattle and sheep. The former are nearly of the same kind as those of Devon, and like them are worked in the yoke, being strong and active in their labour, and prove excellent beef when fattened. The sheep, by the care of some judicious breeders, yield heavy fleeces, of a superior quality; are hardy in the fold, fatten quickly, and when killed produce mutton of a fine flavour; they are deservedly becoming the favourite breed all over the Island. The AGRICULTURE is in general good, and of late years has been very much improved: the soil produces, on the heavier lands, wheat, beans, cabbages and oats; whilst the barley and turnips grown on those of a lighter staple are equal to any produced in England.—The CLIMATE of Sussex on the south side of the South Down hills, is very warm, and exceedingly favourable to vegetation; but, upon the exposed and bleak situation of the hills open to the south-west, the winds are frequently so boisterous as to strip the thatch from buildings and corn-stacks, and blow the corn out of the ear at harvest: these winds, when they are impregnated with saline particles, occasioned by the western blast beating the spray against the beach, destroy all hedges and trees,—every leaf, and in general every thing green, being discoloured into an unsightly brown; the hedges are cut by the spray, on the side open to the wind, in the same manner as if done by an artificial process.—The MANUFACTURES of this county are neither various nor extensive. At Battle, gunpowder is made, and in some other towns paper, being all that can with propriety be placed under this head; but the local and shipping trade of many of the towns is flourishing, and ship building, &c., employs many hands at some of the yards on the coast.

RIVERS.—The principal rivers of Sussex are the ARUN, the ADUR, the OUSE, the ROTHER and the CUCKMERE; there are also a few other less considerable streams which rise within the limits of this county, as the Lavant, the Ashbourn and the Asten. The Arun has its origin in St. Leonard's Forest, near Horsham; and, after running a few miles westward, turns due south, visits Arundel (where it becomes navigable to the sea), and falls into the British Channel about three miles south of that town; this river is also made navigable, for boats and barges, from near Midhurst, through several parishes, to Petworth—and, by a navigable cut, to some other neighbouring districts: in the Arun are caught vast quantities of trout, mullet and eels. The Adur (sometimes called the Beeding,) also rises in the same forest as the Arun; and, running almost parallel with that river, passes by Steyning and Bramber; from the latter place to the sea, at New Shoreham, (where it discharges itself) it is called the 'Bramber Water.' The Ouse is chiefly formed of two branches,—one rising in St. Leonard's Forest, near the spring of the Adur, and the other in the Forest of Worth, north of Cuckfield; these uniting not far from Cuckfield, the river runs south by Lewes, and, falling into the British Channel, forms the harbour called Newhaven, about eight miles south of Lewes: this river is navigable for large boats, from Newhaven to within five miles of Cuckfield. The Cuckmere has its source near Hailsham, and, flowing south-south-west, passes several considerable villages, and falls into the Channel at the haven of its name.

CIVIL and ECCLESIASTICAL DIVISIONS.—Sussex is in the Province of Canterbury and Diocese of Chichester; is included in the Home Circuit, and divided into the six 'Rapes' of ARUNDEL, BRAMBER, CHICHESTER, HASTINGS, LEWES and PEVENSEY; these are subdivided into 66 hundreds, containing 310 parishes, one city and county town town (Chichester), three of the Cinque Ports (Hastings, Rye and Winchelsea), and 17 market towns. The whole county returns 28 Members to Parliament, namely, two each for the three CINQUE PORTS before named, two each for ARUNDEL, BRAMBER, CHICHESTER (City), EAST GRINSTEAD, HORSHAM, LEWES, MIDHURST, NEW SHOREHAM, SEAFORD and STEYNING, and two for the COUNTY.

POPULATION.—According to the census of 1821, there were houses inhabited in the county, 36,283; uninhabited, 1,272; and houses building, 576. The number of families then resident in the county was 43,565; comprising 116,705 males, and 116,314 females; total, 233,019: and by a calculation made by order of Government, which included persons in the army and navy, for which was added after the ratio of about one to thirty prior to the year 1811, and one to fifty for that year and the census of 1821, to the returns made from the several districts; the population of the county, in round numbers, in the year 1700, was 91,400—in 1750, 107,400—in 1801, 164,600—in 1811, 196,500—and in 1821, 237,700. The increased population in the 50 years, from the year 1700, was 16,000—from 1750 to 1801, the increase was 57,200—from 1801 to 1811, the increase was 31,900—and from 1811 to 1821, the augmented number of persons was 41,200: the grand total increase in the population of the county, from the year 1700 to the census of 1821, being about 146,300 persons.

Index of Distances from Town to Town in the County of Sussex.

THE NAMES OF THE RESPECTIVE TOWNS ARE ON THE TOP AND SIDE, AND THE SQUARE WHERE BOTH MEET GIVES THE DISTANCE.

	Arundel	Battle	Brighton	Chichester	Cuckfield	Eastbourne	East Grinstead	Hailsham	Hastings	Horsham	Lewes	Midhurst	Petworth	Rye	Shoreham	Steyning	Uckfield	Winchelsea	*Distance from London.*
Arundel																			56
Battle	53																		56
Brighton	20	33																	52
Chichester	11	64	30																61
Cuckfield	24	38	14	35															39
Eastbourne	42	18	22	53	32														60
East Grinstead	37	34	27	47	13	31													29
Hailsham	40	14	21	52	26	7	26												59
Hastings	60	8	40	71	46	18	42	20											64
Horsham	22	50	20	30	12	43	18	39	54										36
Lewes	28	25	8	38	14	18	21	13	34	26									50
Midhurst	12	62	29	12	28	51	36	50	70	21	37								50
Petworth	11	59	23	14	24	46	33	44	64	16	31	5							49
Rye	71	15	51	81	53	30	48	29	11	66	40	77	72						63
Shoreham	15	39	6	26	19	28	32	27	46	20	14	27	26	57					56
Steyning	14	45	12	25	12	34	25	33	51	14	20	22	17	63	6				50
Uckfield	36	26	17	48	13	21	13	13	33	25	9	40	35	42	23	25			41
Winchelsea	69	13	49	79	51	28	46	27	9	64	38	75	70	2	55	61	40		64
Worthing	9	45	12	20	21	34	34	33	52	20	20	21	20	63	6	9	29	61	56

[*See over.*

Additional information relating to the County of Sussex.

—ooo—

POPULATION.—By the Census for 1831 this county contained 135,326 males, and 137,002 females—total 272,328, being an increase, since the returns made in the year 1821, of 39,309 inhabitants; and from the Census of 1801 to that of 1831 the augmentation amounted to 113,017 persons.

REPRESENTATION.—By the *Reform Bill* the boroughs of BRAMBER, EAST GRINSTEAD, SEAFORD, STEYNING, and WINCHELSEA have been disfranchised, and ARUNDEL, HORSHAM, MIDHURST, and RYE deprived of one member each: by the same Act, the privilege of election has been conferred upon BRIGHTON, which returns two members, and two others, in addition, have been bestowed on the county. By these alterations the whole county, now, sends *eighteen* representatives to Parliament, instead of *twenty-eight*, as before the passing of the Bill. The new *Boundary Act* divides Sussex into two parts, respectively called the *Eastern Division* and the *Western Division*; the former includes the rapes of Lewes, Hastings, and Pevensey, and the latter, those of Arundel, Bramber, and Chichester. The election of members for the eastern division is held at LEWES, and for the western division at CHICHESTER: besides the place of election, the eastern division polls at EAST GRINSTEAD, BATTLE, and MAYFIELD; and the western division (besides the place of election) polls at ARUNDEL, STEYNING, PETWORTH, and HORSHAM.

RAILWAY.—The LONDON and BRIGHTON passes about two miles to the east of *Crawley* and *Cuckfield*, to *Brighton*. From this line there will be a branch to Lewes, another to Newhaven, and a third to Shoreham. The Brighton line communicates with the SOUTH EASTERN RAILWAY (to *Dover*), about two miles to the east of *Reigate*. The route of the South Eastern, from Reigate to Dover, will be seen under 'Kent.'

SUSSEX.
Explanation.
Mail Roads
Turnpike Roads with the distance from one Market Town to another across the Road, as
Cross Roads
Rivers
Canals
Towns with the distance from London, as PETWORTH 49
Villages as Linchmere
Division of the Rapes
Division of the Hundreds
Division of the Counties according to the Reform Bill
The number of Members returned by each Borough, as RYE
Polling Places
Rail Roads
CHICHESTER CATHEDRAL.
REFERENCE to the HUNDREDS.
THE LARGER FIGURES ON THE MAP.
CHICHESTER RAPE
1 Dumford
2 Easebourn
3 Westbourn and Singleton
4 Bosham
5 Manhood
6 Box and Stockbridge
7 Aldweeke
ARUNDEL RAPE
8 Rotherbridge
9 Wst Easwrith
10 Poleing
11 Bury
12 Avisford
BRAMBER RAPE
13 Tarring
14 Est Easwrith
15 Brightford 15* Patching
16 Steyning
17 West Grinsted
18 Singlecross
19 Fishersgate
20 Burbeach
21 Tipnoake
22 Windham & Ewhurst
LEWES RAPE
23 Buttinghill
24 Street
25 Poynings
26 Deane
27 Preston
28 Whalesbone
29 Younsmere
30 Holmstrough
31 Swanborough
32 Barcombe
PEVENSEY RAPE
33 Ringmer
34 Rushmonden
35 Burleigh Arches
36 Hartfield
37 Rotherfield
38 Laxfield Dorset
39 Shiplake
40 Totnore
41 Aleiston
42 Flexborough
43 Longbridge
44 Willingdon
45 Eastbourne
46 Dill
47 Pevensey Liberty
48 Laxfield Pelham
HASTINGS RAPE
49 Hawkesborough
50 Fox Earle
51 Shoyswell
52 Henhurst
53 Netherfield
54 Ninfield
55 Bexhill
56 Baldslow
57 Battel
58 Staple
59 Goldspur
60 Gostrow
61 Guestling
THE ENGLISH CHANNEL
SURREY
KENT
HANTS
CHICHESTER RAPE
ARUNDEL RAPE
BRAMBER RAPE
LEWES RAPE
PEVENSEY RAPE
HASTINGS RAPE
SCALE
10 Miles
Longitude East from Greenwich
Engraved on Steel by Pigot & Co. Manchester

WARWICKSHIRE.

THE County of WARWICK is situated nearly in the centre of the Kingdom, in a north-west direction from the Metropolis; is bounded on the south by Oxfordshire and Gloucestershire, on the west by Worcestershire, on the north by Derbyshire, on the north-west by Staffordshire, on the north-east by Leicestershire, and on the east by Northamptonshire. Its length, from north to south, is about 50 miles; and its breadth, from east to west, nearly 35: its circumference is about 150 miles, comprising about 900 square miles.

NAME and ANCIENT HISTORY.—The name of this county is derived from its county town, Warwick, which was called by the Saxons *Weringscire*, signifying 'a station of soldiers;' by the Anglo-Saxons it was denominated *Werheca*, and in some old records it has been written *Warrewyk*. It is one of the five counties which, in the time of the Romans, were inhabited by the *Cornavii;* and under the Saxon Heptarchy it formed part of the Kingdom of Mercia. Three military ways of the Romans intersect this county; they are, the *Watling-street*, the *Ikenild-street*, and the *Fosse-way*. Connected with the modern history of this county, the most memorable occurrence was the battle of Edge Hill, fought in 1642, between the forces of Charles I. and those of the Parliament,—the event of which was undecisive, each party claiming the victory: Charles I. and his two sons (afterwards Charles II. and James II.) slept at Southam, in this county, the night previous to the battle. In Warwickshire are several towns and objects which forcibly recal the memory to days of old, and are alike interesting to the antiquary and the scientific tourist. The ancient town of Warwick is celebrated for its magnificent and noble Castle, the seat of the Earls of Warwick: this strong majestic erection, the walls of which are ten feet in thickness, was built by Thomas Beauchamp, Earl of Warwick, in 1394; many curiosities are still preserved here with great care, which either did belong, or are supposed to have belonged, to that legendary hero, *Guy*, Earl of Warwick. At Kenilworth the extensive and impressive ruins of its Castle carry the imagination back to centuries that have flitted away, when its walls rung with the revellings of Royalty, as at other periods they re-echoed the moans of suffering captivity. In ancient times, the castle, park and chases of Kenilworth occupied upwards of five square miles: this immense demesne several times reverted, by the attainder of its noble possessors, to the Crown, and was as often bestowed on succeeding favourites,—one of whom, Dudley, Earl of Leicester, here entertained his Royal Mistress, Queen Elizabeth, with all the splendour and romantic pageantry which that age could exhibit, and to which that otherwise masculine-minded Princess was so ridiculously attached: here, too, the imbecile Edward II. was imprisoned by his licentious Queen and her favourites, prior to his inhuman murder in Berkeley Castle. Leamington is in high repute for its medicinal springs, and the beauty of the surrounding country. The town of Stratford-upon-Avon may be traced as remotely as three centuries before the Norman Conquest; but the circumstance which sustains its interest at the present day, with all admirers of inspired genius, is that of being the birth-place of the inimitable and immortal SHAKSPEARE, whose productions have for upwards of two centuries so brilliantly illumined the histrionic hemisphere; here is still shewn the house in which he first drew breath: this unrivalled bard—this 'masterpiece of nature'—died on the 23d of April, (his birth-day,) 1616, aged fifty-two years; and was interred on the north side of the chancel of Stratford church. Birmingham (by far the most populous town in the county,) without recurring to its origin or ancient history, bears an exalted situation,—the modern inhabitants having, by unrelaxed industry, aided by an inventive and persevering genius, raised it perhaps to the *acme* of manufacturing and commercial fame. The city of Coventry (formerly spelled *Coventree,)* is exceedingly ancient, and was in early time surrounded with walls of prodigious strength, having twelve gates and thirty-two towers; few vestiges, however, remain of these defences: in modern days it is chiefly noted as the principal seat of the ribbon manufacture; and for perpetuating the remembrance, by an annual procession, of the important service said to have been rendered the inhabitants of the city, on a certain occasion, by the Lady Godiva, wife of Leofric, Earl of Mercia.

SOIL and CLIMATE, PRODUCE and MANUFACTURES.—Warwickshire is divided into two irregular and unequal portions by the river Avon: the south or smaller portion, which is called 'Feldon,' being a champaign country of great fertility; and the north, termed 'the Woodland,' is generally highly cultivated, but interspersed with wild heaths and moors, and a large portion of it still bears the name of the 'Forest of Arden.' It would require very minute observation to describe exactly the SOIL of this county,—in fact, it would be a task hardly possible to effect, as it varies so much in each district, that two or three different kinds of soil may often be seen in the same field. The northern part has a gravelly soil, and contains coal and lime-stone; but in the middle of the county, clay predominates. Dunsmore Heath, in the part of Feldon, between the Leam and the Avon (now mostly inclosed), was the theatre of some of the fabulous tales related of the celebrated *Guy* before alluded to. On the borders of Oxfordshire is a low ridge, called Edge Hills, below which lies the fruitful vale of 'the Red Horse,' extending towards Warwick. Owing to the large proportion of pasture, Warwickshire is chiefly characterized as a feeding and dairy county, and its breeds of cattle and sheep are of a superior description. Timber of all kinds grows in this county, and is a considerable article of commerce: the elm tree predominates, but oak is plenteous, especially in that quarter which formed the ancient Forest of Arden; and due regulations exist for the management of the woodlands. Flax is grown and manufactured here; the dairy is of high importance; whilst the sheep of Warwickshire are large, and their fleeces both fine and abundant.—The CLIMATE of this county is healthy, mild and pleasant; its salubrity has been improved by the great consumption of wood for the iron works, many districts being entirely cleared, and converted into tillage and pasture. The MANUFACTURES of Warwickshire are of a most multifarious character, and as important as they are diversified: the loom and the forge contend for superiority,—Coventry having manufactures of ribbons, gauzes, other silk fabrics, lastings and thread; Nuneaton partaking of a similar trade; and Birmingham, celebrated all over the globe for its hardware, cutlery, ornamental articles, steam engines, guns, pistols and other implements of war; toys in every metal, glass works, &c. &c. At Kenilworth combs are manufactured, where are also chemical works for making salts and hartshorn; Stratford has a manufacture of silk buttons; and at Warwick are silk-throwing mills; hats also are made here, and it enjoys, in common with some other towns in the county, a very considerable business in malt.

RIVERS, CANALS and MINERAL SPRINGS.—The principal rivers that water this county are the AVON, the LEAM, the TAME and the ARROW. The Avon enters the county from Northamptonshire, in its course giving additional beauty to the delightful territory of Warwick Castle; thence glides on to Stratford-upon-Avon, traverses the great level of Worcestershire by Evesham, and joins the Severn at Tewkesbury. The Leam rises on the eastern borders of the county, and after a winding course falls into the Avon at a small distance from Warwick. The Tame flows out of Worcestershire, and enters Warwickshire near Birmingham; from whence it proceeds to Tamworth, in Staffordshire, receives many rivulets in its course, and finally falls into the Thanet near Coleshill. The Arrow cuts off a narrow slip of the south-west part of the county, and after being joined by the Alne, unites with the Avon at the very extremity where it passes into Worcestershire. The lesser streams are the Anker, the Alne, the Swift and the Stour. The kinds of fish caught in all the rivers are various, and the quantity abundant,—the Avon, in particular, yielding salmon equal to any in England. The CANALS that pass through this county are the 'Birmingham,' the 'Coventry and Oxford,' the 'Warwick and Birmingham,' the 'Ashby-de-la-Zouch,' the 'Stratford-on-Avon,' the 'Worcester and Birmingham,' and the 'Warwick and Braunston.' By these canals, and their various cuts and branches, the transmission and reception of every description of merchandize and manufactures are effected to and from all quarters of the Kingdom. The MINERAL SPRINGS at Leamington have drawn the attention of many distinguished medical men who have pronounced the drinking of the waters to be highly beneficial in cases of rheumatism, gout, scrofula, &c. The waters are of three different kinds, viz. sulphureous, chalybeate and saline.

CIVIL and ECCLESIASTICAL DIVISIONS.—Warwickshire is in the Province of Canterbury, and Dioceses of Worcester, and Lichfield & Coventry; is included in the Midland Circuit, and divided into the four hundreds of BARLICHWAY, HEMLINGFORD, KINGTON and KNIGHTLOW, which are subdivided into two hundred and five parishes, collectively containing one city (Coventry), one county town (Warwick), and thirteen other market towns. The whole county returns six Members to Parliament, viz. two for the city of COVENTRY, two for the town of WARWICK, and two for the SHIRE.

POPULATION.—According to the census of 1821, there were houses inhabited in the county, 55,082; uninhabited, 2,408; and houses building, 403. The number of families then resident in the county, was 60,123; comprising 133,827 males, and 140,565 females: total, 274,392. And by a calculation made by order of Government, which included persons in the army and navy, for which was added after the ratio of about one to thirty prior to the year 1811, and one to fifty for that year and the census of 1821, to the returns made from the several districts, the population of the county, in round numbers, in the year 1700, was 96,600—in 1750, 140,000—in 1801, 215,100—in 1811, 236,400—and in 1821, 280,000. The increased population in the fifty years, from the year 1700, was 43,400—from 1750 to 1801, the increase was 75,100—from 1801 to 1811, the increase was 21,300—and from 1811 to 1821, the augmented number of persons was 43,600: the grand total increase in the population of the county, from the year 1700 to the census of 1821, being about 183,400 persons. Of the 274,392 inhabitants in the county in 1821, 106,722 were returned for the town of Birmingham.

Index of Distances from Town to Town in the County of Warwick.

THE NAMES OF THE RESPECTIVE TOWNS ARE ON THE TOP AND SIDE, AND THE SQUARE WHERE BOTH MEET GIVES THE DISTANCE.

	Alcester	Atherstone	Birmingham	Coleshill	Coventry	Henley-in-Arden	Kenilworth	Kineton	Leamington	Nuneaton	Rugby	Solihull	Southam	Stratford-upon-Avon	Sutton Coldfield	*Distance from London.*
Alcester																103
Atherstone	39															107
Birmingham	19	20														110
Coleshill	24	9	9													103
Coventry	27	14	18	12												91
Henley-in-Arden	8	31	14	24	18											101
Kenilworth	22	18	22	13	5	14										96
Kineton	19	33	31	30	21	19	16									83
Leamington	18	26	22	32	12	11	7	9								90
Nuneaton	34	5	21	12	8	26	13	28	20							100
Rugby	35	26	31	25	13	28	17	21	14	17						85
Solihull	17	21	7	10	14	10	10	23	14	20	27					108
Southam	24	27	30	25	13	20	15	10	8	21	10	23				82
Stratford-upon-Avon	8	32	22	27	19	8	13	11	10	26	24	18	16			95
Sutton Coldfield	25	15	8	10	20	22	19	35	26	21	35	14	34	30		110
Warwick	16	24	20	18	10	9	5	11	2	18	16	12	10	8	24	92

[See over.

Additional information relating to the County of WARWICK.

———ooo———

POPULATION.—By the Census for **1831** this county contained 165,761 males, and 171,227 females—total 336,988, being an increase, since the returns made in the year 1821, of 62,596 inhabitants; and from the Census of 1801 to that of 1831, the augmentation amounted to 128,798 persons.

REPRESENTATION.—By the *Reform Bill* the elective franchise has been bestowed upon BIRMINGHAM, which returns two members, and two additional ones have been given to the county; which, in consequence, sends in the whole *ten* representatives to Parliament, instead of *six*, as before the passing of the Bill. The new *Boundary Act* divides Warwickshire into two parts, respectively called the *Northern Division* and the *Southern Division;* the former includes the hundred of Hemlingford, and the county of the city of Coventry, also the Rugby and Kirby divisions of the hundred of Knightlow; and the southern division comprises the hundreds of Barlichway and Kington, and the Kenilworth and Southam divisions of the hundred of Knightlow. The election of members for the northern division of the county is held at COLESHILL, and for the southern at WARWICK: besides the place of election the northern division polls at BIRMINGHAM, COVENTRY, NUNEATON and DUNCHURCH; and the southern division (besides the place of election) polls at KINETON, STRATFORD, HENLEY, and SOUTHAM.

RAILWAYS.

The LONDON and BIRMINGHAM RAILWAY passes through *Rugby* and *Coventry* to *Birmingham;* from the latter town the GRAND JUNCTION proceeds to the great towns of *Manchester* and *Liverpool.* We have noticed the London and Birmingham more fully under Middlesex—so have we the Grand Junction under Lancashire, and the Rugby Extension under Staffordshire. From *Rugby* the MIDLAND COUNTIES' RAILWAY runs to *Nottingham, Derby,* &c. The WESTERN UNION passes from *Birmingham* to *Gloucester* by the route detailed under the county of Worcester; and the BIRMINGHAM and DERBY line joins the London and Birmingham at *Hampton,* and by another branch, near *Coleshill,* to *Birmingham.* The BIRMINGHAM and GLOUCESTER RAILWAY will go by *Bromsgrove, Worcester, Tewkesbury* and *Cheltenham,* to *Gloucester.* A branch Railway, from the Coventry station of the London and Birmingham line to Leamington, is about being commenced.

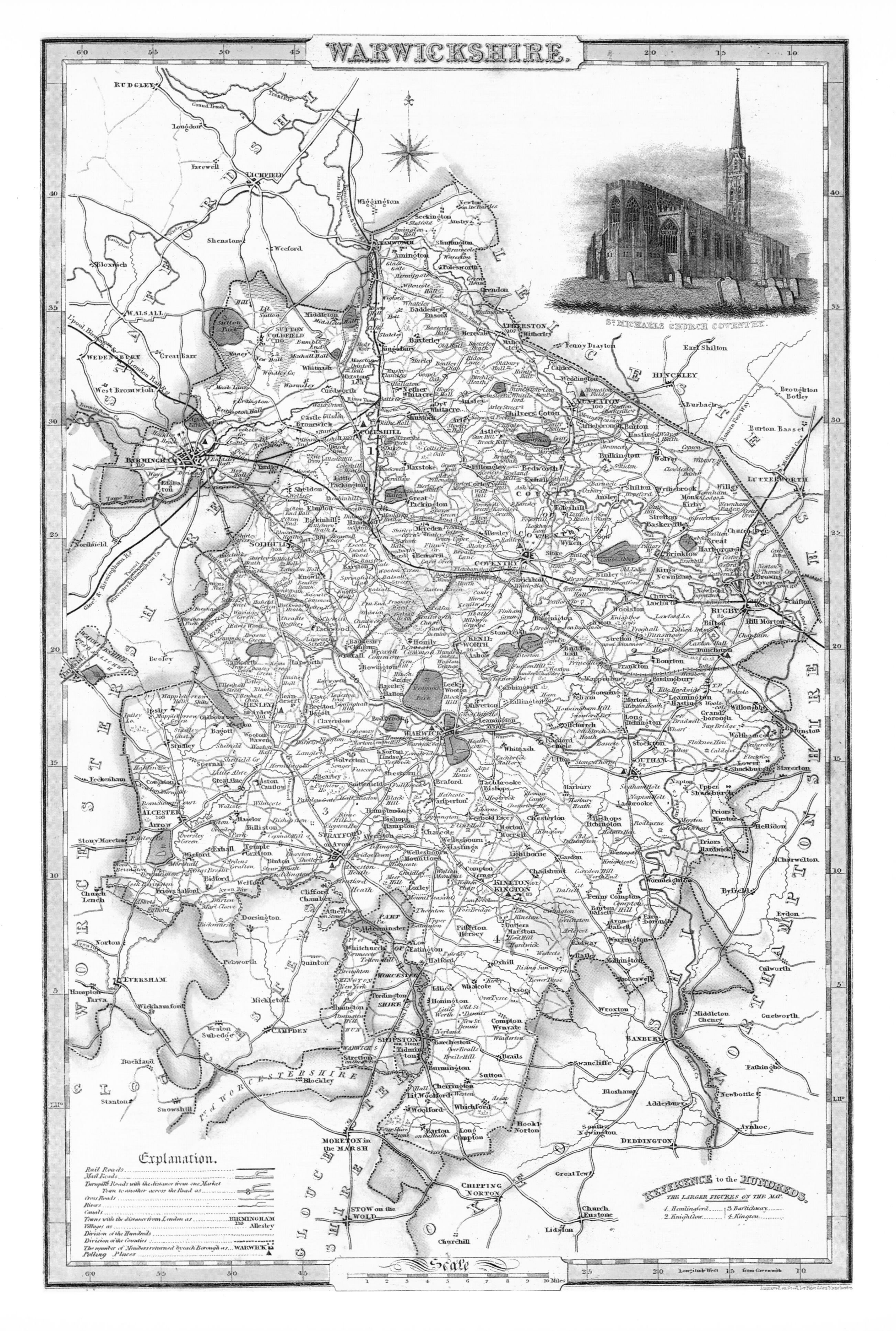
WARWICKSHIRE.
S.T MICHAELS CHURCH COVENTRY.
Explanation.
Rail Roads
Mail Roads
Turnpike Roads with the distance from one Market Town to another across the Road as
Cross Roads
Rivers
Canals
Towns with the distance from London as BIRMINGHAM 110
Villages as Allesley
Division of the Hundreds
Division of the Counties
The number of Members returned by each Borough as WARWICK 2
Polling Places
REFERENCE to the HUNDREDS.
THE LARGER FIGURES ON THE MAP.
1. Hemlingford
2. Knightlow
3. Barlichway
4. Kington
Scale
10 Miles
Longitude West from Greenwich
BIRMINGHAM
COVENTRY
WARWICK
STRATFORD on Avon
RUGBY
KENILWORTH
SOLIHULL
COLESHILL
NUNEATON
ATHERSTONE
TAMWORTH
LICHFIELD
WALSALL
SOUTHAM
ALCESTER
HENLEY in Arden
SHIPSTON on Stour
BANBURY
HINCKLEY
LUTTERWORTH
EVESHAM
CAMPDEN
MORETON in the MARSH
CHIPPING NORTON
STOW on the WOLD
DEDDINGTON

WESTMORELAND.

THE County of WESTMORELAND is an inland one, being bounded on the north and north-west by Cumberland, on the east by Durham and Yorkshire, and on the south and south-west by Lancashire. It is about thirty miles in length from north to south; and in breadth from east to west, at its narrowest part, it does not exceed twelve miles, while its greatest width is about thirty-six miles: the ambit of the county is computed at about one hundred and forty-five miles, and its area as comprising 763 square miles.

NAME and ANCIENT HISTORY.—Westmoreland received its name from its situation being westward, and from the principal part of it being formerly moorish barren land. It is one of those counties which, in the time of the Romans, was inhabited by that tribe of the ancient Britons denominated the *Brigantes*. By the Romans it was incorporated with the province of MAXIMA CÆSARIENSIS; and under the Saxon Heptarchy, it formed part of the kingdom of Northumberland. Traces of two Roman roads are still visible; one from Carlisle to Appleby; and the other from the Picts' Wall, in Cumberland, by Kendal, to Lancaster. Amongst the towns deserving notice as connected with the early history of this county, may be mentioned Appleby, the *Aballaba* of the Romans, a station of considerable consequence to that nation. In the Scotch wars, in the 22d year of Henry II, it was consumed by fire; and again suffered that calamity in the 11th of Richard III. At Brough are the ruins of a fortress of Roman origin, which must at one period have been of great strength and extent. Kendal, the principal town for population and size in the county, also possesses the remains of an ancient and once noble castle, erected by the first Barons of Kendal; this is one of the most picturesque and conspicuous objects in Westmoreland.

SOIL and CLIMATE, PRODUCE and MANUFACTURES.—This county is divided into two unequal portions, called 'the Baronies of Westmoreland, and Kendal:' the former, although abounding with hills, and characterized by a general inequality of surface, is, nevertheless, comparatively an open country; the latter is extremely mountainous, containing numerous bleak and barren hills, usually termed the 'fells.' Not half a century has elapsed since scarcely one-fourth part of the whole county was under cultivation; the greater proportion still remains free from the labours of the husbandman and agriculturist; and the parts productive are chiefly applied to the growth of oats, the proportion of wheat and barley being very small. Some of the mountains yield good pasturage for sheep, and are stored with grouse, which induces an influx of sportsmen in the shooting season; on the hills graze herds of black cattle, and on the moors great numbers of geese are bred. The vallies in which the rivers run are tolerably fertile; and it is in such districts that dairying is pursued to advantage, and a great deal of fine butter is made for the London markets. The western mountains contain mines of copper, and in some places have been discovered veins of gold, but not sufficient to answer the expense of working. Slate and lime-stone quarries, in this county, are productive; and near to Kendal a beautiful variegated marble is found, which is susceptible of a very high polish, and is worked into chimney-pieces, ornaments, &c. The hams of Westmoreland, as a delicacy, are in high estimation, and are cured in many of the towns.—The CLIMATE of this county, taken generally, must be considered as healthy: the air is pure, and varies in its keenness according to local situation; upon the hills it is sharp and piercing, but in the vallies it is mild, genial and serene.—The MANUFACTURES of Westmoreland are of a similar character to those of its neighbouring county, York, being woollen goods of different kinds. The principal manufactories are at Kendal, where are produced kerseymeres, serges, baizes, carpetings, knit woollen caps and jackets, waistcoatings, &c. The marble works here are a very important branch, and embrace all the purposes of statuary. Paper and gunpowder are also manufactured, to some extent, in the neighbourhood of Kendal; as are carpets and blankets at Kirkby Lonsdale, and at Kirkby Stephen knit hose.

RIVERS, LAKES & CANALS.—This county is plentifully watered with rivers, the principal of which are the EDEN, the EIMOT, the LEN (Lon, or Lune), and the KEN (or Kan); besides these, there are several other streams, chiefly tributary to those just named. The Eden, which is the most considerable river of the county, has its source near the middle of it, not far from the borders of Yorkshire; and, passing the town of Appleby, runs by a north-west course into Cumberland. The Eimot flows out of Ulles-water Lake, and forms the boundary of this county and that of Cumberland, until it meets the Eden. The Len has its source near to that of the last-named river; and, becoming a boundary to the West Riding of Yorkshire, passes by Kirkby Lonsdale, when it leaves this county and enters Lancashire: the scenery adorning the course of this river is extremely beautiful, and very much admired by tourists. The Ken runs nearly south, by Kendal, and soon after falls into the estuary near Morecamb Bay.—The principal LAKES are WINANDER-MERE and ULLES-WATER. The first-named is the largest lake in England, being fifteen miles in length; it serves as a boundary, for its whole extent, to this county and Cumberland: in width it may be taken to average about a mile; and its greatest depth, near Ecclesrig Crag, has been found to be upwards of 200 feet. Winander-mere abounds with delicate fish, the chief of which is the char; and its sides are skirted with scenery beautifully romantic,—the general effect being heightened by several small islands, some of them ornamented with castellated buildings. Ulles-water, a lake of great beauty, is partly situated in this county and partly in Cumberland: its whole length is about nine miles, but its greatest width is little more than one,—and in its second reach a vast rock projects, so as to reduce it to less than a quarter of a mile. These are its reputed admeasurements; but the eye loses the power of judging even of the breadth, confounded by the boldness of the shores, and the grandeur of the fells rising beyond the proportions; yet the water retains its dignity, notwithstanding the vastness of the accompaniments. The rocks of Ulles-water and its vicinity are celebrated for reverberating sounds; and the echoes produced from firing a cannon (for which purpose there is a vessel on the lake, provided with brass guns,) are exceedingly grand, being thrown from rock to rock, and repeated six or seven times. The introduction of a few French horns and clarionets procures a continuation of musical echoes, which, travelling round the lake, are exquisitely melodious in their several gradations, and produce countless symphonies, playing in concert from every point;—the variety of notes is inconceivable, and the ear is not equal to their innumerable combinations. In short it has been most appositely observed, that every rock is vocal, and the whole lake transformed into a kind of magical scene, in which every promontory seems peopled with aerial beings, answering each other in celestial music. Ulles-water abounds with fish of various kinds, but particularly with trout, perch and eels; the trout and eels are of great size,—of the former, some are not unfrequently taken of 30 lbs. weight; char and gwinniard are likewise caught here, the latter in considerable quantities. Wild ducks, in immense numbers, breed by the sides of the lake; and in the month of October thousands may be seen, with their new broods.—The 'LANCASTER CANAL' is the only work of artificial inland navigation by which Westmoreland is immediately benefited: its course is nearly due north, commencing at West Houghton; and its entire length is about 76 miles, exclusive of cuts communicating with other canals in its progress.

CIVIL and ECCLESIASTICAL DIVISIONS.—Westmoreland is in the Province of York and Diocese of Carlisle; is included in the Northern Circuit, and divided into the four Wards of EAST, WEST, KENDAL and LONSDALE; these are subdivided into thirty-two parishes, collectively containing one borough and county town (Appleby), and nine other market towns. The number of Members returned to Parliament for Westmoreland are four, namely, two for the town of APPLEBY, and two for the COUNTY.

POPULATION.—According to the census of 1821, there were houses inhabited in the county, 9,243; uninhabited, 301; and houses building, 113. The number of families then resident in the county was 10,438; comprising 25,513 males, and 25,846 females; total, 51,359: and by a calculation made by order of Government, which included persons in the army and navy, for which was added after the ratio of about one to thirty prior to the year 1811, and one to fifty for that year and the census of 1821, to the returns made from the several districts; the population of the county, in round numbers, in the year 1700, was 28,600—in 1750, 36,300—in 1801, 43,000—in 1811, 47,500—and in 1821, 52,400. The increased population in the 50 years, from the year 1700, was 7,700—from 1750 to 1801, the increase was 6,700—from 1801 to 1811, the increase was 4,500—and from 1811 to 1821, the augmented number of persons was 4,900: the grand total increase in the population of the county, from the year 1700 to the census of 1821, being about 23,800 persons.

Index of Distances from Town to Town in the County of Westmoreland.

THE NAMES OF THE RESPECTIVE TOWNS ARE ON THE TOP AND SIDE, AND THE SQUARE WHERE BOTH MEET GIVES THE DISTANCE.

Town	Ambleside	Appleby	Brough	Burton	Kendal	Kirkby Lonsdale	Kirkby Stephen	Milnthorpe	Distance from London
Ambleside									276
Appleby	33								270
Brough	38	8							261
Burton	26	31	33						251
Kendal	14	21	26	11					261
Kirkby Lonsdale	26	33	28	5	12				252
Kirkby Stephen	38	13	5	29	24	24			266
Milnthorpe	22	29	34	4	8	9	32		254
Orton	27	9	14	24	13	24	12	21	275

[See over.

Additional information relating to the County of WESTMORELAND.

———ooo———

POPULATION.—By the Census for **1831** this county contained 27,594 males, and 27,447 females—total 55,041, being an increase, since the returns made in the year 1821, of 3,682 inhabitants; and from the Census of 1801 to that of 1831, the augmentation amounted to 13,424 persons.

REPRESENTATION.—By the *Reform Bill* the borough of APPLEBY has been disfranchised, and one member given to the town of KENDAL: so that the whole county returns but *three* representatives to Parliament, instead of *four*, as heretofore. The election of members for the county is held at APPLEBY, and (besides that town) the polling takes place at KIRKBY STEPHEN, SHAP, AMBLESIDE, KENDAL and KIRKBY LONSDALE.

RAILWAYS.

There is a line of Railway proposed from *Lancaster* to *Carlisle*—*see* the account of Railways under CUMBERLAND.

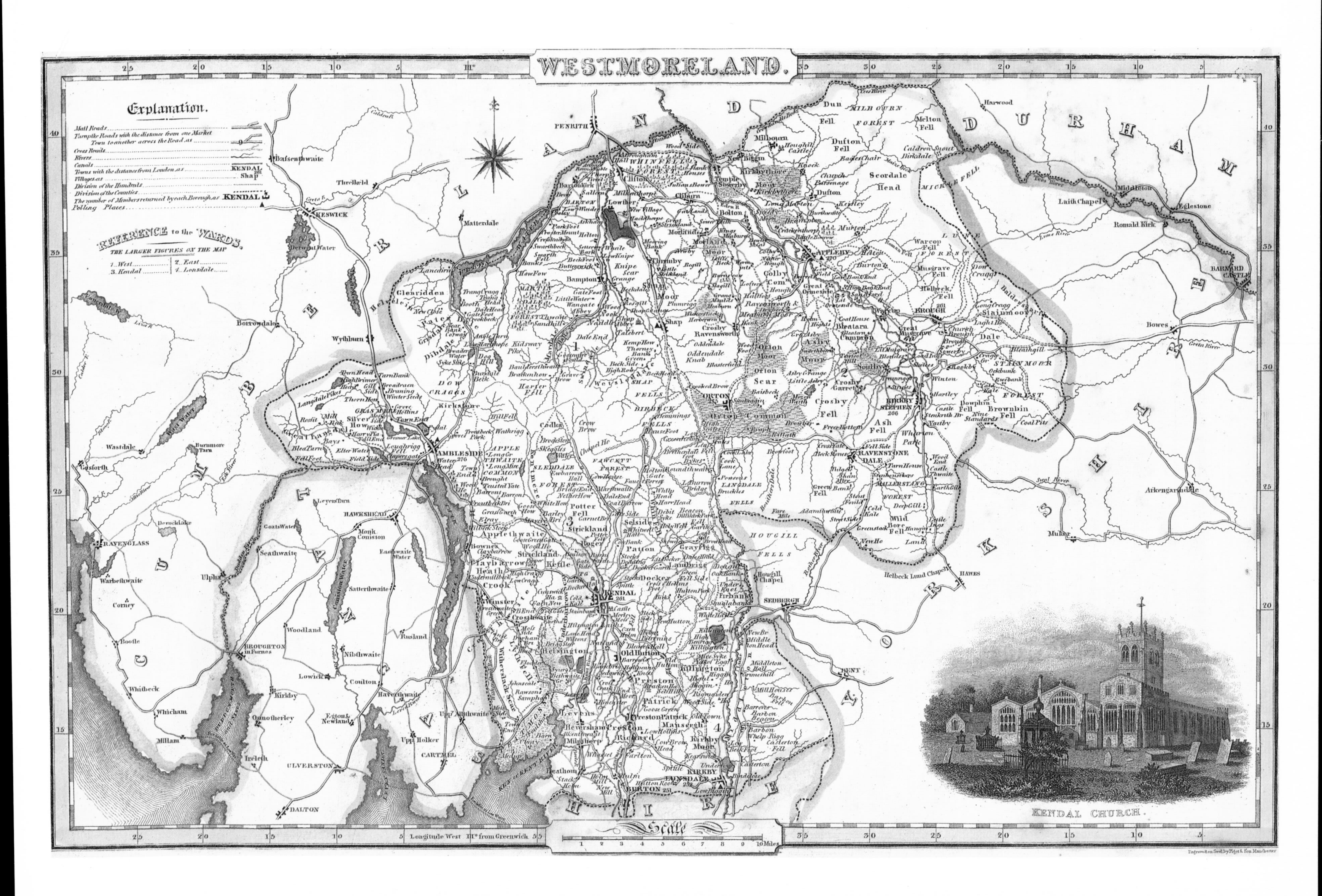
WESTMORELAND.
Explanation.
Mail Roads
Turnpike Roads with the distance from one Market Town to another across the Road as
Cross Roads
Rivers
Canals
Towns with the distance from London as KENDAL 261
Villages as Shap
Division of the Hundreds
Division of the Counties
The number of Members returned by each Borough as KENDAL
Polling Places
REFERENCE to the WARDS,
THE LARGER FIGURES ON THE MAP
1. West
2. East
3. Kendal
4. Lonsdale
DURHAM
YORKSHIRE
LANCASHIRE
CUMBERLAND
PENRITH
APPLEBY
BROUGH
KIRKBY STEPHEN
ORTON
AMBLESIDE
KENDAL
KIRKBY LONSDALE
BURTON
SEDBERGH
KESWICK
HAWKSHEAD
ULVERSTON
DALTON
RAVENGLASS
BROUGHTON in Furness
BARNARD CASTLE
Scale
10 Miles
Longitude West III° from Greenwich
KENDAL CHURCH.
Engraved on Steel by Pigot & Son Manchester

WILTSHIRE.

WILTS is an inland county, bounded on the north by Gloucestershire, on the east by Berkshire and Hampshire, on the south by Dorsetshire, and on the west by Somersetshire and Gloucestershire. In length, from north to south, (exclusive of a small portion almost surrounded by Gloucestershire, at its northern extremity), it is about 48 miles; in breadth, from east to west, it is 36; and its area contains 1,379 square miles.

NAME and ANCIENT HISTORY.—This county, at the time of the invasion of Britain by the Romans, was part of the territory of the *Belgæ;* and the northern portion was inhabited by an allianced tribe of this people, distinguished from the general body by the name of the *Cangii.* During the existence of the Saxon Heptarchy, the modern Wiltshire constituted part of the Kingdom of the West Saxons. By some early writers, this county is called *Severnia,* and *Provincia Serverorum,* from *Servia,* a name by which Old Sarum was formerly known; it derives its present appellation from the town of Wilton, which was formerly the most considerable town in the county, but now a place to which but little importance is attached. Besides its City, Wiltshire contains within its limits many large and populous towns, amongst which are some possessing considerable interest from having well-founded claims to antiquity. Salisbury (City), or New Sarum, appears to have erected its subsequent consequence and celebrity upon the fallen dignity of Old Sarum, accomplished by the removal of the Cathedral from the latter to the more modern town, and the seizure of its castle (which had theretofore formed a part of the possessions of the Church,) by King Stephen. Old Sarum was one of the ten British cities admitted to the privileges of the Latian law: of this once distinguished place, nothing now remains but its venerable ruins. Chippenham, in the days of Alfred, was one of the finest and strongest cities in the Kingdom; its capture by the Danes, about the year 880, was the principal cause of the sudden retreat and temporary seclusion of that truly great Monarch,—who afterwards, however, unexpectedly re-appearing at the head of his countrymen, totally defeated the ferocious invaders in a sanguinary battle at Eddington, south of Devizes. This latter town, when in the possession of the Romans, was a military station of great strength; it was inclosed by a *vallum* and ditch, and defended by a castle: the latter, in after-times, was rendered almost impregnable by Roger, Bishop of Salisbury; it is now nearly destroyed, but the *vallum* and ditch are still discernible, having been converted into a road. Malmesbury at one period was a place of considerable distinction as a fortified place, having been surrounded by walls, within which was a strong castle; but its principal consequence arose from its celebrated Abbey, which was the largest in the county, and its Abbot sat in Parliament; the remains of this religious edifice present a beautiful specimen of ancient architecture.

SOIL and CLIMATE, PRODUCE and MANUFACTURES.—A very obvious difference exists between the face of the south and east parts of this county and the north and west portions: the former are composed of a broken mass of chalk hills, entering the county from Berkshire, Dorsetshire and Hampshire, and terminating in an irregular line of bold breaks and disjointed elevations, intersected by deep valleys, formed by rivulets and brooks rising within this district; the west and north parts consist chiefly of a rich tract of vale land, stretching north-east and south-west under the hills, but rising gradually in the north-west quarter till it joins the high land of Gloucestershire. The Wiltshire Downs have two principal subdivisions, called 'Marlborough Downs' and 'Salisbury Plain:' the former occupy a considerable tract on the north-east side, towards the Berkshire border; below the middle of the county begins that extensive tract, great part of which bears the name of SALISBURY PLAIN—the most remarkable spot of the kind in England. Over these wilds, stretching beyond the limits of the eye, wander vast flocks of sheep, attended by their solitary shepherds; and ruins of Roman, Saxon, Danish and ancient British monuments are scattered throughout this district, among which the venerable and mystical STONEHENGE rises distinguished to the view. The soil of this uncultivated waste is said to be naturally good, producing wild burnet and fine grasses, forming excellent herbage for sheep; of these (including the whole summer stock,) there are said to be annually 500,000. The north-west district of this county is particularly famed for its cheese,—first introduced under the name of 'Gloucester' cheese, but now so generally known and esteemed as to be distinguished by its own name, and to obtain a higher price. Cattle are likewise fattened in these parts; great numbers of swine are reared, and Wiltshire has ever been celebrated for its bacon: the breed of hogs, till lately, was that of the long-eared large kind; these have, however, given way to the more profitable smaller pig, which will fatten on less meat, and make more delicate bacon and hams. The horses bred in this county are remarkably fine, but kept at a great expense; and the breed of cows is not confined to any particular species. The agriculture of Wiltshire is, generally speaking, good, and some of the Norfolk systems are gradually being adopted; the culture of sanfoin is perfectly understood; in wet seasons the wheat is fine and heavy, and the barley is equal to that of any other part of the Kingdom. The use of covered drains has been long known in many parts of this district; they have been made in different modes,—with turf, with wood and with stone, but chiefly with the latter, on account of the facility of getting it, there being but few parts without stone of some kind or other within a moderate distance. There are no mines in this county, nor any mineral production requiring particular notice. At Chelmark, near Hindon, there have been stones of immense dimensions dug out of the quarries, lying in beds, sixty feet long and twelve feet thick, without a flaw. In the parish of Box, about seven miles from Chippenham, there are quarries of that beautiful stone called 'Bath stone,' great quantities of which are dug up and sent to various parts of the country. CLIMATE.—The air of Wiltshire, like that of most other English counties, is various, according to the local situations of different parts of it; but, on the whole, it is salubrious and agreeable. On the Downs, and higher parts of the county, it is sharp and clear; in the vallies, mild and temperate, even in winter. MANUFACTURES.—Wiltshire, not many years since, stood conspicuous as a flourishing manufacturing county; and was celebrated for producing fabrics, from flax and the fleece, to a most important extent, and of superior qualities. A great depression has, however, for some time back been experienced by the manufacturing establishments throughout the county: different causes have been assigned for this falling off; but it is well ascertained, that in proportion as the West of England manufactures have retrograded in consequence, those of Yorkshire have advanced in importance. The manufactures which at present exist comprise thin, fine and coarse woollen cloths, serges and other woollen stuffs, coarse linens and thicksets; and Wilton is still noted for its carpets. Bradford was, at no very distant period, the centre of the greatest fabric of superfine cloths in England.

RIVERS and CANALS.—The principal rivers that have their source in, or pass through this county, are, the ISIS (afterwards the THAMES), the UPPER and LOWER AVON, the NADDER, the WILLY (or Wiley), the BOURNE and the KENNET; the lesser rivers are the Calne, the Were and the Deverill. The Thames enters the north part of the county, and runs eastward into Berkshire. The Lower Avon enters Wiltshire near Malmesbury, and at Chippenham is joined by the Calne, when, after passing Bradford, it leaves the county. The Upper Avon rises among the hills near Devizes and at Salisbury receives the Willy and Nadder; then flows into Hampshire, and makes its exit in the British Channel. The Nadder rises in Dorsetshire, and falls into the Willy at Wilton. The Willy has its source near Warminster, and, after receiving the Nadder, falls into the Upper Avon as before mentioned. The Kennet rises near the source of the Upper Avon, and runs eastward, by Marlborough, into Berkshire.—Of the CANALS, the principal is the 'Wilts and Berks,' which commences on the banks of the Isis, near Abingdon; passes through Swindon, Wootton Bassett and Melksham; and joins the canal from the river Kennet to the river Avon at Trowbridge. From this canal collateral cuts are made to Wantage, Calne and Chippenham.

CIVIL and ECCLESIASTICAL DIVISIONS.—Wiltshire is in the Province of Canterbury and Diocese of Salisbury; is included in the Western Circuit, and divided into twenty-eight hundreds, which are subdivided into 300 parishes; these contain one city (Salisbury), one county town (Wilton), and twenty other market towns. The whole county returns thirty-four Members to Parliament, viz. two each for BEDWIN, CALNE, CHIPPENHAM, CRICKLADE, DEVIZES, DOWNTON, HEYTESBURY, HINDON, LUDGERSHALL, MALMESBURY, MARLBOROUGH, the CITY OF SALISBURY, OLD SARUM, WESTBURY, WILTON, WOOTTON BASSETT, and two for the SHIRE.

POPULATION.—According to the census of 1821, there were houses inhabited in the county, 41,702; uninhabited, 1,129; and houses building, 294. The number of families then resident in the county, was 47,684; comprising 108,213 males, and 113,944 females: total, 222,157. And by a calculation made by order of Government, which included persons in the army and navy, for which was added after the ratio of about one to thirty prior to the year 1811, and one to fifty for that year and the census of 1821, to the returns made from the several districts, the population of the county, in round numbers, in the year 1700, was 153,900—in 1750, 168,400—in 1801, 191,200—in 1811, 200,300—and in 1821, 226,600. The increased population in the fifty years, from the year 1700, was 14,500—from 1750 to 1801, the increase was 22,800—from 1801 to 1811, the increase was 9,100—and from 1811 to 1821, the augmented number of persons was 26,300: the grand total increase in the population of the county, from the year 1700 to the census of 1821, being about 72,700 persons.

Index of Distances from Town to Town in the County of Wilts.

THE NAMES OF THE RESPECTIVE TOWNS ARE ON THE TOP AND SIDE, AND THE SQUARE WHERE BOTH MEET GIVES THE DISTANCE.

Town	Amesbury	Bradford	Calne	Chippenham	Cricklade	Devizes	Highworth	Hindon	Lavington	Malmesbury	Marlborough	Melksham	Salisbury	Swindon	Trowbridge	Warminster	Westbury	*Distance from London.*
Amesbury																		78
Bradford	27																	100
Calne	23	13																88
Chippenham	32	11	6															94
Cricklade	38	30	17	20														84
Devizes	16	13	8	10	24													89
Highworth	35	34	20	23	8	25												76
Hindon	17	20	30	24	47	26	51											97
Lavington	10	17	14	16	30	6	31	22										94
Malmesbury	46	21	16	9	12	20	20	44	26									96
Marlborough	19	24	13	19	19	14	16	36	20	23								75
Melksham	22	5	8	6	26	8	26	22	12	16	21							96
Salisbury	8	33	30	33	46	22	43	16	18	52	28	30						81
Swindon	29	27	16	18	9	19	6	45	25	16	11	22	38					80
Trowbridge	22	3	13	13	30	10	33	17	12	27	24	6	30	29				99
Warminster	18	11	21	15	38	17	42	9	13	30	31	13	22	36	8			96
Westbury	20	7	17	15	34	15	39	13	9	26	28	9	26	33	4	4		100
Wootton Bassett	32	22	10	12	8	16	12	42	22	10	12	17	39	6	22	30	26	89

[*See over.*

Additional information relating to the County of Wilts.

———ooo———

Population.—By the Census for 1831 this county contained 117,118 males, and 122,063 females—total 239,181, being an increase, since the returns made in the year 1821, of 17,024 inhabitants; and from the Census of 1801 to that of 1831, the augmentation amounted to 54,074 persons.

Representation.—By the *Reform Bill* the following boroughs have been disfranchised, namely, Great Bedwin, Downton, Heytesbury, Hindon, Ludgershall, Old Sarum, and Wootton Basset; and the boroughs of Calne, Malmesbury, Westbury and Wilton now send one member each instead of two: by the same Act, the privilege of returning two members has been conferred upon Bradford, and two additional ones are given to the county. By these alterations the whole shire sends *twenty* representatives to Parliament, instead of *thirty-four*, as before the passing of the Bill. The new *Boundary Act* divides the County into two parts, respectively called the *Northern Division* and the *Southern Division;* the former comprises the several hundreds of Chippenham, North Damerham, Bradford, Melksham, Potterne and Cannings, Calne, Selkley, Ramsbury, Whorwelsdown, Swanborough, Highworth, Cricklade and Staple, Kingsbridge, and Malmesbury; the southern includes the hundreds of Kinwardstone, Heytesbury, Branch and Dole, Elstub and Everley, Amesbury, Warminster, Mere, South Damerham, Downton, Chalk, Dunworth, Cawden and Cadworth, Frustfield, Alderbury, Underditch, and Westbury. The election of members for the northern division is held at Devizes, and for the southern at Salisbury: besides the place of election, the northern division polls at Melksham, Malmesbury, and Swindon; and the southern division (besides the place of election) polls at Warminster, East Everley, and Hindon.

Railways.—The Great Western runs a little to the north of *Swindon;* thence, after passing through *Chippenham*, and leaving *Bradford* about five miles to the south (or left), enters the city of *Bath* upon its southern side, and thence proceeds to *Bristol;* from the latter city commences the Bristol and Exeter line, of which notice has already been taken, both under Devonshire and Gloucestershire. A connexion with the London and Southampton Railway will be effected by a line from Salisbury, through Romsey, to Basingstoke. A Railway is projected to commence from the Great Western, at or near Reading, in Berkshire; thence, leaving Newbury on the north, will pass near Kingsclere and Andover, to Salisbury; and thence, by Wincanton and Somerton, will join the Bristol and Exeter Railway to the north of Taunton, in Somersetshire.

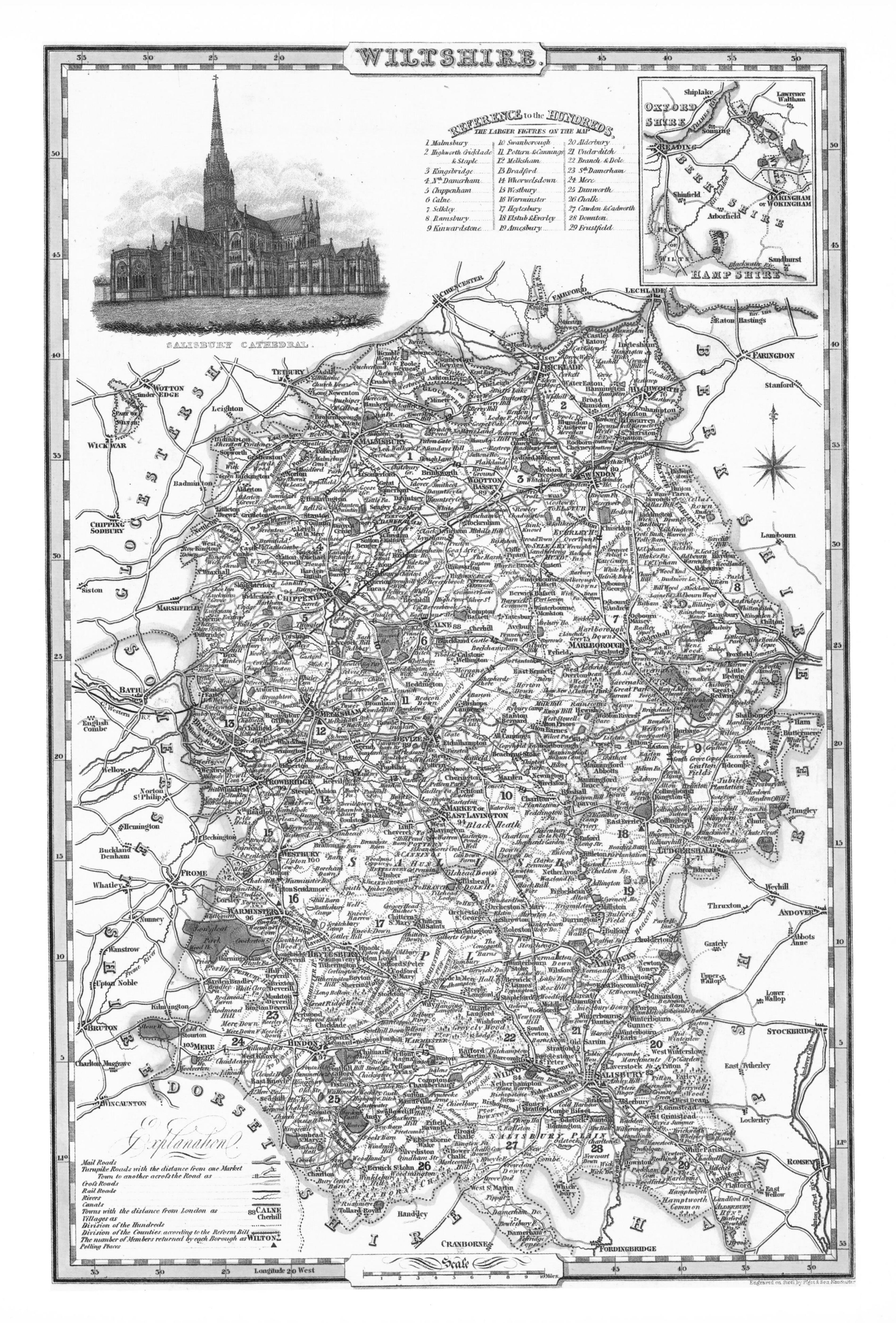
WILTSHIRE.
SALISBURY CATHEDRAL
REFERENCE to the HUNDREDS,
THE LARGER FIGURES ON THE MAP
1 Malmsbury
2 Highworth Cricklade & Staple
3 Kingsbridge
4 Nth. Damerham
5 Chippenham
6 Calne
7 Selkley
8 Ramsbury
9 Kinwardstone
10 Swanborough
11 Pottern & Cannings
12 Melksham
13 Bradford
14 Whorwelsdown
15 Westbury
16 Warminster
17 Heytesbury
18 Elstub & Everley
19 Amesbury
20 Alderbury
21 Underditch
22 Branch & Dole
23 Sth. Damerham
24 Mere
25 Dunworth
26 Chalk
27 Cawden & Cadworth
28 Downton
29 Frustfield
OXFORD SHIRE
BERKSHIRE
HAMPSHIRE
GLOCESTERSHIRE
DORSETSHIRE
SALISBURY PLAIN
Explanation
Mail Roads
Turnpike Roads with the distance from one Market Town to another across the Road as
Cross Roads
Rail Roads
Rivers
Canals
Towns with the distance from London as 88 CALNE
Villages as Cherhill
Division of the Hundreds
Division of the Counties according to the Reform Bill
The number of Members returned by each Borough as WILTON
Polling Places
Longitude 2 0 West
Scale
10 Miles
Engraved on Steel by Pigot & Son Manchester

WORCESTERSHIRE.

WORCESTER is reckoned among the middle counties of England; and is bounded on the north by Staffordshire, on the north-west by Shropshire, on the west by Herefordshire, on the east and north-east by Warwickshire, and on the south by the county of Gloucester. The shape of this county is extremely irregular, having upon almost every side small portions detached and insulated by the adjoining counties; and the boundaries form numberless indentures, resembling bays, promontories and peninsulas. The principal detached districts are those locally situate in the counties of Gloucester, Warwick and Stafford, the latter county surrounding the town of Dudley. Without taking into account such separated portions, the length of the county, from about Stourbridge on the north to Bredon on the south, is thirty miles; and in breadth from east to west, at its widest part, it is about twenty-eight miles. From the numerous abrupt angles which present themselves on the borders of this county, some difficulty has arisen in computing its circumference; it may, however, be stated at two hundred and fifty miles including the projecting points, and exclusive of them at about one hundred and twenty-five: the area of the county is stated by Government to comprise 729 square miles,—which, it is presumed, does not take in those parts before referred to as situated in other counties.

NAME and ANCIENT HISTORY.—The name of this county has its origin from that of its city, Worcester; the which is said to be deduced from *Wire-cester*, a Saxon term, signifying, by its first syllable, 'a place of wears;' but the remaining part (and indeed the whole of the name) is subject to doubt; and *how* its present appellation was obtained is sunk so deep in obscurity, as hitherto to elude the prying search of the etymologist.—Antecedent to the invasion of this country by CÆSAR, and under the dominion of his successors, Worcestershire was inhabited by the *Cornavii*, and was comprised by the Romans in the province of FLAVIA CÆSARIENSIS; during the Heptarchy it belonged to Mercia, when it was the frequent scene of sanguinary contests between the Saxons and the Danes. To *Dudo*, a famous Saxon, may be ascribed the origin of the town of *Duddeley*, now 'Dudley:' this warrior raised a strong fortress here, the venerable remains of which are to this day justly admired, as well from their beautiful situation as their extensive and picturesque contour. Evesham, in the days of monastic grandeur, was celebrated for its Abbey, then one of the largest and most stately in the Kingdom; and was originally founded by Egwin, third Bishop of Worcester, A. D. 702;—one of the most remarkable battles recorded in the English annals was fought in the Vale of Evesham, in the year 1265, between Simon de Montford, Earl of Leicester, and Prince Edward, afterwards Edward I, in which the Earl and most of his adherents were slain. The ancient city of Worcester was possessed by the Britons and Romans before the arrival of the Saxons; but by whom, or at what period, it was first founded, are circumstances as doubtful as is the derivation of its name. The original Cathedral was established in 680; but in the year 983, Oswald, the great patron of the monks, completed the building of a new and more stately edifice: Bishop Wulstan laid the foundation of the present Cathedral in 1084. From having been enlarged, repaired, and many parts rebuilt by subsequent Prelates, its interior as well as exterior presents a great variety of systems of architecture, but which, taken as a whole, forms a beautiful and noble pile of building. It was at this city that Cromwell, in 1651, obtained what he called his '*crowning* victory' over the Scottish army.

SOIL and CLIMATE, PRODUCE and MANUFACTURES.—The SOIL of this county, though various, is generally rich and fertile; producing grain and fruit in the greatest profusion, and abundant pasturage. Between Worcester and the Vale of Evesham, the soil is composed partly of red marl, and partly of a strong loamy clay,—the beautiful valley of Evesham consisting of a deep rich earth. On the borders, and in the various parts of the Coteswold Hills, lime-stone predominates, particularly in the more elevated regions, while the lower are covered with a rich loam. From Worcester to the Malvern Hills, the surface is clay and gravel; westward, deep clay forms the upper stratum in some parts; in others, a loose stony soil.—The AIR of this county is mild, warm and healthy, there being but few lakes, and very little swampy ground. The inhabitants enjoy a most salubrious and temperate climate; a circumstance which, conjointly with the beautiful, rich and picturesque scenery which they furnish, contributes not a little to induce multitudes of loungers to make the villages of Great and Little Malvern, situated upon the eastern side of these hills, the temporary theatres of their gaieties.—The principal MANUFACTURES of this county are seated in its city; they consist in the making of gloves to a great extent, and beautiful porcelain and cabinet ware. In other towns in the county are considerable tanneries, glass and iron works; many hands are also employed in the combing and spinning of wool, linen weaving, the making of needles, nails, fish-hooks, &c. Kidderminster has long been famed for its carpets, and also for the manufacture of worsted stuffs, and fabrics of silk and worsted. This county is also noted for its fine cider, perry and hops; and beautiful salt is obtained from the springs at Droitwich: the antiquity of the manufacture of this article here has been traced prior to the Norman Conquest, and at the present day it is its staple trade. At Dudley all kinds of ornamental and cut glass are got up in the most elegant style of workmanship. The iron works for manufacturing various descriptions of heavy hardware are very extensive; and the nail trade employs an immense population in Dudley and the neighbouring parishes: the stranger, approaching this district in the evening, is much struck with the innumerable lights seen in every direction issuing from furnaces, forges, collieries, &c.; giving not only to the face of the earth, but to that of the firmament also, an appearance of one universal illumination. The town of Redditch is almost entirely supported by the needle and fish-hook trade; there seldom being fewer than thirty flourishing establishments, employing numerous hands in the manufacture of these minute and useful articles.

RIVERS, CANALS and MINERAL SPRINGS.—The principal rivers of this county are the noble SEVERN, the AVON and the STOUR: many streams of little note, but of no inconsiderable utility to the farmer, water this county, beside the rivers just mentioned, but do not form sufficiently striking features to demand particular description. The Severn enters this county at Bewdley, and, turning nearly south, passes the city of Worcester, and also, further below it, the town of Upton; after which it enters Gloucestershire at Tewkesbury, and thence proceeds onward to the Bristol Channel. The Avon traverses the south-east part of the county, and falls into the Severn at Tewkesbury. The Stour passes the towns of Stourbridge and Stourport, to which it gives name; on the south side of the latter town it falls into the Severn, which is here joined by the Staffordshire and Worcester Canal, where are extensive basins and warehouses; and from these circumstances it is aptly denominated the 'Port of Worcestershire.'—The CANALS that pass through Worcestershire, and furnish to its inhabitants the facility of inland navigation, and communication with distant counties, are, the 'Droitwich,' the 'Worcester and Birmingham,' the 'Dudley Extension,' and the canal above mentioned.—The SPRINGS in this county which are said to possess MEDICINAL properties, are those of the Wells, at Malvern, which have acquired a reputation for curing many disorders, and especially for relieving persons suffering from scrofula, or scurvy: their efficacy has, however, been denied by many; and the relief experienced by patients, under different complaints, has been ascribed to the cheering influence of beautiful scenery, pure and bracing air, simple diet and regular exercise.

CIVIL and ECCLESIASTICAL DIVISIONS.—Worcestershire is in the Province of Canterbury and Diocese of Worcester, and included in the Oxford Circuit; it is divided into the five hundreds of BLAKENHURST, DODDINGTREE, HALFSHIRE, OSWALDSLOW and PERSHORE, which are subdivided into 171 parishes, containing collectively one city and county town (Worcester), and 12 other market towns. The whole county returns nine Members to Parliament, viz. two for the city of WORCESTER, two each for DROITWICH and EVESHAM, one for BEWDLEY, and two for the SHIRE.

POPULATION.—According to the census of 1821, there were houses inhabited in the county, 34,738; uninhabited, 980; and houses building, 232. The number of families then resident in the county was 39,006; comprising 90,259 males, and 94,265 females; total, 184,424: and by a calculation made by order of Government, which included persons in the army and navy, for which was added after the ratio of about one to thirty prior to the year 1811, and one to fifty for that year and the census of 1821, to the returns made from the several districts; the population of the county, in round numbers, in the year 1700, was 88,200—in 1750, 108,000—in 1801, 143,900—in 1811, 165,900—and in 1821, 188,200. The increased population in the 50 years, from the year 1700, was 19,800—from 1750 to 1801, the increase was 35,900—from 1801 to 1811, the increase was 22,000—and from 1811 to 1821, the augmented number of persons was 22,300: the grand total increase in the population of the county, from the year 1700 to the census of 1821, being about 100,000 persons.

Index of Distances from Town to Town in the County of Worcester.

THE NAMES OF THE RESPECTIVE TOWNS ARE ON THE TOP AND SIDE, AND THE SQUARE WHERE BOTH MEET GIVES THE DISTANCE.

Distance from Birmingham.	Town	Bewdley	Bromsgrove	Droitwich	Dudley	Evesham	Kidderminster	Malvern	Pershore	Redditch	Shipston	Stourbridge	Stourport	Tenbury	Upton-upon-Severn	Distance from London.
20	Bewdley															129
13	Bromsgrove	13														116
19	Droitwich	15	6													118
10	Dudley	14	14	20												126
29	Evesham	30	17	15	31											96
17	Kidderminster	3	9	10	13	28										126
32	Malvern	22	20	15	32	17	22									120
34	Pershore	23	15	14	32	6	24	12								102
12	Redditch	18	6	8	20	18	15	21	21							111
33	Shipston	44	26	26	40	15	36	32	21	26						83
12	Stourbridge	10	10	16	6	27	7	28	24	16	25					126
22	Stourport	3	10	9	16	24	4	17	19	16	35	10				124
37	Tenbury	14	26	21	32	35	19	19	27	32	49	24	14			133
35	Upton-upon-Severn	24	23	17	38	14	24	8	8	24	29	31	20	24		111
26	Worcester	14	13	7	28	15	14	7	9	19	29	21	11	20	10	111

[*See over.*

Additional information relating to the County of WORCESTER.

---ooo---

POPULATION.—By the Census for **1831** this county contained 103,367 males, and 107,989 females—total 211,356, being an increase, since the returns made in the year 1821, of 26,932 inhabitants; and from the Census of 1801 to that of 1831, the augmentation amounted to 72,023 persons.

REPRESENTATION.—By the *Reform Bill* the borough of DROITWICH has lost one of its members; the towns of KIDDERMINSTER and DUDLEY have obtained the right of returning one each, and two additional members have been bestowed on the county; the whole shire, in consequence, now sends *twelve* representatives to Parliament, instead of *nine*, as before the passing of the Bill. The new *Boundary Act* divides the county into two parts, respectively called the *Eastern Division* and the *Western Division;* the former comprises the divisions of Stourbridge, Dudley, Droitwich, Northfield, Blockley, and Pershore; and the western portion includes the divisions of Upton, Worcester, Hundred House, and Kidderminster. The election of members for the eastern division of the county is held at DROITWICH, and for the western at WORCESTER: besides the place of election, the eastern division polls at PERSHORE, SHIPSTON and STOURBRIDGE; and the western division (besides the place of election) polls at UPTON, STOURPORT and TENBURY.

RAILWAYS.—The WESTERN UNION RAILWAY opens a communication between *Gloucester* and *Birmingham;* from the latter town it will pass to the east of *Bromsgrove* and *Droitwich*—thence, leaving *Worcester* city on the right and *Pershore* on the left, it pursues its route by *Cheltenham* to *Gloucester*. From Gloucester, on the south, it proceeds to *Cirencester;* and leaving *Cricklade* on the east, it joins the Great Western line, near *Swindon*, in Wiltshire.

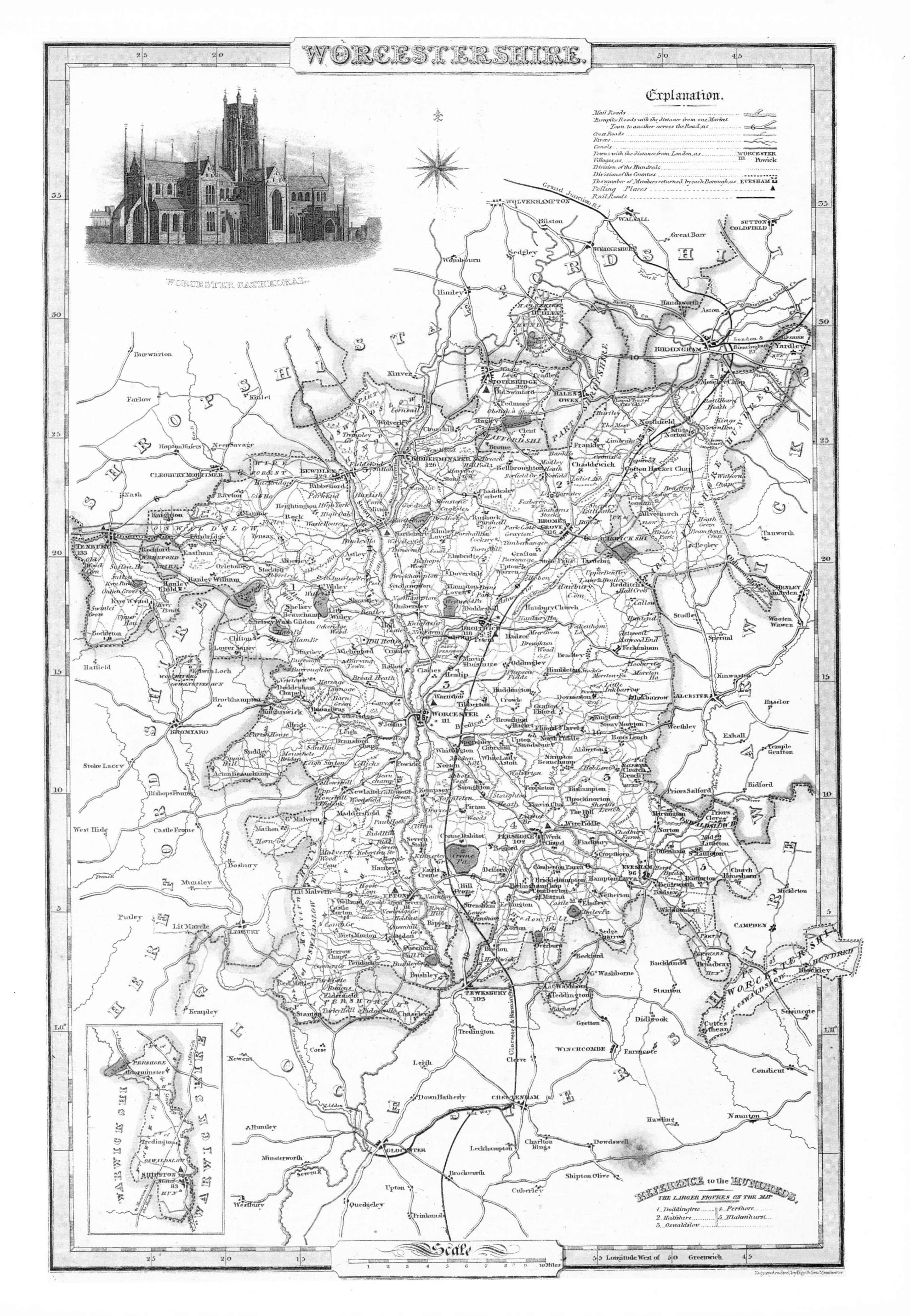
WORCESTERSHIRE.
WORCESTER CATHEDRAL.
Explanation.
Mail Roads
Turnpike Roads with the distance from one Market Town to another across the Road, as
Cross Roads
Rivers
Canals
Towns with the distance from London, as
WORCESTER
Villages, as
Powick
Division of the Hundreds
Division of the Counties
The number of Members returned by each Borough, as
EVESHAM
Polling Places
Rail Roads
REFERENCE to the HUNDREDS,
THE LARGER FIGURES ON THE MAP.
1. Doddingtree
2. Halfshire
3. Oswaldslow
4. Pershore
5. Blakenhurst
Scale
Miles
Longitude West of
Greenwich
WOLVERHAMPTON
WALSALL
SUTTON COLDFIELD
WEDNESBURY
BIRMINGHAM
STOURBRIDGE
HALES OWEN
KIDDERMINSTER
BEWDLEY
CLEOBURY MORTIMER
TENBURY
BROMSGROVE
DROITWICH
WORCESTER
BROMYARD
PERSHORE
EVESHAM
UPTON
TEWKESBURY
LEDBURY
WINCHCOMBE
CHELTENHAM
GLOCESTER
ALCESTER
CAMPDEN
SHIPSTON

YORKSHIRE.

THE County of YORK is a maritime one, and the largest of all the English counties, being in length upwards of ninety miles from east to west, eighty from north to south, and its area comprising about 5,960 square miles. It is bounded on the north by the counties of Durham and Westmoreland, on the east by the German Ocean, on the west by part of Westmoreland and Lancashire, and on the south by Cheshire, Derbyshire, Nottinghamshire and Lincolnshire. From its great extent, Yorkshire has been arranged into three divisions, respectively denominated the 'NORTH RIDING,' the 'WEST RIDING,' and the 'EAST RIDING.' The North Riding comprehends the whole northern part of the county from side to side, descending to its capital in the centre; divided from the East Riding by the river Derwent, and from part of the West by the river Ure. The West Riding is bounded on the north by the North Riding, on the east by the East Riding and part of Lincolnshire, on the south by Derbyshire and Nottinghamshire, and on the west by Cheshire, Lancashire, and a small part of Westmoreland. The East Riding comprehends the south-east part of the county; and is bounded on the north-west and north by the North Riding, on the north-east and east by the German Ocean, on the south by Lincolnshire, from which it is separated by the river Humber, and on the west (until it approaches its northern extremity,) by the West Riding.

NAME and ANCIENT HISTORY.—The name of the County is derived from that of its City (York), which, according to Camden, was named by the Britons *Cær Effroc;* by the Saxons, *Evorwic;* by Nennius, *Carr Ebrauc,* which, the latter historian asserts, originated from its first founder, King Ebraucus; Camden, however, more discriminatingly suggests that the word *Eboracum* implies the situation of the town on the river Ure, now the Ouse, and that by gradual corruption *Eborac* or *Euorwic* became *Yorc,* or 'York.' Yorkshire was included by the Romans, in their division of the Island, in the province of MAXIMA CÆSARIENSIS. After the departure of the Romans, Yorkshire formed part of the Saxon 'Northumberland,' (a denominative title which the latter intruders founded upon the local *Northumbria* of the former, signifying the territory north of the river *Humber,* or *Umber,)* and continued so until the extinction of the Heptarchy, when all the States were united under Egbert. The north-eastern coast was the district that first suffered under the devastating ravages of the Danes; and Yorkshire, with the adjacent counties, primarily experienced, what the greater portion of England eventually did, the sanguinary scourge of these invaders. After the Conquest, this country was divided among some of the great Norman Barons, who were sworn to prevent the incursions of the Scots: the English, however, detesting the Norman tyranny, fled in considerable numbers to Scotland, and assisted King Malcolm *Canmore* in his invasion of the northern borders. Yorkshire exhibited a prominent character during the destructive contentions between the Houses of York and Lancaster, and however singular it may now appear, a great proportion of the population frequently signalized themselves under the banner of the 'Red Rose.' In the reign of Edward IV. the county was involved in a formidable rebellion, originating in the intrigues of the Nobility, which was not suppressed until a considerable time had elapsed, and some thousands of lives lost. In the reign of Henry VIII. the peace of the county was again disturbed by an insurrection, fomented by the Clergy, which merely hastened the dissolution of monasteries and other religious houses: by this measure, many families who rented small farms under the convents were reduced to utter ruin: driven in despair to take up arms and endeavour to retaliate, they marched from the centre of the county to Doncaster—their numbers increasing until they amounted to 40,000; and the residences of the Nobility, and the inhabitants of several villages through which this formidable body passed, underwent all the spoliation that an infuriated and licentious mob could inflict. These commotions were not hushed to peaceful silence even during the short succeeding reign of Edward VI, nor until the enactment of the poor laws, under Queen Elizabeth. With the early history of the county that of the City of York is intimately connected and involved: it appears to have been founded, or at least aggrandized, by Agricola, about the year 80, after his final subjugation of the *Brigantes;* he established in it the head-quarters of the Roman legions under his command, and succeeding Generals continued this distinction; it even became the temporary residence of Severus and several succeeding Roman Emperors. Upon the declension of the Imperial power in Great Britain, this city fully participated with the surrounding country in the barbarous inflictions of the German tribes,—at a subsequent period writhed under the yet more atrocious scourge of the Scandinavian hordes, and groaned under repeated misfortunes for upwards of six hundred years; notwithstanding which, York as repeatedly arose out of its ashes, and recovered at least a portion of its former splendour. In less than a century after it had been razed to the ground, in consequence of its uncompromising resistance, by the Norman Conqueror, it was rebuilt, and a Parliament summoned thither by Henry II; after which it was honoured with the presence and occasional residence of most of our Kings, from Henry III. to Charles I: in these successive ages, at different periods, parliaments and conventions were held, coronations, Royal marriages and interviews took place, in this city. Charles I. for the last time visited it in 1640; shortly after, it was garrisoned for that Monarch, but surrendered to the authority of the Parliament on the 16th July, 1646. In modern days the great object of attraction to the stranger in this city is its justly celebrated Cathedral,—the largest, as it is the most superb Gothic edifice in the Kingdom: its origin is too remote to be satisfactorily traced; but, as it now stands, it is decidedly pre-eminent, and the preservation of it in its pristine beauty seems to be the gratifying and praiseworthy province of those who are clothed with the important powers of improving this interesting and ancient city. By the act of one Martin, a maniac incendiary, the Minster sustained considerable damage, in the month of February, 1829, the fire having destroyed the noble organ, choir, &c.: by the employment, however, of the most talented architects, and aided by general and liberal subscriptions, the work of renovation was prosecuted so ably and so assiduously, that but few marks of the deed of the sacrilegious fanatic are now apparent in the venerable pile.—To the historian and the antiquary, Yorkshire, from its recorded events, and its numerous ancient relics of monasteries, abbeys, churches, &c., cannot fail to afford an almost endless source of information and delight; and perhaps in no part of England can there be found so many objects to gratify curiosity, please the imagination, or awaken national recollections. To the mineralogist a wide field displays itself, replete with numbers of subjects for attention not to be found elsewhere.

SOIL, CLIMATE, and AGRICULTURAL PRODUCE.—The SOIL of the NORTH RIDING is a brownish clay and loam, and the hills along the coast abound with allum shale. The district of Cleveland, on the west side of the eastern moors, has a very fertile clay, and fine red sandy soil; the Vale of York, both in soil and fertility, is very variable; Swaledale, on each side of the river Swale, is extremely fertile. The eastern moorlands is a wild and extensive tract of mountain, occupying a space of land about twenty miles in length and fourteen in breadth; the surface of some of the higher hills is entirely covered with large free-stones, and extensive morasses and peat-bogs, highly dangerous to pass; some of the dales among these moors are very extensive, the bottoms being mostly narrow, and the land is well cultivated for nearly a mile up the hills. The western moorlands are a part of that long range of mountains extending north from Stafford into Scotland. Of about 1,311,000 acres of land embraced by this Riding, about 443,000 are cultivated,—the remainder being open fields and moors, woods and roads. Along the coast next the German Ocean the land is very hilly; the cliff rises from the sea to the height of from fifty to one hundred and fifty feet; and from this the country attains a very rapid elevation, in the space of half a mile, of three or four hundred feet. The soil of the WEST RIDING varies from a deep strong clay, or loam, to the worst peat earth: the face of this portion of the county is also very irregular; the north and west parts are hilly and mountainous, but intersected with numerous vales; the rest of the district is flat: the whole is almost completely inclosed with stone dikes and hedges. The contents of this Riding are about 1,568,000 square statute acres,—having about 700,000 acres pasturage, and 350,000 arable. This division of the county is noted for the extent of its manufactures, for which it is every way admirably adapted, as well from the abundance of the raw materials, coals, &c., as from the means of conveying its produce and manufactures, by canals, &c., to all parts of the Kingdom. In the EAST RIDING, the shore for fifteen miles round Flamborough is high; and behind that lies the sheep district of the Yorkshire Wolds, containing upwards of 300,000 acres; the soil is a light loam, having a mixture of gravel. The country extending between the Wolds and the Ouse and Humber, to Hull, has a good fertile soil; and towards the Spurn Head, along the side of the Humber, it is also flat, with a strong soil: the produce of corn in this district is more than adequate to its consumption; but there is very little wood, and with coal it is chiefly supplied from Wakefield and Leeds. The PRODUCE and exports of this Riding are vast quantities of wool, grain, bacon, butter and cattle; of the latter, with horses, great numbers are bought at the York and Howden fairs by the London dealers. The horses of this part have long been noted for their excellence; the prevailing species are those adapted to the coach and saddle. The horned cattle of this Riding, and indeed of the county generally, are not surpassed in number or quality by those of any other division of England: there are also many descriptions of sheep bred, most of which are famous both for their size and goodness; great quantities of the Scotch breed are fed in the low part of the country. The contents of this Riding are about 819,200 square statute acres; having about 350,000 in pasturage, and 150,000 in arable.—The CLIMATE of Yorkshire is, on the whole, considered salubrious, although as variable as that of any other county in the Kingdom. In the North Riding, along the coast next the German Ocean, which is very hilly, it is bleak and cold; at the same time, the air is pure and bracing: upon the moors, also, as may be expected from their height, the cold is severely felt. The climate in the West Riding is in general moderate and pleasant, except in the eastern part, where it is reckoned unhealthy, from its low situation and its damps and fogs. In the East Riding, that part adjoining the sea, extending from the Humber to the North Riding, the air is very bleak, and the spring very backward; from the Spurn Head to Bridlington, nearly forty miles, the shore is low, and the effect of the cold winds is not so much experienced.

MANUFACTURES, and MINES and MINERALS.—As a manufacturing district, Yorkshire must be acknowledged to be the second in the Kingdom. The manufacture of woollen cloths of every description has been brought to such a degree of perfection, as to be considered equal, and in many respects superior, to those made in other places. The iron works, which contribute materially to the opulence of the county, are very extensive, and furnish employment to multitudes of mechanics, miners, &c. Sheffield is the ancient seat of the cutlery manufacture; and Chaucer, who penned his best authenticated pieces so far back as the reign of Henry III, and who has been styled 'the Father of English Poetry,' mentions this town as being famous for the production of knife-blades; for, in describing a character in one of his poems, he say, *'A Shefeld thwytel bare he in his hose:'* a 'thwytel' or 'whittle,' was a knife, such as was carried about the person so late as the time of Charles I. Every kind of article in cutlery at the present day is furnished by Sheffield; besides joiners' tools of all denominations, plated works, Britannia metal goods, &c.: these productions, for excellence of quality, variety of pattern and amount of quantity, no other place in the world can vie with. The principal towns in the county in the woollen trade are Leeds, Bradford, Halifax, Wakefield and Huddersfield, with the wide district of Saddleworth: these places may be said to have almost monopolized the entire woollen manufacture of the Kingdom, and been the means of sinking into comparative insignificance many towns in Wiltshire, Somersetshire and Devonshire, which not many years ago prospered entirely by this business. At Barnsley the manufacture of linens is extensive; Dewsbury is famous for its blankets and flushings, as Rotherham is for its glass and iron works; while Hull, Whitby, Goole & Scarborough are celebrated commercial sea-ports, and have extensive yards for ship-building, &c.,—the latter place being also noted for its medicinal waters. There are some towns in the county which partake with Lancashire in the cotton manufacture; others where carpets are made; and the city of York has a considerable and reviving trade in glove making, and horn, ivory and tortoise-shell combs.—The principal MINERAL PRODUCTIONS consist of copper, pyrites, copper combined with iron and sulphur, lead ores in great variety and abundance, ores of zinc, &c. The North and East Ridings abound with various sorts of stone for building, slate and lime-stone; and many parts of the county also possess very material advantages, and high importance, from the numerous coal mines, which yield abundance of fuel for the various manufactories.

RIVERS, CANALS and MINERAL SPRINGS.—The principal rivers of Yorkshire are the OUSE, the DON, the CALDER, the WHARFE, the AIRE, the NIDD and the RIBBLE; these may be said to belong to the West Riding:

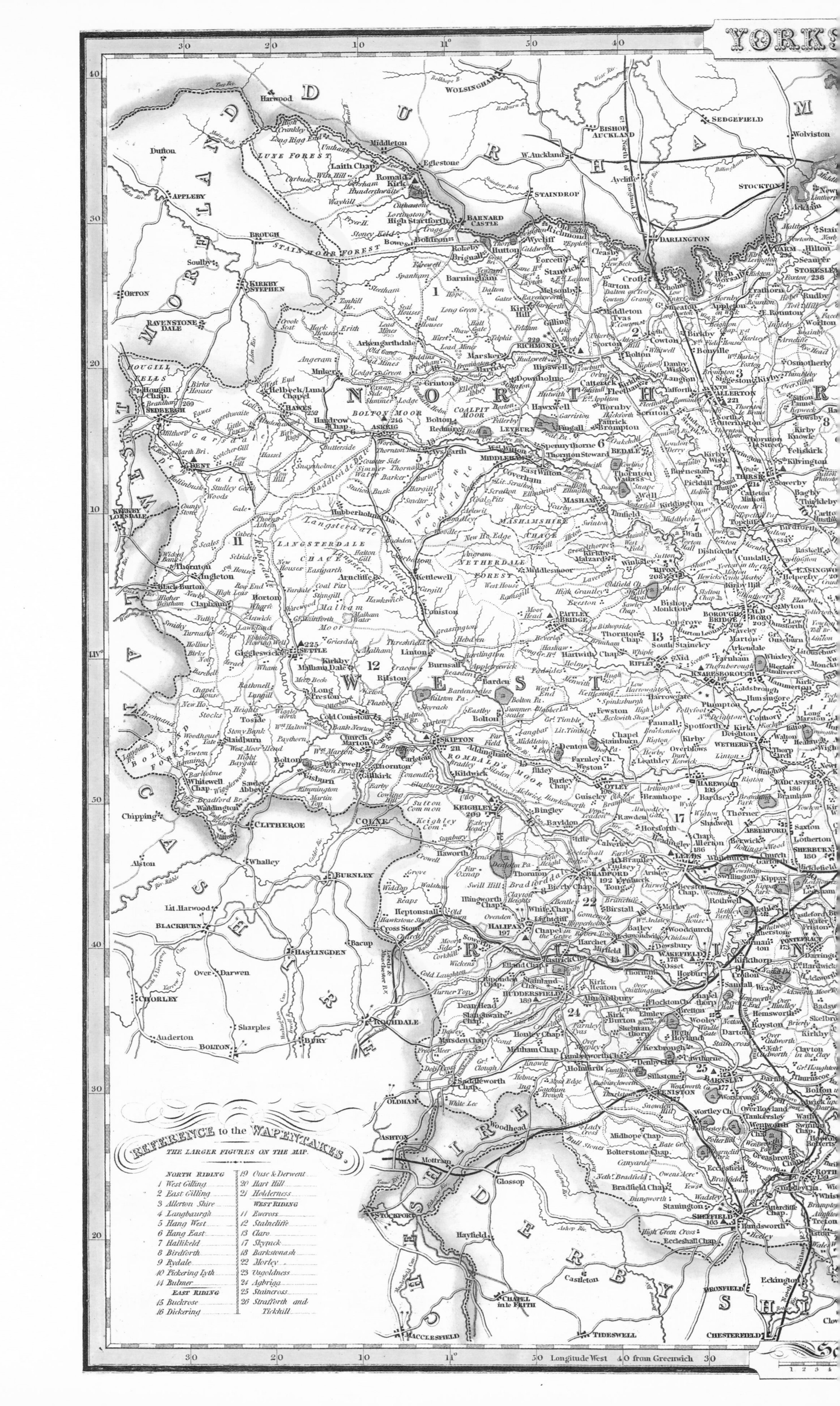
YORKS
REFERENCE to the WAPENTAKES.
THE LARGER FIGURES ON THE MAP.
NORTH RIDING
1 West Gilling
2 East Gilling
3 Allerton Shire
4 Langbaurgh
5 Hang West
6 Hang East
7 Hallikeld
8 Birdforth
9 Rydale
10 Pickering Lyth
14 Bulmer
EAST RIDING
15 Buckrose
16 Dickering
19 Ouse & Derwent
20 Hart Hill
21 Holderness
WEST RIDING
11 Ewcross
12 Stalncliffe
13 Claro
17 Skyrack
18 Barkstonash
22 Morley
23 Usgoldness
24 Agbriga
25 Staincross
26 Strafforth and Tickhill
Longitude West from Greenwich
DURHAM
WESTMORELAND
LANCASHIRE
CHESHIRE
DERBYSHIRE
NORTH
WEST RIDING
LANGSTERDALE CHACE
MASHAMSHIRE CHACE
NETHERDALE FOREST
LUNE FOREST
STAINMOOR FOREST
ROMBALDS MOOR
BISHOP AUCKLAND
SEDGEFIELD
STOCKTON
DARLINGTON
BARNARD CASTLE
RICHMOND
NORTH ALLERTON
THIRSK
RIPON
BEDALE
MASHAM
LEYBURN
HAWES
ASKRIG
SEDBERGH
SETTLE
SKIPTON
KEIGHLEY
OTLEY
KNARESBOROUGH
WETHERBY
HAREWOOD
TADCASTER
LEEDS
BRADFORD
HALIFAX
HUDDERSFIELD
WAKEFIELD
PONTEFRACT
BARNSLEY
PENISTONE
SHEFFIELD
ROTHERHAM
CHESTERFIELD
KIRKBY STEPHEN
APPLEBY
BROUGH
KIRKBY LONSDALE
CLITHEROE
COLNE
BURNLEY
BLACKBURN
HASLINGDEN
CHORLEY
BOLTON
BURY
ROCHDALE
OLDHAM
ASHTON
STOCKPORT
MACCLESFIELD
CHAPEL in le FRITH
TIDESWELL
WOLSINGHAM
STAINDROP
PATELEY BRIDGE
BOROUGHBRIDGE
ALDBOROUGH
RIPLEY
SHERBURN

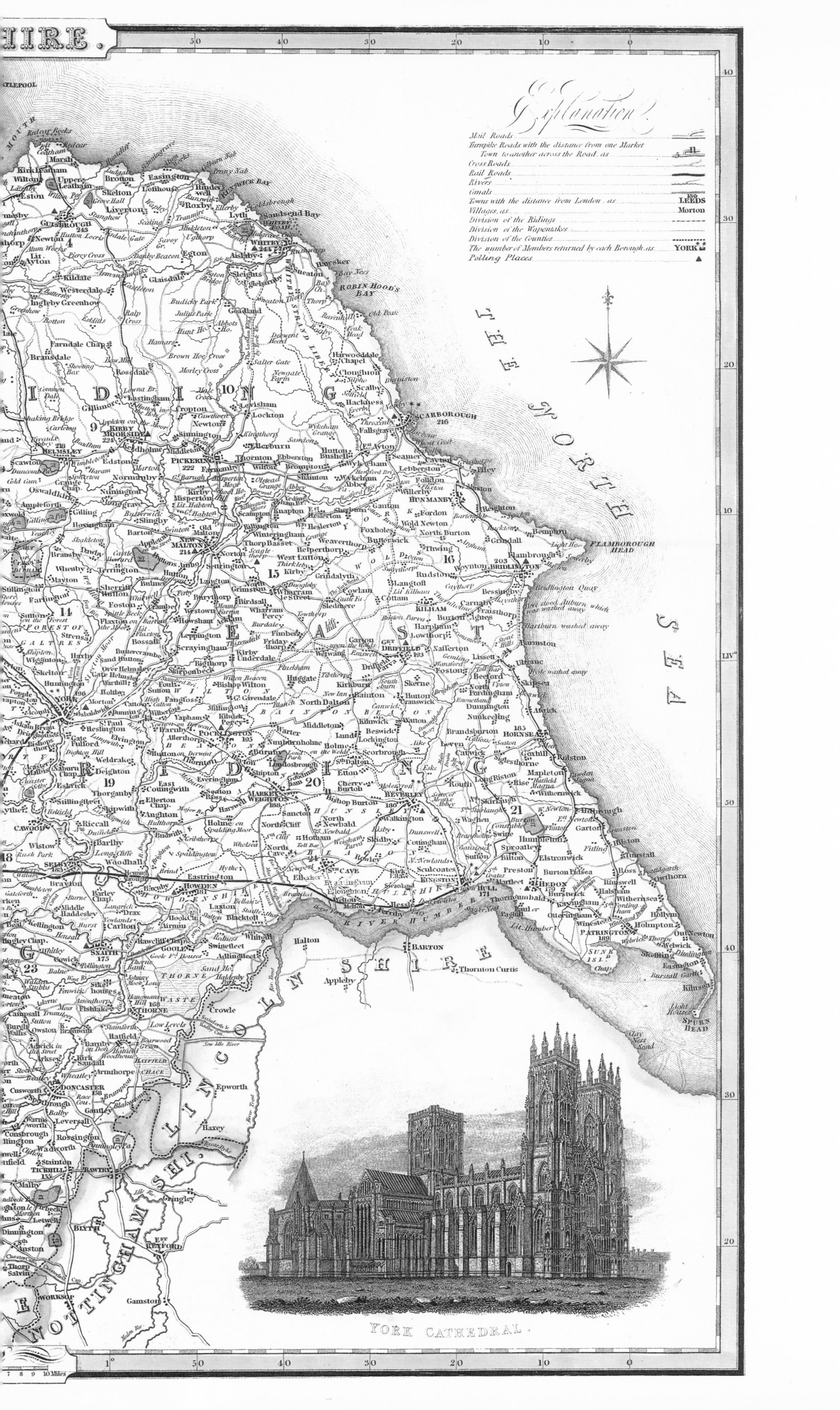

HIRE.
Explanation.
Mail Roads
Turnpike Roads with the distance from one Market Town to another across the Road, as
Cross Roads
Rail Roads
Rivers
Canals
Towns with the distance from London, as
LEEDS
Villages, as
Morton
Division of the Ridings
Division of the Wapentakes
Division of the Counties
The number of Members returned by each Borough, as
YORK
Polling Places
THE NORTH SEA
FLAMBOROUGH HEAD
SPURN HEAD
RIVER HUMBER
LINCOLNSHIRE
NOTTINGHAMSHI.
SCARBOROUGH
WHITBY
BRIDLINGTON
BEVERLEY
HULL
YORK
PICKERING
NEW MALTON
DONCASTER
SELBY
GOOLE
HOWDEN
HEDON
PATRINGTON
YORK CATHEDRAL.

the others have connection for the most part with the North and East Ridings,—and are, the HULL, the TEES, the DERWENT, the SWALE, the URE and the FOSS. Besides those already named, there are, the Cover, the Greta, the Wisk, the Leven, the Rical, the Dove, the Seven and the Costa, with a multitude of other insignificant streams, which merely serve the purpose of turning a few mills. The Ouse (which takes this name at York, being before its arrival there called the Ure,) rises near the borders of Westmoreland, and, after collecting many tributary streams in the North Riding, flows on to the Humber. The Don rises near Barnsley, and passing by Sheffield, Rotherham, Doncaster and Thorne, loses itself in the Aire at Snaith. The Calder has its source in Lancashire, and, running eastward, passes Wakefield, five miles below which town it falls into the Aire. The Wharfe springs from the foot of the Craven Hills, and, after a course of more than fifty miles across the Riding, discharges itself into the Ouse. The Aire is a large river, issuing out of the mountain Penigent, in this county; it visits Leeds, Pontefract and Snaith, and joins the Don near to the last-named town. The Nidd rises in Madesdale Forest, near the source of the Aire; and, passing Ripley and Knaresborough, becomes tributary to the Ouse a few miles above York. The Hull descends from the eastern edge of the Wolds, and, pursuing a southerly course, passes the town of Beverley (to which it is united by a navigable cut), and falls into the Humber at Hull, contributing to form the port. The Tees rises between the counties of Westmoreland and Durham; through its whole course it divides the latter county from the North Riding, and is navigable for vessels of thirty tons from the ocean to Yarm. The Derwent has its source in the eastern moorlands within about four miles of the sea, with which it is parallel, in a southerly direction, until it comes to the foot of the Wolds, when it alters its course, and passes the town of Malton, to which it is navigable from the Humber. The Swale rises in the district called Swaledale, on the borders of Westmoreland, and, flowing east by Richmond, takes a south course; being joined by the Wisk from Northallerton, and several smaller rivers, it thus increased adds to the waters of the Ure, below Aldborough. The Ure rises near the borders of Westmoreland, and collecting, during its course through the beautiful Vale of Wensley, numerous tributary streams, loses its name in that of the Ouse, near York (as before mentioned), and which in its turn is lost in that of the Humber. The Foss is an inconsiderable river, which originates near the western end of the Howardian Hills, and unites with the Ouse at York.—The CANALS which intersect this county are numerous, and of the first importance to its manufactures and commerce: by their means communications are formed between the Irish Sea and the German Ocean, as well as with its great and navigable rivers. The canals of the West Riding are, the 'Leeds and Liverpool,' 130 miles in length; the 'Barnsley Canal,' which joins the river Calder below Wakefield; the 'Dearne and Dove,' commencing at the cut of the Don Navigation, between Swinton and Mexbrough, and communicating with the Barnsley canal; the 'Stainforth and Keadby,' which joins the river Trent, and is about fifteen miles in length; and the 'Huddersfield Canal,' which unites with the Ashton and Oldham canal on the south side of Ashton, in length nearly twenty miles. The canals of the North and East Ridings are, the 'Foss Navigation,' thirteen miles in length; the 'Market Weighton Canal;' and a canal from Great Duffield to Hull, about seven miles in length.—There are several MINERAL SPRINGS in different parts of Yorkshire, the most celebrated of which are at the fashionable towns of Scarborough and Harrogate. The waters of the former are chalybeate and saline; and are a compound of vitriol, iron, alum, nitre and salt. The springs of Harrogate comprise several of sulphureous and chalybeate properties; they are numerously visited, and are highly esteemed by the faculty for curing scorbutic, cutaneous and chronic disorders.

CIVIL and ECCLESIASTICAL DIVISIONS.—Yorkshire is in the Province and Diocese of York, with the exception of the Deaneries of Boroughbridge and Catterick, a few parishes bordering on Lancashire, and that part called 'Richmondshire.' It is included in the Northern Circuit, and divided (as has been before stated) into three Ridings. The East Riding is apportioned into five Wapentakes, including 'Howdenshire,' the Liberty of St. Peter at York, and the Ainsty of the City of York; York City, and the 'Town and County of the Town of Kingston-upon-Hull:' the whole Riding containing 237 parishes. The North Riding is divided into ten Wapentakes, comprising 183 parishes. The West Riding is distributed into nine Wapentakes, in which are included the Liberties of Ripon and Leeds, and the Borough and Soke of Doncaster; the entire Riding containing 193 parishes. The whole county contains 613 parishes, one city and county town (York), and sixty other market towns. Yorkshire sends thirty-two Members to Parliament, viz. four for the SHIRE, two for the CITY OF YORK, and two each for the towns of ALDBOROUGH, BEVERLEY, BOROUGHBRIDGE, HEDON, KINGSTON-UPON-HULL, KNARESBOROUGH, NEW MALTON, NORTHALLERTON, PONTEFRACT, RICHMOND, RIPON, SCARBOROUGH and THIRSK.✻

POPULATION.—According to the census of 1821, there were houses inhabited in the county, 224,469; uninhabited, 9,342; and houses building, 1,613. The number of families then resident in the county, was 240,696; comprising 580,000 males, and 592,731 females: total, 1,173,187. And by a calculation made by order of Government, which included persons in the army and navy, for which was added after the ratio of about one to thirty prior to the year 1811, and one to fifty for that year and the census of 1821, to the returns made from the several districts, the population of the county, in round numbers, in the year 1700, was 431,500—in 1750, 564,200—in 1801, 887,200—in 1811, 1,019,200—and in 1821, 1,197,100. The increased population in the fifty years, from the year 1700, was 132,700—from 1750 to 1801, the increase was 323,000—from 1801 to 1811, the increase was 132,000—and from 1811 to 1821, the augmented number of persons was 177,900: the grand total increase in the population of the county, from the year 1700 to the census of 1821, being about 765,600 persons.

The proportion of the population belonging to the three divisions, by the census of 1821, in round numbers, was thus: in the NORTH RIDING, 187,400; in the EAST RIDING, 194,300; and in the WEST RIDING, 815,400.

Index of Distances from Town to Town in the County of York.

THE NAMES OF THE RESPECTIVE TOWNS ARE ON THE TOP AND SIDE, AND THE SQUARE WHERE BOTH MEET GIVES THE DISTANCE.

Distance from Manchester	Town	Distances (to the towns above, in order from Askrig)	Distance from London
68	Askrig		
37	Barnsley	82	246
92	Beverley	85 61	177
66	Boroughbridge	38 44 48	180
35	Bradford	58 24 64 30	202
106	Bridlington	95 87 23 57 75	192
33	Dewsbury	71 16 60 33 9 72	203
51	Doncaster	82 16 46 44 34 63 26	184
96	Driffield (Great)	80 76 13 48 63 12 61 58	159
76	Easingwold	46 52 42 10 40 44 43 50 28	193
107	Guilsborough	56 56 70 41 71 58 74 86 60 38	208
27	Halifax	60 26 70 38 8 83 10 36 73 48 79	243
57	Harrogate	43 35 51 10 20 75 24 44 52 20 51 28	194
102	Hedon	103 72 17 65 72 28 74 57 26 61 80 80 68	200
71	Howden	77 40 22 38 39 39 38 26 28 33 69 48 37 32	179
25	Huddersfield	68 17 67 41 14 81 8 33 71 51 82 8 32 78 46	175
94	Hull	95 64 9 57 64 32 62 49 22 52 52 72 60 8 24 70	189
39	Keighley	48 36 69 30 10 79 19 44 69 40 71 12 20 82 50 20 74	171
95	Kirkby Moorside	58 78 38 30 64 39 64 66 34 20 26 72 41 60 49 70 51 62	202
59	Knaresborough	44 37 48 7 23 59 26 39 49 17 48 31 3 65 37 34 57 22 39	221
41	Leeds	57 19 52 25 10 65 8 28 55 35 66 18 16 62 30 16 54 20 54 18	197
83	Market Weighton	75 52 10 37 53 27 50 36 16 31 68 60 41 27 12 58 19 58 38 38 44	186
84	New Malton	66 58 28 30 53 29 51 55 18 19 42 61 40 46 38 59 38 57 13 37 43 23	187
82	Northallerton	31 63 62 19 47 65 52 63 55 18 24 55 29 79 52 60 71 46 27 26 44 51 37	214
45	Otley	53 29 58 20 10 68 18 38 59 30 61 18 10 72 40 26 64 10 50 13 10 48 47 37	221
112	Patrington	113 82 27 75 82 38 80 67 36 71 96 90 78 10 42 88 18 92 70 75 72 37 56 89 82	196
92	Pickering	65 65 36 36 61 32 61 63 27 26 31 69 48 53 46 67 45 65 6 45 51 31 8 33 55 63	189
47	Pontefract	69 16 45 31 23 63 15 15 51 37 73 25 29 55 23 23 47 33 53 27 13 35 42 50 23 65 50	222
93	Richmond	18 71 74 27 59 81 60 72 71 32 35 64 36 91 64 68 83 52 42 34 52 64 53 16 47 101 47 58	173
68	Ripon	32 47 54 6 30 60 35 50 54 14 41 38 11 71 45 43 63 30 32 12 27 43 36 17 20 81 37 37 25	229
47	Rotherham	89 13 56 56 37 79 29 12 70 62 98 37 48 69 38 28 61 51 78 49 32 48 67 75 47 79 75 20 84 59	208
12	Saddleworth (from the Junction Inn)	84 28 80 54 21 94 20 38 84 63 95 12 43 91 59 13 83 25 82 46 28 71 72 73 31 101 79 34 81 51 30	159
106	Scarborough	82 80 35 48 75 18 73 77 22 42 42 83 62 47 49 81 44 79 24 59 65 36 22 54 69 57 17 64 72 54 89 94	184
61	Selby	64 39 32 32 30 49 28 26 44 27 63 38 28 42 10 36 34 40 43 28 20 21 32 46 30 52 40 15 59 36 37 47 54	216
50	Settle	22 60 88 40 36 99 45 69 89 49 76 38 37 105 58 46 97 26 67 40 41 78 77 52 31 115 72 54 40 35 72 51 89 61	177
41	Sheffield	90 14 64 58 38 88 30 18 77 66 102 34 49 74 42 26 66 46 82 51 33 54 71 77 43 84 79 30 85 60 6 29 93 44 76	225
43	Skipton	36 44 74 32 20 85 29 53 74 42 67 22 20 87 55 30 79 10 62 22 25 63 62 51 15 97 63 38 51 26 56 35 84 45 16 56	163
60	Snaith	77 31 30 39 37 53 29 18 36 33 69 39 35 40 8 36 32 46 49 40 26 20 38 52 39 42 46 13 64 45 31 47 57 7 67 36 51	211
98	Stokesley	47 76 61 32 62 60 65 79 51 29 9 75 42 78 63 73 70 62 20 39 57 56 33 16 52 88 28 63 26 32 89 85 44 56 68 90 58 62	175
56	Tadcaster	57 29 39 19 25 50 23 27 40 23 59 33 15 56 22 31 48 30 39 14 15 29 28 38 19 66 36 14 46 25 39 42 50 13 50 43 34 20 51	238
78	Thirsk	39 56 52 12 42 54 46 56 47 10 29 50 21 70 44 53 62 42 20 19 37 42 28 9 30 80 25 43 25 12 68 66 46 37 47 69 39 43 20 31	186
66	Thorne	85 25 34 46 43 57 34 11 46 41 77 44 42 46 14 41 38 53 57 48 34 26 46 60 44 56 54 21 73 52 22 49 65 14 75 29 59 7 70 27 51	214
38	Wakefield	66 10 54 34 14 71 6 20 59 44 78 16 25 64 32 13 56 24 58 27 9 44 47 53 19 74 55 9 61 36 23 25 69 24 48 24 34 22 66 19 45 28	165
57	Wetherby	50 34 44 12 24 55 24 31 45 22 53 33 8 61 30 32 53 25 42 7 16 34 33 32 15 71 41 19 40 18 48 43 55 20 44 49 30 27 44 7 24 34 24	178
113	Whitby	78 86 44 57 82 37 82 84 40 47 23 90 69 60 66 88 64 86 27 66 72 55 28 47 76 80 20 71 57 60 96 100 20 61 95 100 91 66 31 57 48 75 76 62	190
98	Yarm	40 82 69 32 78 70 78 80 65 31 14 86 42 89 64 84 81 62 28 39 57 62 41 17 52 99 38 63 22 32 92 85 55 57 67 90 64 64 8 53 20 71 66 44 36	244
66	York	56 39 29 15 35 40 35 37 30 13 49 43 22 46 21 41 38 39 29 19 25 19 18 32 29 56 26 24 44 24 49 53 40 14 59 53 44 20 42 10 23 28 29 15 47 43	235
			196

Additional information relating to the County.

POPULATION.—By the Census for 1831 this county contained 677,601 males, and 693,695 females—total 1,371,296, being an increase, since the returns made in the year 1821, of 198,109 inhabitants; and from the Census of 1801 to that of 1831, the augmentation amounted to 512,404 persons. According to the last returns (1831) the population of the respective ridings was as follows; EAST RIDING, 168,646; NORTH RIDING, 190,873; WEST RIDING, 976,415; and the CITY and AINSTEY, 35,362 (total as above 1,371,296).

✻ REPRESENTATION.—By the *Reform Bill* the boroughs of ALDBOROUGH, BOROUGHBRIDGE and HEDON are disfranchised, and one member taken from NORTHALLERTON, and THIRSK: under the same Act the following towns have obtained the right of representation, namely, BRADFORD, HALIFAX, LEEDS and SHEFFIELD; these return two members each; and HUDDERSFIELD, WAKEFIELD and WHITBY one each; each Riding now sends two members, making six county (or Riding) members, instead of four, as heretofore. The whole shire, by these alterations, returns *thirty-seven* representatives to Parliament, instead of *thirty-two*, as before the passing of the Bill. The election of members for the East Riding is held at BEVERLEY, and the polling takes place, besides, at HULL, DRIFFIELD, POCKLINGTON, BRIDLINGTON, HOWDEN, HEDON and SETTRINGTON; the North Riding elects at YORK, and polls, besides, at MALTON, SCARBOROUGH, WHITBY, STOKESLEY, GUILSBOROUGH, ROMALDKIRK, RICHMOND, ASKRIGG, THIRSK, NORTHALLERTON and KIRKBY-MOOR-SIDE; and the West Riding elects at WAKEFIELD, and polls also at SHEFFIELD, DONCASTER, SNAITH, HUDDERSFIELD, HALIFAX, BRADFORD, BARNSLEY, LEEDS, KEIGHLEY, SETTLE, KNARESBOROUGH, SKIPTON, PATELY BRIDGE, and DENT.

RAILWAYS THROUGH YORKSHIRE.

The MANCHESTER and LEEDS RAILWAY.—The act for this Railway was first applied for in 1830, when it encountered a violent opposition by the various canal companies whose interests would be affected by the line; and, uniting with powerful land owners, they succeeded in throwing out the bill. A second application was made in 1836, when, after a severe struggle, the bill was passed. In 1837 parliament sanctioned an application to amend the act. A work to which we are much indebted for some interesting and valuable informaiton upon the subject of Railways, says—" this is one of the most important Railways in England, as well as one of the best investments." It commences at Manhester, and runs to *Rochdale* and *Littleborough*—through a densely populated and manufacturing district to *Todmorden*, and, by *Hebden Bridge, Elland, Brighouse, Dewsbury* and *Wakefield*, to *Normanton*, where it joins the North Midland Railway, which proceeds to *Leeds*—and by means of the York and North Midland, and the Leeds and Selby, and along the Hull and Selby, to *Hull*. The line includes the traffic connected with the towns of Rochdale, Oldham, Halifax, Huddersfield, Bradford, Wakefield and Dewsbury; and forms a connecting link of communication (by Manchester) with the port of Liverpool, and (by Leeds) with that of Hull. On its southern route, after joining the York and North Midland, the line communicates with *Sheffield* and *Rotherham*, and at the latter town unites with the North Midland Railway.

The LEEDS and SELBY RAILWAY, which is about twenty miles in length, runs from *Leeds*, by *Sherburn* and *Hambleton*, to *Selby*. From the latter town the HULL and SELBY RAILWAY proceeds to *Hull*, passing to the north of *Howden* and to the south of *South Cave*. A Railway is projected from Halifax to Leeds, by way of Bradford, and, proceeding in the direction of Ovenden, will pass into Bradford Dale.

The WHITBY and PICKERING RAILWAY was opened on the 26th May, 1836. The scenery of the whole line of road (about twenty miles) is wild, romantic and picturesque in the highest degree. This is a prosperous line, the gross receipts being equal to 9 per cent. per annum on the paid up capital of the proprietors.

The SHEFFIELD and MANCHESTER RAILWAY (which we have already noticed under Lancashire), runs from *Sheffield*, by *Penistone, Glossop*, and near *Ashton*, to *Manchester*. A Railway is projected from the modern port of Goole, which will pass to the north of Thorne, and, by Barnsley and Silkestone, to Penistone, where it will unite with the Sheffield and Manchester line. The SHEFFIELD and ROTHERHAM RAILWAY was opened on the 31st October, 1838: the total length of the line is five miles, seven furlongs and twenty-five yards. This line, as before mentioned, communicates with the North Midland Railway.

The NORTH MIDLAND RAILWAY, for which a bill was obtained in 1836, encountered a severe opposition from the inhabitants of Sheffield, and from the Aire and Calder Canal Company—both parties proposing different lines, according to their several interests; the opposing schemes were, however, unsuccessful, and the proprietors are now actively proceeding upon their original plan. This Railway is seventy-two miles in length, and runs for upwards of sixty miles through one of the best and most productive coalfields in England. The line proceeds from Leeds to *York*, leaving *Sherburn* and *Tadcaster* on the left: on its western route it communicates with *Rotherham* and *Sheffield*; proceeds, by *Chesterfield*, to *Derby* and *Nottingham*, and continues, through *Leicestershire*, to *Rugby*, where it joins the London and Birmingham Railway: it also unites with the Birmingham and Derby line at Derby. This may be considered the main line of Railway from Edinburgh, Newcastle, York, Leeds, Halifax, Huddersfield and Bradford, to London and the south—and to Birmingham, Bristol, Gloucester, Worcester, and the south-west of England.

The YORK and NORTH MIDLAND.—The bill for this Railway also was opposed by the Aire and Calder Company, but was passed in 1836, and some amendments were carried through parliament in the session of 1837. It commences at *York*, and passes about three miles to the south of *Tadcaster*, where it crosses the river Wharfe, and at Milford passes under the Leeds and Selby Railway, with which it communicates by branches running towards Selby: it passes at no great distance from *Pontefract*, and joins the North Midland at *Methley*, as before mentioned. This Railway is twenty-three miles in length, exclusive of branches. From Methley to the Leeds and Selby Railway this line forms the only communication from Manchester and Liverpool to the port of Hull; it also forms a portion of railway communication from London to Newcastle-on-Tyne and Edinburgh; likewise from Leeds to the north; as also effecting a communication between York, Scarborough, Whitby and the East Riding of Yorkshire—whilst, by its connexion with the North Midland at Methley, it accomplishes a communication with Leeds, Manchester and Liverpool, and with the north-east of England. The traffic upon this line will, it is anticipated, be very considerable when the Manchester and Leeds Railway comes into operation—besides enjoying a vast traffic between York and Leeds.

The GREAT NORTH OF ENGLAND RAILWAY, for which an act was obtained in 1836-7, commences at the city of *York*—passes about five miles to the west of *Easingwold*—and, leaving *Thirsk* and *Northallerton* a little to the right, runs on to *Darlington*, and from thence, by *Durham*, to *Newcastle-upon-Tyne*. This Railway will form a large portion of the great main line of railway from London to Edinburgh, as also from York, Leeds, Manchester, and Birmingham, by means of its immediate connexion with the York and North Midland line. The Great North of England, on its route between Croft and Newcastle, intersects the Stockton and Darlington Railway—likewise the Clarence, and the Durham and Sunderland Railways; it forms a communication with the Hartlepool line, and afterwards crosses the Stanhope and Tyne Railway. None of these Railways are competing lines, being principally used for the conveyance of coal.

Thus it will be seen that the Great North of England line, in conjunction with that of the York and North Midland, and the latter with the North Midland Railway, will effect the grand communication between the capitals of England and Scotland. Persons of acknowledged commercial and statistical knowledge are of opinion, however, that one line will not prove sufficient for the traffic between the two cities, and that another, on the west, must eventually be formed, either by private companies or by government, for the accommodation of Liverpool, Manchester, and the districts immediately communicating with Carlisle and Glasgow. Railways are already in progress from Preston to Lancaster, and from Lancaster to Carlisle; the bay of Morecambe has been surveyed, with a view to construct a line across the sands, and onwards to Whitehaven. These operations may be considered as indications of an embryo design to carry a Railway along the western coast to the city of Glasgow. A line, indeed, between Carlisle and Glasgow, has been surveyed; its route being by Gretna, then to pass between Annan and Ecclefechan, on to, or near, Dumfries, and thence to Kilmarnock, where the line is proposed to unite with the Ayr and Glasgow Railway. Under 'Northumberland' has been noticed, two projected lines from Newcastle to Edinburgh.

PUBLISHED BY PIGOT & Co. FLEET STREE